W9-AOP-984

Information Processing Research
in Advertising

INFORMATION PROCESSING RESEARCH IN ADVERTISING

Edited by
RICHARD JACKSON HARRIS
Kansas State University

LEA LAWRENCE ERLBAUM ASSOCIATES, PUBLISHERS
1983   Hillsdale, New Jersey   London

Lawrence Erlbaum Associates, Inc., Publishers
365 Broadway
Hillsdale, New Jersey 07642

Library of Congress Cataloging in Publication Data
Main entry under title:

Information processing research in advertising.

    Includes bibliographies and indexes.
    1. Advertising—Psychological aspects.   2. Human
information processing.   3. Advertising, Fraudulent.
I. Harris, Richard Jackson.
HF5822.I52   1983   659.1   82-24172
ISBN 0-89859-204-6
Printed in the United States of America
10 9 8 7 6 5 4 3 2 1

Contents

Preface

The idea for this book arose several years ago from the frustration I felt as an experimental cognitive psychologist trained in basic research. When I decided to begin applying basic information-processing theories and methodology to the problem of deceptive advertising, I found very little relevant literature in my own field and few accessible routes to explore advertising research in other fields. Thus this book is dedicated to helping bridge the interdisciplinary gap among psychologists, marketing researchers, linguists, and communications scientists. We have all been studying advertising in some similar ways but we have not always known that much about what each other is doing.

Thanks are expressed to many people who helped make this book possible, most especially the contributors. Obviously this book would not exist without them. I have appreciated their patience during several delays and their encouragement to me in times when the entire project looked in question.

Thanks to Larry Erlbaum and his staff at Lawrence Erlbaum Associates for sharing the vision of this project and taking a chance on publishing it. It is somewhat a departure from their usual basic psychology research publication.

In a more personal vein, I would like to express appreciation to Henry Loess and Al Hall of the College of Wooster; without them I would have never been drawn into psychology. Thanks also to Bill Brewer of the University of Illinois; although he always warned me about wandering into applied psychology, under his tutelage I became a competent basic researcher in psycholinguistics.

Finally, thanks to all my present and former students active in our advertising research project at Kansas State University: Kris Bruno, Tony Dubitsky, Greg Monaco, Cindy Ellerman, Jim Connizzo, Mark Larson, Karen Perch, Steve Snook, Larry Letcher, Sue Thompson, Bruce Monroe, Rick Cameron, Gail Burgess, Terri Faubion, and Ross Teske. Their interest and dedication sustained my interest in the project.

Richard Jackson Harris
Manhattan, Kansas

Information Processing Research in Advertising

ADVERTISING AS A PROBLEM IN INFORMATION PROCESSING

Introduction

Richard Jackson Harris
Kansas State University

In considering the many and varied effects of advertising, a very central issue is how the information in an ad is processed, that is, how people understand and remember what an ad said. Although this suggests that cognitive psychology could contribute directly to the study of advertising, such has not really been the case in any substantial way until recently. Scientific approaches to advertising research have been fragmented, and only in the last few years has this framework called information processing become a heuristic approach toward studying advertising. It is this approach that this book develops and explores, through examination of research on a variety of problems. In pondering the title of this volume, two questions may came to mind. First of all, what is information processing anyway and second, what does it have to do with advertising?

THE INFORMATION PROCESSING PARADIGM

Although there is no consensually definitive statement of information processing, probably the most complete and definitive description exists in the landmark cognitive psychology text by Lachman, Lachman, and Butterfield (1979). Whereas they argue that information processing is an established paradigm in psychology, in the sense of philosopher-of-science Thomas Kuhn (1962), the discussion below draws heavily on Lachman et al.'s description of the information processing approach, without any necessary commitment to whether or not it is a scientific paradigm in the Kuhnian sense.

There are a number of basic characteristics of information-processing psychology. One of the most basic is the conception of a human mind as a symbol manipulator with certain similarities to a general purpose machine. For example, a few basic symbolic computational operations such as encoding, storing, comparing, and locating may ultimately describe what we call thought or intelligence. Such an information-processing system is, however, very complex and

5

not amenable to any simple mechanistic model, such as simple S-R psychology or a nonrecursive Markov model of sequential information processing.

The use of the so-called "computer metaphor" is popular in information processing psychology. In many, perhaps most, cases it is used at the level of a metaphor, that is, there are certain properties of computers which have certain features in common with some aspects of information processing (e.g., input, output, recursive process, and graphic representation by flowchart) and thus are useful in describing such processes, but there is no necessary implicit assumption that the processes of the computer and the mind are identical or even similar in any significant way. Use of the computer as a metaphor is characteristic of many of the authors of this book. Sometimes, however, the computer is taken more literally to be an analogy or even a simulation of thought processes; although such approaches have become popular recently in basic research in information processing, they have not had any great effect on advertising research for the most part and thus are not considered further here.

Another very central feature of information processing psychology is that there is some sort of internal representation of reality, on which information processes operate. All knowledge must be representable in whatever form this representational system takes (e.g., propositions, images, concepts), a condition that insures this system will be quite complex. This cognitive representation is never directly observable and must always be inferred, which naturally makes studying it far from easy. In spite of this difficulty, however, the problem of representation is central to information-processing research.

Another emphasis is that of a "systems approach." This involves conceiving of intelligent behavior as an emergent characteristic of the interactions among a system of components and processes interacting with each other and with the environment. Whereas the outcome end-product of such intelligent behavior may be studied (e.g., attitudinal or behavioral response to an ad), the emphasis is more heavily on the processes used by the mind to generate that outcome (e.g., inference-drawing, reasoning).

In this sense, information-processing views the human mind as an active information-seeker, rather than a passive responder to environmental events. Information processing is thus constructive, in that representations to be stored in memory are constructed through the interactions of the environmental stimulus and what the person already knows about that information (see Spiro, 1980). For example, how a consumer interprets and remembers an ad will be determined by the interaction of the stimulus of the ad and the knowledge one already has about that product and product class, as well as one's own needs, interests, and past experience. The representational system is continually being added to, through its interaction with new external information. When information is to be retrieved from long-term memory for later use, processes of reconstruction occur. Like construction, these processes are dynamic and interactive, not a passive playback of a tape recording of past events.

The assumption that a series of processing stages can be identified, at least in principle, implies that information processing takes place in real time. Inferences about the nature of these processes may be made from timing the length of their occurrence and examining characteristics of their output. A clearer understanding of the stages of the processes involved in responding to advertisements would certainly have practical as well as theoretical importance.

Information processing generally assumes that there are some innate abilities which are probably species-specific to humans. Although this assumption is less central than some others, it is important in that it tends to discourage thinking and description in terms of laws and principles applicable to all species. Thus there is, for example, little interest in describing advertising comprehension as a process of classical conditioning, merely because such a process is frequently observed in a variety of species, although such an explanation may still be useful in more sophisticated form (e.g., Rossiter & Percy, this volume).

The methodology of information processing is basically empirical, with the experimental method being the modal approach. However, there is some trend in the basic research of the last few years to develop broad comprehensive global theories using rational methods rather than the traditional empirical ones, but this new trend has yet to have significant impact on advertising research and it may eventually have only an oblique relevance. In spite of the use of the experimental method, the primary interest is still in non-directly-observable phenomena. Thus one uses the data from a well-controlled experiment and the methodological principles of experimental design and control to infer the nature of unobservable processes.

Information processing has a number of intellectual antecedents inside and outside psychology which have influenced its development (Lachman et al., 1979). The neobehaviorist (S-R) school in psychology contributed its use of the experimental method and its emphasis on operationism and nomothetic explanations. At the same time, however, information processing rejected the neobehaviorist emphasis on logical positivism, environmentalism, the use of stimuli and responses as the basic ''building blocks'' of all behavior, and the extrapolation of research on lower animals to human behavior. From the verbal learning tradition in psychology came several laboratory measures and techniques as well as a large data base of information about memory. Information processing, however, expanded beyond the problem of memory and beyond the S-R assumptions behind verbal learning psychology.

From human engineering and communication engineering have come the analogies of the person as an information transmitter carrying multiple communication channels. Techniques such as signal detection and theoretical constructs such as serial versus parallel processing have grown out of these influences to pervasively influence information processing. From computer science comes the idea of humans as symbol-manipulating systems performing complex intelligent behavior. In addition, certain computational concepts, simulation techniques, and an emphasis on specifying underlying processes as a means of explanation also show the computer science influence.

The science of linguistics has been influential in information processing through its emphasis on complex and abstract representational systems and operations that could not be explainable in any simple behavioral model of observable behavior. The work in describing linguistic competence as systems of rules has been a model for other areas of information processing, such as inference-drawing and reasoning.

INFORMATION PROCESSING IN ADVERTISING

Certainly not all writers of chapters in this book would agree with all the assumptions and principles of information processing above. Indeed, some of them may not even consider themselves to be in the information processing tradition. Labels are not the issue here, however. All the chapters do represent attempts to examine advertising as a problem in information processing. The consumer hearing or seeing ads is processing information in the truest sense of the word and as such is an active organizer and interpreter of pictorial and verbal information. Thus the question of what an ad means or what effect it has is largely an issue of information processing, subject to empirical study using the methodology and theoretical tools of information-processing psychology.

A major difficulty in working with the research literature in advertising is the way it is so fragmented by disciplines. Much of its appears in places like *Journal of Marketing Research, Journal of Consumer Research, Journal of Advertising,* or *Journal of Advertising Research,* which are not necessarily read by psychologists or advertising law scholars. Other work, especially by psychologists, may appear in the *Journal of Applied Psychology* or be presented at the American Psychological Association and never be seen by market researchers. Linguistics papers might appear in conference volumes or, worse still, circulate unpublished in the "linguistics underground" for years, virtually inaccessible to anyone outside the field. Much marketing research is in proprietary research reports and thus effectively lost to the academic research community, as well as to government agencies like the Federal Trade Commission. It is hoped that this book will play a significant role in advancing progress in studying advertising from an information processing perspective by bringing together researchers in different fields who are approaching the same problems within different theoretical and disciplinary frameworks. Such convergence is especially important as researchers continue to have more and more input into legislation and regulation (Preston, 1980; Rotfeld & Preston, 1981).

This book is divided into three major sections. The first (this chapter) offers an introduction to the work. The second is a set of papers exploring issues in the processing of advertisements by the consumer from the point of view of current issues, theories, and findings in information-processing psychology. The authors attempt to relate current basic research in perception, memory, and marketing to the applied problem of advertising. Recent work in information processing such as levels-of-processing research, imagery, and models of various memory stores are shown to be useful in understanding how we process advertisements.

The third section of the book takes one particular issue and examines it in more depth from an information-processing point of view. The issue examined here is misleading advertising. This particular issue has the advantage of having long been considered both in the public mind and the consumer research literature. This is an advertising issue that seems especially amenable to an information-processing approach, which focusses on whether the consumer is misled, rather than on the less tractable issues of whether or not the advertiser had a fraudulent intent to deceive or whether or not the ad content is literally false. It is also an issue with very clear policy ramifications (Armstrong, Gurol, & Russ, 1980; Brandt & Preston, 1977; Preston, 1975; Reed & Coalson, 1977). The chapters in Part III represent approaches by linguists (Garfinkel, Coleman), psychologists (Harris et al., Monaco & Kaiser), consumer researchers (Shimp), and communications scientists (Rotfeld, Preston).

We who have been writing this book have learned a lot from each other and profited greatly from the interdisciplinary interchange this project has offered. Our hope is that our readers will do likewise.

REFERENCES

Armstrong, G. M., Gurol, M. N., & Russ, F. A. Defining and measuring deception in advertising: A review and evaluation. In J. H. Leigh & C. R. Martin Jr. (Eds.), *Current issues and research in advertising 1980*. Ann Arbor: University of Michigan Graduate School of Business Administration Division of Research, 1980.

Brandt, M. T., & Preston, I. L. The Federal Trade Commission's use of evidence to determine deception. *Journal of Marketing*, 1977, *41*, 54–62.

Kuhn, T. S. *The structure of scientific revolutions*. Chicago: University of Chicago Press, 1962.

Lachman, R., Lachman, J. L., & Butterfield, E. C. *Cognitive psychology and information processing*. Hillsdale, N.J.: Lawrence Erlbaum Associates, 1979.

Preston, I. L. *The great American blow-up*. Madison: University of Wisconsin Press, 1975.

Preston, I. L. Researchers at the Federal Trade Commission—Peril and promise. In J. H. Leigh & C. R. Martin, Jr. (Eds.), *Current issues and research in advertising 1980*. Ann Arbor: University of Michigan Graduate School of Business Administration Division of Research, 1980.

Reed, O. L., & Coalson, J. L. Eighteenth-century legal doctrine meets twentieth-century marketing techniques: FTC regulation of emotionally conditioning advertising. *Georgia Law Review*, 1977, *11*, 733–782.

Rotfeld, H. J., & Preston, I. L. The potential impact of research on advertising law. *Journal of Advertising Research*, 1981, *21*(2), 9–17.

Spiro, R. J. Constructive processes in prose comprehension and recall. In R. J. Spiro, B. C. Bruce, & W. F. Brewer (Eds.), *Theoretical issues in reading comprehension*. Hillsdale, N.J.: Lawrence Erlbaum Associates, 1980.

II

BASIC INFORMATION-
PROCESSING PRINCIPLES
IN ADVERTISING RESEARCH

1 Cognitive Processes Initiated by Exposure to Advertising

Andrew A. Mitchell
Carnegie-Mellon University

INTRODUCTION

Research on communication effects, as with most research areas, may be viewed as progressing through a series of research stages. Each stage is defined by a particular research focus that has resulted both from the knowledge gained and the theoretical or methodological problems identified in the previous stage. In examining communication effects, each successive stage has moved toward a more detailed exposition of the mental processes that intervene between exposure to a communication and its resulting impact on an individual's evaluation of or reaction to the communication topic.

At the first stage of research on communication effects, primary emphasis was directed at examining the effect of alternative message structures (i.e., fear appeals, one and two sided communications) on an individual's evaluation of the communication topic (e.g., Hovland, Janis, & Kelley, 1953). Receiver characteristics (i.e., education level) were frequently examined as possible mediators of these effects. Although some of the relationships that were discovered at this stage have been consistently replicated (e.g., source effects), many other relationships have not (e.g., fear appeals—Higbee, 1969; and sleeper effects—Gillig & Greenwald, 1974; Capon & Hulbert, 1973).

These inconsistent results led to an examination of alternative mediators of the relationship between exposure to a communication and the resulting effect on an individual's evaluation of the communication topic. At the second research stage, effort was concentrated on the evaluative thoughts (e.g. counterarguments) generated during exposure to a communication (Greenwald, 1968;

Wright, 1973) and the beliefs formed or changed by the communication (Lutz, 1975; Olson & Mitchell, 1975). Both have been shown to mediate the effect of communications and, recently, effort has been directed at integrating these two approaches (Lutz & Swasy, 1977; Olson, Toy, & Dover, 1979).

Recent research, however, indicates that these two variables may not be the only mediators of communication effects, First, it has been argued that the reception of many communications occur under conditions of "low involvement" and under these conditions very few, if any, evaluative thoughts may occur (e.g., Ward, 1974). Mitchell, Gardner and Russo (1981), for instance, have discussed an information acquisition process that results in little evaluative processing. In an experiment, they examined attitude formation with this process and under conditions where individuals actively evaluate the information in an advertisement. Their results indicate that different attitudes may be formed under these two conditions and that counterarguments and support arguments do not mediate all of the attitudinal differences. Second, Mitchell and Olson (1981) have shown that product attibute beliefs may not be the only mediator of advertising effects on the formulation of brand attitudes.

These problems suggest the possibility of a third research stage for examining communication effects. This stage would take a more fine grained view of the information acquisition process. It would, for instance, focus on all the mental activities or cognitive processes that occur during exposure to a communication or advertisement instead of just the verbal evaluative thoughts. In addition, the dependent variables of interest would be the content and organization of information acquired after exposure to a communication, instead of just structured belief scale measures and attitudes toward the communication topic.

Research in cognitive psychology has indicated that these mental processes mediate the content of information stored in long-term memory, how it is organized and the ability to retrieve this information at a later point in time (e.g., Anderson & Reder, 1979; Hyde and Jenkins, 1969; Craik & Tulving, 1975; Smith, 1981). Since it is generally agreed that information stored in long-term memory has an important effect on consumer decision making (Bettman, 1979; Chestnut & Jacoby, 1977; Mitchell, 1978), it is important to understand the effect of a communication on the contents and organization of information in memory, instead of on just attitudes and intentions.

The purpose of this chapter is twofold. The first is to present a review of the current literature on memory and cognitive processes. This review is organized into a theoretical framework for understanding the information acquisition process. The second is to use this framework for understanding advertising effects at the individual level. The theoretical framework is developed to a greater degree than may seem necessary given our current understanding of advertising effects. It is hoped, however, that this framework will provide a better understanding of advertising effects and suggest a number of areas for future research.

The chapter is divided into two sections. The first section presents the theoretical framework based on the review of memory and cognitive processes. The second section applies this framework to communication effects and identifies first level and second level factors that will affect the cognitive processes that occur during exposure to a communication.

THEORETICAL FRAMEWORK

In this discussion of the information acquisition process, special attention will be directed at those points in the process where the individual exerts control over the process and on the physical constraints of the system that may affect the process. Also, a distinction is made between structure and process. Structure refers to the state of the system at any point in time and process represents the dynamics of the system that operate on or within these structures. For instance, the amount, content and organization of information in memory about a particular concept or object (e.g., a particular brand of creamed peas) is an example of a psychological structure. The retrieval of information about an object is an example of a process. A distinction is also made between high-level and low-level processes. Low level processes are basic to the system and define how it operates whereas, high-level processes are generally under the control of the individual.

The Information Acquisition Process

Multi-Store Model. During the information acquisition process, stimulus energies from the environment (e.g., sounds) are processed, encoded and stored in memory. Originally, this process was decomposed into three stages with each stage conceptualized as a separate memory—sensory store, short-term store and long-term store. This conceptualization was based on the belief that the three memories differed in terms of capacity, codes used to store information and forgetting rates. For instance, it was believed that the sensory stores held sensory information, the short-term store held acoustic information, and the long-term store held semantic information.

Specific mechanisms were required, under this view, to "move" information between the different memory stores. For instance, attention was required to "move" information between the sensory stores and short-term memory and rehearsal was required to "move" information between short-term and long-term memory (Fig. 1.1). Information that was not attended to in the sensory store or rehearsed in short-term memory was lost from the ssytem. Consequently, both attention and rehearsal acted as filters.

This particular conceptualization, which is based on a computer analogy, was formally developed into a model by Atkinson and Shiffrin (1968). In this model, special attention was directed at "control processes"—processes that are under the control of the individual which determine what information is processed and

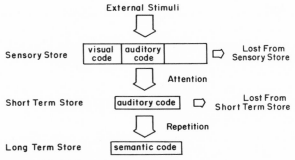

Fig. 1.1.   Multi-store model of information acquisition.

how it is processed. As mentioned previously, examples of these are attention and rehearsal.

For a number of reasons, this multi-store conceptualization of the information acquisition process has undergone considerable change during the past ten years. First, experimental research produced conflicting estimates as to the capacity and forgetting rates in the three different memory stores (Craik & Lockhart, 1972; Postman, 1975). Second, the different memory stores were found to hold information in codes other than those originally hypothesized. Third, the model was developed to explain the findings of verbal learning experiments, and it was not clear how it could be extended to explain the acquisition of generalized knowledge (Lachman, Lachman, & Butterfield, 1979). Finally, research on attention had produced conflicting evidence as to where control processes occur in the information-acquisition process (i.e., Deutsch & Deutsch, 1963; Triesman, 1960).

Process Orientation.   The first change in this conceptualization was the combining of the sensory store and the short-term store into a single component (Shiffrin, 1975, 1976). This change occurred, as mentioned earlier, because empirical research had indicated conflicting results as to where attention occurred in the process. In his original formulation, Broadbent (1958) hypothesized that attention was required at the sensory level to "move" information from the sensory stores to the short-term store. However, subsequent research by Moray (1959) and Triesman (1960) indicated that attention may also occur at later stages in the process (e.g., semantic stages).

Recent research has indicated that attention may occur at a number of different locations in the process. To explain these seemingly conflicting findings, Schneider and Shiffrin (1977) and Shiffrin and Schneider (1977) differentiated between automatic and controlled processes. Automatic processes require little attention and can be executed in parallel with other cognitive processes. Driving an automobile, for example, is an automatic process for most individuals. We can drive and execute other tasks, such as carrying on a conversation, while we are driving. Controlled processes, on the other hand, require attention and are generally executed serially.

In processing information from the environment, attention may occur at a number of different points in the process depending on the extent to which automatic processes are available. For instance, in processing information about a familiar stimulus like a dog, we are probably not aware of the processing that occurs until the stimulus is labeled as a dog. With less familiar stimuli, we may become aware of the processing that occurs at an earlier stage. Consequently, whether the processing that occurs is automatic or controlled is dependent on the contents of long-term memory. In order to automatically label a particular stimulus as a dog, we must first have knowledge about the qualities of dogs stored in long-term memory.

When processes are automatic, it is difficult for individuals to override these processes even when it may be in their best interest to do so. This is aptly demonstrated by the Stroop effect. This effect occurs when subjects are presented with stimuli that contain the names of different colors printed in different colored ink. Subjects are asked to either state whether the color name matches a physical color or name the ink color. In each case, either the ink color or the color name interferes with the task and produces longer response times than conditions where the color name and ink color are the same. When subjects are asked to name the ink color, they should avoid reading the color name, but cannot do so because reading the color name is an automatic process. The reverse happens in the matching task.

Most current models of the information acquisition process do not consider short-term memory and long-term memory to be separate components (Norman, 1968; Shiffrin & Schneider 1977). Instead, short term memory is that portion of long-term memory that is currently accessible or activated. As we process information from the environment, this information activates portions of long-term memory which are then used to interpret the new information. As demonstrated by the Stroop effect, much of the initial processing of a stimulus is automatic, however, at later points in the process individuals may control which portions of long-term memory are activated.

In summary, then, information acquisition is viewed as a process where information from the environment is interpreted and a representation of this information is stored in long-term memory. In this process, which is illustrated in Fig. 1.2, the processing proceeds through a series of levels ranging from basic sensory levels to more semantic levels.

Processing Levels.   The first level of the process is sensory analysis. At this level, the individual words of the phrase "The boy carried the cat" are recognized. At the phrase analysis level, the words are organized into a phrase and then interpreted for their semantic content. This semantic content is then stored in long-term memory. In Fig. 1.2, this semantic knowledge is represented as a

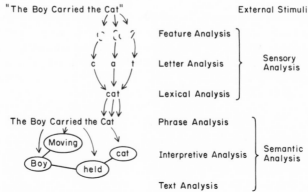

Fig. 1.2.   The information acquisition process.

network of associations. It is important to note that it is the semantic interpretation of the phrase that is stored in semantic memory not the actual phrase. For instance, in our example, the verb "carried" implies that the boy was "moving" and that he "held" the cat. In order to make these semantic interpretations, however, the individual must activate the appropriate knowledge structures. Finally, at the next level of analysis, text analysis, the meaning of the phrase is integrated with related phrases to obtain an understanding of the text material.

At each level of the information acquisition process, portions of long-term memory are activated which are then used to process the information. These processes may be either automatic or controlled. For instance, in reading, processing may begin by interpreting different patterns of light and dark on a page and then proceed through a feature analysis, letter analysis and then a lexical analysis (LaBerge & Samuels, 1974). Models of higher level cognitive processes involving text comprehension have also been recently developed (e.g., Kintsch & van Dijk, 1978).

The information acquisition process, as described above, is essentially a serial process with the individual playing a passive role. As such, it is an example of what Norman and Bobrow (1975), term a data driven process. In many situations, however, the individual plays a more active role. Navon (1977), for instance, has suggested that individuals first attempt to obtain a global understanding of the stimulus and then proceed to a more local feature analysis. The global understanding of the stimulus is used to process the information at the local level. This latter type of processing has been called a conceptually driven process (Norman & Bobrow, 1975). With this type of processing, the individual uses prior expectations to actively process the new information. Norman (1979) has recently suggested that in most cases, information acquisition results in both data and conceptually driven processes.

Recently, McClelland and Rumelhart (1980) have proposed a model based on the cascade model by McClelland (1979) which captures these ideas. In this model, processing of information occurs at the different levels simultaneously. Information from each level is partially processed and used to form expectations through activation and inhibitory processes. The best conclusions from this partial processing is then passed on to the next level while processing continues at the current level.

Long-Term Memory

Long-term memory contains an individual's knowledge of the external world. It is currently believed that long-term memory has an infinite capacity and that all the information acquired by an individual is stored. Forgetting only occurs because an individual is unable to retrieve a particular piece of information.

In discussing long-term memory, the critical question concerns how information is represented (Palmer, 1978). The question of representation can be broken down further into questions of what information is stored in memory and how it is organized. In discussing these questions, a distinction is frequently made between declarative knowledge and procedural knowledge. Declarative knowledge may be thought of as data and procedural knowledge as the programs that operate on this data.

Procedural knowledge is organized into production systems. Within these systems, knowledge is represented by a series of condition-act statements (e.g., Newell, 1973). If a particular condition is recognized, then a particular action is taken. Production system models have been developed to represent procedural knowledge in memory scanning (Newell, 1973), language comprehension (Anderson, Kline & Lewis, 1977) and solving geometry problems (Neves & Anderson, 1981). All automatic processes imply the availability of a production system to execute these processes. Consequently, most individuals will have production systems for labeling an animal with a particular shape as a horse or a particular sound as coming from a dog.

With declarative knowledge, a distinction is frequently made between episodic and semantic memory (Kintsch, 1980; Tulving, 1972). Episodic memory contains a temporal and spatial recording of experienced events. These events may be recorded in the sequence that the events were experienced, and under these conditions, retrieval involves a temporal search similar to the rewinding of a film (Jacoby, 1974). According to this distinction, semantic memory contains our generalized knowledge.

Over the years, this distinction has blurred. Much of our semantic knowledge and episodic knowledge seems to be linked. For instance, when we think about a particular concept (e.g., houses), frequently both generalized knowledge and episodic knowledge are activated. Episodes may be stored in the sequence that they were experienced, however, some episodes seem to be linked to our generalized knowledge. (e.g., Schank, 1980).

It is generally agreed that our declarative knowledge can be represented by an associative network (e.g., Hollan, 1975; Wickelgren, 1981). Within this network, concepts are represented by nodes and the strength of the associations are represented by arcs. For every idea that we can represent in our minds, there is a node or a set of nodes that represent this idea. Consequently, both verbal and nonverbal information may be represented by nodes (Wickelgren, 1981). Bower (1981), for instance, has recently suggested that moods may be represented by nodes in an associative network model.

Several formal network models have been developed. In these models, propositions are the basic representations of knowledge. The most important of these models are by Anderson and Bower (1973), Kintsch (1974), after Norman, Rumelhart and the LNR Group (1975) and Anderson (1976). These models differ primarily as to how propositions are represented in the model and restrictions on the type of links allowed. Recently, there has been considerable debate as to whether propositions are the only form of representation for knowledge (e.g., Anderson, 1978; Kosslyn, 1981; Pylyshyn, 1973, 1981). Consequently, it will be assumed that other representations are possible.

Much of our declarative knowledge seems to be organized into packets of information. Within these packets, the strength of the associative links are stronger than between packets. Different types of these packets have been suggested in the literatures. Examples of these include schemata (Rumelhart & Ortony, 1977), frames (Minsky, 1975), scripts (Schank & Abelson, 1977) and memory organization packets (Schank, 1980). Each of these packets differ conceptually. For instance, a frame is a structure with a set of slots. Each slot has an associated set of properties which may take different values. A frame for a house, for example, may have slots for each room. Scripts are knowledge structures for generalized events and contain information about the temporal flow of actions within a generalized event. A restaurant script, for example, might contain generalized information about the temporal events that occur when eating at a restaurant. Finally, memory organizational packets are similar to scripts; only information about specific events associated with the generalized event are linked within this packet of information.

Consumers probably have packets of information about different brands and about specific products. An example of a packet of information about a Ford Fiesta is shown in Fig. 1.3. Note that it is organized into a network of associations.

Finally, semantic memory is probably layered with information stored at different levels of generality (e.g., Ortony, 1980; Rosch, 1978). For instance, we probably have information about specific automobiles (e.g., automobiles that we have owned) and generalized knowledge about specific models (e.g., Buick Skylark), brands (e.g., Ford) and types of automobiles (e.g., small, compact automobiles). Within this system, there are probably both horizontal and vertical linkages.

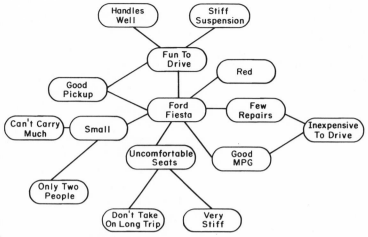

Fig. 1.3. A packet of information about Ford Fiestas.

Learning.   Learning is defined here as any change in the content or organiza-tion of information in long-term memory. Based on this definition, learning may occur in a number of different ways. For instance, simply experiencing an event may result in a trace of that event being recorded in episodic memory. Also, simply repeating a task may change the production system for that task which allows for its faster execution in the future (e.g., Anderson, 1980; Brucks & Mitchell, 1981).

Here, however, we are primarily concerned with the learning of declarative knowledge. There are at least four different types of learning that may occur. First, linkages between specific concepts may be strengthened. At some point, two concepts may become so tightly linked that they become a single chunk of information (Hayes-Roth, 1977). Second, new linkages may be formed. For instance, new information about a particular brand may be acquired. Third, new packets of information may be formed by generalizing from previous experi-ences. For instance, after visiting a McDonald's restaurant a number of times, an individual may abstract information from these experiences to form a packet of generalized knowledge about McDonald's. Finally, new packets of information may be formed by analogical reasoning (e.g., Rumelhart & Norman, 1981). For instance, if an individual has never visited a Burger King restaurant, but has a generalized packet of information about McDonald's, he or she may adapt the McDonald's information to fit Burger King. This would involve reasoning that Burger King is just like McDonald's, but the waitresses have brown uniforms and you can have anything you want on the hamburger. (e.g., Schank, 1980).

Retrieval.   Retrieval of declarative knowledge occurs through activation (Collins & Loftus, 1975), which is an example of a low-level process. One node within the network is activated and this activation then spreads through the network. The nodes that are most strongly associated with the activated node will be activated first, and only a limited number of nodes can be activated at one time. Finally, more than one node may be activated initially. Activating more than one node will generally result in the activation of different portions of the network. For instance, activating automobile and V-8 engine may result in the activation of the Ford node whereas activating automobile and Germany may result in the activation of the Volkswagen node.

Some information in long-term memory is readily available to us and retrieval is almost instantaneous (e.g., direct access). For instance, almost everyone can easily retrieve information about cats—what sounds they make, what they look like, etc. In these situations, we can quickly locate our node in memory for cats and this activates our packet of information about cats.

Other information, such as the name of our high school chemistry teacher, is harder to retrieve. In these situations, we need to develop a strategy for retrieving a particular piece of information. Frequently, this first involves retrieving information related to the critical information. For instance, in the example of trying to retrieve the name of our high school chemistry teacher, we may try to remember what she looked like, what kind of car she drove, and so on. Norman and Bobrow (1979) call this strategy the formation of a description. Within a network model of memory, this strategy may be interpreted as finding as many nodes as possible that may be linked to the critical node. Activating these nodes increases the probability of activating the critical node, thereby obtaining the information the individual is trying to retrieve.

Cognitive Processes

Attention.   Under the conceptualization of the information acquisition process discussed earlier, short term memory is thought of as a process (Craik & Jacoby, 1975) and the primary structure in the information processing system is long-term memory. Also, under this conceptualization, attention becomes a subset of short-term memory since short-term memory also contains automatic processes which do not require attention. Therefore, attention as opposed to short term memory becomes a scarce resource, so only a limited number of information chunks can be attended to at one time.

These attentional processes are shown in Fig. 1.4. Here stimulus energies from different stimuli enter the information processing system and are processed automatically (Wavy lines). The system constantly monitors the outcomes of these processes to determine where attention should be focused.

Finally, attentional processes may involve separate channels for verbal and visual information. A number of studies indicate that executing a verbal task seems to interfere with the acquisition of verbal information, but not visual information and executing a visual task interferes with the acquisition of visual

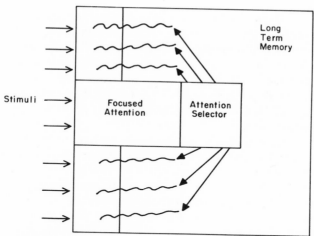

Fig. 1.4.   Attentional processes.

information but not verbal information (e.g., Brooks, 1968; Nelson & Brooks, 1973).

Process-Permanence Frameworks.   Considerable research has been directed at examining the relationship between the type of controlled processing that occurs during the information-acquisition process and the likelihood of recalling this information. One of the original frameworks used to explain this relationship was "depth of processing" proposed by Craik and Lockhart (1972). Within this framework, it was originally hypothesized that information is processed through a series of discrete levels similar to the ones discussed earlier (e.g., sensory level) and that increasing the number of levels used in processing a stimulus increases the likelihood of recalling that stimulus at a later point in time. Consequently, information that is processed to a semantic level is more likely to be recalled than information that is only processed to a sensory level.

Experiments within this framework presented a series of words to the subjects. Preceding each word was a question which was used to create a specific level of processing. For instance, to create processing at a sensory level, subjects would be asked if the word begins with a "b." To create processing at a semantic level subjects would be asked if the word was an animal. After completing this task, the subjects are asked to recall as many of the presented words as they can.

The results of the experiments indicated that information processed to a semantic level was more likely to be recalled than information processed to a sensory level, however, it was also found that in the semantic task, more words were recalled when the subjects answered yes to the question than no. This led Craik and Tulving (1975) to suggest that the amount of elaboration during the processing task also affects recall.

Anderson and Reder (1979) have recently suggested that the amount of elaboration may also explain why words processed at a semantic level are more likely to be recalled than words processed at a sensory level. Processing information at a semantic level allows the individual to make more links between the new information and the old information stored in long-term memory. This increase in the number of linkages increases the probability that the individual will be able to retrieve the information at a later point in time.

The "depth of processing" framework made an important distinction between maintenance rehearsal or the continual rehearsal of a piece of information and elaborative processing (Craik & Watkins, 1973). Because maintenance rehearsal did not result in the processing of information to "deeper" levels, it should not improve recall. An initial study confirmed this hypotheses (Craik & Watkins, 1973), however, a study by Nelson (1977) indicated that maintenance rehearsal did improve recall. In another study, Woodward, Bjork and Jongeward (1973), found that maintenance rehearsal improved recognition, but not recall.

A second framework relating the type of processing to the likelihood of recall is dual coding (Paivio, 1971). Within this framework, it is hypothesized that information may be encoded and stored in two different ways—verbally or nonverbally. The two different coding systems are partially interconnected and have an additive effect on performance. In other words, information that is encoded and stored both verbally and nonverbally is more likely to be retrieved than information that is encoded only verbally or nonverbally. Some stimuli (e.g., concrete words) generally produce a dual code whereas others (e.g., abstract words) produce only a single code. The effects of multiple coding have been shown to hold with both verbal and visual stimuli (e.g., Murry & Newman, 1973).

A third framework is the sensory-semantic model proposed by Nelson, Reed and McEvoy (1979). This framework emphasizes the ability of the sensory qualities of words and pictures to enhance recall. For instance, pictures are generally remembered better than their verbal labels. However, these results can be reversed if the words are phonemically distinctive and the pictures visually confusing (Nelson, 1979). Based on the results of a series of studies, Nelson (1979) has suggested that the likelihood of recalling a particular stimulus is primarily a function of the "distinctiveness" of the resulting memory trace.

These three frameworks strongly suggest that a relationship exists between the type of processing that occurs during exposure to a stimulus and the abilty to recall that stimulus, however, the precise nature of this relationship is not well understood. Two studies have recently examined both the depth of processing and the dual-coding hypotheses (D'Agostino, O'Neill & Paivio, 1977; Hunt, Elliott & Spence, 1979). The results of these two studies indicate reliable main effects for both "depth" and type of stimuli (e.g., concrete vs. abstract) on recall. However, one study (D'Agostino, O'Neill, & Paivio, 1977) also found an interaction that indicated that the depth of processing hypothesis held only with concrete words.

Each of these frameworks hypothesizes that the type of processing creates certain characteristics of the resulting memory trace which affects recall. Tulving and Thompson (1973), however, have emphasized the importance of the similarity between the type of processing that occurs during exposure to the stimulus and the retrieval cues used to recall that stimulus. For instance, if a particular word was processed at a sensory level (e.g., does the word begin with a "b"?) then sensory retrieval cues (e.g., what words began with a "b"?) should improve recall. A number of studies have confirmed this hypothesis (e.g., Tulving, 1979), however, even after taking into account the similarity of retrieval cues, processing to a semantic level still seems to result in superior recall (Fisher & Craik, 1977). Finally, a number of criticisms have been directed at the depth-of-processing framework recently (e.g., Baddeley, 1978; Nelson, 1977; Postman, Thompkins, & Gray, 1978). Many of these criticisms involve the failure to find a measure of depth that is independent of the experimental task.

Summary.   In the information acquisition process, then, the individual has control over the process in three critical ways. The first is simply whether an individual choses to expose himself to the information. The second is the amount of attention that the individual devotes to the information. For instance, in the model proposed by Kahneman (1973), an individual has control over the amount of attention devoted to a particular stimulus, and the amount of attention is directly related to the amount of arousal evoked by the stimulus. Finally, individuals exert control over how they process the information. As mentioned previously, the depth of processing, the amount of elaboration, the type of coding and the retrieval cues all seem to affect recall. Currently, however, the exact relationship between these variables and the permanence of the trace is not clearly understood (Craik, 1979b).

The research reviewed here also suggests that a relationship exists between the type of processing that occurs during exposure to a stimulus and how that information is stored in memory. First, the type of processing should affect how the information is coded in memory (Tulving, 1979; Tulving & Thompson, 1973). Information that is processed at a sensory level may be stored nonverablly whereas information processed to a semantic level may be stored with a verbal code. Second, the type of processing that occurs should have an effect on how that resulting information is organized in long-term memory. Maintenance rehearsal should primarily strengthen existing links in memory whereas elaborative processing may add new concepts or links within a particular structure (Anderson & Reder, 1979; Mandler, 1979). Finally, there is a relationship between the type of processing that occurs during exposure and the effectiveness of specific retrieval cues in recalling information. This relationship can also be explained using an associative network model. During processing, linkages may be made between the new information and the context in which these processes occurred. For instance, Bower (1981) has suggested that linkages may be made between the new information and the mood of the individual during processing. The mood of the individual may be represented as a node in the resulting network and may act as a retrieval cue if activated during recall.

ADVERTISING EFFECTS

In this section, the theoretical framework developed in the previous section is used to examine advertising effects at the individual level. This will be done in two parts. In the first part, factors that directly affect the cognitive processes that occur during exposure to an advertisement are discussed. These are called Level One factors. In the second section, factors that affect Level One factors are discussed.

Information Acquisition Process

The information acquisition process with advertising is, of course, essentially the same as the process discussed in the previous section. In this discussion, however, the process is extended at certain points so that it pertains specifically to advertising. One of these extensions concerns the modality in which the information is presented (e.g., visual vs. auditory) and the way in which the information is presented (e.g., verbal vs. nonverbal). Theoretically, these differences should cause processing differences primarily at the sensory analysis level. Once the information in the advertisement is converted into verbal information, the levels and the effect of the additional processing levels should remain the same.

The processing of information from an advertisement is illustrated in Fig. 1.5. Here the phrase "Prevent colds, buy Fuzz Cold Medicine" is presented both acoustically and visually. As before, exposure to the advertisement activates portions of long-term memory, which in turn, is used to process the information in the advertisement. We again assume that the type of processing that occurs is a result of an interaction between the individual and the stimulus and that processing at the sensory stages is automatic. At this level of processing, the stages for acoustic and visual information differ. With acoustic information, a phonemic level is included while for visual information there is a letter-analysis level.

The next levels involve semantic processing. Generally these levels will be controlled processes and require the activation of the appropriate knowledge structures. First, the message is comprehended which results in the formation of message beliefs. In Fig. 1.5, this is represented by the formation of the belief that "The advertisement claims that Fuzz Cold Medicine prevents colds." These message beliefs are then evaluated using prior information stored in memory.

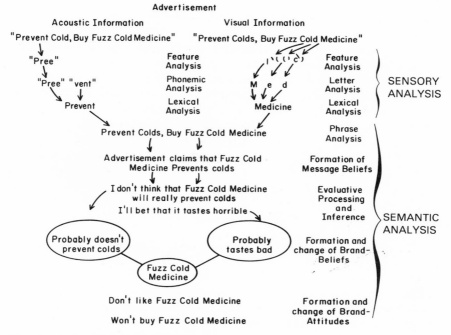

Fig. 1.5.   Verbal processing of advertising information.

This comparison results in evaluative semantic processing (e.g., the generation of couterarguments and support arguments), which causes or blocks changes in attitudes and beliefs about the advertised brand. In addition, inferences may be formed at this stage (Olson, 1978a). In our example, a counterargument is generated against the message belief and an inference that the product "tastes horrible" is formed. These processes result in the linking of these two pieces of information with Fuzz Cold Medicine in long-term memory. This represents the belief formation and change stage. After these linkages are made, it is generally believed that attitudes and intentions are formed.

Finally, although it is not illustrated in Fig. 1.5, it is hypothesized that the individual initially attempts to make a global interpretation of the advertisement which basically involves a labeling response. For instance, individuals probably identify the advertisement as an advertisement for Budweiser Beer or an advertisement for a small car. The purpose of this labeling response is to activate the appropriate packet of information in long-term memory. If the individual has seen the same advertisement before, or similar advertisements from the same campaign, this labeling response may be automatic. It is also possible, that in some situations, affective judgements are also made at this point (Zajonc, 1980).

Mediators of Attitude Formation and Change

Much of the previous research examining advertising or communication effects has concentrated on controlled verbal processes and their resultant effects on the beliefs and attitudes toward the advertised brand. For instance, the cognitive response approach to examining advertising effects concentrates on the amount and type of evaluative verbal processing (e.g., the generation of counterarguments and support arguments). The cognitive structure approach has emphasized the beliefs about the brand that are formed or changed after exposure to the advertisement. These two approaches concentrate on the verbal processing that occurs during exposure to the advertisement and the verbal knowledge about the brand that is stored in memory, respectively. Theoretically, there should be a close relationship between the verbal processing that occurs during exposure to the advertisement and the formation or change in the verbal knowledge structure for the brand.

In experiments that involve exposing subjects to advertisements for new products and then measuring cognitive responses or cognitive structure, the typical findings is that each of these factors explains between 15 and 30 percent of the variance in attitudes (i.e., Edell & Mitchell, 1978; Olson, Toy, & Dover, 1979). In addition, we have found that attitudes toward new products have a reliability of between .6 and .7, which means that somewhere between 35 and 50 percent of the variance in these scores is reliable and therefore, predictable. If we assume that cognitive-structure measures and cognitive-response measures explain approximately the same variance in attitudes, then how do we account for the remaining 20 to 30 percent of the variance?

One possible explanation is the standard one of measurement error. Our methods of measuring cognitive responses and cognitive structure may be poor measures of the actual verbal responses that occur during exposure and of the actual verbal knowledge associated with a brand. For instance, retrospective cognitive responses are frequently used in these types of studies, and they may be poor measures of the actual thought processes that occurred during exposure. Roberts and Maccoby (1973) provide some evidence that this may be true. In their study, the number of counterarguments and support arguments generated toward a particular communication differed if retrospective or concurrent measures were used. Similarly, structured questionnaires are generally used to measure cognitive structures and these are also likely to be very imprecise measures of what information is actually stored in memory. However, even though there is measurement error with both of these measures, it seems unlikely that it would account for all the unexplained variance.

A second explanation is that our models of how information is integrated to form attitudes may be incorrect. With cognitive response measures, usually the number of support arguments minus the number of counterarguments is used to predict attitudes. With cognitive structure measures, the Fishbein attitude model is generally used to predict attitudes (Fishbein & Ajzen, 1975). These may be incorrect models. However, alternative weighting schemes have been used with cognitive-response measures to predict attitudes and the general conclusion is that they seem to add little in terms of predictive power (i.e., Edell & Mitchell, 1978; Greenwald, 1968; Wright, 1973). In addition, a number of alternative models have been tested against the Fishbein model and, in most cases, the Fishbein model provides the best prediction of attitudes (i.e., Bettman, Capon & Lutz, 1975). Consequently, the models that are currently used to predict attitudes have generally been found to have the greatest predictive power. The possibility remains, however, that other models that have yet to be proposed, may turn out to be better predictors of attitudes.

A third and final explanation is that there may be other mediators of the attitude formation and change process. These mediators may not involve verbal brand information. One mediator that has been suggested is attitude toward the ad, a measure of affective feelings about the advertisement (Mitchell & Olson, 1981). Although we do not have a complete understanding of this mediator, it may represent the transfer of affect through a nonverbal channel (Fig. 1.6). For instance, affect may be transferred from the advertisement to the advertised brand by principles of classical conditioning (Staats & Staats, 1958). A photograph that evokes positive feelings may be paired with a brand in an advertisement and over time these positive feelings may be transferred to the brand.

Support for this position comes from a study by Mitchell and Olson (1981) in which subjects saw a number of different advertisements (e.g., visual vs. verbal) for hypothetical facial tissue brands. In attempting to explain differences in attitudes toward the different brands, predicted scores from the Fishbein attitude model were used as covariates. After covarying out these effects, significant differences remained in the attitudes toward the different brands. However, when

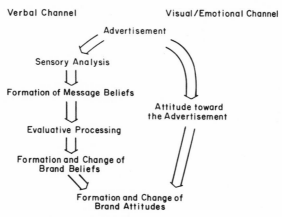

Fig. 1.6.   Dual channel processing of advertising information.

both the predicted attitudes scores from the Fishbein model *and* attitude toward the advertisement scores were used as covariates, all significant differences in attitudes toward the brands was eliminated. These results indicate that attitude toward the advertisement may also be a mediator of the effects of advertising on brand attention.

In summary, then, three mediators have currently been identified as explaining the effect of advertising on attitude formation and change. These are cognitive responses, cognitive structure and attitudes toward the advertisement. Next, we examine the factors that may affect how these mediators affect attitudes.

LEVEL ONE FACTORS

As discussed earlier, individuals have control over the information acquisition process in three ways. First, they may deliberately choose not to expose themselves to the stimulus. Second, they can control the amount of attention they devote to the stimulus, and third they can control the type of processing that they use during exposure to the stimulus. The first factor is relatively uninteresting, so we now concentrate on the latter two factors; amount of attention and type of processing.

Attention Levels.   A number of studies in social psychology have examined the effects of different attention levels during exposure to a persuasive communication (e.g., Petty, Wells, & Brock, 1976). These studies were conducted within the distraction paradigm which examined the effect of a distraction on the persuasion process and the mediators of this process. Within this paradigm, both attention levels and processing goals (e.g., evaluate the personality of the speaker) were manipulated.

Studies that manipulated attention levels found that reduced attention levels affect the amount of attitude change by blocking evaluative processing (i.e., the generation of counterarguments and support arguments) [Baron, Baron, & Miller, 1973]. If, under conditions of full attention, the persuasive communication causes subjects to generate mostly support arguments, then partial attention will result in a less positive attitude. However, if the communication causes counterarguments to be generated during conditions of full attention, then partial attention will result in more positive attitudes (Petty, Wells, & Brock, 1976). These results, however, occur only if the reduced attention level blocks the generation of counterarguments and support arguments, but not the comprehension of the message.

Different types of messages may require differing amounts of attention in order to comprehend the message. For instance, messages that have a higher level of meaning generally require more attention (Britton, Westbrook, & Holdredge, 1978). Consequently, for a relatively simple message, a particular level of attention may allow for comprehension of the message, but block the generation of counterarguments and support arguments. However, the same attention level may inhibit the comprehension of a more complex message (Regen & Cheng, 1973).

There is a second dimension that must also be taken into account in determining the effect of a particular distracting stimuli. This is whether the distractor effectively blocks the verbal channel or the visual channel. A distractor that effectively blocks the verbal channel may still allow visual information to be received (e.g., Mitchell, 1980).

The type and amount of distraction will not only have an effect on attitude formation but also on the amount of brand information stored in memory. If the distractor task only blocks the generation of counterarguments and support arguments, there will still be a considerable amount of information from the message stored in memory. However, as the distractor task takes up greater amounts of attention, the amount of information from the message stored in memory will be reduced. In addition, under these latter conditions, the resulting memory structure may be fragmented. In other words, associated concepts may be only weakly linked to the brand.

Processing Strategy.   The strategy dimension concerns how individuals process information from the advertisement. One strategy, which has been called a brand strategy (Mitchell, Gardner, & Russo, 1981), is to actively process the information from the advertisement with the goal of forming an overall evaluation of the advertised brand or to acquire information about the advertised brand. Alternatively, individuals may have some other goal during exposure to the advertisement, such as simply enjoying the entertainment aspects of the advertisement. We have called these nonbrand strategies. When executing a nonbrand strategy the individual will generally not activate the appropriate brand or product schema in memory and consequently will generate few, if any product related thoughts, counterarguments or support arguments.

These two processing strategies will generally cause differences in the resulting content and organization of information from the advertisement in memory. Both strategies cause a trace of the advertisement to be retained in memory, however, the brand strategy also results in a well-integrated network of concepts organized about the brand. In contrast, a nonbrand strategy appears to result in a weakly linked set of knowledge about the brand. In a previous study, these two types of strategies resulted in differences in the amount of time required to verify information about the brands and the resulting attitudes toward brands. The group executing the nonbrand strategy took longer to verify information about the brands and formed more positive attitudes (Mitchell, Gardner, & Russo, 1981).

These two different types of strategies are conceptually similar to the distinction between intentional and incidental learning that is frequently made in psychology (McLaughlin, 1965; Postman, 1975). The brand strategy may be thought of as intentional learning whereas a nonbrand strategy represents incidental learning. In order to produce a nonbrand strategy in the laboratory, subjects must be given a task other than a brand task while exposed to the advertisement. In the previously mentioned study, we had subjects evaluate the attention-getting value of each advertisement. This is similar to a Type II incidental-learning task which is frequently used in the levels-of-processing paradigm (Postman, 1975).

Although conditions of reduced attention with a brand strategy that results in comprehension of the message but blockage of evaluative processing may on the surface seem similar to a nonbrand strategy under full attention, there are important conceptual differences between the two. A brand strategy with low attention levels should result in a network of associations that are strongly linked to the brand whereas a nonbrand strategy under conditions of full attention may result in a weakly linked network of associations. These conceptual differences also result in empirical differences. In the previously mentioned study (Mitchell, Gardner, & Russo, 1981), the use of the number of counterarguments, support arguments and source derogations as covariates did not eliminate the differences in attitudes between groups executing a brand and nonbrand strategy. This is in contrast to the results of experiments examining differences in attention levels, where the use of either the number of counterarguments or support arguments as covariates eliminates any between group differences in attitude (Insko, Turnbull, & Yandell, 1974; Osterhouse & Brock, 1970). In addition, the preliminary results of an experiment examining differences in the effects of a brand strategy with reduced attention levels and a nonbrand strategy with full attention indicated between group differences in attitudes (Mitchell, 1980).

These two factors, attention and strategy, provide a useful means of understanding the effect of involvement on the processing of information from advertisements. Although different levels of involvement are believed to result in differences in advertising effects (e.g., Krugman, 1965), these differences are not well understood nor are the cognitive processes well defined at a conceptual level.

In previous papers, I defined involvement as the motivational state of an individual induced by a particular stimulus or situation (Mitchell, 1979, 1981). Consequently, this definition of involvement has two dimensions: intensity and direction. When applying this definition to advertisements, the amount of attention devoted to the advertisement indicates intensity whereas the type of processing strategy used indicates direction.

Learning with Controlled Processes

The different stages of the information acquisition process and the two dimensions of level of attention and processing strategy suggest three alternative models of learning with controlled processes (Fig. 1.7). The first model involves

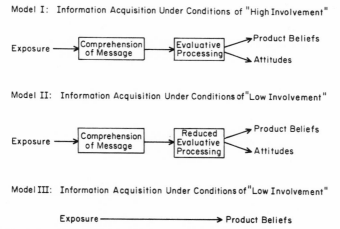

Fig. 1.7.   Alternative models of the acquisition of verbal information.

learning under conditions where information from the advertisement is actively processed and evaluated with the goal of forming an overall evaluation of the brand. Here individuals activate the appropriate knowledge structures and fully comprehend the message. This might be thought of as model of "high involvement" information processing. We would expect cognitive responses and product specific beliefs to be the primary mediators of attitude formation and change. However, even under these conditions, if an affect-laden stimulus is used in the advertisement, attitude toward the advertisement may also be a mediator.

In the second model, attention deficits block the amount of evaluative processing that occurs, however, the individual activates the appropriate knowledge structures so the message is comprehended. This condition, as mentioned previously, has been studied extensively in social psychology. This research indicates that cognitive responses are the only mediator of attitude formation and change; however, these results were obtained by using highly rational verbal stimuli (e.g., arguments for raising college tuition). It is hypothesized that if, for instance, an affect-laden stimulus appeared in the advertisement, attitude toward the advertisement might also be a mediator.

The third model occurs when the appropriate knowledge structures are *not* activated so the individual does not fully comprehend the message in terms of its implications about the advertised brand. This may occur because individuals are executing a nonbrand evaluation strategy or because the attention deficit impedes the comprehension of the message. The individual acquires some information about the brand and a trace of the advertisement exists in memory. Later, if the individual forms an attitude toward the advertised brand, this attitude will probably be based on the fragmentary information acquired and the trace of the advertisement. Previous research suggests that cognitive responses are not the only mediator under these conditions (Mitchell, Gardner, & Russo, 1981). Alternative mediators under these conditions may be attitude toward the advertisement and the few brand-specific beliefs that are formed. These latter two models might be thought of as representing "low involvement" information processing.

Learning with Automatic Processes

The current discussion has centered on the effect of advertising under conditions of different controlled processes. However, in many situations, exposure to advertisements may involve little controlled processing. For instance, after individuals have been exposed to the same advertisement a number of times, additional exposures may result in little controlled processing.

Most of the literature indicates that repetition of the same print advertisement has little, if any, effect on immediate attitude measures, however, it does have a positive effect on recall (e.g., Mitchell & Olson, 1977; Ray & Sawyer, 1971). One study which examined the effect of message repetition on delayed attitude measures found differences in delayed measures of attitudes, but no differences in immediate measures of attitudes when the message was repeated (Johnson & Watkins, 1971). Also, another study found that different advertisements for the same brand had an effect on attitudes (McCollough & Ostrom, 1974).

One interpretation of these results is that when the same advertisement is presented to individuals a number of times, they used automatic processing to determine whether they have already seen the advertisement. This automatic processing may facilitate access to the packet of information about the brand and the automatic activation of the associated concepts may also strengthen these links. Consequently, recall would be facilitated and the organization of information would become more tightly organized. This, in turn, may cause attitudes to be more stable over time.

LEVEL TWO FACTORS

In the previous section, factors which affect the cognitive processing that occurs during exposure to an advertisement (Level One) were discussed. In this section, we will discuss factors that affect the amount of attention that is devoted to the advertisement and the strategy that is used to process the information from the advertisement. These factors are divided into three groups: Individual Factors, Environmental Factors and Stimulus Factors (Fig. 1.8).

Individual Factors.   These factors, which are internal to the individual, include his or her brand and product related knowledge structures and current goals. As illustrated in Fig. 1.8, they affect both the amount of attention devoted to the advertisement and the processing strategy that is used. The amount of prior information that an individual has about a particular brand and product category

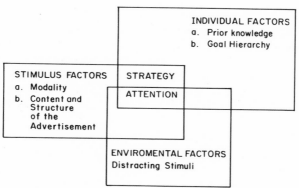

Fig. 1.8.   Level two factors.

should affect his or her ability to comprehend and evaluate the information in the message. For instance, with little stored information, an individual will have difficulty comprehending a complex and highly technical advertisement. This difficulty in comprehending the message will also affect his or her ability to evaluate the information in the message. Edell and Mitchell (1978), for instance, found that subjects with little product class knowledge generated significantly fewer counterarguments than more knowledgeable subjects.

An individual's current goals will primarily affect the strategy that the individual uses in processing information from advertisements. If an individual is planning to purchase an automobile in the near future and is interested in acquiring information about different brands of automobiles, he or she is likely to execute a brand strategy during exposure to an automobile advertisement. However, if an individual does not have a goal to purchase or acquire information about the product being advertised, he or she will probably execute a nonbrand strategy.

Environmental Factors.   These factors center the number of distracting stimuli in the environment during exposure to the advertisement. Both the amount of distraction and the type of distraction will have an affect on the amount of attention devoted to the advertisement. As the amount of distraction increases, the amount of attention available for processing the information from the advertisement will decrease. This will first reduce the amount of evaluative processing and then comprehension of the message. In addition, the type of distraction may also affect processing. A distraction, for instance, that requires verbal processing such as listening to the conversation of another person will interfere with the verbal processing of information from the advertisement.

Stimulus Factors.   These factors include the modality used to present the advertisement and the content and structure of the advertisement. They will affect the processing strategy that is used (Fig. 1.8). Modality affects the amount of time that the individual has to process the information from the advertisement. With print advertisements, the individual can spend as much time as he or she would like processing the information, however, with broadcast the individual has only a limited amount of time to process the information. In the only carefully controlled study in the area, Wright (1974) found that fewer counterarguments were generated when the same information was presented auditorily as opposed to visually.

Modality effects also have been found on recall tasks where a greater recency effect is found for auditorily presented items than for visually presented items immediately after presentation (e.g., Penny, 1975). However, with a delayed recall test, Engle and Mobley (1976) found the opposite—a greater recency effect for visually presented items. These results suggest that structural differences may exist in the visual and the verbal channels and that modality may cause processing differences as Wright (1974) demonstrated, or a combination of both.

The content and structure of an advertisement may also be important. The content of an advertisement refers to what information is presented in the advertisement and the structure refers to how the information is presented (e.g., verbally or visually). Both of these factors may affect how easily the message is comprehended and the amount of attention devoted to the advertisement. For instance, processing visually presented information may require less attentional capacity than processing verbal information. In addition, information that is presented in a unique way will probably cause the individual to devote more attention to the advertisement.

Finally, it should be noted that important interactions will probably occur between these factors. For instance, the current goals of the individual will interact with the amount of distraction in the environment to affect processing. If the need for information about a particular brand is a relatively low-level goal, then relatively unimportant stimuli from the environment may cause a distraction effect, however, if the goal is important, the distracting stimuli may have little effect.

SUMMARY

In this chapter, a theoretical framework for examining advertising effects is presented. This framework focuses on the cognitive processes that occur during exposure to an advertisement and the effect of these processes on the content and organization of brand related information in memory. A review of the literature on memory and cognitive processes indicated that dual channels may exist for verbal and visual information. In addition, a number of different approaches were discussed which indicate a relationship between the type of processing that occurs during the information acquisition process and the permanence of the memory trace for this information. Finally, this review indicated that individuals may exert control over this acquisition process in two ways. First, they control the amount of attention devoted to a stimulus, and second, they control the strategy used in processing the information.

In applying this framework to understand advertising effects, it was suggested that the typical mediators that have been examined in the past were only tapping information acquisition through the verbal channel. For this reason, they may be explaining only part of the reliable variance in attitudes. It was suggested that attitude toward the advertisement may be a mediator of the visual channel and that this mediator may explain the remaining amount of reliable variance of attitudes.

The attention and strategy distinction was then used to examine three alternative models of the information acquisition process. Suggestions as to how the different mediators may affect attitude formation and change were discussed, along with the effect of the different models in the content and structure of information about the advertised brand in memory. Finally, factors that may affect attention levels and processing strategies were discussed. These were grouped into individual factors, environmental factors and stimulus factors.

ACKNOWLEDGMENT

This research was partially supported by Grant DAR76-81806 from the National Science Foundation. The author thanks Linda Alwitt, Jim Bettman, Eric Johnson, Jerry Olson and Terrence Smith for their many helpful comments on an earlier version of this chapter.

REFERENCES

Anderson, J. R. *Language, memory and thought.* Hillsdale, N.J.: Lawrence Erlbaum Associates, 1976.

Anderson, J. R. Arguments concerning representations for mental imagery. *Psychological Review,* 1978, *85,* 249–277.

Anderson, J. R. *Cognitive psychology and its implications.* San Francisco: W. H. Freeman and Co., 1980.

Anderson, J. R., & Bower, H. G. *Human associative memory.* Washington, D.C.: Winston & Sons, 1973.

Anderson, J. R., Kline, P. J., & Lewis, C. A production system model for language processing. In P. Carpenter & M. Just (Eds.), *Cognitive processes in Comprehension.* Hillsdale, N.J.: Lawrence Erlbaum Associates, 1977.

Anderson, J. R., & Reder, L. M. An elaborative processing explanation of depth of processing. In L. S. Cermak & F. I. M. Craik (Eds.), *Levels of processing in human memory.* Hillsdale, N.J.: Lawrence Erlbaum Associates, 1979.

Atkinson, R. C., & Shiffrin, R. M. Human memory: A proposed system and its control processes. In K. W. Spence & J. T. Spence (Eds.), *Advances in the psychology of learning and motivation: Research and theory, Vol. 2.* New York: Academic Press, 1968.

Baddeley, H. D. The trouble with levels: A reexamination of Craik and Lockhart's framework for memory research. *Psychological Review,* 1978, *85,* 139–152.

Baron, R. S., Baron, P. H., & Miller, N. The relation between distraction and persuasion. *Psychological Bulletin,* 1973, *80,* 310–323.

Bettman, J. R. *An information processing theory of consumer behavior,* Reading, Mass.: Addison-Wesley, 1979.

Bettman, J. R., Capon, N., & Lutz, R. J. Cognitive algebra in multi-attribute models. *Journal of Marketing Research,* 1975, *12,* 151–164.

Bower, G. H. Mood and memory. *American Psychologist,* 1981, *36,* 129–148.

Britton, B. K., Westbrook, R. D., & Holdredge, T. S. Reading and cognitive capacity usage: Effects of text difficulty. *Journal of Experimental Psychology: Human Learning and Memory,* 1978, *4,* 582–591.

Broadbent, D. E. *Perception and communication.* London: Pergamon Press, 1958.

Brooks, L. R. Spacial and verbal components of the act of recall. *Canadian Journal of Psychology,* 1968, *22,* 349–350.

Brucks, M., & Mitchell, A. A. Knowledge structures, production systems and decision strategies. In K. Monroe (Ed.), *Advances in consumer research, Vol. 8,* Ann Arbor, Mich.: Association for Consumer Research, 1981.

Capon, N., & Hulbert, J. The sleeper effect: An awakening. *Public Opinion Quarterly,* 1973, *37,* 56–72.

Chestnut, R. W., & Jacoby, J. Consumer information processing: Emerging theory and findings. In A. G. Woodside, J. N. Sheth, & P. D. Bennett (Eds.), *Consumer and industrial buying behavior.* New York: North Holland, 1977.

Collins, A. M., & Loftus, E. F. A spreading-activation theory of semantic processing. *Psychological Review,* 1975, *82,* 407–428.

Craik, F. I. M. Levels of processing: Overview and closing comments. In L. S. Cermak & F. I. M. Craik (Eds.), *Levels of processing in human memory,* Hillsdale, N.J. Lawrence Erlbaum Associates, 1979. (b)

Craik, F. I. M., & Jacoby, L. L. A process view of short-term retention. In F. Restle et al. (Eds.), *Cognitive theory, Vol. 1,* Hillsdale, N.J.: Lawrence Erlabum Associates, 1975.

Craik, F. I. M., & Lockhart, R. S. Levels of processing: A framework for memory research. *Journal of Verbal Learning and Verbal Behavior,* 1972, *11,* 671–684.

Craik, F. I. M., & Tulving, E. Depth of processing and the retention of words in episodic memory. *Journal of Experimental Psychology: General,* 1975, *104,* 268–294.

Craik, F. I. M., & Watkins, M. J. The role of rehearsal in short term memory. *Journal of Verbal Learning and Verbal Behavior,* 1973, *12,* 599–607.

D'Agostino, P. R., O'Neill, B. J., & Paivio, A. Memory for pictures and words as a function of level of processing: Depth or dual code? *Memory and Cognition,* 1977, *5,* 252–256.

Deutsch, J. A., & Deutsch, D. Attention: Some theoretical considerations. *Psychological Review,* 1963, *70,* 80–90.

Edell, J., & Mitchell, A. A. An information processing approach to cognitive responses. In S. C. Jain (Ed.), *Research frontiers in marketing: Dialogues and directions* Chicago: American Marketing Association, 1978.

Engle, R. W., & Mobley, L. A. The modality effect: What happens in long-term memory? *Journal of Verbal Learning and Verbal Behavior,* 1976, *15,* 519–527.

Fishbein, M., & Ajzen, I. *Belief attitude, intention and behaivor.* Reading, Mass.: Addison Wesley, 1975.

Fisher, R. P., & Craik, F. I. M. Interaction between encoding and retrieval operations in cued recall. *Journal of Experimental Psychology: Human Learning and Memory,* 1977, *3,* 701–711.

Gillig, P. M., & Greenwald, H. G. Is it time to lay the sleep effect to rest? *Journal of Personality and Social Psychology,* 1974, *29,* 132–139.

Greenwald, A. G. Cognitive response to persuasion and attitude change. In A. G. Greenwald, T. C. Brock, & T. M. Ostrom (Eds.), *Psychological foundations of attitudes,* New York: Academic Press, 1968.

Hayes-Roth, B. Evolution of cognitive structures and processes. *Psychological Review,* 1977, *84,* 260–278.

Higbee, K. L. Fifteen years of fear arousal: Research on threat appeals: 1953–1968. *Psychological Bulletin,* 1969, *72,* 426–444.

Hollan, J. D. Features and semantic memory: Set theoretic or network model? *Psychological Review,* 1975, *82,* 154–155.

Hovland, D., Janis, J. L., & Kelley, H. H. *Communication and persuasion.* New Haven, Conn.: Yale University Press, 1953.

Hunt, R. R., Elliott, J. M., & Spence, M. J. Independent effects of process and structure on encoding. *Journal of Experimental Psychology: Human Learning and Memory,* 1979, *5,* 339–347.

Hyde, T. S., & Jenkins, J. J. Differential effects of incidental tasks on the organization of recall lists of highly associated words. *Journal of Experimental Psychology,* 1969, *82,* 472–481.

Insko, C. A., Turnbull, W., & Yandell, B. Facilitative and inhibiting effects of distraction on attitude change. *Sociometry,* 1974, *37,* 508–528.

Jacoby, L. L. The role of mental contiguity in memory: Registration and retrieval effects. *Journal of Verbal Learning and Verbal Behavior,* 1974, *13,* 483–496.

Johnson, H. H., & Watkins, T. A. The effect of message repetitions on immediate and delayed attitude change. *Psychonomic Science,* 1971, *22,* 101–103.

Kahneman, D. *Attention and effort.* Englewood Cliffs, N.J.: Prentice-Hall, Inc., 1973.

Kintsch, W. *The representation of meaning in memory.* Hillsdale, N.J.: Lawrence Erlbaum Associates, 1974.

Kintsch, W. Semantic memory: A tutorial. In R. S. Nickerson (Ed.), *Attention and performance, VII,* Hillsdale, N.J.: Lawrence Erlbaum Associates, 1980.

Kintsch, W., & van Dijk, T. A. Toward a model of text comprehension and production. *Psychological Review,* 1978, *85,* 363–394.

Kosslyn, S. M. The medium and the message in mental imagery: A theory. *Psychological Review,* 1981, *88,* 46–66.

Krugman, H. E. The impact of television advertising: Learning without involvement. *Public Opinion Quarterly,* 1965, *29,* 349–356.

LaBerge, D., & Samuels, S. J. Toward a theory of automatic information processing in reading. *Cognitive Psychology,* 1974, *6,* 293–323.

Lachman, R., Lachman, J. L., & Butterfield, E. C. *Cognitive psychology and information processing,* Hillsdale, N.J.: Lawrence Erlbaum Associates, 1979.

Lutz, R. J. Changing brand attitudes through modification of cognitive structure. *Journal of Consumer Research,* 1975, *1,* 49–59.

Lutz, R. J., & Swasy, J. L. Integrating cognitive structure and cognitive response approaches to monitoring communication effects in W. D. Perreault, Jr. (Ed.), *Advances in Consumer Research.* Vol. 4, Atlanta: Association for Consumer Research, 1977.

Mandler, G. Organization and repetition: Organizational principles with special reference to rote learning. In L. Nilsson (Ed.), *Perspectives on memory research,* Hillsdale, N.J.: Lawrence Erlbaum Associates, 1979.

McClelland, J. L. On the time relations of mental processes: An examination of systems of processes in cascade. *Psychological Review,* 1979, *86,* 287–330.

McClelland, J. L., & Rumelhart, D. E. An interactive activation model of context in perception: Part I. *Psychological Review,* 1981, *88,* 375–407.

McCollough, J. L., & Ostrom, T. M. Repetition of highly similar messages and attitude change. *Journal of Applied Psychology,* 1974, *11,* 283–287.

McLaughlin, B. "Intentional" and "incidental" learning in human subjects: The role of instructions to learn and motivation. *Psychological Bulletin.* 1965. *63,* 359–376.

Minsky, M. A. Framework for representing knowledge. In P. H. Winston (Ed.), *The Psychology of Computer Vision.* New York: McGraw-Hill, 1975.

Mitchell, A. A. An information processing view of consumer behavior. In S. C. Jain (Ed.), *Research frontiers in marketing: Dialogues and directions.* Chicago: American Marketing Association, 1978.

Mitchell, A. A. Involvement: A potentially important mediator of consumer behavior, in W. Wilkie (Ed.), *Advances in consumer research, Vol. 6.* Ann Arbor, Mich.: Association for Consumer Research, 1979.

Mitchell, A. A. The use of an information processing approach to understand advertising effects. In J. C. Olson (Ed.), *Advances in consumer research, Vol. 7.* Ann Arbor, Mich.: Association for Consumer Research, 1980.

Mitchell, A. A. The dimensions of advertising involvement. In K. Monroe, (Ed.), *Advances in consumer research, Vol. 8.* Ann Arbor, Mich.: Association for Consumer Research, 1981.

Mitchell, A. A., & Olson, J. C. Cognitive effects of advertising repetition. In W. Perreault (Ed.), *Advances in consumer research, Vol. 4.* 1977.

Mitchell, A. A., & Olson, J. C. Are product attribute beliefs the only mediator of advertising effects on brand attitudes? *Journal of Marketing Research,* 1981, *18.*

Mitchell, A. A., Gardner, M., & Russo, J. E. *Strategy-induced low involvement processing of advertising messages.* Working Paper, Graduate School of Industrial Administration, Carnegie-Mellon University, Pittsburgh, PA, August, 1982.

Moray, N. Attention in dichotic listening: Affective cues and the influence of instructions. *Quarterly Journal of Experimental Psychology,* 1959, *11,* 56–60.

Murry, D. J., & Newman, F. M. Visual and verbal coding in short term memory. *Journal of Experimental Psychology,* 1973, *100,* 58–62.

Navon, D. Forest before trees: The precedence of global features in visual perception. *Cognitive Psychology,* 1977, *9,* 353–383.

Nelson, D. L. Remembering pictures and words: Appearance, significance and name. In L. S. Cermak & F. I. M. Craik (Eds.), *Levels of processing in human memory.* Hillsdale, N.J.: Lawrence Erlbaum Associates, 1979.

Nelson, D. L., & Brooks, D. H. Independence of phonetic and imaginal features. *Journal of Experimental Psychology,* 1973, *97,* 1–7.

Nelson, D. L., Reed, V. S., & McEvoy, C. L. Learning to order pictures and words: A model of sensory and semantic encoding. *Journal of Experimental Psychology: Human Learning and Memory,* 1979, *5,* 292–314.

Nelson, T. O. Repetition and depth of processing. *Journal of Verbal Learning and Verbal Behavior,* 1977, *16,* 151–172.

Neves, D. M., & Anderson, J. R. Knowledge compilations: Mechanisms for the automatization of cognitive skills. In J. R. Anderson (Ed.), *Cognitive skills and their acquisition,* Hillsdale, N.J.: Lawrence Erlbaum Associates, 1981.

Newell, A. Production Systems: Models of control structures. In W. G. Chase (Ed.), *Visual information processing.* New York: Academic Press, 1973.

Norman, D. A. Toward a theory of memory and attention. *Psychological Reivew,* 1968, *75,* 522–536.

Norman, D. A. Perception, memory and mental processes. In L. Nilsson (Ed.), *Perspectives on memory research*, Hillsdale, N.J.: Lawrence Erlbaum Associates, 1979.

Norman, D. A., & Bobrow, D. G. On data-limited and resource limited processing. *Cognitive Psychology*, 1975, *7*, 44–64.

Norman, D. A., & Bobrow, D. G. Descriptions: An intermediate stage in memory retrieval. *Cognitive Psychology*, 1979, *11*, 107–123.

Norman, D. A., Rumelhart, D. E., and LNR Research Group. *Exploration in cognition*. San Francisco: W. H. Freeman, 1975.

Olson, J. C. Inferential belief formation in the cue utilization process. In H. K. Hunt (Ed.), *Advances in consumer research, Vol. 5*. Ann Arbor, Mich.: Association for Consumer Research, 1978.(a)

Olson, J. C., & Mitchell, A. A. The process of attitude acquisition: The value of a developmental approach to consumer attitude research. In M. J. Schlinger (Ed.), *Advances in consumer research, Vol. 2*. Chicago: Association for Consumer Research, 1975.

Olson, J. C., Toy, D. A., & Dover, P. A. *Do cognitive responses mediate the effects of advertising content on cognitive structure?* Working Paper, College of Business Administration Pennsylvania State University, June 1979.

Ortony, A. Remembering, understanding and representation. *Cognitive Science*, 1980, *2*, 53–69.

Osterhouse, R. A., & Brock, T. C. Distraction increases yielding to propaganda by inhibiting counterarguing. *Journal of Personality and Social Psychology*, 1970, *15*, 344–358.

Paivio, A. *Imagery and verbal processes*. New York: Holt, Rinehart & Winston, 1971.

Palmer, S. E. Fundamental aspects of cognitive representation. In E. Rosch & B. B. Lloyd (Eds.), *Cognition and categorization*, Hillsdale, N.J.: Lawrence Erlbaum Associates, 1978.

Penny, C. G. Modality effects in short-term verbal memory. *Psychological Bulletin*, 1975, *82*, 68–84.

Petty, R. E., Wells, G. L., & Brock, T. C. Distraction can enhance or reduce yielding to propaganda: Thought disruption versus effort justification. *Journal of Personality and Social Psychology*, 1976, *34*, 874–884.

Postman, L. Verbal learning and memory. *Annual Review of Psychology*, 1975, *26*, 291–335.

Postman, L., Thompkins, B. A., & Gray, W. D. The interpretation of encoding effects in retention. *Journal of Verbal Learning and Verbal Behavior*, 1978, *17*, 681–705.

Pylyshyn, Z. W. What the mind's eye tells the mind's brain: A critique of mental imagery. *Psychological Bulletin*, 1973, *80*, 1–24.

Pylyshyn, Z. W. The imagery debate: Analogue media versus tacit knowledge. *Psychological Review*, 1981, *88*, 16–45.

Ray, M. L., & Sawyer, A. G. Repetition in media models: A laboratory technique. *Journal of Marketing Research*, 1971, *8*, 20–29.

Regen, D. T., & Cheng, J. Distraction and attitude change: A resolution. *Journal of Experimental Social Psychology*, 1973, *9*, 138–147.

Roberts, D. F., & Maccoby, N. Information processing and persuasion: Counter arguing behavior. In P. Clarke (Ed.), *New Models for Communication Research*. Beverly Hills: Sage Publications, 1973.

Rosch, E. Principles of categorization. In E. Rosch & B. B. Lloyd (Eds.), *Cognition and Categorization*. Hillsdale, N.J.: Lawrence Erlbaum Associates, 1978.

Rumelhart, D. E., & Norman, D. A. Analogical processes in learning. In J. R. Anderson (Ed.), *Cognitive Skills and their acquisition*, Hillsdale, N.J.: Lawrence Erlbaum Associates, 1981.

Rumelhart, D. E., & Ortony, A. The representation of knowledge in memory. In R. C. Anderson, R. J. Spiro, & W. E. Montague (Eds.), *Schooling and the acquisition of knowledge*, Hillsdale, N.J.: Lawrence Erlbaum and Associates, 1978.

Schank, R. C. Language and memory. *Cognitive Science*, 1980, *4*, 243–284.

Schank, R. C., & Abelson, R. P. *Scripts, plans, goals and understanding.* Hillsdale, N. J.: Lawrence Erlbaum Associates, 1977.

Schneider, W., & Shiffrin, R. N. Controlled and automatic human information processing I: Detection, search and attention. *Psychological Review,* 1977, *84,* 1–66.

Shiffrin, R. M. Short-time store: The basis of a memory system. In F. Restle et al. (Eds.), *Cognitive theory, Vol. 1,* Hillsdale, N.J.: Lawrence Erlbaum Associates, 1975.

Shiffrin, R. M. Capacity limitations in information processing, attention and memory. In W. K. Estes (Ed.), *Handbook of cognitive learning and cognitive processes: Attention and memory.* Hillsdale, N.J.: Lawrence Erlbaum Associates, 1976.

Shiffrin, R. M., & Schneider, W. Controlled and automatic human information processing: II, Perceptual learning, automatic attending, and a general theory. *Psychological Review,* 1977, *84,* 127–190.

Smith, E. E. Organization of factual knowledge. In J. H. Flowers (Ed.), *1980 Nebraska Symposium on Motivation,* Lincoln, Nebraska: University of Nebraska Press, 1981.

Staats, A. W., & Staats, C. K. Attitudes established by classical conditioning. *Journal of Abnormal and Social Psychology,* 1958, *57,* 37–40.

Treisman, A. M. Contextual cues in selective listening. *Quarterly Journal of Experimental Psychology,* 1960, *12,* 242–248.

Tulving, E. Episodic and semantic memory. In E. Tulving & W. Donaldson (Eds.), *Organization and memory,* New York: Academic Press, 1972.

Tulving, E. Cue-dependent forgetting. *American Scientist,* 1974, *62,* 74–81.

Tulving, E. Relation between encoding specificity and levels of processing. In L. S. Cermak & F. I. M. Craik (Eds.), *Levels of processing in human memory,* Hillsdale, N.J.: Lawrence Erlbaum Associates 1979.

Tulving, E. & Thompson, D. M., Encoding specificity and retrieval processes in episodic memory. *Psychological Review,* 1973, *80,* 352–373.

Ward, S. A discussion of Wright's paper. In G. D. Hughes & M. L. Ray (Eds.), *Buyer/consumer information processing.* Chapel Hill: University of North Carolina Press, 1974.

Wickelgren, W. A. Human learning and memory. *Annual Review of Psychology,* 1981, *32,* 21–52.

Woodward, A. E., Bjork, R. A., & Jongeward, R. H. Jr. Recall and recognition as a function of primary rehearsal. *Journal of Verbal Learning and Verbal Behavior,* 1973, *12,* 608–617.

Wright, P. L. The cognitive processes mediating acceptance of advertising. *Journal of Marketing Research,* 1973, *10,* 53–62.

Wright, P. L. Analyzing media effects on advertising responses. *Public Opinion Quarterly,* 1974, *38,* 192–205.

Zajonc, R. D. Thinking and feeling: Preferences need no inferences. *American Psychologist,* 1980, *35,* 151–175.

2

Effects of Involvement and Message Content on Information-Processing Intensity

Robert E. Burnkrant
Alan G. Sawyer
The Ohio State University

The position taken in this chapter is that a major determinant of what and how much we learn from our exposure to communications is a function of the intensity with which we process the information we confront. At some times and in some situations people devote a considerable proportion of their cognitive capacity to taking in, interpreting and understanding what is being said. At other times little, if any, cognitive capacity is allocated to message processing. This variation in the intensity with which information is processed is a major determinant of the learning which takes place when people are exposed to information.

The focus of this chapter is on determinants and consequences of information processing intensity. Evidence is beginning to emerge which suggests that this intensity is a function of two types of variables. First, it seems to be directly related to the task or goal orientation of the individual receiving the message. Second, it seems to be a function of the structural characteristics of the message itself. These two types of factors interact with one another to determine information processing intensity. This intensity, in turn, is a major determinant of the learning which takes place when people are exposed to information.

In this chapter we first consider the goal or task determinants of information processing. This is followed by a consideration of message characteristics. We then review evidence that suggests that information-processing intensity is determined by an interaction of both task and message factors. The final section of this chapter attempts to draw out the implications of these findings and suggests directions for future research.

INFORMATION-PROCESSING INTENSITY

Before proceeding, it would seem advisable to consider further what we mean by information-processing intensity. We assume that people have a limited processing capacity. This capacity is allocated by the individual to processing tasks of all kinds from those oriented to scanning the environment to those that are concerned more directly with the attainment of specific informational goals (Bettman, 1979; Kahneman, 1973). The amount of this capacity allocated to a specific processing task determines information-processing intensity. Thus, information-processing intensity is wholly consistent with what others have called cognitive effort. This construct has been defined as ''the amount of the available processing capacity central processor utilized in performing an information processing task'' (Tyler, Hertel, McCallum, & Ellis, 1979, p. 608). It is shown that the amount of learning which takes place when people are exposed to a message is directly related to the intensity with which they process that information contained in the message.

One of the major advantages of information-processing intensity over such related constructs as depth of processing, is that the former construct is amenable to measurement procedures which are independent of learning. This can be accomplished by monitoring responses to a secondary task. The time required to respond to this secondary task is taken as a measure of the amount of cognitive effort devoted to the primary task (Kerr, 1973). Tyler, Hertel, McCallum, and Ellis (1979) employed this procedure to measure cognitive effort and found that the time required to respond to the secondary task (tone recognition) was directly related to recall of information processed in the primary task.

INVOLVEMENT AND OTHER GOAL ORIENTATIONS

There are several different conceptualization of involvement in the communication literature. They all imply that an individual high in involvement is more likely to intensively process information than an individual low in involvement. Cognitive psychology also manipulates people's processing intensity, but this is typically accomplished by varying the information processing task. After reviewing these areas, we propose the concept of need for information—a goal orientation that bears some similarity to the following concepts but is likely to be more directly related to information processing intensity.

Krugman (1965, p. 355) defined involvement as, ''The number of conscious 'bridging experiences', connections or personal references per minute that the viewer makes between his own life and the stimulus.'' However, rather than attempting to explicate the determinants and consequences of this variable, Krugman's work has focused primarily on supporting his contention that television and print media differ in their involvement of the audience (i.e., Krugman,

1966–67, 1971). Many other treatments of involvement have been proposed (i.e., Clarke & Belk, 1978; Houston & Rothschild; 1978; Lastovicka & Gardner, 1978; Ray, Sawyer, Rothschild, Heeler, Strong, & Reed, 1973; Tyebjee, 1979), but there has been little agreement among them in terms of either their definitions or their operationalizations.

Issue Involvement

There have been two approaches to involvement that have been developed more systematically than the treatments referred to above. The first approach considers involvmement to be the personal importance or commitment of the individual to an *issue*. Research examining the effects of this *issue involvement* on subjects' attitudes has tended to show that when the subjects' position on the issue is discrepant from the position advocated in a message, increasing involvement decreases attitude change (Apsler & Sears, 1968; Rhine & Severance, 1970; Sherif & Hovland, 1961). Occasionally a boomerang effect occurs so that increasing involvement leads to attitude change in a direction opposite the one advocated by the message (Dean, Austin, & Watts, 1971).

In contrast to these largely negative findings, more recent research suggests that increasing issue involvement can lead to greater attitude change if the arguments contained in the message are particularly persuasive. Petty and Cacioppo (1979b) hypothesized that involved subjects focus their thoughts on message content whereas subjects less involved in the topic of the message are more apt to process information other than the message's content. To test this prediction, Petty and Cacioppo presented subjects with counter-attitudinal messages containing either strong ("logically sound, defensible and compelling") or weak ("more open to refutation and skepticism") arguments under conditions of high- or low-issue involvement. Consistent with the hypotheses, increased involvement increased the production of counter-argument cognitive responses to weak arguments and increased supportive thoughts to strong arguments. These differences in cognitive responses coincided with greater persuasion of strong arguments than weak arguments for involved subjects. However, as also predicted, less-involved subjects exhibited no statistically significant differences in either cognitive responses or persuasion.

The explanation of the above results was that those low in involvement were less likely to intensively process the messages. Such an explanation is supported by other experiments. Two experiments manipulated issue involvement, message quality, and characteristics of the sources of the message (Petty & Cacioppo, 1981). In the first experiment, a high-credible spokesperson for a message advocating comprehensive exams for college seniors was more persuasive than a low-credible spokesperson as was the stronger arguments message. In addition, statistically significant interactions of involvement with both credibility and message quality were found. Spokesperson credibility produced much more persuasion for low-involved subjects than those highly involved, whereas the high-quality arguments message was much more persuasive for those high in involvement than those less involved. A second experiment manipulated the attractiveness of models in a shampoo advertisement, in addition to involvement and message quality. Essentially the results were the same as those in the first experiment except that the involvement by message source interaction, although directionally similar to the previous one, was not statistically significant. The two experiments support the contention that, for an involved audience, message information will be intensively processed and nonmessage cues such as source credibility or attractiveness will be less likely to be processed. For an uninvolved audience, cues more easily attended than message cues (such as source characteristics) are likely to dominate processing.

Another experiment indicated that message quality interacts with issue involvement and whether attributes are expressed in the form of a rhetorical question. Petty, Cacioppo, and Heesacker (1981) hypothesized that rhetorical questions would cause a person to increase the intensity of message processing. However, when a subject is already intensely processing a message; such as when involved with a message topic, the disruption in information processing caused by the rhetorical questions might result in either no further processing or an actual decrease. As predicted, there was a three-way interaction of involvement, message quality, and whether arguments were expressed by ending with rhetorical questions or summary statements. When message arguments were summarized in statement form, the strong arguments were more effective than weak arguments in increasing attitude and decreasing counter-arguments of high-involvement subjects. This result was similar to the overall results of Petty and Cacioppo (1979b) and the results collapsed across credibility conditions of Petty and Cacioppo (1981). However, an opposite interaction of message quality and involvement was found when each message argument was summarized by a rhetorical question. Strong arguments with rhetorical questions were only slightly more effective than weak arguments under high involvement but were much more effective with low involvement. Petty, Cacioppo, and Heesacker concluded that the rhetorical questions appeared to enhance low-involved subject's processing of the messages and hence led them to react more positively to the stronger arguments. However, this enhanced processing was not needed by the involved subjects because they were already intensely processing the message. In this condition the rhetorical questions appeared to distract from processing the differences in argument quality.

Involvment is likely to also differentially influence the processing of other characteristics besides the cogency or number of message arguments. Petty and Cacioppo (1979a) manipulated issue involvement and whether subjects were forewarned about the message's attempt to persuade them on the topic (adoption of senior comprehensive exams). In addition to a negative effect of forewarning on persuasion, an interaction of forewarning and involvement was found. Forewarning produced a more negative effect on attitudes for involved than for less-involved subjects. Similarly, involved subjects produced more counterarguing cognitive responses and less supportive thoughts due to forewarning, but there were no statistically significant differences in cognitive responses for low-involved subjects. Finally, subjects expecting to discuss an issue with an opponent generated more supportive thoughts in anticipation of that discussion when the attitude issue was of high rather than low personal relevance (Cialdini, Levy, Herman, Kozlowski, & Petty, 1976).

Although the prior research suggests that high issue involvement can lead to greater attitude change through more intensive processing of message arguments, this finding may be very dependent on the particular type of issue under consideration. Several of the previously reviewed negative findings seem to have been obtained with messages that employed reasonably strong arguments. Zimbardo (1960, p. 91) has pointed out that "since arousal of issue-involvement is dependent upon a cluster of antecedent factors, which generally cannot be analyzed separately, it tends to be a rather unreliable independent variable." Furthermore, because the individual who is highly involved in an issue is likely to be highly committed to a position on that issue (e.g., Dean, Austin, & Watts, 1971; Sherif & Hovland, 1961) and probably has already developed a well-defined cognitive structure to support that position, it is not at all clear that he would be open to and actively process information on the topic. Rather, he may well be expected to defensively avoid and engage in other behaviors designed to minimize his confrontation with the ramifications of exposure to information.

Response Involvement

An alternative, less frequently employed treatment of involvement, uses this construct to account for the personal importance to the individual of an impending decision or *response*. Response involvement may be a more appropriate construct than issue involvement for researchers interested in marketing communications. In most product purchase situations, it is the implications of one's response rather than the topic per se that is important or not important. Zimbardo (1960) told people in a high-involvement condition that the responses they were about to make to a case study would be important indicators of their social values and personality whereas he led those in the low-involvement treatment to believe that their resonses would be unimportant. He found that when both groups were subsequently exposed to a case study on juvenile deliquency, the high-involvement group exhibited greater attitude change than the low-involvement group. However, Freedman (1964) manipulated response involvement and found that high-involvment subjects exhibited less opinion change than low-involvement subjects. Thus, it appears that the effect of response involvement on attitude is indeterminate. It has been suggested that whether high-response involvement favors more or less attitude change depends on which attitudinal position is most conducive to the maximization of the subjects' rewards (Petty & Cacioppo, 1979b).

More recent research has examined the effects of response involvement on the processing of message content. Wright (1974) found that high-involvement subjects exposed to print advertising engaged in more counter-arguing and less source derogation than low-involvement subjects. Similar results were obtained by Hass (1972). Chaiken (1980) found an interaction among response involvement, the number of message arguments, and source likeability. Opinion change for involved subjects was influenced by the number of arguments but not by the likeability of the source, whereas low-involved subjects were influenced by the source but not the arguments. Furthermore, high-involvement subjects recalled more arguments than low-involvement subjects. She also measured the persistence of opinion change and found greater persistence of opinion change in the high-involvement condition compared to the low-involvement condition. Presumably, this greater recall and persistence were due to more intense processing of the message content in the high-involvement condition and a greater likelihood of those more positive thoughts being stored in long term memory.

Finally, Gardner, Mitchell, and Russo (1978) told subjects to process advertisements in either an evaluative high-involvement manner "as though they were planning a purchase of the product class of the brand in the advertisement" (p. 585) or in a low-involvement manner in which the ads were attended to but were assessed for the ad's attention getting ability. Response times for recall of evaluative statements were shorter for the high-involvement group than the low-involvement group, and an opposite result was found for statements about the ads' attention-drawing abilities. Although this result was essentially a confirmation of the manipulations, the results of more accurate responses of all types for the high-involvement group indicated the likelihood of more intensive processing in that condition.

In summary, there is evidence to suggest that more intensive processing of message content occurs under high-response involvement than low-response involvement conditions. However, this may not invariably be the case. No evidence was provided to suggest that the more highly involved subjects in Freedman's (1964) study processed information any more intensively than the uninvolved subjects. Furthermore, a situation may be envisioned in which an individual is confronted with an important task but is quite confident that he can accomplish the task without exposure to additional information. Under these conditions increasing task involvement would not be likely to increase information processing, and it may well have a retarding effect on message processing if the information is expected to be inconsistent with the reader's prior beliefs. What is needed, if we are to obtain more consistent relationships between manipulations of personal importance and information processing, is a treatment that focuses more directly on the information contained in the message, rather than the response or issue dealt with in the message. It is, after all, the importance of the information contained in the message and not the importance of an issue or response per se which should determine message processing intensity.

Depth of Processing

Further insight into the nature of the individual's message orientation may be obtained from a consideration of the depth of processing literature in cognitive psychology. Task is also employed as a manipulation in this literature. However, rather than manipulating the importance of the task *per se,* this research manipulates the extent to which the individual must deal with and grasp the meaning of the information contained in a message or other stimulus material in order to perform satisfactorily on the task (i.e., Craik & Lockhart, 1972; Jacoby, Bartz, & Evans, 1978). For example, Craik and Tulving (1975) found that when subjects were asked about word meaning and then briefly exposed to the word they showed greater recall of these words than subjects who were asked about the physical properties of the words. Similarly, subjects who were asked to rate each paragraph for degree of difficulty exhibited greater recall of this paragraph than subjects who were asked to count the number of four-letter words in the passage (Schallert, 1976). Other researchers (Hyde & Jenkins, 1973; Walsch & Jenkins, 1973) have also found that tasks requiring people to process information as meaningful units generate greater recall than tasks which do not require subjects to deal with the meaning of information.

Rogers, Kuiper, and Kirker (1977) have found that tasks requiring individuals to indicate whether or not information describes them (self-reference task) generate greater recall than tasks requiring people to rate whether information is meaningful (semantic task). Rogers et al. attribute this to the involvment of the self schema in the former task. This self schema is presumed to operate as a powerful retrieval cue in the self-reference task. If this were true we would expect that schema-consistent information would be remembered better than schema-inconsistent information. However, when Rogers et al. (1977) examined the proportion of recalled words rated yes vs. no, there was no significant yes-no difference within the self-reference task.[1] An alternative possible explanation for the superiority of the self-reference task over the semantic task is that, because subjects' responses in the self-reference task are reflective of their own self concepts, they feel it is more important to accurately process and interpret the information in the self-reference task than in the semantic task. This greater desire to take in and accurately interpret the information in the self-reference condition may lead subjects in that condition to devote greater cognitive effort to the processing task. This greater cognitive effort, or information-processing

---

[1]Rogers, Kuiper, and Kirker (1977) did find a significant yes-no recall difference for self reference ratings before adjusting for the number of yes and no responses; but, as they point out, this effect could be due merely to a differential number of yes responses as a function of rating task.

intensity, may then cause the superior recall results demonstrated for the self-reference task. Tyler, Hertel, McCallum, and Ellis (1979) showed that effort can be varied within levels of processing and that effort is an important determinant of subsequent recall performance.

The preceding literature all seems to focus on the orientation the individual brings to the message. The involvement research emphasized the personal importance to the individual of an issue or impending response. Although this literature seems to bear an indeterminate relationship to attitude change, several studies suggested that involvement is directly related to the intensity with which the content of a message is processed. It was pointed out that this intensive processing would only be expected to occur to the extent that interest in an *issue or a response* covaries with interest in *additional information* about that issue or response. The depth of processing literature is related to the involvement literature (and especially response involvement) in that it too is concerned with the task or goal orientation confronting the individual. However, depth of processing research focuses directly on the kind of *information processing task* the individual is asked to perform. Learning seems to be facilitated to the extent the task requires the individual to grasp the *meaning* of the information conveyed in the message.[2] More recent research suggests that semantic tasks may differ in the amount of learning they generate. The amount of learning which occurs appears to be directly related to the magnitude of cognitive effort expended when processing information.

NEED FOR INFORMATION

What is needed is a conceptualization that recognizes cognitive effort, or information-processing intensity, as a major determinant of learning and ties individual task or goal orientation directly to this information-processing intensity. It appears that the crucial aspect of the manipulations employed in the involvement and depth of processing literature that leads to more intensive processing is the personal importance, not of the task or decision or issue, but of understanding and correctly interpreting the information itself. It is the importance to the individual of correctly grasping the meaning or content of the message that determines information-processing intensity.

This personal importance to the individual of understanding the meaning of the message may be regarded as a need for information (Burnkrant, 1976). Kagan (1972) defines need as a cognitive representation of a goal state that is desired. In this case, however, the goal state that is desired is greater certainty or

---

[2]Other research suggests that this may not be due so much to the inherent superiority of semantic processing but rather to the tendency of most testing situations to favor semantic processing (Bransford, Franks, Morris, & Stein, 1979).

understanding regarding the task or message under consideration. This is what is meant here by a need for information. Need for information may be defined, then, as the desire for an increase in understanding, and it is usually, but not necessarily, topic specific.

This need is inferrable from information-seeking and processing behavior. Howard and Sheth (1969) point out that, when "confidence" is low, the individual's behavior is directed at information seeking, which continues until confidence is sufficiently high for the individual to make a decision. At that point, information seeking ceases and is replaced by behavior in which this information is put to use. The observable seeking of information and the observed ceasing of this seeking after some degree of information acquisition provides a basis for inferring a need for information. In marketing, this need is generally topic-specific. It arises out of an individual's desire to make a purchase in a product class about which he or she has less knowledge than desired. At this point the person is likely to seek information relevant to that purchase. Bennett and Mandell (1969) found an inverse relationship between the amount of purchasing experience consumers have and the amount of information seeking they engage in prior to purchase. Swan (1969) also found an inverse relationship between certainty and information seeking.

An individual with an aroused need for information about a type of product would be likely to process communications about that product more intensively than an individual whose need is not so aroused. Among the available communications that he would process more intensively are advertisements on the needed topic. Need for information, then, predicts more intensive processing of a whole set of communications—those advertisements and other messages relevant to the topic on which information is desired.

This need may also be specific to an individual message, and it is in this sense that it is relevant to the recently reviewed information processing literature. When people are asked to indicate whether a passage is meaningful (i.e., semantic task) they would be expected to have a greater need to understand that passage than would other people who are asked to indicate whether the words contained in the passage are long or short (i.e., structural task). Similarly, it would be likely that when people are asked to indicate whether a word or phrase is descriptive of themselves (i.e., self-referent task) they would have a greater need to correctly understand and categorize the information than if they were merely asked to specify whether or not the word or phrase is meaningful. The former task would be much more reflective of their own personal characteristics than the latter task. Hence, the cost of erring may also be greater in the former task than in the latter task.

Need for information must be ascertained independently of recall and information-processing intensity if it is to be a useful explanatory variable in the sense suggested here. A methodology has been proposed elsewhere to help accomplish this objective (Burnkrant, 1976). It employs both experimental manipulations and paper-and-pencil tests. Dermer and Berscheid (1972) have shown that self reports of arousal including paper and pencil tests can be valid indicators of need states. In an experimental test employing this methodology need for information was found to be directly related to belief acquisition and change (Burnkrant, 1974). Cohen (1957) obtained similar results with need for cognition. There is also evidence to indicate that physiological arousal is directly related to information processing intensity (i.e., Cacioppo, 1979; Kroeber-Riel, 1979). Further validation of the mediating role of need for information would be desirable.

The use of "need for information" as a determinant of information-processing intensity has several advantages over the previously discussed alternative treatments. First, it explicitly treats the informational need arousal likely to underlie effective manipulations of response or issue importance. As a result, it should help to explain discrepancies in findings in the involvement literature and help integrate them with literature on information processing. Second, rather than suggesting that task manipulations have qualitative effects on the way information is processed, it suggests that processing intensity varies on a continuum and that the subject's position on this continuum is a function of the degree of his information need arousal.

Need for information has been derived from a broader literature on motivation (i.e., Atkinson, 1964; Tolman, 1951). As a result, the antecedents and consequences of this construct should be more clearly and systematically explainable by reference to this literature than has been accomplished thus far with the more general issue and response involvement constructs. The literature on motivation suggests other variables that should interact with need for information to produce information-processing intensity effects. Most treatments of motivation consider the strengths of behavioral tendencies to be derived from the interaction of personal and environmental factors impinging on the individual. Similarly we consider information-processing intensity to result from interaction of need for information and message structural and contextual factors. We now turn to a consideration of these message related factors.

MESSAGE CONTENT

Research reviewed earlier on the topic of involvement shows that message characteristics (Petty & Cacioppo, 1979b; Petty & Cacioppo, 1981; Petty, Cacioppo, & Heesacker, 1981) interact with involvement. These interactions show that message content has a greater impact, both on persuasion and cognitive response, under high-involvement information-processing conditions than under low-involvement conditions. For the high-involvement subjects, messages that employ convincing arguments produce greater persuasion than messages containing relatively weak arguments. This seems to occur because the high-quality messages elicit more support arguments and fewer counterarguments than low-quality messages. Little evidence has been generated by the preceding research to suggest that high-quality messages produce more intensive information processing than low-quality messages. Rather, it appears that information-processing intensity is affected by involvement and the *content* of that information processing is determined by the characteristics of the message.

Other research is beginning to emerge, however, which suggests that message content factors may also affect the intensity with which people process information. Petty, Harkins, and Williams (1980) found that subjects exposed to a high-quality message reported the expenditure of more cognitive effort processing that message than did subjects given a low-quality message. Argument quality was also directly related to support arguments and attitude change and inversely related to counterarguments.

The number of speakers conveying a message has also been found to impact on information processing. Harkins and Petty (1981) found that three speakers conveying three arguments produced more attitude change and more support arguments than one speaker conveying the same three arguements. When the arguments were weak three sources conveying these arguments led to more negative attitudes and more counterarguments than one source conveying the same three arguments. These results were not due to the belief that arguments were shared by more than one person. Rather they seem to have been due to the more intensive processing of message content provided by three sources than one source. Harkins and Petty suggest their results may be due to more elaborative processing of information provided by three sources than by one source. They leave open the question of why three sources may produce more processing than one. It may be that subjects expect the different sources to convey new or different information and that this expectation about the message leads to more intensive processing of message content in the three source condition than in the one source conditions. Sears and Freedman (1965) found that the mere belief that a message would contain new information led to more opinion change after reading that message than occurred when people did not have that expectation.

More direct evidence regarding the effects of message content on information-processing intensity and learning is provided by literature in cognitive psychology. Britton, Holdredge, Curry, and Westbrook (1979) used a secondary task technique (discussed earlier) to measure the amount of cognitive effort employed to process a series of messages. The messages were identical except that in one condition a meaning enhancing title (or picture) was provided at the beginning of the passages. In a second condition, subjects were exposed to the same message without the title. Each passage was constructed so that its meaning would be relatively difficult to comprehend in the absence of a title. The title (and in one case, the picture) gave subjects a semantic context to which they could relate the material provided in the passage. It was found, using the secondary task technique, that greater cognitive effort was devoted to processing message content when titles (or a picture) were provided than when they were not provided. In a second experiment, these authors employed messages in which the meaning of the passage was clearly provided without the title. In this case, presence or absence of a title had no effect on the allocation of cognitive capacity to the processing task. Thus, it is not the presence or absence of a title, *per se*, which affects information processing. Title only effects the intensity with which information is processed when it increases the meaning of the passage for the individual.

This information-processing intensity is directly related to the amount of learning that occurs when people are exposed to a message. The passages used in the Britton et al. (1979) research included several that had previously been used by other researchers (i.e., Bransford & Johnson, 1972; Dooling & Lachman, 1971). Both of these other researchers found that the recall of message content was higher when the titles (and picture) used by Britton et al. (1979) preceded the passages than when they did not.[3] It has also been found that, when a meaning enhancing title is provided at the end of the message rather than in front of it, subjects show no better recall than those who were not exposed to the title at all (Dooling & Mullet, 1973). We may conclude that the presence of a meaning enhancing title or clarifying picture at the beginning of a passage increases both the intensity with which that passage is processed and the recall that results from that processing.

Further clarification of the conditions under which introductory material increases learning is provided by Morris, Stein, and Bransford (1979). They found that prior information, in this case an introductory paragraph, facilitated learning of later information only when it permitted subjects to elaborate and make sense of the subsequent information based on their own past knowledge of the world. For example, recall of a sentence like, "The group felt sorry for the fat man but couldn't help chuckling about the incident" was facilitated by prior exposure to a sentence indicating that the fat man had become stuck in a cave (Morris, Stein, & Bransford, 1979, p. 254). This introductory material allowed people to use their knowledge of fat and cave to elaborate, and process more effectively, the new information. It was also found that, when prior information is not consistent with one's general knowledge of the world, the prior information does not enhance recall. This research shows, then, that clarifying introductory material such as a paragraph, sentence, title, or picture will only increase learning to the extent it

---

[3]It should be pointed out that Britton et al. also measured recall and were unable to demonstrate a significant title effect with recall. However, it may be argued that this failure to achieve a recall effect may have been due to their method of measuring recall. "For each passage, 5-11 important content words were chosen. The passage was retyped with the words deleted and replaced by a line the length of the word. . . . The subject's task was to replace the missing words" (Britton et al., 1979, p. 265). In contrast to this procedure Bransford and Johnson (1972) and Dooling and Lachman (1971) asked subjects to freely recall as much as they could about the passage.

allows the reader to elaborate the information in the passage by tying it in more ways and/or more thoroughly to what the reader already knows.

The message content research reviewed to this point suggests that introductory material (i.e., paragraph, sentence, title, picture) may be used to increase the meaningfulness of the message to which subjects are subsequently exposed. This meaningfulness may be regarded as the ease and extent to which a message or message unit permits the formation of new and/or more distinctive linkages with the individual's past (Johnson, 1974). It is our contention that increasing meaningfulness leads to more intensive information processing and that this more intensive processing leads, in turn, to the greater learning of message content.

Introductory material may also bias the direction that information processing takes. Kozminsky (1977) has suggested that a title serves as a signal or pointer to the reader permitting assembly of his/her present knowledge on a topic in order to more readily integrate and further elaborate expected new information with what he/she already knows. If introductory material facilitates or increases the likelihood that this will occur then this should lead to more intensive processing of message content and greater learning. If, instead, the introductory material merely changes the topic or subject of the knowledge structure called up within the individual, this will change the *direction* of information processing but not necessarily its intensity. Kozminsky (1977) found, when biasing titles were provided at the beginning of textual material, that recall was systematically biased in the direction of the title. Similar results were obtained by Schallert (1976). She provided subjects with ambiguous paragraphs. However, rather than being ambiguous in the sense that they were low in meaningfulness, they were ambiguous in the sense that, although meaningful, they could be given two different meanings (e.g., the same paragraph could be interpreted as being about "worries of a baseball team manager" or "worries of a glassware factory manager" [Schallert, 1976, p. 622]). She gave the paragraph to one group in the context of one title and to a second group in the context of the other title. A control group was given no title. She found that, although the groups did not differ in terms of the total number of paragraph units recalled, learning was biased in the direction of the title with which the subjects were provided. These results show, then, that introductory material can bias the *direction* of the learning which takes place by making a knowledge structure on one topic more accessible than knowledge structures on other topics.

The manipulations of meaningfulness referred to above all made use of variations in introductory material. However, meaninguflness may also be manipulated by systematically varying the structure and content of the prose passage itself. Marslen-Wilson and Tyler (1976) manipulated the meaningfulness of messages by constructing some paragraphs that had semantic meaning and by creating others that were semantically anomalous. They found that meaningful prose was recalled better than the semantically anomalous prose. Aulls (1975) found a direct relationship between the meaningfulness of paragraph content and the recall of idea units contained in the paragraph. Johnson (1974) asked some subjects to rate the meaningfulness of prose subunits while others were given a recall test over the same material. He obtained a direct relationship between subunit meaningfulness and recall. These results show that meaningfulness is also directly related to recall when it is manipulated by systematically varying the structure of prose passages. We would expect, given the preceding discussion, that these manipulations would also yield a direct relationship between meaningfulness and information-processing intensity.

MESSAGE CONTENT INTERACTS WITH NEED FOR INFORMATION

There is reason to believe that neither goal orientation manipulations nor message content variations produce independent effects on learning. Rather it is beginning to appear that message meaningfulness and need for information have an interactive effect on lerning. Jacoby, Bartz, and Evans (1978) manipulated depth of processing, repetition, and the meaningfulness of consonant-vowel-consonant trigrams in a factorial design. They found that both meaningfulness and depth of processing were directly related to recall. Furthermore, an interaction was obtained between depth of processing and meaningfulness such that the advantage in recall of the high-meaningfulness stimulus material over low-meaningfulness material was greater under deep processing instructions than under shallow processing instructions.

Seamon and Murray (1976) obtained similar results. They manipulated the meaningfulness of words and the task confronting subjects. They found that there was more recall with the semantic task than the structural task and that, within the semantic group, high-meaning words were recalled better than low-meaning words. A similar pattern of results was also obtained with recognition.

Meaning-enhancing titles should also interact with depth of processing in the same manner that word meaningfulness does. Shallert (1976) conducted a study (discussed earlier) in which she manipulated both depth of processing and message title. She obtained a direct relationship between depth of processing and number of idea units recalled, but the main effect for title and the interaction between depth of processing and title failed to reach significance. It was pointed out earlier, however, that her manipulation of title was not likely to have increased the meaningfulness of the message. Rather, it appears to have had the effect of changing the direction of the meaning attributed to the passage. For example, under one title a passage was about a baseball team manager, whereas under the other title the same passage was about a glassware factory manager. In this case we would not expect title to have an effect on the amount learned. Instead it should affect the direction of the learning that occurs, and Schallert's results are consistent with this expectation.

She obtained a significant task by title interaction as well as task and title main effects when the mean proportion of recognitions consistent with the less likely title was employed as the dependent variable. Semantic processing led to a higher proportion of correct recognitions than nonsemantic processing. The proportion of correct recognitions was biased in the direction of the title. The task by title interaction was such that, in the deep processing conditions, more correct (i.e., title consistent) recognitions were made after subjects read the message with the appropriate title than after they read the passage with either an alternative title or no title. In the shallow processing tasks, however, subjects were not sensitive to passage title.

These results suggest that information-processing task and meaningfulness of message content should have an interactive effect on the amount of learning that occurs when people are exposed to a communication. Learning should be maximal when people deeply process a highly meaningful communication. This is what occurred when meaningfulness was manipulated at the word and consonant-vowel-consonant levels. The Schallert (1976) research does not address this issue, because it manipulated the direction of meaning rather than the amount of meaning derivable from the employed passages. Nevertheless, the same results that were obtained for manipulations of meaningfulness at the word and consonant-vowel-consonant levels would be expected to hold for manipulations at the passage level. This would suggest that message meaningfulness would have a stronger effect on learning at relatively deep levels of processing than at shallower levels. Learning should be greatest when people are confronted with a high-meaning message under conditions likely to lead to relatively deep processing. Finally, we would expect that effects would be obtained for information-processing intensity which parallel those anticipated for recall.

DISCUSSION

The literature reviewed in this chapter implies that two types of variables underlie and determine both information-processing intensity and the amount of learning that occurs when people are exposed to a communication. These variables are shown more explicitly in Fig. 2.1 First, an information-processing task or goal orientation seems to account for the amount learned when people confront a message. Evidence (i.e., Tyler et al., 1979) was reviewed earlier which showed that depth of processing was directly related to both information-processing

Fig.2.1. A model of information-processing intensity.

intensity and learning. Manipulations of involvement and processing depth seem to have in common the characteristic that they vary the strength of the individual's desire to understand and meaningfully process information. It was pointed out earlier, however, that involvement in an issue or response would not necessarily lead to a desire for more information about that issue or response. *Need for information* was proposed as a construct that would be more closely and consistently related to information processing than issue or response involvement. Rather than implying a series of qualitatively different levels of processing, it represents the magnitude of the individual's desire for an increase in certainty or understanding. This need may be general, or it may be specific to a topic or even a particular message. It is consistent with more general treatments of motivation to expect need for information to be directly related to the intensity with which information is processed (Burnkrant, 1976). The direct relationship between information-processing intensity and recall has been shown by research reviewed earlier (e.g., Tyler et al., 1979).

Little research exists at present to directly validate our contention that a need for information mediates the effects of involvement and depth of processing on information-processing intensity and learning. Research directed at this issue would be feasible, however. One approach to the attainment of this evidence might be to employ experimental designs in which involvement and/or depth of processing are manipulated and measurements of need for information, information-processing intensity, and learning are obtained. The first step would be to determine whether information-processing intensity and recall are directly related to involvement and/or depth of processing. If positive results were obtained, it would then be desirable to partial out the effects of need for information on the dependent variables. We would expect that this would eliminate the obtained effects. A similar procedure could also be employed to determine whether information-processing intensity mediates the amount recalled. We would expect that partialling out processing intensity would eliminate the recall effect.

The second major variable considered in this chapter is the *meaningfulness of message content*. It was referred to as the ease and extent to which the communication content permits the establishment of new and/or stronger, more distinctive, linkages between the new to-be-learned information and what has already been learned (Johnson, 1974). Introductory paragraphs, titles, pictures, and message structure have all been employed to manipulate meaningfulness. Evidence has been reviewed which indicates that this construct is directly related to both information processing intensity (i.e., Britton et al., 1979) and recall (i.e., Bransford & Johnson, 1972; Dooling & Lachman, 1971; Morris, Stein, & Bransford, 1979). Substantially more research was available to link meaningfulness to recall than to tie it to information-processing intensity. Further research directed at examining the mediating effect of meaningfulness on processing intensity and learning would be desirable. Procedures similar to those suggested for validation of need for information would also be feasible here. Manipulations of meaningfulness could be employed at the passage level. Measures of meaningfulness, information-processing intensity, and recall would permit one to validate the linkages proposed among these constructs.

Research was reviewed earlier which indicated that the subject's goal or task orientation (i.e., need for information) interacts with meaningfulness to determine the amount learned. At high levels of need for information, meaningfulness manipulations generate a larger difference in the amount learned than at low levels of need. The multiplicative nature of this interaction accords well with more general models of motivation (Atkinson, 1964; Burnkrant, 1976). We believe that this interaction between need for information and meaningfulness will determine the intensity of information processing and that information processing intensity will be directly related to the amount learned. Evidence reviewed earlier showed a direct relationship between task orientation and both information-processing intensity and recall. Other research supported the same relationship between meaningfulness and both information-processing intensity and recall. Evidence was also reviewed which supported an interaction between task orientation and meaningfulness when recall was the dependent variable. Unfortunately this research did not manipulate meaningfulness at the passage level, and it did not employ information-processing intensity as a dependent variable. If both dependent variables were used in research that included manipulations of goal orientation and passage level meaningfulness, we would expect that both main effects would be significant and consistent with direct relationships. Furthermore, a significant interaction consistent with a multiplicative relationship would be anticipated. The form of this interaction and its consistency with a multiplicative model could be tested through an application of functional measurement procedures (Shanteau & Anderson, 1972). Although the bulk of the research we have reviewed has examined either task orientation or meaningfulness in isolation, evidence supporting the existence of an interaction between these variables strongly suggests that in future research these variables should be used together in designs capable of ferreting out interaction effects.

Most of the research we have examined employed recall as a dependent variable. We would expect, however, that the proposed model would also predict the extent to which the content of the communication is evaluated. Evaluation involves a cognitive comparison of statements made in the message with one another and with beliefs already held by the receiver. Processing intensity should determine the extent to which the receiver responds cognitively to the material, evaluating it in terms of what he/she already believes. It should determine the extent to which arguments and their implications are grasped by the receiver and combined with other beliefs on the topic in long-term memory. Whether this leads to positive or negative or large or small attitude change will also depend on the logic of the message and the recipient's prior opinion. Finally a direct-relationship would be anticipated between information-processing intensity and the retention of any belief or attitude change. The impact of the communication, in other words, should be directly related to the intensity with which it is processed.

CONCLUSION

We began this chapter by making the contention that the cognitive effort people employ when they process information varies considerably as a function of both the goal orientation of the processor and the content of the communication being processed. We then reviewed research that supports that contention and proposed a model to help account for the obtained results.

The model proposed here stresses the importance of the individual's need for information and the meaningfulness of message content as major determinants of the amount learned when people confront a communication. When meaning enhancing material is provided at the beginning of a passage, rather than being omitted or provided at the end, it will lead to more intensive processing of message content and greater recall. The effect of this meaningfulness will be greatest when informational needs are high, but it should hold whenever people semantically process information. Anything advertisers can do at the beginning of the advertisement to provide information about the focus of the communication should have a facilitating effect on the processing of that advertisement. The presence of an explanatory title, rhetorical question, or picture at the outset of the advertisement tying the communication to the information to be conveyed in the message would be likely to have a facilitating effect on learning.

It may well be that message content that follows an order of support will be more effective than content that follows an order of climax. The former type of message begins with an initial general statement of the subject or idea. This idea is then developed and supported in the remaining portions of the message. Messages of this type tend to make the topic clear at the very beginning of the communication, rather than letting the topic become clear as the message unfolds. We would expect that exposure to the initial portion of an order of support message may provide the same meaning enhancing function that was provided in the research reviewed above by title and other introductory material.

It may be that advertising can be effectively directed at increasing the need for information. A creative message introduction may stir the consumer out of his perceived optimal information state and induce further processing (Ray, 1979). Lutz (1979) proposes several ways to heighten the prominence of decision structures and, in effect, the need for information; but he also suggests that achieving greater involvement is likely to be very difficult. Among the alternative possibilities would be to stress the heterogeneity of brands in the product class and the importance of information in guiding the individual's purchase. It may be possible to suggest that people who seek information before purchase are more likely to be satisfied with the product after purchase. Finally, it may be possible to increase the need for information by telling people they could be tested on the information or by portraying a subject being tested in the advertisement. The important point is that it may be possible to increase a person's need for information on a topic by providing him with information about the importance of the decision or by making his own lack of information more salient.

There are likely to be many other ways that advertisers can increase the effectiveness of their communications by increasing message meaningfulness and by either attempting to reach people when their informational needs are high or trying to increase those needs. Our major goal in writing this chapter was to show that these variables are important determinants of the amount people learn when they confront a communication.

REFERENCES

Apsler, R., & Sears, D. O. Warning, personal involvement, and attitude change. *Journal of Personality and Social Psychology,* 1968, *9,* 162–166.

Atkinson, J. W. *An introduction to motivation.* New York: Van Nostrand Reinhold, 1964.

Aulls, M. W. Expository paragraph properties that influence literal recall. *Journal of Reading Behavior,* 1975, *7,* 391–400.

Bennett, P. D., & Mandell, R. M. Prepurchase information seeking behavior of new car purchasers—The learning hypothesis. *Journal of Marketing Research,* 1969, *6,* 430–433.

Bettman, J. R. *An information processing theory of consumer choice.* Reading, Mass.: Addison-Wesley, 1979.

Bransford, J. D., Franks, J. J., Morris, C. D., & Stein, B. S. Some general constraints on learning and memory research. In Laird S. Cermak & Fergus I. M. Craik (Eds.), *Levels of processing in human memory.* Hillsdale, N.J.: Lawrence Erlbaum Associates, 1979.

Bransford, J. D., & Johnson, M. K. Contextual prerequisites for understanding: Some investigations of comprehension and recall. *Journal of Verbal Learning and Verbal Behavior,* 1972, *11,* 717–726.

Britton, B. K., Holdredge, T. S., Curry, C., & Westbrook, R. D. Use of cognitive capacity in reading identical texts with different amounts of discourse level meaning. *Journal of Experimental Psychology: Human Learning and Memory,* 1979, *5,* 262–270.

Burnkrant, R. E. *Toward a motivational theory of information processing.* Unpublished doctoral dissertation, University of Illinois, 1974.

Burnkrant, R. E. A motivational model of information processing intensity. *Journal of Consumer Research,* 1976, *3,* 21–30.

Cacioppo, J. T. Effects of exogenous changes in heart rate on facilitation of thought and resistance to persuasion. *Journal of Personality and Social Psychology,* 1979, *37,* 489–498.

Chaiken, S. Heuristic versus systematic information processing and the use of source versus message cues in persuasion. *Journal of Personality and Social Psychology,* 1980, *39,* 752–766.

Cialdini, R., Levy, A., Herman, P., Kozlowski, L., & Petty, R. Elastic shifts of opinion: Determinants of direction and durability. *Journal of Personality and Social Psychology,* 1976, *34,* 663–672.

Clarke, K., & Belk, R. W. The effects of product involvement and task definition on anticipated consumer effort. In W. L. Wilkie (Ed.), *Advances in consumer research, Vol. VI.* Ann Arbor: Association for Consumer Research, 1979.

Cohen, A. R. Need for cognition and order of communication as determinants of opinion change. In C. I. Hovland (Ed.), *The order of presentation in persuasion.* New Haven, Conn.: Yale University Press, 1957.

Craik, F. I. M., & Lockhart, R. S. Levels of processing: A framework for memory research. *Journal of Verbal Learning and Verbal Behavior,* 1972, 11, 671–684.

Craik, F. I. M., & Tulving, E. Depth of processing and the retention of words in episodic memory. *Journal of Experimental Psychology: General,* 1975, *104,* 268–294.

Dean, R. B., Austin, J. A., & Watts, W. R. Forewarning effects in persuasion: Field and classroom experiments. *Journal of Personality and Social Psychology,* 1971, *18,* 210–221.

Dermer, M., & Berscheid, E. Self report of arousal as an indicant of activation level. *Behavioral Science,* 1972, *17,* 420–429.

Dooling, D. J., & Lachman, R. Effects of comprehension on retention of prose. *Journal of Experimental Psychology,* 1971, *88,* 216–222.

Dooling, D. J., & Mullet, R. L. Locus of thematic effects in retention of prose. *Journal of Experimental Psychology,* 1973, *97,* 404–406.

Freedman, J. L. Involvement, discrepancy, and change. *Journal of Abnormal and Social Psychology,* 1964, *69,* 290–295.

Gardner, M. P., Mitchell, A. A., & Russo, J. E. Chronometric analysis: An introduction and an application to low involvement perception of advertisements. In H. K. Hunt (Ed.), *Advances in Consumer Research,* Chicago: Association for Consumer Reserach, 1978.

Harkins, S. G., & Petty, R. E. Effects of source magnification of cognitive effort on attitudes: An information-processing view. *Journal of Personality and Social Psychology,* 1981, *40,* 401–414.

Hass, R. *Resisting persuasion and examining message content: The effect of source credibility and recipient commitment on counterargument production.* Unpublished doctoral dissertation, Duke University, 1972.

Houston, M. J., & Rothschild, M. L. *A paradigm for research on consumer involvement.* Unpublished working paper, University of Wisconsin, 1978.

Howard, J. A., & Sheth. J. N. *The Theory of Buyer Behavior.* New York: Wiley, 1969.

Hyde, T. S., & Jenkins, J. J. Recall for words as a function of semantic, graphic, and syntactic orienting tasks. *Journal of Verbal Learning and Verbal Behavior,* 1973, *12,* 471–480.

Jacoby, L. L., Bartz, W. H., & Evans, J. D. A functional approach to levels of processing. *Journal of Experimental Psychology: Human Learning and Memory,* 1978, *4,* 331–346.

Johnson, R. E. Learners' predictions of the recallability of prose. *Journal of Reading Behavior,* 1974, *6,* 41–51.

Kagan, J. Motives and development. *Journal of Personality and Social Psychology,* 1972, *22,* 51–66.

Kahneman, D. *Attention and effort.* Englewood Cliffs, N.J.: Prentice-Hall, 1973.

Kerr, B. Processing demands during mental operations. *Memory and Cognition,* 1973, *1,* 401–412.

Kozminsky, E. Altering comprehension: The effect of biasing titles on text comprehension. *Memory and Cognition,* 1977, *5,* 482–490.

Kroeber-Riel, W. Activation research: Psychobiological approaches in consumer research. *Journal of Consumer Research,* 1979, *5,* 251–262.

Krugman, H. E. The impact of television advertising: Learning without involvement. *Public Opinion Quarterly,* 1965, *29,* 349–356.

Krugman, H. E. The measurement of advertising involvement. *Public Opinion Quarterly,* 1966–67, *30,* 583–596.

Krugman, H. E. Brain wave measures of media involvement. *Journal of Advertising Research,* 1971, *11,* 3–9.

Lastovicka, J. L., & Gardner, D. M. Components of involvement. In J. C. Maloney & B. Silverman (Eds.), *Attitude research plays for high stakes,* Chicago: American Marketing Association, 1978.

Lutz, R. J. How difficult is it to change consumer decision structures? In A. D. Shocker (Ed.), *Analytic approaches to product and marketing planning.* Cambridge, Mass.: Marketing Science Institute, 1979, 317–334.

Marslen-Wilson, W., & Tyler, L. K. Memory and levels of processing in a psycholinguistic context. *Journal of Experimental Psychology: Human Learning and Memory,* 1976, *2,* 112–119.

Morris, C. D., Stein, B. S., & Bransford, J. D. Prerequisites for the utilization of knowledge in the recall of prose passages. *Journal of Experimental Psychology: Human Learning and Memory,* 1979, *5,* 253–261.

Petty, R. E., & Cacioppo, J. T. Effects of forewarning of persuasive intent and involvement on cognitive responses and persuasion. *Personality and Social Psychology Bulletin,* 1979, *5,* 173–176. (a)

Petty, R. E., & Cacioppo, J. T. Issue involvement can increase or decrease persuasion by enhancing message-relevant cognitive responses. *Journal of Personality and Social Psychology,* 1979, *37,* 1915–1926. (b)

Petty, R. E., & Cacioppo, J. T. Issue involvement as a moderator of the effects on attitude of advertising content and context. In Kent B. Monroe (Ed.), *Advances in consumer research, Vol. VIII.* Ann Arbor: Association for Consumer Research, 1981.

Petty, R. E., Cacioppo, J. T., & Heesacker, M. Effects of rhetorical questions on persuasion: A cognitive response analysis. *Journal of Personality and Social Psychology,* 1981, *40,* 432–440.

Petty, R. E., Harkins, S. G., & Williams, K. D. The effects of group diffusion of cognitive effort on attitudes: An information-processing view. *Journal of Personality and Social Psychology,* 1980, *38,* 81–92.

Ray, M. L. Involvement and other variables mediating communication effects as opposed to explaining all consumer behavior. In W. L. Wilkie (Ed.), *Advances in Consumer Research,* Vol. VI. Ann Arbor: Association for Consumer Research, 1979, 197–199.

Ray, M. L., Sawyer, A. G., Rothschild, M. L., Heeler, R. M., Strong, E. C., & Reed, J. B. Marketing communication and the hierarchy of effects. In P. Clarke (Ed.), *New models for mass communication research.* Beverly Hills, Calif.: Sage, 1973.

Rhine, R. J., & Severance, L. J. Ego-involvement, discrepancy, source credibility, and attitude change. *Journal of Personality and Social Psychology,* 1970, *16,* 175–190.

Rogers, T. B., Kuiper, N. A., & Kirker, W. S. Self-reference and the encoding of personal information. *Journal of Personality and Social Psychology,* 1977, *35,* 677–688.

Schallert, D. L. Improving memory for prose: The relationship between depth of processing and context. *Journal of Verbal Learning and Verbal Behavior,* 1976, *15,* 621–632.

Seamon, J. G., & Murray, P. Depth of processing in recall and recognition memory: Differential effects of stimulus meaningfulness and serial position. *Journal of Experimental Psychology: Human Learning and Memory,* 1976, *2,* 680–687.

Sears, D. O., & Freedman, J. L. Effects of expected familiarity with arguments upon opinion change and selective exposure. *Journal of Personality and Social Psychology,* 1965, *2,* 420–426.

Shanteau, J., & Anderson, N. H. Integration theory applied to judgments of the value of information. *Journal of Experimental Psychology,* 1972, *92,* 266–275.

Sherif, M., & Hovland, C. I. *Social judgment: Assimilation and contrast effects in communication and attitude change.* New Haven, Conn.: Yale University Press, 1961.

Swan, J. E. Experimental analysis of predecision information seeking. *Journal of Marketing Research,* 1969, *6,* 192–197.

Tolman, E. C. A psychological model. In T. Parsons & E. A. Shils (Eds.), *Toward a general theory of action.* Cambridge, Mass.: Harvard University Press, 1951.

Tyebjee, T. T. Response time, conflict, and involvement in brand choice. *Journal of Consumer Research,* 1979, *6,* 295–304.

Tyler, S. W., Hertel, P. T., McCallum, M. C., & Ellis, H. C. Cognitive effort and memory. *Journal of Experimental Psychology: Human Learning and Memory,* 1979, *5,* 607–617.

Walsch, D. A., & Jenkins, J. J. Effects of orienting tasks on free recall in incidental learning: "Difficulty," "effort," and "process" explanations. *Journal of Verbal Learning and Verbal Behavior*, 1973, *12*, 481–488.

Wright, P. L. Analyzing media effects on advertising responses. *Public Opinion Quarterly*, 1974, *38*, 192–205.

Zimbardo, P. G. Involvement and communication discrepancy as determinants of opinion conformity. *Journal of Abnormal and Social Psychology*, 1960, *60*, 86–94.

3 Strategies That Influence Memory For Advertising Communications

Kathryn Lutz Alesandrini
University of Iowa

Research on strategies that facilitate learning and memory can be useful in understanding and predicting the effectiveness of advertising communications. The two classes of memory strategies of particular significance for advertising include (1) visual strategies, which are techniqeus that use pictures and other means to elicit mental visualization in the viewer; and (2) organizational strategies, which are techniques that provide a unifying framework for the advertising message. Some techniques suggested by the research findings on visual and organizational strategies are presently used in advertising, whereas other techniques have yet to be investigated or applied in the advertising context. A memory strategy perspective can be useful whether the purpose is to regulate advertising or improve advertising effectiveness. This chapter discusses research on visual and organizational memory strategies and considers how these strategies have been or could be used in advertising communications. The use of visual strategies in advertising has probably increased since the FTC ruled in 1971 that product claims in advertising must be substantiated. According to an FTC Task Force, ads since that time make more "subjective claims" and provide less information to consumers (FTC, 1979). The Task force's view as well as public policy on affirmative disclosure, nutrient labeling, and substantiation of claims are based on the assumption that information is primarily verbal and consumers' responses to information are primarily verbal. Yet research evidence is accumulating to the contrary as this chapter discusses. Visual strategies are being used in advertising and their effects are probably better assessed by visual rather than verbal measures. Yet verbal measures are often used. In the 1960s, George Gallup instituted a survey to assess the verbal recall of commercials during prime-time TV shows. On the average, only 12% of the viewers could verbally recall the average commercial on the following day. However, Krugman (1975) reported that viewers who are later shown photoscripts of TV commercials weeks after exposure were able to correctly recognize nearly half of the commercials they had seen. One advertising researcher concluded that consumers have information about products and brands that cannot be verbally reported so he asked children to draw colored pictures of breakfast cereals to investigate the relationship between visual and verbal knowledge of cereal products (Rossiter, 1976). Children at several age levels included a great deal of information and details in the drawings that were not reported verbally. Rossiter called for greater reliance on visual outcome measures in advertising research based on the results.

VISUAL MEMORY STRATEGIES

Visual memory strategies are techniques that elicit mental imagery in the learner and include (1) pictorial strategies; (2) concreteness; and (3) mental imagery instructions. In general, the empirical evidence indicates that visual strategies facilitate learning and memory (see review by Alesandrini, 1982).

Pictorial Strategies

This subsection presents the general findings on using pictures as aids to learning and memory and notes advertising implications. A related chapter provides a more in-depth discussion of research on specific picture characteristics such as color and realism as well as on the function that pictures in advertising serve relative to the viewer's thoughts and attitudes (Alesandrini & Sheikh, in press). The reader is also referred to a more general review and critique of picture research (Alesandrini, 1982). The research is selectively cited in the following section and advertising implications discussed.

Pictorial Equivalents.   In general, a number of studies provide evidence that pictures are remembered better than words (see Paivio, 1971). Moreover, memory for pictures does not fade as quickly over time as does verbal memory, a phenomena researchers have termed "hypermnesia" (Erdelyi & Becker, 1974). Memory for pictures in advertising has been investigated by Shepard (1967). He showed people 612 illustrations from magazine ads and found that the viewers were able to recognize a median of 98.5 percent of the pictures that they had been shown.

The literature indicates that memory for words can be increased by presenting a picture along with its verbal counterpart (see review by Paivio, 1971). Words are later recognized or recalled better if they were originally presented pictorially as well as verbally.

The use of pictures to supplement words has been tested in an advertising context. Several types of pictures in logos were selected from the Yellow Pages of a metropolitan phone directory and shown to viewers who recalled more company and brand names if they saw a picture depicting the name (Lutz & Lutz, 1977). Only logos that included a pictorial depiction of the brand name facilitated recall. Logos that showed only the product, such as example D of Fig. 3.1 for All State Tree Surgery, may be interesting but did not help the viewer remember the company names, whereas pictures of the company name like example A in Fig. 3.1 for Jack's Camera Shop did result in better recall of brand and company names.

Pictorial Associates.   Not all companies have the kind of names that readily lend themselves to pictorial depiction. Some names are more concrete and easily pictured whereas others are more abstract. The companies with concrete names in our study were able to use pictorial "equivalents" of the brand or company name and include, for example, Acorn, Arrow, Bird, King, Rhino, and Rocket. Some of the companies had more abstract names but used a picture strategy by showing a pictorial "associate" rather than pictorial equivalent of the name. For example, the following companies used the picture indicated in parentheses to

INTERACTIVE IMAGERY

PICTURE INTERACTION   **LETTER ACCENTUATION**

A.   Jack's Camera   **B.**   Magic Mushroom Cyclery

NON-INTERACTIVE IMAGERY

BRAND OR COMPANY NAME   **PRODUCT OR SERVICE**

C.   Western Glass Co.   **D.**   All State Tree Surgery

Fig. 3.1.   Examples of pictorial strategies in advertising.

depict the brand or company: Gonzales-Murphy (sombrero with clover leaves on it), King (crown), Weisz (owl), and Western (cactus cowboy). The logo for Western Glass shown in Fig. 3.1 is an example of a pictorial associate. The pictorial associate should be obvious or familiar to the intended viewing audience, however, or the benefits of this strategy will probably be lost.

Pictorial associates can also facilitate memory for product attributes according to a study that compared the effectiveness of pictorial and verbal strategies to communicate the attribute of "softness" in hypothetical brands of facial tissue (Mitchell & Olson, 1981). In one ad version the attribute of softness was communicated by showing a colored photograph of a fluffy kitten, a pictorial associate for softness. The other ad versions, either stated the claim verbally or showed colored photographs that were conceptually irrelevant to the product attribute. The effects of repetition were also investigated in the study by presenting each ad either 2, 4, 6, or 8 times. After the ads were presented, viewers completed rating scales that reflected their belief strength about various product attributes including softness, their attitude toward the brand, and their intentions to purchase the brand. Results indicate that viewers had stronger beliefs that the brand of tissue was soft when they saw the kitten photograph, regardless of the number of times that the other ads had been presented. This result suggests that a pictorial associate strategy is more effective than verbal repetition even when the verbal message is repeated two and three times more often than the visual message. The ad containing the pictorial associate also resulted in more favorable attitudes toward the brand than did the other ad versions.

Picture Interaction.   There are many studies in paired-associated learning which indicate that an interactive picture helps the learner remember two items to be learned (see Reese, 1965). An interactive picture figurally integrates the two items to be associated in some mutual or reciprocal action. When the picture is not interactive and the items are depicted side by side, paired-associate learning is not facilitated in spite of the pictorial presentation (see, for example, Neisser & Kerr, 1973).

Interactive pictures facilitate memory for ads according to the study described earlier which used company-product pairs and their accompanying pictorial logos from ads in the Yellow Pages of a telephone directory (Lutz & Lutz, 1977). In that study, the group seeing the interactive pictures recalled significantly more company names than those who viewed the non-interactive pictures. The interactive logos integrated the brand and product in one picture whereas non-interactive logos showed the brand and product separately.

An interactive picture strategy appears to be the most effective strategy according to our study and can be used by companies with portrayable names (although it may require some ingenuity to create a pictorial depiction for some names). Picture-interaction logos unite a depiction of the brand along with a picture of the product or service in one picture. The logo for Jack's Camera Shop is an example of how both the company name and service can be shown pictorially in one integrated image (see example A in Fig. 3.1). That example shows a playing card jack (a clever way to picture "Jack") holding a movie camera to his eye. Some of the picture logos used in the non-interactive condition were unique and memorable in their own right, such as the depiction of Western shown in Fig. 3.1. However, the company or brand was not associated with the product (in this case, glass) because the logo did not graphically depict the product and brand interacting.

One dimension of an interactive picture not yet investigated is the "dynamism" or animation of the interaction. Interactive pictures may be either dynamic or static, with dynamic interactions presumably being the more memorable type. Research on attention and reinforcement indicates that a visual stimulus change in the environment elicits attention to that action by the viewer (Kish, 1966). Television ads provide examples of dynamic interactive pictures in which the interaction between brand and product is animated. The use of action in a commercial can focus the viewer's attention on the important interaction between the brand and the product or service and make the picture much more memorable. An example of this type of visual strategy is the ad for Hunt's Tomato Sauce in which thick tomato sauce is slowly poured into the "u" in "Hunt." The ad uses a letter-accentuation technique that is useful for brand names that cannot be depicted pictorially. An example of an animated pictorial strategy which may not direct attention to the brand-product interaction is an ad for American Motors that shows a number of interesting pictures appearing next to a moving, flashing line. The line holds the viewer's attenion very well, but the viewer may fail to notice what brand was advertised. Thus, the ad may not direct the viewer's attetion to the critical information.

Letter Accentuation.   Some company or brand names are not suited to using either a pictorial equivalent or associate to represent the name but may still benefit from an interactive visual strategy by converting one or more letters in the name to a pciture of the product or service. A letter accentuation strategy is typically applied to the first letter of the name. One example is the logo for Cooper Donut Shop in which the *C* in *Cooper* looks like a donut with a bite out of it. Another is the logo for Vernon Diamond Company in which a side view of a diamond replaces the *V* in *Vernon*. The strategy can also be used with middle or ending letters. The logo for Magic Mushroom Cyclery shown in example B of Fig. 3.1, uses a letter accentuation strategy on the middle letters by showing the *oo* in *Mushroom* as two wheels of a bicycle.

A letter accentuation strategy may be combined with either a pictorial equivalent or a pictorial associate strategy in portraying the product or service. The preceeding products (donuts, diamonds, and cycles) used pictorial equivalents in their letter accentuation strategies. Purcell Employment Agency uses a pictorial associate for its letter accentuation strategy which shows two workers standing in line as the two *l*'s in *Purcell*.

The interactive picture group in our study described earlier actually saw two types of logos, including picture-interaction logos and letter-accentuation logos (see Fig. 3.1). Participants in the study recalled more company names with accompanying picture-interaction logos than companies using letter-accentuation logos. However, both types of interactive logos—completely pictorial interactions and letter accentuations—facilitated brand-name memory more than the all-verbal control condition. So companies with names that have no pictorial equivalent or associate can still capitalize on interactive imagery benefits by using a letter-accentuation logo to show the brand name and product together.

Letter Inclusion.   Similar to letter accentuation, letter inclusion is a strategy that may be used with brand names that are difficult to picture. Using this technique, the letters in the brand name visually include an important characteristic of the product. Letter inclusion is used in the logo for Mullin Lumber Company which depicts the letters of *Mullin* as woodgrained boards arranged as letters. Other researchers report that this type of strategy facilitates learning (Lippman & Shanahan, 1973).

Other Techniques for Visual Communication.   In addition to depicting brands and products pictorially, ads can communicate attributes, characteristics, and concepts via pictures. Researchers have explored the statement that "A picture is worth a thousand words" (e.g., Mandler & Johnson, 1976) and discovered that viewers can learn more quickly and effectively from information presented pictorially rather than verbally (see review by Alesandrini, 1982). In addition to increased memorability of visual information, research on picture communication indicates that viewers are more influenced by pictorial information, so that pictures and concrete examples are more influential than abstract information in decision-making (Nisbett, Borgida, Crandall, & Reed, 1976).

Advertising messages can use visuals in a variety of ways to communicate product information or company characteristics. Graphs and pictographs are one way to convey certain types of quantitative information and concepts of equivalence. One example is a pictograph used by Life breakfast cereal showing a pictorial "equation" that a bowl of Life cereal equals an egg plus a strip of bacon. Pictorial simulation is another way to communicate difficult concepts visually. One ad uses pictorial simulation to convey the idea of high gas mileage. A TV ad for Plymouth Champ on the West Coast visually communicates the feature of high mileage—43.4 miles per gallon—by showing their car starting in Los Angeles with 10 gallons of gasoline, driving through Santa Barbara, and arriving in San Francisco having traveled a distance of 434 miles on the 10 gallons of gasoline. Symbol substitution is another technique to visually communicate information. This technique involves using a pictorial symbol in place of verbal material to more effectively and efficiently convey the message. A good example of this technique is the ad for Ford Motor Company which visually communicates its claim to have a better idea by showing a light bulb turning on (often in place of the *o* in *Ford*), the visual symbol in this culture for having a good idea.

Research on modeling and demonstration in advertising indicates that these techniques can also affect viewers. Wright (1979) attempted to increase the reading of warning labels on over-the-counter drugs (antacids) by visually showing and concretely describing such behavior in ads for the drugs. To do this, Wright modified several ads for antacid products adding 5-second messages about reading warning labels to the end of several 30 second commercials. The 5-second messages either showed the product or showed a consumer reading the label on the product while a verbal message, that was either general or concrete, told the viewer to read the warning on the product's label. Viewers who saw ads with the concrete message and demonstration of a person actually reading the warning subsequently spent more time reading in-store warnings and package labels of antacids before buying them compared with viewers who had not seen the demonstrations in the ads. The demonstrations only affected viewers who shopped immediately after seeing the ads and not viewers who delayed shopping for 40 minutes or more after exposure to the ads. Nevertheless, the results are noteworthy because the pictorial strategy was so short in duration (5 seconds) yet affected actual behavior.

Concretization Techniques

Concretization refers to making information more memorable by making it more concrete. The variable of concreteness or "imagery value" refers to the likelihood that a word will elicit a mental image in the mind of the reader. Imagery values for hundreds of words have been established by asking readers to rate the ease with which a word arouses sensory images. Imagery values are based on mean ratings and are available for nouns (Paivio, Yuille, & Madigan, 1968), for verbs (Lippman, 1974), and for words frequently used by children (Van der Veur, 1975). According to these ratings, words like "desk" and "chair" are more concrete with higher imagery values whereas words such as "idea" and "quality" are most abstract with lower imagery values. Research results indicated that words high in imagery value are remembered better than words of low imagery value (see review by Paivio, 1969).

Concrete Names.   The implication of research on concreteness for advertising design is that brand names that are concrete should be more memorable than names based on abstract words, proper nouns, or abbreviations. If a new brand name were being selected, concrete nouns would probably be the best choice. Examples of concrete brand names include *Sunrise* (instant coffee) and *Camel* (cigarettes). Of course, viewers may recall abstract names quite well if the ad uses other memory strategies such as repetition of the name. Some companies use action verbs as brand names that may also result in rather memorable names. Examples include *Tickle* (deodorant) and *Shout* (cleaner). Abstract and proper nouns, though often used as brand names, are not as memorable unless the ad uses other memory strategies. Examples include *Glory* (rug cleaner) and *Folgers* (coffee). (Both of these brands use other strategies that are very effective, however.) Brand names based on stative or abstract verbs are also not the most memorable names. An example is *Vanish* (cleaner). The use of adjectives as brand names is probably one of the least effective approaches, according to concretization research, yet it seems to be widely used. Although research has not specifically compared the memorability of nouns, verbs, and adjectives (holding other factors constant), a visual inspection of tabled imagery values indicates adjectives are low in imagery value, making adjectives one of the poorer choices for a brand name. Brands such as *Gleam* (toothpaste) and *Arid* (deodorant) may seem to convey an important or preferred characteristic but are not memorable names. An exception may be to combine an adjective with a concrete noun so that the combination is easily pictured as in *Green Giant* (vegetables). However, the use of adjectives as brand names is popular because of the assumption that important characteristics about the product are being communicated by the adjective. Consider, for example, the intended message behind *Kool* cigarettes.

So how does the advertiser effectively communicate desirable product characteristics in the brand name? One approach is to select a concrete noun that has desirable, associated attributes. The automobile industry sets a good example in selecting names that convey desirable attributes. The implications of concrete names such as Audi *Fox* and Ford *Mustang* are clear compared to more abstract names such as Chevy *Citation* and Oldsmobile *Omega*. An added benefit of using concrete brand names is that concrete nouns lend themselves more readily to pictorial ad campaigns based on the characteristics of the concrete noun.

Concrete Connective Words.   Several studies varied the kind of connective words used to relate word pairs and found that verbs were more effective in facilitating memory for the pair than conjunctions or prepositions (Reese, 1965; Rohwer, Lynch, Levin, & Suzuki, 1967). Although imagery values for the connecting words were not compared, it seems quite likely that the verbs had much higher imagery values than the conjunctions and prepositions used in those experiments, based on a visual inspection of the tabled values.

The use of concrete connectives in advertising messages has not yet been investigated experimentally. However, the preceding evidence suggests that messages that use concrete words to relate brand names and product claims should be more memorable. Furthermore, because a visual inspection of the tabled values indicates that action verbs are more concrete than linking verbs, the more effective ad may tell what the product *does* (its usage benefits) rather than what the product is (its attributes). An ad may be more memorable if it uses high-imagery verbs such as attack, break, climb, fall, fly, itch, jump, kick, laugh, run, scream, shout, smile, and tickle rather than verbs with lower imagery values such as be, contain, do, get, has, is, keep, set, try, use, and will.

Concrete Stories and Other Concrete Materials.   A number of researchers have used sentences, passages, and texts to study the effects on memory of concreteness. Some of these studies tested response latency and recognition, whereas some investigated recall in order to determine how people encode, store, and retrieve concrete versus abstract information. Results from this research indicate that concrete information is recognized and verified faster than abstract information (see review of research on concreteness by Alesandrini, 1982). The reviewer concludes that studies investigating verbal recall show that concreteness correlates highly with recall. The variable of concreteness was directly manipulated in several studies; results show that sentences that contain concrete adjectives and modifiers were recalled better by adults than sentences with the equivalent but abstract adjectives and modifiers. In other experiments, concrete versions of prose passages were better remembered than otherwise equivalent, abstract passages (the passages were constructed by the experimenters). And finally, one study found that concrete passages taken from a sample of published texts from a variety of subject matter topics were comprehended better by the readers than were passages that were rated as being more abstract.

After considering the evidence concerning the effectiveness of concreteness, the FTC Task Force on Consumer Information Remedies suggested that abstract warning messages such as "this product could be hazardous to your health" be changed to more concrete warnings such as "consuming this product will increase the user's chance of death by 5%" (FTC, 1979).

Several studies have attempted to investigate the use of concrete language in advertising. Unfortunately, both studies appear to have confounded concreteness with amount of information. Wright (1979) conducted a study, discussed in an earlier section, that varied the wording of a message about reading the warnings on drug labels before purchasing the drug. According to Wright, the verbal message given in the ad was either more abstract, "Read the package warnings" or more concrete, "In the store, before buying, read the package warnings." Comparing the two messages reveals that the two versions of the message differ more in terms of amount of information rather than only on the dimension of concreteness-abstractness. There was no main effect for the message manipulation in the study although the combination of the longer message and the pictorial demonstration of the action did result in the consumers spending more time reading drug labels. The other study in the field is frought with similar problems. Rossiter and Percy (1978) originally described their study as an investigation of abstract and concrete messages in a print ad for a hypothetical beer. Abstract messages in the ad included statements such as "Affordably priced" and "Great Taste." Concrete versions of these messages were "Affordably priced at $1.79 per six pack of 12 of bottles" and "Winner of 5 out of 5 taste tests in the U.S. against all major American beers and leading imports." Obviously, these messages differ more on the factor of amount of information than on the concreteness-asbtractness dimension. In a later version of the report, the researchers referred to the manipulation as explicitly-stated claims and implicitly-stated claims, which correspond to the concrete and abstract conditions, respectively (Rossiter & Percy, 1980). The explicit claims fostered more favorable attitudes toward the hypothetical brand than did the ad versions with the implicit claims. The most effective version was a combination of the explicit verbal claims and a larger sized picture of the product.

The effects of concrete and vivid stories in advertising has also not been empirically investigated but the implication of this research is that vivid, concrete stories and scenarios will be more memorable than abstract descriptions or stories. An FTC Task Force notes the effectiveness of beer commercials which "show the actors participating in some Herculean sports event which brings on a 'good sweat', and ultimately, a beer. This is likely to make the viewer think of the last episode in his or her life where s/he worked up a good sweat, and either had, or would have liked to have had an ice-cold beer" (FTC, 1979, p. 103).

Imagery Instructions and Inducements

The results of numerous studies on mental imagery instructions are reviewed and discussed by Paivio (1971). The research indicates that giving learners imagery instructions—telling them to mentally visualize the information to be remembered—facilitates learning and the effects on memory are much like picture effects. The interactive feature of the mental image remains a necessary condition for maximum effectiveness. Learners told to mentally imagine two objects in interaction remember more word pairs than learners told to mentally picture the objects side by side or on opposite sides of a room. One advantage of eliciting mental imagery in the viewer as opposed to showing the viewer interactive pictures is that the self-generated mental imagery will probably be more "bizarre" and personally meaningful. Memory experts claim that bizarre, unique, individualized mental images are most effective (Lorayne & Lucas, 1974), although this claim has not been supported by empirical investigation (Nappe & Wollen, 1973). In fact, people may take longer to form bizarre mental images than "common" images with no associated memory benefits. Although the bizarreness of a mental image may not affect memory, the "vividness" of the image is related to recall according to Higbee (1979) who reviewed a number of studies that investigated the effects of vividness, defining a vivid image as one that is clear, distinct, and strong. Mowen (1980) tested an imagery strategy in an advertising context by showing consumers an ad for a hypothetical brand of shampoo that either included instructions to imagine themselves using the product or contained no such instructions. Viewers who were given the imagery instructions later reported no stronger intentions to try the product than viewers who had not seen the imagery instructions. However, the imagery instructions may have been too contrived and overstated to elicit a positive response from the viewers.

Although there are no studies on the effects of imagery instructions on remembering brand names and product claims in advertising, several ads provide examples of how to induce a simple, yet distinctive, image. An ad by Johnston's Yogurt directs the listener to "look for the sunny yellow cups," probably eliciting a mental image in the listener that is easy to visualize but is distinctive from appeals used by other advertisers of that type of product. Another way for an ad to elicit mental imagery is to tell listeners to picture themselves in a situation. The ad campaign by a life insurance company to "imagine yourself *out* of the picture" is a variant of this approach.

Caution should be used in adopting imagery strategies in print media advertising. There is a problem with trying to induce the reader to use mental imagery while reading. Findings suggest that imagery generation is a more successful strategy when applied during listening rather than during reading (Brooks, 1967). Telling an advertising audience to form mental images while hearing or reading an advertising message has not been empirically tested, but the literature on imagery inducement suggests that imagery instructions should generally facilitate memory for an ad and may be especially effective with nonprint such as radio and television.

ORGANIZATIONAL MEMORY STRATEGIES

Visual memory strategies are only one general class of strategies that are relevant in the advertising context. Organizational strategies may also be useful in understanding and predicting advertising effects. Organizational strategies put discrete parts of an information presentation together into a meaningful whole, helping the viewer see the bigger picture. The research on several organizational techniques are selectively discussed along with the implications for advertising.

Chunking: The Basis of Organizational Strategies

People can remember only a limited number of information units or "chunks" in short-term memory at any one time, that number ranging from 5 to 9 bits of information (Miller, 1956). For example, most people can temporarily remember a 7-digit number but probably cannot remember several unfamiliar phone numbers simultaneously without some sort of memory strategy such as rehearsing the numbers. Although short-term memory limits the number of chunks that can be processed simultaneously, the number of information bits contained in those chunks is not restricted to that limit. Information chunks may range in complexity from a single bit of information to many bits. Memory can be increased by chunking the information—combining separate bits of the information into larger patterns or groups. The new groups or chunks are then easier to remember than all the separate items.

Chunking can dramatically increase the power of memory, as demonstrated by studies comparing the memory of chess experts to novices for locations of chess pieces on the board (de Groot, 1965). After briefly viewing chess pieces arranged as if a game were in progress, chess experts recall the location of many more pieces than do novices. However, after viewing randomly arranged pieces, novices and experts remember about the same number of pieces. When viewing a game, the chess experts are able to chunk chess pieces into meaningful patterns or groups that can be recognized as quickly as the novice recognizes each separate chess piece. When the board is randomly arranged, there are no meaningful patterns, so that the expert must look at each piece separately just as the novice does.

Chunking may be the most important strategy in promoting advertising effectiveness, especially when combined with visual strategies. Brand names, slogans, logos, and jingles can all be powerful chunks that communicate a great many "bits" of information. The brand can summarize the main characteristics of the product that the advertiser wishes to communicate. An example of a name which chunks together a number of bits of information is Kellogg's *Most* cereal; the ad campaign shows how various components—wheat germ, fiber, iron, and vitamins—combine to produce the *most* in cereal.

The FTC realized that a brand name can summarize a number of qualities about a product, some of which may be deceptive. Based on the realization that Listerine mouthwash ads created the impression that the product had medicinal qualities, the Commission required corrective advertisements that explicitly stated that Listerine is not an effective treatment for colds and sore throats. The Commisssion also realizes that corrective disclosures may be needed for products with similar brand names such as Listermint mouthwash or Listerine throat lozenges since consumers chunk beliefs about medicinal qualities with the name (FTC, 1979). When consumers have beliefs embedded in a holistic chunk about a product, it may be difficult to correct misconceptions, however,

Slogans and jingles are another approach to chunking information. Budweiser's slogan summarizes its campaign and tries to create a chunk of the brand name: "When you've said 'Bud,' you've said it all." Similarly, many advertisers end an ad by telling the viewers that all they need think of is the brand name rather than the many attributes. MacDonald's slogan that "We do it all for you" is a way of chunking or summing up their ad campaign.

The use of the proper type of logo can be the most effective way to chunk information and promote memory. The interactive pictures discussed earlier are good examples of effective chunking strategies. For example, the logo for Arrow Pest Control Company shows a bug killed by an arrow. In one chunk of information the logo communicates the brand name as well as the service of extermination.

Advance Organizers

An advance organizer is an overview that cues the listener or viewer to the topic and main points of the information to be presented, thereby providing the "bigger picture" and eliciting the proper mental set. An advance organizer is usually in the form of a short, verbal introduction. Ausubel conducted many of the earlier studies on advance organizers and found that learners remembered more when they read an abstract and general introduction to a passage rather than an historical introduction (Ausubel, 1962). Two recent reviews cite over a dozen studies confirming the facilitative effect of using abstract introductions as advance organizers, but another half dozen studies failed to find any benefits of using advance organizers (Faw & Waller, 1976; Hartley & Davies, 1976). The reviewers criticized the research for lack of adequate controls and for using nonreplicable procedures in creating the advance organizers.

Although the use of advance organizers in advertising should result in better memory, listeners or readers of the ad could "turn off" to the ad if the topic and introduction were not of interest to them. Therefore, this strategy may not always promote memory especially if it can't hold the viewer's attention beyond the introduction. Verbal advance organizers in ads may include catchy titles for the ad such as "Free" or "Find Out How to Win Money."

Several studies in the literature indicate that visual advance organizers are also facilitative (see Weisberg, 1970). A visual advance organizer presents a picture or scenario that cues the viewer to the content or importance of the subsequent message. Commericals may use a visual advance organizaer in several ways; for example, the ad can cue the viewers and capture their attention by posing a situation that the viewers want to know about such as a problem that can be solved or a positive situation that can be achieved by watching the ad. An ad that uses a visual organizer is a commercial for heavy duty trash bags which begins by showing how other brands of garbage bags break and spill their contents, a situation that can be avoided by watching the commercial to learn about the advertised brand.

Analogies

Giving a learner analogies or comparisons between new information and something more familiar is a strategy that facilitates learning and memory (see Larkin & Reif, 1976). Analogies as well as metaphors are powerful ways to relate new information to familiar information (Davidson, 1976). In fact, some learning theorists claim that relating new information to prior knowledge is a necessary condition of meaningful learning (Wittrock, 1974).

The use of analogies in advertising campaigns is common, although no studies have tested the effectiveness of this strategy in an advertising context. Many brand names are selected to suggest an analogy between the product and a familiar referent with desirable characteristics. There are many examples in the area of car names in which an object or animal name is selected because it is associated with speed, power, sure-footedness, and so on. Such brands include, for example, Mustang, Cougar, Pinto, and Rabbit. Many product names are selected to suggest an analogy between the product and a particular attribute rather than an analogous object. A few examples include Sure deodorant, Gleam toothpaste, Long 'n Silky hair products, Kool cigarettes, and Downy fabric softener. The FTC has sometimes required disclosures in ads where the product name suggests an analogy that gives a false impression about the product. For example, Manchurian Linsee Oil had to be labeled as "not imported" and makers of "Cashmora" had to list their constituent materials conspicuously, which did not include Cashmere (FTC, 1979).

Many of the analogies in television advertising are visual so that both visual and organizational strategies are incorporated. Products named after an analogous object rather than attribute are more easily portrayed graphically. One example of an effective use of visual analogy is the ad for Audi Fox which superimposes a real, running fox and the automobile to communicate the speed, turning, and handling capabilities of the car. The ad for Ford Mustang uses a similar technique. Print media can also make use of a visual analogy strategy. For example, a savings and loan institution uses a visual analogy in their newspaper ad for home equity loans. The ad campaign is "tap your assets" and the visual analogy shows a faucet pouring money out of a house. This type of visual analogy is probably a very effective way to communicate a rather abstract concept.

Context

Providing a context for information is another strategy for getting the viewer to see the bigger picture rather than specific, unorganized bits of information. Jenkins (1974) emphasizes the importance of context in learning and points out that learning and memory are constructive processes in which what is remembered depends heavily on the context. Advertisers know this when they show cigarette smokers in front of a waterfall or out on the open plains rather than in a hot, stuffy, smoke-filled room. The kind of visual context in which a product is shown can have major effects on what the viewer learns and remembers from the message according to the research on picture effects. Because no studies have tested the effects of an ad's visual context, such as a cigarette smoker in a refreshing setting, we don't know how much influence the context has. The FTC has acknowledged the potential impact that visual context can have on beliefs and attitudes toward the product. For example, the Commission is questioning whether the ad for Belair cigarettes, showing a happy couple frolicking in the surf, communicates the message that Belairs will make the user healthy and happy, a message that might be considered deceptive if stated verbally in the ad (Crock, 1978).

One technique for embedding information in a context is to use a scenario or story format. Research indicates that people recall stories better than other kinds of information probably because stories have a familiar and useful structure that aids memory (Gordon, Munro, Rigney, & Lutz, 1978). Television ads use a story technique more often than other media because a short story or scenario can be developed very quickly via pictorial communication. Miller beer ads, for example, often portray a story which involves characters, a plot, setting, purpose, attempt, and outcome—the outcome always being ''It's Miller time.''

Inserted Questions

Another technique to help organize the message is to ask learners general questions, a technique referred to as adjunct or inserted questioning. The effects of inserted questions on learning and memory has been extensively researched. Several articles reviewed the effects of inserted questions and the conditions under which they facilitate learning (Anderson & Biddle, 1975; Faw & Waller, 1976). The reviewers concluded that inserted questions generally facilitate learning because the learner expends cognitive effort in order to answer the question.

Questioning is used in advertising, often as a technique for chunking the main points. One example is the question in a 7-Up ad about which other soft drinks contain no caffeine. Viewers give this question some thought and probably remember the claim that ''7-Up contains no caffein'' better than they would have if the claim were made explicitly.

SUMMARY AND DISCUSSION OF VISUAL AND ORGANIZATIONAL STRATEGIES

Visual and organization strategies have obvious implications in the control, prediction, and assessment of advertising effects. The use of visual strategies in ads is hardly a new idea to advertisers, who have relied on illustrations for years to achieve more interesting and persuasive advertising campaigns. However, the research on visual strategies provides a richer perspective on the issue of using pictures to communicate. Some illustrations are more effective than others. Research supports the use of interactive pictures, wherein a brand name is pictorially portrayed in relation to the product or its attributes. In contrast, memory for the critical relationship between a brand name and its product category is not facilitated by a pictorial presentation that does not show the two items united in a figural interaction. The concept of interactive imagery suggests that it is not enough that an illustration be memorable but that it must also depict the relationship between the brand and its proffered benefits.

The concept of organizational strategies is also an important one in predicting or assessing advertising effectiveness. Organizational strategies are independent from visual strategies so that either visual or verbal information may be presented in a more organized way, although combining visual and organizational strategies may be most effective approach. Organizational strategies used in advertising include making analogies, embedding the information in a context such as a story format, summarizing the information by using a slogan or jingle, questioning the viewer about the topic or point of the information, and giving advance organizers that introduce the general topic of the information. Visual and organizational strategies are combined in ads that use visual analogies, show logos involving interactive imagery, and embed information in a visually-presented context.

Both types of strategies should ideally be brought to bear in advertising decisions such as in the selection of a brand name. A brand name will be most memorable if it (1) has a direct visual equivalent (can be depicted graphically); (2) has a high concreteness value (typically arouses mental sensory images), (3) relates to an analogous object that possesses desirable attributes; and (4) serves as a chunk of information that has many associated, favorable bits of information. An example of a name which meets these four criteria is Audi's *Fox* automobile while a poor choice of name according to these criteria is *Glory* rug cleaner.

Other aspects of advertising design can benefit from a memory strategy perspective. For example, the creation of logos and slogans can capitalize on visual as well as organizational strategies. Logos and slogans serve as summaries or chunks of information about the brand and/or product and can be most memorably when portrayed graphically. Other aspects of an ad that can follow the principles of memory strategies include the language used in the ad, the context in which the product is shown, and the introduction and closing sections of the ad. These elements of an advertising message should be concrete and suggest familiar analogies wherever possible. The message should open and end with a unifying or summarizing message that is concrete or graphic if possible.

Conclusion.   This chapter has presented some of the empirical evidence favoring the use of visual and organizing memory strategies and has discussed the implications for advertising. In addition to helping the advertising designer create more effective ads, a memory strategy perspective can also help an evaluator or regulatory agency determine the effects that a particular advertising message has on a viewer. For example, the evaluator can suspect that the context in which a product is shown can have an effect on the viewer. Information presented pictorially will probably be better remembered than verbal information and analogies can affect how a consumer comprehends and remembers information about the product. Much emphasis is currently given to regulating verbal advertising claims, but the potentially more powerful effects of pictorial presentation have received less attention by those concerned with advertising deception. More recently, an FTC Task Force has suggested that surveys be conducted to determine what meaning the consumer actually derives from the total advertisement, including the nonverbal elements of the ad (FTC, 1979). Future research and evaluations concerning advertising communications would benefit from adopting a memory strategy perspective and considering the possible effects of visual and organizational strategies.

REFERENCES

Alesandrini, K. L. Imagery-eliciting strategies and meaningful learning. *Journal of Mental Imagery*, 1982, *6*, 125–140.

Alesandrini, K. L., & Sheikh, A. A. Research on imagery: Implications for advertising. In A. A. Sheikh (Ed.), *Imagery: Current theory, research and application*. New York: Wiley, in press.

Anderson, R. C., & Biddle, B. B. On asking people questions about what they are reading. In G. Bower (Ed.), *Psychology of learning and motivation, Vol. 9*. New York: Academic Press, 1975.

Ausubel, D. P. A subsumption theory of meaningful verbal learning and retention. *Journal of General Psychology*, 1962, *66*, 213–224.

Brooks, L. R. The suppression of visualization by reading. *Quarterly Journal of Experimental Psychology*, 1967, *19*, 289–299.

Crock, S. FTC is seeking way to decide if pictures in advertising convey false impressions. *The Wall Street Journal*. August, 1978, p. 6.

Davidson, R. E. The role of metaphor and analogy in learning. In J. R. Levin & V. L. Allen (Eds.), *Cognitive learning in children. Theories and strategies*. New York: Academic Press, 1976.

DeGroot, A. D. *Thought and choice in chess*. The Hague: Mouton, 1965.

Erdelyi, M. H., & Becker, J. Hypermnesia for pictures: Incremental memory for pictures but not words in multiples recall trial. *Cognitive Psychology*, 1974, *6*, 158–171.

Faw, H. W., & Waller, T. G. Mathemagnenic behaviors and efficiency in learning from prose materials: Review, critique and recommendations. *Review of Educational Research*, 1976, *46*, 691–720.

Federal Trade Commission. *Consumer Information Remedies*. Washington, D.C.: U.S. Government Printing Office, 1979.

Hartley, J., & Davies, I. K. Preinstructional strategies: The role of pretests, behavioral objectives, overviews, and advance organizers. *Review of Educational Research*, 1976, *46*, 239–265.

Higbee, K. L. Recent research on visual mnemonics: Historical roots and educational fruits. *Review of Educational Research*, 1979, *49*, 611–629.

Jenkins, J. J. Remember that old theory of memory? Well, forget it! *American Psycholgist*, 1974, *29*, 785–795.

Larkin, J. H., & Reif, F. Analysis and teaching of a general skill for studying scientific text. *Journal of Educational Psychology*, 1976, *68*, 431–440.

Lippman, M. Z. Enactive imagery in paired-associate learning. *Memory & Cognition*, 1974, *2*, 385–390.

Lippman, M. Z., & Shanahan, M. W. Pictorial facilitation of paired-associate learning: Implications for vocabulary training. *Journal of Educational Psychology*, 1973, *64*, 216–222.

Lorayne, H., & Lucas, J. *The memory book*. New York: Stein & Day, 1974.

Lutz, K. A., & Lutz, R. J. The effects of interactive imagery on learning: Application to advertising. *Journal of Applied Psychology*, 1977, *62*, 493–498.

Mandler, J. M., & Johnson, N. S. Some of the thousand words a picture is worth. *Journal of Experimental Psychology: Human Learning and Memory*, 1976, *2*, 529–540.

Miller, G. A. The magical number seven, plus or minus two: Some limits on our capacity for processing information. *Psychological Review*, 1956, *63*, 81–97.

Mitchell, A. A., & Olson, J. C. Are product attribute beliefs the only mediator of advertising effects on brand attitude? *Journal of Marketing Research*, 1981, *18*, 318–332.

Mowen, J. C. The availability heuristic: The effect of imaging the use of a product on product perceptions. In J. C. Olson (Ed.), *Advances in Consumer Research* (Vol. VII.) Ann Arbor: Association for Consumer Research, 1980.

Nappe, G. W., & Wollen, K. A. Effects of instructions to form common and bizarre mental images on retention. *Journal of Experimental Psychology*, 1973, *100*, 6–9.

Neisser, U., & Kerr, N. Spatial and mnemonic properties of visual images. *Cognitive Psychology*, 1973, *5*, 138–150.

Nisbett, R. E., Borgida, E., Crandall, R., & Reed, H. Popular indiction: Information is not necessarily informative. In J. B. Carroll & J. W. Payne (Eds.), *Cognition and social behavior*. Hillsdale, N.J.: Lawrence Erlbaum Associates, 1976.

Paivio, A. Mental imagery in associative learning and memory. *Psychological Review*, 1969, *76*, 241–263.

Paivio, A. *Imagery and verbal processes*. New York: Holt, Rinehart & Winston, 1971.

Paivio, A., Yuille, J. C., & Madigan, S. A. Concreteness, imagery, and meaningfulness values for 925 nouns. *Journal of Experimental Psychology Monograph*, 1968, *76* (1, Pt. 2), 1–25.

Reese, H. W. Imagery in paired-associate learning in children. *Journal of Experimental Child Psychology*, 1965, *8*, 290–296.

Rohwer, W. D., Lynch, S., Levin, J. R., & Suzuki, N. Pictorial and verbal factors in the efficiency learning of paired-associates. *Journal of Educational Psychology*, 1967, *58*, 278–284.

Rossiter, J. R. Visual and verbal memory in children's product information utilization. In B. B. Anderson, (Ed.), *Advances in Consumer Research* (Vol. III). Chicago: Association for Consumer Research, 1976. pp. 523–527.

Rossiter, J. R., & Percy, L. Visual imaging ability as a mediator of advertising response. In H. K. Hunt (Ed.), *Advances in Consumer Research* (Vol. V.). Ann Arbor, MI: Association for Consumer Research, 1978, 621–628.

Rossiter, J. R., & Percy, L. Attitude change through visual imagery in advertising. *Journal of Advertising*, 1980, *9*, 10–16.

Shepard, R. N. Recognition memory for words, sentences and pictures. *Journal of Verbal Learning and Verbal Behavior*, 1967, *6*, 156–163.

Van der Veur, B. W. Imagery rating of 1,000 frequently used words. *Journal of Educational Psychology*, 1975, *67*, 44–56.

Weisberg, J. S. The use of visual advance organizers for learning research science concepts. *Journal of Research in Science Teaching*, 1970, *7*, 161–165.

Wittrock, M. C. Learning as a generative process. *Educational Psychologist*, 1974, *11*, 87–95.

Wright, P. Concrete action plans in TV messages to increase reading of drug warning. *Journal of Consumer Research*, 1979, *6*, 256–269.

4 Visual Communication in Advertising

John R. Rossiter
Larry Percy
Columbia University
Creamer, Inc.

INTRODUCTION

The role of visual communication in advertising is finally coming to be appreciated for its theoretical and practical importance. Early studies of advertising effects (reviewed by Hendon, 1973) focused on visual characteristics of print advertising and their effects on recognition scores but did not attempt to advance any theory as to how advertising communicates visually. Not until the mid-1960s and the pioneering ideas of Krugman (1966–67) did any theory of advertising effects make reference to visual processes, and even in Krugman's theory the processes were poorly specified and have remained so in later versions of his theory. In 1975 one of the authors published a paper (Rossiter, 1975) that contained the first reference to *visual information processing* in advertising. This was followed by a theoretical paper (Rossiter & Percy, 1978) on visual information processing. There have been several speculative papers (Calder, 1978; Calder, Robertson, & Rossiter, 1975; Krugman, 1977; Lutz & Lutz, 1978) and a few empirical studies (Holbrook & Moore, 1981; Lutz & Lutz, 1977; Rossiter, 1976; Rossiter & Percy, 1980; Wright, 1979) concerning visual communication in advertising. However, more centrally to this book, few of these studies have contributed to the *theoretical* understanding of visual information processing in advertising. The paper by Rossiter and Percy (1978) stands as the sole attempt at a comprehensive theory development in this area.

The study of visual communication in advertising is also gaining in importance from a practical perspective. The Federal Trade Commission is planning to devote more of its advertising regulation activities to "subjective claims" in advertising as expressed through "nonverbal images." An example is a cigarette

83

advertisement cited by FTC Bureau of Consumer Protection Deputy Director Tracy Westen as potentially misleading and deceptive because of its visual communication implications (the picture in the ad shows a healthy-looking couple frolicking in the surf). According to Mr. Westen, the words in the advertisement, which state that the cigarettes "take you all the way to fresh," appear to be "trivial throwaways." The real message, he continues, may be that this brand of cigarettes will make you "healthy" and "happy," a message that could be deceptive if stated in words (Crock, 1978).

Actually, the FTC has long been interested in visual communication in advertising and, over the years, has formulated trade regulation rules to prohibit "white jacket" depictions for medicinal products, which may imply endorsement by the medical profession; use of American symbols, such as the flag or eagle, which might imply connection with the U.S. government; foreign scenes, such as the Tower of London, which might imply imported products; selected "before-and-after" pictures, which may imply that the product, on average, works better than it does; and product displays showing items not sold with the product, which may imply more value than is actually obtained (Engel, Blackwell, & Kollat, 1978).

The FTC's interest in visual communication in advertising has accelerated recently, however, in part because of its own actions in requiring advertiser substantiation of verbal claims, which may force advertisers into nonverbal alternatives (FTC, 1979; Hendon, 1973).

Other non-academics have also contributed interest in visual communication in advertising. For instance, an unscientific book by Key (1973) claiming that advertisers were using subliminal "implants" of sexual stimuli, death symbols, and so forth, generated wide public interest, raising fears of "subliminal seduction" through visual communication in advertising. More recently, speculations about the "visual and emotional right hemisphere" and the "verbal and logical left hemisphere" have gained similar notoriety. Several respected academicians have embraced this notion. For example, "hemisphere theory" is now a central part of Krugman's high- versus low-involvement notions of advertising effects (Krugman, 1977) and is offered by several academically staffed research firms as a basis for pretesting advertising (Mariani, 1979). Practitioners are particularly interested in new ways of testing "image" advertising because its emotional (often visual) aspects are not represented well in traditional advertising testing methods.

Where does this new interest in visual communication in advertising lead us? What *is* known about visual communication processes? The purpose of this chapter is to provide a rigorous update of this exciting field from a theoretical and empirical standpoint.

The chapter is organized into four sections. Section I discusses visual communication with the purpose of providing an overall framework applicable to advertising. Section II examines visual information processing from a short-term memory or "cognitive response" perspective. Section III turns attention to stored visual information in the form of longer-term memory responses or "communication effects" that, when retrieved, enter into purchase decisions. Section IV integrates short-term and long-term memory responses by postulating four basic mechanisms through which visual communication in advertising can occur.

I. VISUAL COMMUNICATION: AN OVERVIEW

Currently, the dominant conceptualization of communication is the information processing approach. Communication, in information processing terms, is basically a four-stage process in which: (1) an external stimulus or set of stimuli, for example, an advertisement, is encountered; (2) initial information processing, encompassing subprocesses such as attention, decoding, and encoding, then occurs in the recipient's short-term or active memory; (3) the initial processing forms or alters stored responses, such as awareness, preference, and so on, in the recipient's long-term or permanent memory; and (4) these stored responses are later retrieved into short-term or active memory where they enter into decisions regarding behavioral courses of action with regard to the original object of communication, for example, the advertised product. The major unknowns in this general communication process relate to the form and content of initial processing and the form and content of stored responses. It is our contention that many of these phenomena are visual. In Fig. 4.1 we have outlined a communication framework applicable to advertising which isolates the hypothesized role of visual phenomena. The details of the framework are expanded upon in the sections that follow. However, it is useful to provide a general description here.

In the first component of the framework, visual stimuli are seen to comprise a major mode of advertising input. Visual stimuli, of course, can occur in all advertising media except radio. Visual stimuli consist of static pictorial stimuli, such as illustrations and visual symbols; dynamic pictorial stimuli, as in TV video; and linguistic stimuli in the form of written words and numbers. Three things may be noted about this classification of visual stimuli in advertising. One is that linguistic visual stimuli could be divided into static and dynamic subcategories. Although static words and numbers are most common, examples such as mobile "supers" in TV commercials of "ticker tape" advertising on electronic scoreboards or billboards indicate that linguistic stimuli can also be dynamic. However, the static-dynamic distinction for visually presented linguistic stimuli has little theoretical relevance so we have not included it in the framework. Another consideration is that the distinction between pictorial and linguistic stimuli, as well as the distinction, in the auditory mode, between

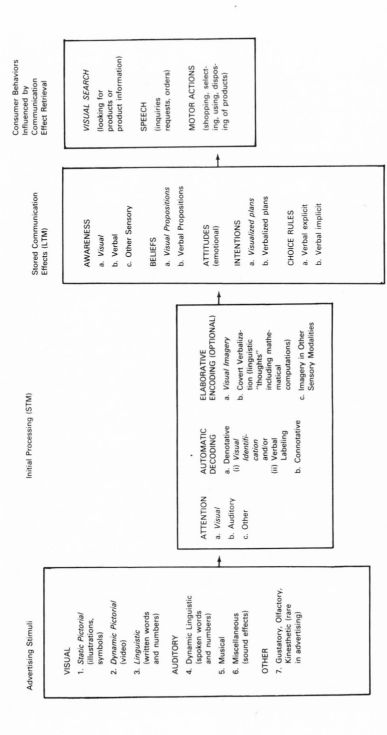

FIG. 4.1. Advertising communication framework illustrating the hypothesized role of visual phenomena (*italicized*).

Advertising Stimuli

VISUAL

1. *Static Pictorial* (illustrations, symbols)
2. *Dynamic Pictorial* (video)
3. *Linguistic* (written words and numbers)

AUDITORY

4. Dynamic Linguistic (spoken words and numbers)
5. Musical
6. Miscellaneous (sound effects)

OTHER

7. Gustatory, Olfactory, Kinesthetic (rare in advertising)

Initial Processing (STM)

ATTENTION
a. *Visual*
b. Auditory
c. Other

AUTOMATIC DECODING
a. Denotative
   (i) *Visual Identification and/or*
   (ii) Verbal Labeling
b. Connotative

ELABORATIVE ENCODING (OPTIONAL)
a. *Visual Imagery*
b. Covert Verbalization (linguistic "thoughts" including mathematical computations)
c. Imagery in Other Sensory Modalities

Stored Communication Effects (LTM)

AWARENESS
a. *Visual*
b. Verbal
c. Other Sensory

BELIEFS
a. *Visual Propositions*
b. Verbal Propositions

ATTITUDES (emotional)

INTENTIONS
a. *Visualized plans*
b. Verbalized plans

CHOICE RULES
a. Verbal explicit
b. Verbal implicit

Consumer Behaviors Influenced by Communication Effect Retrieval

VISUAL SEARCH (looking for products or product information)

SPEECH (inquiries requests, orders)

MOTOR ACTIONS (shopping, selecting, using, disposing of products) linguistic, musical and miscellaneous stimuli, is not entirely objective. These distinctions depend, in part, on some initial processing in the form of preliminary feature analysis on the part of the recipients and are thus partly subjective. However, the distinctions can be independently verified in most cases on the basis of the physical form of the stimulus without any elaborate semantic analysis, so we have included them as stimulus characteristics. Also worth noting is that many other stimulus dimensions could be identified, such as intensity, duration, color, and so forth. However, these would unduly complicate the diagram in Fig. 4.1 and, instead, they are discussed in the text when an important difference on these other dimensions occurs.

In the second component of the framework, initial processing is conceptualized as consisting, potentially, of three subprocesses, each with its own subcomponents. Attention is assumed to occur first, and is regarded primarily as a sensory focusing response or set of responses. Next, we propose that a process called decoding automatically occurs in which the stimulus is analyzed or evaluated for meaning in the manner proposed by Osgood, Suci, and Tannenbaum (1957) and Osgood (1971). Decoding consists of a denotative or identificatory response which may be visual, verbal, or both, and a closely occurring connotative or emotional meaning response in which evaluation, potency and activity features are automatically registered. Thereafter, a third process called elaborative encoding *may* take place (note that we do not consider elaborative encoding as a necessary condition for communication effects to occur). Elaborative encoding, if it does occur, and this depends on previous learning as well as the recipient's current motivational state, may take the form of visual imagery, covert verbalizations or "thoughts," or imagery in other sensory modalities, as in imagined tasting, smelling or feeling responses. Elaborative encoding corresponds with what others have termed "cognitive responses," except that we take a broader view of these responses by including imagery. The hypothesized distinction between automatic decoding and "voluntary" elaborative encoding plays a major role, we believe, in low- and high-involvement learning, as is explained later.

In the third component of the framework, various communication effects in the form of stored, product-related responses are identified. Here we propose an associative network of responses centering around *awareness* as the basic and minimal communication response. Awareness may be visual (especially in product recognition), verbal (especially in product recall) or both. Attached to these basic awareness responses are various *preferential* responses, including beliefs, attitudes (in the global affect sense) and intentions. Beliefs and intentions, we propose, may be stored as visual responses, although they more often are stored as verbal responses. Attitudes, on the other hand, are purely emotional responses that do not directly contain visual or verbal components. The awareness response itself may be attached, along with awareness responses to other brand alternatives, to a choice rule response, which is implicitly or explicitly verbal and which applies to the product category or brand set as a whole. These proposals are elaborated later. However, one aspect is worth noting here, and that is our use of "verbal" as distinct from "propositional," "semantic," or "conceptual" responses. We regard communication effects as responses that are capable of being directly manifest in overt behavior (e.g., visual awareness → looking, or verbal belief → stating reason for buying the product). Thus they are described in the output mode that is, visual or verbal, rather than the input mode, that is, visual, auditory, and so forth, or in some other hypothetical abstract mode, that is, conceptual, propositional, or semantic.

The fourth component of the framework comprises retrieval of various communication effects and a decision that results in overt consumer behaviors. For reasons that might be obvious given the categorization in the foregoing components of the model, we have categorized consumer behaviors in terms of visual search, such as looking for products or for product information; speech, such as inquiring about, requesting or ordering products; and motor actions, such as shopping, physically selecting, using or disposing of products. Our purpose is to indicate how visual communication effects resulting from advertising can mediate these types of behavior.

The emphasis in this chapter is on visual processes that contribute to each component of the framework. Two components are given extensive treatment because they represent to this point major unknowns: visual information processing (Section II) and visual communication effects (Section III). Links between these and other components are referred to throughout and are later summarized into four overall mechanisms (Section IV). We begin with visual information processing as the initial step resulting from advertising stimulus input.

II. VISUAL INFORMATION PROCESSING

Visual information processing refers to hypothesized short-term memory (Broadbent, 1958) or active memory (Lewis, 1979) phenomena that mediate storage of communication effects and which are phenomenologically visual in nature. It should be emphasized that visual information processing can occur as an internal response to *any* mode of stimulus input; it is not confined to visual or pictorial stimuli. We review in this section the conditions under which visual information processing is likely to occur to linguistic stimuli (visual *or* auditory) as well as to pictorial stimuli. It may, of course, occur to stimuli input through other sensory modalities but, as noted, these other modalities are not characteristic of advertising. Also, we devote particular attention to the notion of "cognitive response," broadening this concept to include visual imagery phenomena as well as covert verbal "thoughts." First, however, some theoretical considerations about information processing are necessary. These pertain to what we have called, in Fig. 4.1, automatic decoding and elaborative encoding.

A. Automatic Decoding

Virtually all information processing models postulate attention responses as a precursor to actual processing. As Kellogg (1980) has recently shown, this need not be active or "conscious" attention, but some sense-organ response is necessary. We assume an attention response and move on to where these models differ: which is, in the nature of "processing" itself. We hypothesize that the first processing step following attention consists of automatic decoding. The decoding step is hypothesized to be automatic, that is, to always occur when a stimulus is attended to (in contrast, the second processing step, elaborative encoding, is not automatic and may or may not occur depending on other factors discussed below). We conceptualize decoding, in the same way that Osgood et al. (1957) did in their landmark analysis of meaning, as consisting of denotative responses and connotative responses.

Denotative Responses.   Denotative responses are essentially identificatory responses of the type "That is a _____." The identification may occur in any sensory modality. Perhaps the most common type of identificatory response is a verbal labeling or naming of the stimulus. Verbal labeling naturally occurs in response to linguistic stimuli but it also occurs frequently in response to pictorial stimuli except among pre-school children (Kunen, Green, & Waterman, 1979). Pezdek and Evans (1979) review evidence that suggests that all except the most complex and novel pictorial stimuli are automatically assigned a verbal label by older children and adults. Paivio's (1971) well-known dual coding theory is also consistent with this viewpoint. Alternatively, denotative responses may consist of an automatic *image:* notably, a "mental snapshot" if the input stimulus modality is visual (pictorial *or* linguistic); or an "echoic" image if the stimulus is linguistic (visual or auditory); or even "smelling," "tasting," or "feeling" images for stimuli that are habitually identified through these other sensory modalities. Of particular importance is the fact that linguistic stimuli in advertising (especially visually presented brand names) can be denoted by a visual image as well as by verbal labeling. This is important for the distinction between recognition and recall in product awareness measures and consumer search behavior to be discussed later in this chapter.

We regard imaging responses in the decoding phase as "conditioned sensations," a term first proposed by Leuba (1940) and extensively analyzed by Mowrer (1960, 1977). Denotative images are involuntary classically conditioned responses of an identificatory nature made automatically, rapidly, and often transiently; that is, these images are not necessarily available for "conscious scanning" (see Bugelski, 1977, for an expansion of this point) and may pass simply into long-term memory without further elaboration. Thus, according to our conceptualization, any stimulus attended to in advertising will be denotatively decoded either by means of an automatic verbal label ("literal") or by an image (usually iconic or echoic) or by both types of responses.

Much remains to be investigated regarding denotative responses to complex sets of stimuli, notably compounds of pictorial and linguistic stimuli as found in most advertisements. Whereas denotative responses would occur to individual stimuli within the overall array, it is likely that a summary denotative response occurs to the "Gestalt" array. An early experiment by Kerrick (1955) suggests that pictorial stimuli may dominate the overall denotation. She showed subjects stimuli consisting of mismatched pictures and captions and found that, in the presence of conflicting cues, pictorial cues were more likely to influence the overall stimulus interpretation or denotation. The dependent measure was verbal denotation, and one might expect that pictorial stimuli would be even more dominant in establishing visual denotation.

Connotative Responses. It is further postulated that connotative responses also occur automatically as conditioned reactions during the decoding phase. Here we follow Osgood's (1971) contention, with overwhelming supporting evidence, that stimuli are universally analyzed for "meaning" in terms of three basic dimensions that have biological and cultural survival value: evaluation, potency, and activity (that is, in colloquial terms, it "pays" to decide rapidly how good or bad a stimulus is, whether it is powerful or weak, and whether it is fast or slow).

It is important to note that the semantic differential, as this three-dimensional E-P-A structure of meaning has come to be known, is not merely a way of analyzing verbal stimuli nor is it confined to the verbal mode. For example, Tannenbaum and Kerrick (reported in Osgood et al., 1957) found that pictorial signs of (concrete) nouns produced semantic profiles that correlated, on average, .965 with the semantic profile of the graphological word, for example, Elephant versus a picture of an elephant. Similarly, abstract words, pictures, music, and any other type of stimulus can be represented in this three-dimensional response space. The responses need not even be measured verbally, as indicated by two recent lines of research. French (1977) discusses the development and validation of a "graphic differential" for use with non-literate subjects or in cross cultural studies. For example, the pictorial anchors ☺ _ _ _ _ _ _ ☺ represent the evaluative factor very well (r = .89); the anchors ◉ _ _ _ _ _ _ ⊡ represent the potency factor moderately well (r = .40); and the anchors ∿ _ _ _ _ _ _ ⊟ represent the activity factor moderately well (r = .46). The high correlation for evaluation is interesting in that children's researchers in consumer behavior (e.g., Wells, 1965) and other fields had previously adopted the "smiling faces" type of scale for measuring children's overall evaluations or attitudes.

There has been a long line of research aimed at establishing physiological correlates of connotative responses, particularly evaluative responses, beginning with Watson's early experiments using equipment attached near the vocal chords, and continuing with later work using galvanic skin response measures (GSR) and pupillary dilation measures (PDR). Apparently without realizing the history, Cacioppo and Petty (1979b) recently confirmed Watson's early ideas about "subvocal" thought using electromyographic (EMG) recording of speech muscles during an attitude change experiment. In another study, Chapman, McCrary, Chapman, and Bragdon (1978) appear to have identified reliable electroencephalograph (EEG) patterns corresponding to Osgood's E-P-A dimensions. This research indicates that there is a distinct pattern of cortical responses to a "good" stimulus versus a "bad" stimulus as well as to the other two dimensions of connotative meaning. Physiological research of this type is extremely important to the validation of automatic connotative decoding because it is quite likely that the occurrence of these responses cannot be reported due to their speed and basically emotional nature. What is measured on semantic differential questionnaires, we would argue, are long-term memory communication effects, not the short-term memory responses that may have produced these effects in the first place. Given the instantaneous and often microscopic amplitudes of these connotative short-term memory phenomena, it is probable that they can only be validated physiologically and not by overt report.

"Left Brain-Right Brain" Research.   The sophisticated physiological research exemplified by the Chapman et al. (1978) study should be carefully distinguished from speculations based on "right brain-left brain" research. Although it is true that the right cortical hemisphere is more physiologically specialized for processing visual, musical, and emotional information whereas the left hemisphere is more physiologically specialized for processing linguistic information (e.g., Anderson, Garrison, & Anderson, 1979; Corballis, 1980), the cortical mechanisms are much more complicated than recent popular accounts (e.g., Krugman, 1977; Mariani, 1979; Weinstein, 1979, 1980) would have us believe. First, the hemispheres are not simply dichotomized into linguistic and nonlinguistic specialties. Rather, the two hemispheres tend to exhibit somewhat different types of processing for any type of stimulus, linguistic or otherwise. One theory, and it is only a theory, is that the left hemisphere tends to follow an "idiots savants" form of processing whereas the right hemisphere tends to follow an "impractical layman" form of processing (Goldberg, Vaughan, & Gerstman, 1978). However, the picture is vastly complicated by a tendency toward bilaterality in women, who of course constitute over 50% of the population and in left-handers, about 9% of the population, particularly those with a family history of left-handedness (McGee, 1979). Moreover, laterality is not a singular phenomenon; for example, there are separate eye, ear, and limb factors

that argue against a single hemispherical laterality mechanism (Porac, Cohen, Steiger, & Duncan, 1980).

Second, it is clear that *both* hemispheres *cooperate* (antagonistically as well as reciprocally) most of the time in processing information, including emotional information (Tucker, 1981). Cooperation poses a significant problem for attempts to localize cortical processing (e.g., Krugman, 1977). Recognition of human faces, for example, which constitute complex stimulus arrays not unlike those found in most pictorial content in advertising, depends on physiological events occurring in both sides of the cerebral cortex (Geschwind, 1979). This is true also for decoding pictures (Nguy, Allard, & Bryden, 1980) and concrete words (Day, 1977). Words in music cause different cortical activity than words in text, and so forth (Anderson et al., 1979). Naive experiments attempted by nonphysiologists are likely to be extremely misleading. Metallinos and Tiemens (1977), for instance, claim to have found that pictorial stimuli placed on the left side of a TV screen, and thus presumably being projected to the right cortical hemisphere, are better recalled. However, they failed to control for the simple fact of "scanning" or saccadic eye movements, and also learned left-to-right (in our culture) reading patterns which would confound a "hemisphere" explanation.

Perhaps the greatest shortcoming of right-brain left-brain theory and research to date, however, has been the inability to measure the content of neurological responses (the Chapman et al., 1978, study appears to be the sole exception to this). Sheer activity in each hemisphere, even if this could be correlated with meaningful communication effect measures such as subsequent recognition or recall of the advertisement or advertised product (which has not been done in any published investigations to date), is likely to prove un-informative for advertising diagnostic purposes. Furthermore, comparisons of advertising across media are likely to be confounded by conditioned arousal responses (Rossiter, 1980). "Brain" research as yet does not have clear implications for advertising and much remains to be done before physiological research of any kind can revolutionize the field.

B. Elaborative Encoding

The final step in our hypothesized information processing phase consists of elaborative encoding. Unlike automatic decoding, elaborative encoding is conceptualized as a voluntary (operant) type of response. It is akin to what communication theorists have called "cognitive response." Cognitive responses in the current psychological and consumer research literature have been conceptualized as purely *verbal*. For example, Greenwald (1968a) refers to cognitive responses as subjectively produced "thoughts" or "arguments." Similarly, Olson, Toy, and Dover (1978) refer to cognitive responses as "internal subvocal" responses.

Calder (1978) has been one of the few to recognize that cognitive responses may also be *visual,* that is, visual imagery responses. To this we would add that cognitive responses may include imagery in any modality; for example, "hearing" a jingle suggested by a brand name, "tasting" a cold beer shown in an advertisement, "smelling" country style cooking in an advertisement, "feeling" the texture of luxurious upholstery in an automobile commercial, and so on. Our framework in Fig. 4.1 (earlier) reflects the multimodal possibilities for cognitive responses.

Greenwald (1968a), in discussing the nature of verbal cognitive responses, noted an analogy between his "cognitive" approach and traditional learning theory; in fact, he regards his now highly influential model of persuasion as "a combination of cognitive process theory and learning theory." His 1968a paper proposed that cognitive responses are similar to classically conditioned responses. However, in a subsequent summary in the same volume (Greenwald, 1968b) he changed this position slightly, referring to cognitive responses as responses that are repeated by subjects because they have been "successful in similar previous situations." This puts cognitive responses of the elaborative type, to which Greenwald is referring, in the category of *operantly* learned responses, not classically conditioned responses. This is the way we regard them in our two-phase conceptualization: there may be a second phase of information processing (following decoding, which is automatic) consisting of cognitive responses which are operantly or instrumentally learned. These responses— covert verbalizations, elaborative imagery, and so on—are instrumental in deciding what further to do about the stimulus (i.e., in forming or changing "attitudes" in the traditional sense). Because operants are "free responses," there is much less likelihood that they will be standard across subjects for the same stimulus, or that they will be learned in the first place. This certainly characterizes the empirical evidence on cognitive responses in that there is high intersubjective variability and no guarantee that such responses will in fact occur (e.g., Calder, 1978; Petty, 1977). To the extent that they do occur, of course, cognitive responses have been found to be powerful determinants of preferential communication effects: beliefs, attitudes, and intentions.

An additional theoretical point remains to be addressed about elaborative encoding. When the cognitive responses involved are verbal, it is reasonably clear what "elaborative" means. Any covert verbalizations, reported overtly to the experimenter or written down as a protocol, which are not verbatim statements or close paraphrases of linguistic content in the advertisement or simple descriptions of pictorial content, would presumably qualify as elaborative. This definition could be transferred to visual imagery responses. Any visual images that are not iconic "replays" of the pictorial content, of an illustration in print advertising or a video sequence in television advertising or of written words, would qualify as elaborative visual imagery. However, an obvious problem arises in measuring elaborative visual imagery. To be recorded, the imagery would have to be translated into a verbal description or else drawn visually on paper. Both methods involve expressive difficulties such that errors might tend to be mistakenly counted as elaborative (Evans, 1980). This is a significant measurement problem although it poses no threat to the theoretical distinction between iconic denotative visual imagery and the more subjective visual imagery characteristic of elaborative encoding.

Assuming that advertisers might want to design advertisements that stimulate visual imagery and not just verbal cognitive responses, how might they facilitate the visual imagery process? Three possible ways would be to: (1) use stimuli or stimulus manipulations known to increase the probability of generating visual imagery; (2) instruct consumers to form visual images, for example, "Imagine how you will look . . ."; or (3) try to capitalize, in target audience selection, on individual differences in visual imaging ability. Recent comprehensive research in which all three methods were compared (Slee, 1978) and the first and third were compared (McKelvie & Demers, 1979) indicate that stimulus-based procedures are far more effective than either instructions or individual differences in visual imaging ability. Stimulus-based procedures are also the easiest for advertisers to institute. Accordingly, we review below some of the stimulus variables that have been shown to increase visual imagery responses. The review covers the three main types of stimuli chosen by advertisers: static pictorial stimuli, as in print ad illustrations; dynamic pictorial stimuli, as in TV video; and linguistic stimuli, usable in all advertising.

C. Static Pictorial Stimili

Three primary variables which appear to affect visual imagery generation in response to static pictorial stimuli are picture size, exposure duration, and number of exposures.

Picture Size.   Picture size has long been known in advertising research as a variable that increases print ad recognition (see Hendon, 1973, and Holbrook & Lehmann, 1980, for reviews). A likely explanation is that larger pictures relative to the total advertising layout are more likely to stimulate visual denotative responses and visual imagery than smaller pictures, where relatively larger copy may "push" information processing into the verbal mode (cf. Kerrick's 1955 study of pictorial and linguistic cue dominance). Also, larger pictures may produce larger visual images that make it easier for consumers to "read off" details such as brand names for later recognition or recall. Takeda (1977) had subjects form visual images of common objects "within" circles on a screen of various sizes which projected visual angles of 1°, 10°, and 30°. When asked to report whether or not the object possessed various properties, the very small images produced a high error rate. Similarly, Kosslyn and Alper (1977) found that larger reported visual images of words produced better retention of the words. In an experiment to be described later by Rossiter and Percy (1980) a larger picture of an advertised product produced stronger persuasion effects than an identical but smaller picture, which we feel can be attributed to stronger visual imagery effects, although no direct measure of visual imagery was taken. In general, then, picture size would seem to be a likely stimulus variable moderating the production of visual imagery.

Exposure Duration.   Loftus and Kallman (1979) recently proposed a model of picture recognition which hypothesizes that longer exposure duration increases the likelihood of encoding more details of the picture. They hypothesize that recognition responses are based on an overall familiarity or recognition response plus recognition of specific details. In our terms, the "encoding" of details (which is for us decoding) would simply result in a more detailed denotative visual image. Most importantly for our conceptualization, Intraub (1979) has shown that exposure duration positively influences picture recognition and also recall performance *independently* of the opportunity to verbally label the picture. Thus at least part of the duration effect can be attributed solely to visual information processing phenomena which we believe to be denotative visual imagery. Graefe and Watkins (1980) have shown that people can "rehearse" pictures just as they rehearse words. Picture rehearsal fits our definition of denotative visual imagery exactly.

The general finding in psychology is that exposure duration increases recognition and recall accuracy linearly, up to a duration of about 2 to 4 seconds, depending on the complexity of the pictorial stimulus. For example, using magazine illustrations, Potter and Levy (1969) found only 50 percent could be recognized at a ½-second exposure rate whereas 93 percent were recognized at a 2-second rate. Shepard's classic (1967) experiment in which 97 percent accuracy was obtained for immediate recognition with 90 percent recognition on a 1-week delayed test employed unlimited exposure, though the average chosen by subjects was about 5 seconds. Fleming and Sheikhian (1972) found that longer durations are required with more complex pictures. The exposure duration variable has clear implications for print advertising. Advertisers seeking high recognition scores (the most common method of testing print ad performance, as in the Starch procedure) should try to employ not just attention-getting but rather attention-holding pictures which hold the consumer's attention for at least 2 seconds. In keeping with our notion of denotative visual imagery and also Loftus and Kallman's (1979) detail encoding model, this should guarantee high memorability.

Number of Exposures.   A third variable that appears to influence the effectiveness of static pictorial stimuli is number of exposures (or repetitions). The likelihood is that denotative visual images are fully formed after only 1 or 2 exposures. Shepard (1967) and Standing (1973) provide impressive evidence of 1-trial recognition learning of pictures. Nickerson (1968), using the extremely long retention interval of 1 year, found that 2 exposures produced higher recognition (72 percent) than 1 exposure (60 percent, close to chance). Robinson (1969) found that multiple trials do not add significantly to 1 or 2 trial recognition performance. It should be noted that these experiments used rather long exposure durations (5 seconds or longer) and that under brief exposure conditions more trials may be effective.

Elaborative visual imagery, on the other hand, is more likely to require more than 1 or 2 trials for maximum response strength, as has been found for verbal cognitive responses (Cacioppo & Petty, 1979a). An important consideration, however, pertains to the affective content of the elaborative encoding. "Too many" exposures seem to increase the incidence of negative verbal cognitive responses (counterarguing). Possibly, "overexposure" may also lead to the development of negatively toned visual imagery; for example, imagining what could go wrong with the product. Precisely how many exposures is optimal is an unanswered research problem because cognitive response studies are conducted under laboratory conditions where exposure conditions and exposure intervals may have little generalizability to real-world advertising exposure situations.

In summary, it seems denotative visual imagery (important for recognition and recall) reaches a maximum after 1 or 2 exposures but that elaborative visual imagery (important for preference effects) increases with number of exposures. However, the latter relationship is probably complex. Given the importance of repetition effects in developing advertising media schedules, this relationship is a critical topic for future research.

D. Dynamic Pictorial Stimuli

Visual imagery responses resulting from dynamic pictorial stimuli (represented in advertising by TV video) pose an interesting challenge to the information processing conceptualization proposed in this chapter and indeed for any other visual imagery conceptualization. In the first place TV video presents not *a* picture but a continuous *series* of pictures—at the rate of about 30 per second. Visual imagery responses to each picture, or for that matter verbal labeling of each, is patently impossible. One way around this problem is to propose that people process these sequences as a series of discrete "snapshots" in short-term memory. These discrete "snapshots" may form cartoon-like "scripts" (Abelson, 1976). The denotative visual imagery in this case would be like a brief imaginary "film clip" and the verbal labeling would consist of a "story" rather than a word or two of description. If this proposal is correct, then the verbal labeling process and visual imagery processes applicable to static pictorial stimuli would apply to dynamic pictorial stimuli also.

A further conceptual difficulty arises, however, with elaborative encoding of dynamic pictorial material. It has been shown by a number of investigators (Kieras, 1978; Finke, 1980) that attention to external visual material interferes with visual imagery formulation—just as reading aloud interferes with the generation of other verbal thoughts. Thus, attention to TV video should *prevent* elaborative visual imagery from occurring. There are two ways around this problem. One is to propose that TV video provides "homogenized" elaborative visual imagery for everyone. In this proposal, denotative or iconic visual imagery becomes synonymous with elaborative visual imagery. It is tempting to accept this "provided imagery" explanation for the apparent persuasive superiority of TV commercials over comparable print ads (Grass & Wallace, 1974). Alternatively, it is possible to propose that people do not pay constant visual attention to the video of TV commercials especially after the first few exposures but may keep auditory attention fully or partially focused on the commercial through the sound track. (An independently conducted study for *Newsweek,* 1980, indicates that during the average prime-time commercial break, only 62 percent of the audience stays in the room and only 22 percent, or about a third of those in the room, watch the screen throughout the commercial.) Under these conditions, it would be possible to experience elaborative visual imagery without external visual interference.

The stimulus-based variables that influence visual imagery responses to static pictorial stimuli are not easily transferrable to dynamic pictorial stimuli, but there are some analogies to be considered. First, picture size in TV video is largely homogeneous for most viewers. However, one could perhaps argue that smaller-screen sets are less likely than larger-screen sets to produce visual imagery. Second, exposure duration is complicated by the fixed rapid succession of pictures in video. However, one could infer that particular images that need to be retained by the viewer, such as a close-up of the package, should be "held" on the screen for at least 2 seconds for denotative visual imagery and longer for elaborative visual imagery. In fact Intraub (1980) has shown that successive fixation on rapidly presented ($\frac{1}{10}$ sec.) pictures reduces later recognition of each by about 75 percent, so it is actually better if the viewer looks away after an important frame or at least does not become distracted by novel pictures immediately following it.

The third stimulus-based variable, number of exposures (repetitions), bears more detailed discussion. One might expect that the greater number of pictures ("snapshots") in a TV commercial might require more than 1 or 2 exposures for maximum visual recognition or recall. This is probably true if the purpose is to have consumers *recall* the whole commercial (as, for example, in Burke day-after recall testing). However, it is quite likely that visual *recognition* of TV commercials, and also of details such as brand names, is complete in 1 or 2 trials. This is because recognition is a very easy task when the to-be-recognized stimuli are distinctive, as is the case with TV commercials. Several commercial research services have begun to use a visual recognition measure rather than the more conventional unaided or partially aided verbal recall measure. In this recognition measure, offered in the U.S. by Bruzzone Research Company (BRC), respondents are shown a storyboard of the commercial with package shots and brand names deleted. This is really a recognition measure for the commercial and a highly aided recall measure for the brand name. Stoessl and Clemens (1979) reported some U.K. data on brand recall using this method (Fig. 4.2). Average brand name recall among nonviewers was 30 percent, reflecting a guessing response common with recognition; among light viewers 46 percent; and among heavy viewers a marginally higher 49 percent. Although the independent variable, TV exposure, does not index number of commercial exposures, and although these are aggregate data which undoubtedly contain a ceiling effect due to individuals unexposed to particular commercials, the results are in keeping with the idea that recognition and highly aided recall are complete after only a few exposures.

Pictorial stimuli of all types are particularly likely to generate visual imagery responses because they are themselves visual. Denotative visual images, we have argued, are automatic and inevitable responses to pictures, as is postulated by Paivio's dual coding theory (Paivio 1971, 1978). Elaborative visual imagery, although not inevitable, would seem to follow this same-modality tendency. The interesting and important remaining question is the extent to which elaborative visual imagery is generated by linguistic stimuli (visually or auditorially presented words) and this is addressed next.

D. Linguistic Stimuli

The single most important variable affecting visual imagery as a response to linguistic stimuli is *concreteness*. Concreteness is an attribute reflecting the extent to which a stimulus refers to objects, persons, places, or things that can be experienced by our senses (Toglia & Battig, 1978). The concreteness attribute is very highly related to direct ratings of imagery value (Paivio, 1971). In an

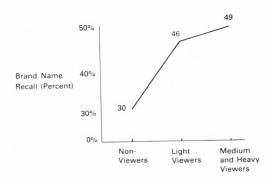

FIG. 4.2. Stoessl and Clemen's (1979) U.K. data showing average TV brand name recall as a function of TV viewing level.

extensive measurement of word ratings, Toglia and Battig defined imagery value as the extent to which a stimulus, in their case, a word, arouses a sensory experience, such as a mental picture or sound, *quickly* and *easily* (these latter requirements would seem to place this type of imagery in our denotative imagery category rather than in our elaborative imagery category). It was found that ratings of word concreteness and word imagery value correlated .88, i.e., the two measures have about 75 percent of their variance in common. Thus, *most* but not all concrete words are high in imagery value and vice versa. It is possible, however, as pointed out by Richardson (1975), to find words that are high in concreteness but low in imagery value (e.g., charlatan, socialist) or low in concreteness but high in imagery value (e.g., fantasy, happiness). Our speculation is that words that are low in concreteness but high in imagery value are words for which visual imagery is either learned as a referent, such as "fantasy" or "dream," or where visual imagery is a common contextual associate in everyday discourse, such as "Imagine how happy you will be." It is not that visual imagery is impossible for these more abstract words but rather that it is less likely unless learned specifically. Moreover, although there is no direct evidence on this, we would guess that most imagery associated with words is indeed visual. Even for obvious exceptions such as onomatopoeic words, where the word's sound suggests its meaning, for example, "hiss," there seems to be a strong likelihood of visual imagery accompanying auditory or other sensory imagery.

Early research on word imagery, as well as most of the current research, employed individual words as stimuli; most often these are nouns (Paivio, Yuille, & Madigan, 1968) although imagery ratings of other parts of speech are emerging in the literature (Berrian, Metzler, Kroll, & Clark-Meyers, 1979; Klee & Legge, 1976; Toglia & Battig, 1978). Research on the imagery value of larger verbal units, such as phrases, clauses, sentences, and paragraphs, however, has been very sparse. This is unfortunate from our point of view since advertising copy usually consists of these larger verbal units.

Larger Verbal Units.   The few studies that have been reported in the psychological literature to date strongly indicate that visual imagery value is an important attribute for larger verbal units as well as individual words. In one study Holyoak (1974) found that sentences rated high in imagery value are significantly easier for people to understand than sentences rated low in imagery value. In a second study Jorgensen and Kintsch (1973) used simple subject-verb-object (SVO) sentences that were prerated as being either high in imagery value or low in imagery value. This variable was then crossed with objective truth or falsehood of sentence content (Table 4.1). It was found that high imagery sentences can be evaluated, on average, 30 percent faster than low imagery sentences. This difference translates to about half a second, which may be a critical difference, when a person is listening to a verbal claim in a broadcast commercial or reading

TABLE 4.1
Results of the Jorgensen and Kintsch (1973) Experiment Showing
that High Imagery Sentences Can Be Evaluated as True or False
Faster Than Low Imagery Sentences (Mean Reaction Times)

	True	*False*
Low Imagery	e.g., Truck has oil 1.9 sec.	e.g., Carrot has stomach 1.9 sec.
High Imagery	e.g., Knife cuts steak 1.3 sec.	e.g., Horse eats sand 1.4 sec.

a claim in a print advertisement, between whether the claim is processed correctly or not. Presumably, claims that advertisers may not wish to have carefully evaluated by consumers, such as mandatory disclosures about unfavorable product characteristics or about conditions or terms attached to the offer, may be more "effective" in being passed over without evaluation if stated in low imagery terms. In contrast, strong, true claims that the advertiser may wish to have evaluated quickly and accurately, should be more effective if stated in high imagery terms. In a third study Williams (1979) found that the syllogisms made up of nouns and adjectives that are high in imagery value are faster and more accurately solved than the same syllogism made up of low imagery nouns and adjectives. This finding has relevance for comparative advertising where claims are frequently stated in syllogistic form (e.g., "Our brand is better than the leading brand, which in turn is better than the other brands, so which should you buy?") in that it implies that claims which arouse visual imagery of the items and relationships readily will be most easily comprehended. In terms of communication effects, this should aid the development of beliefs in a fast and error-free way, and reduce the common risk of comparative claims miscommunicating.

No other variables, as far as we know, have been investigated as potential determinants of visual imagery derived from linguistic stimuli (apart from individual differences, which are minor). However, our category of operantly learned elaborative visual imagery makes it likely that two of the variables identified previously in conjunction with pictorial stimuli might also apply to linguistic stimuli. These are exposure duration and number of exposures. Both variables may increase the opportunity for "free" cognitive responses, including visual imagery, to occur in conjunction with linguistic stimuli, especially advertising claims where pictorial or video stimuli are often also present. The demonstrated power of visual imagery in awareness performance (recognition and recall) as well as the promise in initial research of visual imagery in creating preferential communication effects (such as beliefs and attitudes) make the study of those variables which influence visual imagery as a cognitive response to linguistic stimuli an important avenue for advertising research.

The most complex phenomena in applying visual imagery to advertising research are going to be cross-modality effects, particularly between visual and linguistic content, in both print and TV advertising. In print advertising, Rossiter (1981) found that verbal headline syntax that contains high imagery words is more predictive of subsequent advertisement recognition and brand name awareness than picture size, although the latter variable, as many previous studies have shown, is still a significant predictor. Similarly, an interesting study by Glass, Eddy, and Schwanenflugel (1980) indicates that initial focus on a picture does not interfere with subsequent sentence comprehension (as in body copy) but that the reverse sequence (sentence then picture focus as in reading a headline first) does create interference, particularly if the sentence is high in visual imagery. The latter finding has particular relevance not only for print advertising but also, quite evidently, for TV advertising. Audience focus on high imagery audio content could distract from the processing of video content. In an ingenious but untested interpretation of the psycholinguistic phenomenon of sentence phrase markers, which denote natural pauses in decoding a sentence, Abrams (1981) has proposed that important visual scenes in TV commercials should be placed "in the pauses" to minimize interference. It should be noted along these lines that TV pretest storyboards (which are very much like Abelson's scripts, discussed earlier) usually place the copy in direct coincidence with the main video frames. This points to a possible mistake in TV commercial testing that may or may not be carried over to the finished commercial. Further research on these cross-modality phenomena should prove very insightful for advertising.

III.   VISUAL COMMUNICATION EFFECTS

Communication effects consist of major product-based responses stored in long-term memory that provide relevant information for consumer behavior. They may be generated by advertising or by other sources of marketing information including experience with the product itself. Whatever the external source, these responses are assumed to be formed or altered by responses made, and internal stimulation produced, during initial information processing, the component we have just discussed (see also Fig. 4.1 earlier). Communication effects have been conceptualized in many different ways, although a reasonable consensus is emerging in recent conceptual expositions. Before addressing the role of visual phenomena inherent in various communication effects, it is worthwhile to explicate our particular conceptualization.

A.   A Conceptual Model

One of the most promising conceptualizations of communication effects is based on the associative network model proposed by Anderson and Bower (1974). In this model, "cognitive structures" are formed consisting of nodes representing

concepts and linkages representing the nature and strength of associations between concepts. Olson (1978) has applied the associative network model to
cognitive structures pertaining to products and brands in the following manner
(Fig. 4.3). In his conceptualization, which is being refined, product or brand
concepts are linked to attributes by beliefs of varying strengths or probabilities.
Each attribute contains an evaluative component (not shown) that, when combined with belief strength, contributes to an overall evaluation or attitude toward
the product or brand, respectively. From attitudes follow intentions and overt
behaviors in the manner posited by Fishbein (e.g., Fishbein & Ajzen, 1975).
Thus, the associative network approach is rendered compatible with the multiattribute approach to explain consumer behavior.

There are several problems with the associative network formulation as it
currently stands. First of all, it is not clear what a "concept" is, at least not
operationally. In Fig. 4.3, for instance, what does the box labeled "winter coat"
represent? In our model (Fig. 4.4) the central nodes are conceptualized as awareness responses. Awareness is postulated to be the basic communication effect to
which others (beliefs, attitudes, etc.) are linked. When an external stimulus is
processed in short-term memory and "contacts" a memory trace, it does not
contact a vaguely defined concept; rather it contacts an awareness response—a
visual image of the product or brand or a verbal label of the product or brand,
most often, or else some other response indicating sensory awareness. Awareness is regarded as a base response, in the manner outlined by Hayes-Roth
(1977), which is a necessary precursor of any other product or brand-related
communication effects being activated from long-term memory.

Nor do we use the vague term "concepts" to refer to other parts of our model.
It is evident that communication effects other than beliefs about attributes can be

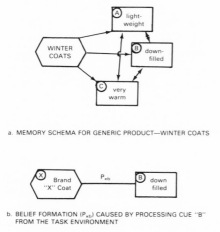

a. MEMORY SCHEMA FOR GENERIC PRODUCT—WINTER COATS

b. BELIEF FORMATION (P$_{xb}$) CAUSED BY PROCESSING CUE "B"
FROM THE TASK ENVIRONMENT

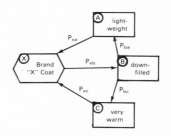

c. BELIEF STRUCTURE (P$_{xb}$, P$_{xa}$, P$_{xc}$) CREATED THROUGH
INFERENTIAL BELIEF FORMATION (arrows indicate
theoretical causal flow).

FIG. 4.3.   Olson's (1978) model of memory schema.

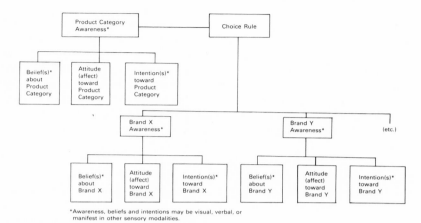

FIG. 4.4.   A conceptual model of communication effects.

connected to awareness responses. This is clearly recognized elsewhere by Olson and other cognitive structure theorists in consumer behavior (e.g., Lutz, 1975). Our model differs in that these communication effects are hypothesized to take various sensory forms rather than being solely "verbal" or "conceptual" as in other models. These communication effects are regarded as covert responses, in sensory form, which have covert stimulus consequences (response-produced stimuli) that can mediate overt behaviors. Osgood (1971) following the pioneering work of Hull (1952) provides a detailed explanation of what is meant here.

Another problem with the associative network model is its "box and arrow" nature. The inadequacy of models that do not translate concepts and their linkages into conventional stimulus and response terms has been pointed out by neobehaviorists such as Berger and Lambert (1968) and Estes (1973). Once stimuli and responses are identified, established conditioning and learning mechanisms can substitute for the "arrows" and a functional process account can emerge. Otherwise, one must assume that some sort of homunculus is present to "rationally" make all the connections. Digressions aside, let us turn specifically to the role of visual responses in communication effects and their relationships with stimuli presented through advertising.

B. Awareness

Percy and Rossiter (1980) define awareness, as an advertising communication effect, as encompassing responses that allow the prospective buyer to identify the product, on cue, in sufficient detail to enable purchase. The phrase "on cue" is critical. Awareness ranges from recognition to recall on a continuum of cue-target similarity. In recognition situations there is typically 100 percent cue-target similarity because the target response is presented as a cue; for example, a detergent package shown in a TV commercial is seen again on the supermarket shelf. In recall situations, on the other hand, the cue may bear varying degrees of similarity to the target response, from 0 percent on upward; for example, a respondent in a day-after TV recall survey may be asked to (1) name the products advertised, (2) name the detergents advertised, (3) name the detergent advertised with the blue and green package, and so on, with increasingly specific "aids," that is, cue-target similarity. Consequently, we simply refer to awareness as a single class of communication effect responses which includes recognition and recall.

The now classic research on awareness (recognition and recall) of various stimuli is that of Paivio (1971, 1978). His general finding was that pictures are retained better than concrete words that in turn are retained better than abstract words (in most experiments the words were presented visually rather than auditory). Paivio's explanation is based on his *dual code theory,* which hypothesizes that stimuli are capable of being represented in two distinct ways in memory: visually or imaginally, and verbally or linguistically. Paivio (1978) concedes the possibility of a third type of code for emotional or evaluative responses rather than memory responses, to stimuli (as in our conceptual model) but argues that this is separate from, rather than superordinate to, visual and verbal representation. Some stimuli, maintains Paivio, are more memorable because they activate both codes or representational systems. Pictures activate both codes most often; concrete words less often; and abstract words rarely. Based on a large number of experiments, Paivio suggests the following indication of the extent to which these three types of stimuli are capable of eliciting either or both types of memory representation (adapted from Eysenck, 1977):

| | Memory Representation | | Total Memory |
	Visual	*Verbal*	*"Weights"*
Pictures	+++	++	5
Concrete Words	+	+++	4
Abstract Words		+++	3

Paivio's "hierarchy" of pictures > concrete words > abstract words holds up well no matter whether the memory or awareness task deals with short- or long-term memory, recall, or recognition (McKelvie & Demers, 1979).

These three types of stimuli, however, pictures, concrete words and abstract words, are far from representing the range of stimuli encountered in advertising (see Fig. 4.1 earlier). Recently there have been several studies expanding on these types of stimuli, both in the psychological and the advertising literature, that allow us to postulate a more comprehensive but decidedly *tentative* hierarchy (Table 4.2). The rankings are tentative due to the fact that only one or two studies have explored various comparisons beyond Paivio's.

Basically the proposed hierarchy favors: (1) pictorial stimuli over verbal stimuli; (2) dynamic (broadcast) presentation over static (print) presentation; (3) concrete stimuli over abstract stimuli; and (4) sentences or phrases over individual words. The research findings leading to the hypothesized ordering are reviewed below.

The top ranking for dynamic concrete pictures, as in TV video, is based on findings and anecdotal evidence from advertising research (almost no research has been done in psychology on the comparative memorability of *sequences* of pictorial stimuli as in video). Grass and Wallace (1974), in an experiment that should have invited further replication given its importance to media decisions, found that TV commercials produced significantly greater recall of message points than specially matched print advertisements which used a "main frame" from the commercial as the pictorial component of the ad and the verbatim audio of the commercial as the copy. Overall recall was superior for TV by 81 percent to 56 percent and recall of the main message point was superior by 75 percent to 39 percent. Grass and Wallace hypothesized that the superior performance of TV commercials over print advertisements was due to greater and easier attention payable to broadcast presentation (both visually and auditory). However, it is possible, following Paivio's dual code theory, that video pictures accompanying the audio message points served to reinforce these points in two memory modalities. In any case, this finding is used here to support the ranking of

TABLE 4.2
Tentative Hierarchy of Advertising Stimuli Ranked in Terms of
Memorability (Awareness)

1. Dynamic concrete pictures (video)
2. Static concrete pictures (print)
3. Dynamic abstract pictures (video)[a]
4. Static abstract pictures (print)
5. Dynamic concrete sentences or phrases (audio)[b]
6. Dynamic abstract sentences or phrases (audio)
7. Dynamic concrete words (audio)
8. Dynamic abstract words (audio)
9. Static concrete sentences or phrases (print)[b]
10. Static concrete words (print)
11. Static abstract sentences, phrases or words (print)

[a]Abstract pictures in video advertising may be infrequent enough to make this category nonexistent for practical purposes.

[b]*Positive* concrete sentences or phrases only, not negative ones (see text).

dynamic pictures *and* verbal material over static presentations, with the concrete versus abstract pictorial exception (ranks 2 and 3) as noted in Table 4.2.

The superiority of video over audio in the dynamic (broadcast) mode is supported by anecdotal evidence and, weakly, by one experiment. O'Barr (1979), who has interviewed many creators and producers of TV commercials, reports that these people believe video to be much more important to the success of TV commercials than the audio (the typical measure of "success" for TV commercials is day-after recall scores, an awareness measure). O'Barr also reports the interesting fact that TV media charges for prime time national advertising are 25 percent if the audio alone is broadcast and 75 percent if the video alone is broadcast, although this practice may date from the early days of TV when audio commercials were sometimes used. One experiment, by Hollander and Jacoby (1973), implies that the video component of TV commercials has a greater effect on awareness (unaided brand recall) than the audio component. In an unusual experiment, these investigators swapped the video and audio tracks of several pairs of commercials. They found the "mismatches" to be more memorable than the normal versions, presumably because of greater attention due to their novelty, and the video to play a somewhat greater role in increasing brand name recall than the audio, although the average difference was slight.

The rankings also favor concrete pictures over abstract pictures in extablishing ranks 1 to 4. Paivio's research generally has not made the concrete-abstract distinction for pictures but only for words, and has generally used rather concrete or realistic pictures (photographs or line drawings with high iconic similarity to some object, person, place or thing). Koen (1969) found that realistic paintings were far more easily recognized than abstract paintings. Nelson (1971) found that recognition memory in children was best for realistic paintings, then abstract paintings, then picture puzzle pieces which, out of context, were presumably most abstract of all. The superiority of concrete pictorial stimuli over abstract pictorial stimuli fits Paivio's dual code theory, by the way, because concrete pictures should be easier for people to describe verbally or label, thus activating verbal representation, although Intraub's recent study (1979), and also an earlier study by Sang and Ross (1970) discrediting the "verbal loop hypothesis" of Glanzer and Clark (1962), suggest that labeling may not be the correct explanation. Advertisers tend to use concrete pictures—usually of products, people or places. This is especially true of TV commercials; it is difficult to think of any really abstract video scenes in commercials (although this could be a problem of recall!). The very highly recalled Levi's commercials that, for a while, held the Burke recall "record," might be described as abstract (they did show people, places, and things but in animated surrealistic style) but their memorability may have been due to novelty rather than abstractness *per se*. Print advertisements more often employ abstract pictures. An example of a picture rated "highly unrelated" to the verbal content, possibly because of its abstractness, in a pilot study by Rossiter and Falsetts (unpublished) is shown in Fig. 4.5. Hendon (1973)

FIG. 4.5   Abstract pictorial content in advertising (courtesy Carillon Importers).

lists several studies that have shown simple, realistic illustrations in magazine advertising to produce higher Starch Noted scores (a visual recognition measure) than more complex, less realistic illustrations. Thus it would seem that the concrete over abstract superiority in awareness holds for pictures as well as words and this ordering is reflected in Table 4.2.

Turning now to differences in memorability between *verbal* (visual-linguistic or auditory-linguistic) stimulus categories, a few recent studies have extended the well-researched concreteness effect beyond single word stimuli to larger word units such as phrases and sentences. Begg and Clark (1975) noted that the concreteness, and also the imagery value, of words may vary according to different context-elicited meanings when used in phrases or sentences; for example, "*view* from the balcony" versus "in *view* of the evidence." Word norm ratings of concreteness also reflect this context effect (e.g., Toglia & Battig, 1978). Phrases or sentences, too, can be rated for "overall" concreteness. It is not surprising, given the well-established word concreteness effect, that concrete phrases are easier to recall than abstract phrases (Paivio, 1975). What is intriguing, however, is that concrete phrases are also easier to recall than concrete single words, that is, in a list. This result alone might suggest that conceptual or semantic units, which are presumably more distinctive for a phrase than for a single word, are responsible rather than concreteness *per se*. However, this "larger verbal unit" effect does not hold for abstract phrases versus abstract single words (Paivio, 1975). (It also may hold only for *positive* concrete sentences or phrases. A 1981 experiment by Smith found that negative concrete sentences produced lower recognition than positive concrete sentences and even abstract sentences of either polarity. Smith suggests that this is because positive concrete sentences such as "The boy hit the girl" refer to an easily imaged event whereas negative concrete sentences such as "The boy did not hit the girl" say virtually nothing about the actual event and are therefore hard to image. Thus an important qualification to our hierarchy is that concrete sentence or phrase superiority applies only to *positive* phrase units.) Paivio suggests that visual images are formed of concrete, but not abstract, phrases that allow subjects to "read off" component words. The implications of this finding for advertising, though based on only one experiment, are significant indeed. Although brand names are usually single words, advertisers also seek copy point recall and slogan recognition. Copy points and slogans usually consist of phrases or sentences and these larger units could easily be rated for concreteness and their related memorability tested. Our tentative ranking lists concrete phrases and sentences ahead of concrete words but, following Paivio (1975), predicts no difference in verbal unit size for abstract verbal material (rank 11).

A very provocative comment by Lutz and Lutz (1978) should be mentioned. These authors suggest that the picture superiority effect may be due to the fact that pictures often are described verbally in several words rather than a single word. Thus, they suggest, memorability of pictures should be compared with memorability of phrases or sentences rather than single words. This comparison was included in the experiment by Shepard (1967). He found a slight picture superiority effect, which accords with Paivio's dual code theory. It is also interesting to note that pictures plus corresponding words may be the most memorable advertising stimulus combination, especially if both types of stimuli are concrete, as they most often are. Levy (1979), in an M.A. thesis completed at the University of Pennsylvania's Annenberg School of Communications, found that comparative advertising claims in print advertising achieved greater attention, better recall of message points, and higher recall of the comparison itself when the comparison was made both pictorially and verbally than when made verbally only. TV commercials, of course, offer an even better combination in terms of our ranking: dynamic, usually concrete, pictures in the video plus dynamic, often concrete, sentences and phrase units in the audio. The stimulus input in this instance is very close to the hypothesized representational unit which Abelson (1976) has called a "script." Scripts, comprising both imagery and verbal labeling components, may be the superior memory code.

This completes our review of the effects of various advertising stimuli on awareness (recall and recognition). Although the evidence is far from complete, it seems safe to conclude that visual-pictorial stimuli in general have greater memorability and are thus capable of generating higher awareness than other types of stimuli. We now review the very small amount of research that has been done on communication effect variables other than awareness.

Our overall framework in Fig. 4.1 lists five main types of communication effects in advertising: awareness, beliefs, attitudes, intentions, and choice rules. The last four communication effects may be described as "preferential" in that they allow consumers to choose between products rather than simply to be aware of them. Whereas awareness, of some type, would seem to be a prerequisite for choice, few would argue that it is sufficient. Consumers usually decide on the basis of differential beliefs held toward product alternatives (e.g., that detergent A washes clothes whiter than detergent B); or on the basis of differential attitudes (e.g., a child may like cereal X more than cereal Y); or on the basis of differential intentions (e.g., to try a new brand); or on the basis of some overall choice rule (e.g., to buy the cheapest brand and size). Frequently, several communication effects are simultaneously involved in product selection, depending on the overall buyer response model exhibited by the consumer (see Rossiter and Percy, in press, for further development of the buyer response model approach). Clearly, advertisers are vitally concerned with these preferential communication effects generated by advertising.

C. Beliefs

Beliefs constitute an interesting theoretical class of communication effects for visual stimuli because of the cross-modality learning involved (beliefs are verbal responses). The Federal Trade Commission's principal interest in visual content in advertising pertains to the potential of visual stimuli to affect beliefs about the product. Examples were given earlier, such as the prohibition of "white coat" advertising, which may stimulate the belief that the product is endorsed by a doctor, and the cigaret advertisement mentioned earlier, which may, according to an FTC spokesman, stimulate the belief that cigarette smoking is a healthy activity. The Federal Trade Commission Act only requires that an advertisement have the *potential* to deceive consumers, that is, the potential to stimulate a belief that is not in accord with objective fact.

Whereas it seems highly probable that visual content in advertisements can affect product beliefs, research evidence on this phenomenon is virtually nonexistent. Only one study, by Mitchell and Olson (1977), has investigated the effects of visual advertising content on product beliefs. Mitchell and Olson developed four advertisements for hypothetical brands of facial tissue. One advertisement was visual-linguistic (i.e., verbal) only, simply stating that "Brand I facial tissues are soft." The other three advertisements were visual-pictorial, consisting only of a brand name plus a picture. The pictorial stimuli used were a kitten, a sunset, and an abstract painting. The target belief in this case was softness. The visual-pictorial "kitten" advertisement generated the strongest softness belief (5.48 on a 1 to 7, highest, scale measuring belief that the brand is "very soft"); the visual-pictorial "sunset" advertisement did as well as the purely "verbal" advertisement, 4.87 and 4.81, respectively; whereas the visual-pictorial "abstract" advertisement generated no softness belief, in that its rating of 3.57 is near the neutral point of 4.0 on the belief measure. Mitchell and Olson also measured attitudes and intentions generated by the four types of advertisements and these results are discussed below in conjunction with the respective communication effects involved.

Given the importance of beliefs as the advertising communication effect of most relevance to the FTC in its monitoring of deceptive advertising, it is surprising that programmatic research on the role of visual content in this regard has not been forthcoming. There is a large body of consumer research on belief structures deriving from verbal advertising stimuli which can serve as a comparative framework. We need to know the extent to which visual advertising stimuli are capable of effecting belief formation, belief maintenance, and belief change. Current interest in the topic by the FTC and by practitioners of "image" advertising indicates that this research effort is likely to emerge soon.

Most of the concern and interest in visual stimuli in advertising pertains to the content of these stimuli. However, another attribute of visual stimuli—color—is also relevant insofar as color may influence consumer beliefs about the nature of the product. Several early studies in advertising investigated the effects of color on product beliefs; however, most of these studies were poorly controlled and are not worth reviewing. One relatively early study conducted by Osgood and Tannenbaum for the Young & Rubicam advertising agency in 1952 (reported in Osgood et al., 1957) is an exception that deserves mention. Osgood and Tannenbaum, as might be expected, used as dependent communication effect variables the three connotative dimensions of the semantic differential: evaluation, potency, and activity. Although evaluation ratings are usually considered as attitudinal, all three can also be considered as beliefs, that is, the product is good, strong, fast, and so on (Wyer, 1974). Consumers were shown "advertisements" for five nationally advertised products, a shirt, a brand of ice cream, a cake mix, a rug, and an auto. The investigators varied either the color of the product or the color of the background in the advertisement. Full results are not reported in the secondary source, unfortunately, so the following findings are incomplete as to the product versus background manipulation. It was found that evaluative ratings showed large product by color interactions; for example, a violet auto was rated favorably but a violet cake unfavorably. Potency ratings for advertising background color were very systematic: the more intense (saturated) the background color, the more potent or powerful the product was rated. Activity ratings were also systematic: background colors toward the red end of the hue spectrum increased ratings of the product as active whereas colors toward the violet end decreased activity ratings, that is, the product was rated as more passive. Whereas the evaluative beliefs have relevance to all products (because they are synonymous with attitudes, discussed below) the potency and activity beliefs may have utility only for certain types of products. For example, it is hard to see the relevance of a "powerful, fast" ice cream, but the same connotative associations for an automobile might be highly appropriate to the advertiser's intended communication goals. Along these lines Wysocki (1979) provides anecdotal evidence of a discount retailer making effective use of the color yellow, not only because yellow is highly visible and attention-getting, but also, according to the retailer's strategy, because it suggests an image (a belief) of "cheapness." Similarly, some proprietary research conducted by the authors with power tools suggested that the "industrial green" favored by one manufacturer connotes a possibly undesirable professional user image to consumers interested in power tools for home handyman applications. Color characteristics in visual stimuli provide an interesting area for belief effect research.

An important methodological consideration in belief effect research with visual stimuli deserves mention. There is mounting evidence that visual stimuli are processed (decoded and encoded) holistically or "configurally" rather than in a step-by-step "linear additive" fashion (Beard, 1980; Holbrook & Moore, 1981). Most multiattribute belief models, including Fishbein's and also conjoint analysis, assume a linear additive process with no configural interactions. These measurement models may need to be replaced by more complex configural models when studying visually induced beliefs.

D. Attitude

A second type of preferential communication effect which may be influenced by visual stimulus characteristics in advertising is attitude. More and more investigators are coming to adopt Fishbein's distinction between beliefs, as judgments about particular characteristics of an item, and attitude, as representing an overall evaluative judgment of the item (e.g., Fishbein & Ajzen, 1975). It is in this sense of overall or global evaluative response that we use the term attitude, here, as a communication effect. Attitude as a communication effect is particularly important in cases where consumers select products based on overall comparative ratings rather than selecting products for superiority on a particular attribute.

Two experiments have studied the effect of visual content in advertising on product attitude. Mitchell and Olson (1977) included an overall product attitude measure in the study described above which tested one "verbal" advertisement against three "visual" advertisements for facial tissues. It may be remembered that one of the visual advertisements, showing only a picture of a kitten along with the brand name, produced the strongest belief rating for the target attribute of softness. When overall product attitude was used as the dependent measure, two of the visual advertisements were superior: "kitten" and "sunset." These two advertisements produced attitude ratings close to 4.0 on the 1 to 5, highest, index used, whereas the visual advertisement with the abstract picture and the verbal advertisement with no picture produced ratings near the neutral point of 3.0. The "kitten" picture was chosen because of its connotative relevance to facial tissue softness; it was, presumably, also an attractive picture. However, the "sunset" picture was chosen simply as a positively evaluated stimulus with no semantic relevance to facial tissue. The fact that the sunset picture influenced attitude without, apparently, influencing beliefs, raises the possibility that attitude, as an essentially emotional rather than cognitive response (in the Fishbein sense) may be susceptible to formation or change through "simple" classical conditioning. In other words, the mere association of a product with a positively evaluated stimulus such as an attractive picture, regardless of the picture's content, may be sufficient to alter attitude toward the product without any "rational" belief change preceding the effect.

This classical conditioning possibility was elaborated in a paper by Rossiter and Percy (1980) based on results obtained in an earlier study (1978). Unfortunately in this earlier study no measures of beliefs were taken so it cannot be established whether attitudinal effects were due to prior belief-based effects. Nevertheless, the capacity of visual context in advertising to influence product attitude was clearly established, as in the Mitchell and Olson study. In the Rossiter and Percy (1978) study, it was found high pictorial emphasis in print advertising, that is, a large picture of the product relative to the space devoted to copy, generated significantly more favorable overall attitude ratings for a new, hypothetical brand of beer than low pictorial emphasis, that is, a small picture of the product with larger size copy. Also varied in this experiment was concreteness of copy claims. Concreteness of the verbal content was also positively related to attitudinal favorability and, consistent with Paivio's dual code theory, there was a large interaction between pictorial emphasis and concrete copy claims such that the combination produced markedly higher product attitude ratings. This experiment needs to be extended over a wider range of visual and verbal parameter values and replicated with other product categories for which attitudes are a relevant communication effect, but the implications of the findings are nevertheless interesting in light of relative ease with which the two content variables can be manipulated in advertising, especially picture size. We have more to say about why the pictorial effect may have been obtained in the next section of the chapter.

E. Intentions

A third type of preferential communication effect that may be influenceable by visual content in advertising is intention. In the traditional definition of attitude, of course, beliefs form the cognitive component of attitudinal dispositions, attitude the affective component, and intentions the conative or action tendency component. Both Mitchell and Olson (1977) and Rossiter and Percy (1978) included intention-to-purchase measures in their studies of visual advertising effects. In both studies similar effects obtained for intentions as they had for attitude; that is, visual emphasis in advertising and also, in the Rossiter and Percy study, concrete copy claims, produced more definite intentions to buy the advertised product. However, the effects for intentions were weaker than for attitudes.

The relatively weaker effect for intentions as a communication effect may reflect the fact that intention to act is an operant rather than a classically conditioned response (Rossiter & Percy, 1980) and, as such, is under the control of variables other than advertising content, for example, expected price, availability, or habitual willingness to try new products. Intentions may therefore be more susceptible to visual advertising content that depicts the target response as a to-be-performed operant. Safety messages would be an obvious example, where safe behavior is shown. The relevance of visual operant depictions to safety messages has been demonstrated by Wright (1979). Over-the-counter drug labels were inspected more often in stores following exposure to public service commercials which showed others doing the same and which also used concrete verbal copy, presumably of high imagery value like the video. More conventional advertising may also use visual operants in an effective way. For example, a TV commercial for WYNY, an FM radio station in New York, shows a radio dial being moved to the "97 spot." This helps because of the problem of remembering FM stations' call signals with the proliferation of them in major markets; however, this could be done auditory or with static alpha-numeric stimuli, such as WYNY-FM 97. The advantage of showing the target response, of actually turning the dial, is that it may additionally encourage imitative trial behavior. Clearly, there is a considerable variety of interesting research that could be conducted on the effects of visual advertising stimuli on consumer intentions.

F.   Choice Rules

A final type of communication effect that may be influenced by visual advertising content is the overall product category choice rule. As defined, for example,
by Percy and Rossiter (1980), choice rules are communication effects that "tell"
the prospective buyer how to choose a particular brand based on other communication effects pertaining to the brands. Examples illustrating the use of other
communication effects in choice rules would be: "Buy the first brand you are
familiar with" (awareness); "Buy the brand with the highest nutritional content
(belief); "Buy the brand you like most overall" (attitude); and "Buy the brand
you planned to buy before visiting the store" (intention). Choice rules pertain to
a total product category but they can be used by brand advertisers to encourage
consumers to use a choice rule that favors the company's brand (Wright &
Barbour, 1975). For example, a brand with the highest nutritional ratings might
promote the belief-based choice rule above as a way of selecting brands within
the overall product category as well as reminding consumers that the brand has
the highest nutritional ratings (a fact that may be irrelevant if most consumers
employ some other choice rule).

No studies, to our knowledge, have investigated the ability of visual content
in advertising to influence choice rules. Choice rules are assumed to be implicit
(tacit) or explicit verbal responses and thus all of the hypothetical strategies for
altering them have been verbal (Wright, 1977). However, visual depictions may
help to dramatize and make more memorable the choice rule. Examples include
video scenes of cars running out of gasoline, to try to encourage good gasoline
mileage as a basis for choosing automobiles; pictures of people having fun, to try
to suggest this as a basis for selecting soft drink brands; and so forth. Choice
rules remain a neglected communication effect in advertising research in general,
so it is not perhaps surprising that choice rule measures have not been included in
research on visual content in advertising.

This completes our review of communication effects. The focus has been on
the capacity of visual stimuli in advertising to influence product-related communication effects in the consumer's long-term memory (see Figs. 4.1 and 4.4) and
particularly on the relative effectiveness of visual-pictorial stimuli versus visual-
linguistic or auditory-linguistic stimuli. We have seen that there is a great need
for the range of stimuli represented in advertising (see Table 4.2) to be systematically investigated and for much more attention to communication effects other
than awareness (recognition and recall). Advertisers are additionally concerned
with preferential communication effects—beliefs, attitudes, intentions, and
choice rules—for which visually based theory and research are almost nonexistent. The promise of visual advertising content is great indeed, but much more
needs to be known.

With the need for knowledge about visual communication *processes* in mind,
the final section of this chapter presents some proposed mechanisms that link

stimulus characteristics, information processing, and communication effects in a functional manner in mediating consumer behaviors. Here we extend well beyond the essentially structural dual coding theory to a more process-oriented approach. In keeping with the central purpose of this chapter, the emphasis is again on visual communication processes.

IV. VISUAL MEDIATING MECHANISMS

In our conceptualization of initial information processing (see Fig. 4.1) we proposed two phases, the first consisting of automatic decoding of a denotative and connotative nature, and the second consisting of a potential elaborative encoding phase in which verbal cognitive responses and elaborative visual or other imagery may occur. In our conceptualization of communication effects, the next major stage, we then proposed five types of product-based, stored responses: awareness, beliefs, attitudes, intentions, and choice rules. We reviewed the role of external stimuli which can be employed in advertising to generate information processing in short-term or active memory and produce communication effects in long-term or permanent memory. However, the overall process relationships (i.e., external stimulus → information processing → communication effect) were not well specified. Our objective in this section is to describe four mechanisms through which entire communication processes may take place. It should be noted that these mechanisms are quite general and do not involve any new principles. However, the specification of the role of visual phenomena in these mechanisms is new.

Two of the mechanisms are relatively passive, requiring little or no consumer-generated activity other than attention and automatic decoding. Accordingly, these mechanisms may be typical of "low involvement" learning. The first two mechanisms are: (1) iconic rote learning and (2) classical affective conditioning. The other two mechanisms are more active or elaborative, requiring mental participation by the consumers, specifically, elaborative encoding during the information processing stage. Accordingly, these two mechanisms may be typical of "high involvement" learning. The last two mechanisms are: (3) verbal propositional reinforcement and (4) visual propositional reinforcement. These are described below along with their implications for the mediation of consumer behaviors.

A. Iconic Rote Learning

The simplest mechanism may be described as iconic rote learning. This requires only automatic *denotative* decoding of external stimuli in the information processing stage. All that is learned is an "icon" or literal image of the external stimulus; for example, a product package image if the denotation is visual or a brand name if the denotation is a verbal label or a visual image. The learning is of the rote "paired associate" type in which the external stimulus is paired with the denotative response in short-term memory. The learning may be sufficiently strong to transfer the denotative response to long-term memory. There, the denotative response would satisfy the conditions for an *awareness* communication effect, that is, a response that allows the consumer to identify the product, on cue, in sufficient detail to enable purchase.

The iconic rote learning mechanism has important implications for the notion of "evoked set" (Howard, 1963, 1977; Howard & Sheth, 1969). The evoked set consists of awareness responses for brands. Critical, however, is the nature of the awareness response stored in long-term memory and the nature of the external cue which evokes these responses. A consumer may have learned a visual denotation only and therefore may only be able to exhibit visual awareness (recognition). In this case point-of-purchase cues may be necessary to evoke awareness of the brand. In contrast, if a verbal denotation has been learned, verbal awareness (recall) can be exhibited. In this case a verbal prepurchase product category cue, for example, "detergent," may produce an evoked set in which brands for which only visual denotation (unless this image clearly includes the brand name) has been learned may be excluded from consideration. The implications for advertising communication strategy should be clear: one must anticipate the likely decision-initiating cues facing the consumer and tailor the requisite type of awareness accordingly by providing the appropriate denotation of the brand in advertising.

It is possible that quite complex sequences of denotations can be learned from advertising. In the auditory linguistic mode, for example, jingles may be learned on a rote basis (Rossiter, 1976). This requires only echoic auditory imagery of the denotative type. The consumer may respond with the jingle, transferred to long-term memory as a verbal awareness response, in response to a product cue, for example, "hamburger" → McDonald's jingle. This may be sufficient to initiate brand choice consideration. Adults may act on children's learned speech behavior in this way even though the child may experience no communication effects about the brand other than awareness (our base communication effect). Complex visual stimulus sequences, as in TV video, may also be learned in rote fashion. Bandura's research on imitative learning, or modeling, (Bandura, 1977) provides plenty of examples of this phenomenon. Thus a consumer may learn consumption styles or how to use a product (motor actions in our framework) from advertising in this relatively simple manner.

B. Classical Affective Conditioning

A second mediational mechanism is classical affective conditioning. This is slightly more complex than rote learning in that it involves a pairing of a denotative decoding response with an evaluative (affective) connotative response. The evaluative connotative response, or more precisely its stimulus consequence in short-term memory, serves as an unconditioned stimulus (UCS) while the stimulus consequence of the denotative response serves as a conditioned stimulus (CS). Effective UCSs may be provided by attractively shown or favorably described products or by connotative evaluative responses to other contextual stimuli such as settings, characters, music, and so forth. Because many of these stimuli are learned rather than innate UCSs, the learning mechanism actually involves higher order classical conditioning but this is a rather technical distinction that need not concern us here.

The communication effect targeted in classical affective conditioning, assuming that the conditioning is successfully transferred to long-term memory, is attitude in sense of global emotional affect (Fishbein & Ajzen, 1975.) Specifically, product or brand attitude becomes the conditioned affective response (CR) for the CS-UCS pairing. No elaborate cognitions about the product or brand are required; this is still a relatively passive and automatic learning process.

Krugman's well-known version of low-involvement learning may operate in this way. Krugman (1966-67) describes a subtle increase in the "perceptual salience" of a brand, due to repetitious advertising, which is triggered by a point-of-purchase (recognition) cue. Note, however, that visual awareness alone would not be a sufficient communication effect to enable brand choice. As noted earlier, recognition is virtually perfect after 1 or 2 exposure trials. Thus all brands would tend to have equal recognition probabilities of 1.0. On the other hand, affective attitudinal responses are likely to be learned to varying degrees of response strength proportional to number of exposure trials, so that an awareness *plus* attitude communication effect "module" (see Fig. 4.4) *could* account for differential brand choice. The attitudinal response may be of low amplitude and, as an emotional response, be below a conscious articulation threshold, in keeping with Krugman's account. Where the brands are highly similar and do not involve high economic or psychosocial risk for "incorrect" choices, this low-involvement learning may well explain consumer brand choice behavior.

The remaining two mechanisms pertain to high-involvement learning, where consumers actively review attributes of brands and deliberate about potential courses of action before purchasing. Both require elaborative encoding and a more detailed module of communication effects associated with each brand.

C. Verbal Propositional Reinforcement

The term "proposition" may be applied to communication effects that include the product or brand as the "subject" of the proposition and some attribute or consequence as the "predicate." By this definition, beliefs, intentions, and choice rules function as propositions. Notice that we are not using the term "propositional" to refer to some abstract or conceptual type of information storage, as in many cognitive theories, notably alternatives to Paivio's dual code theory which propose a single, propositional or conceptual, code (e.g., Anderson & Bower, 1974; Pylyshyn, 1973). Rather we are referring to data meeting the syntactic structure of propositions, as defined above, which are stored as *verbal* responses. That is, we really mean to hypothesize that consumers, albeit covertly, actually articulate these propositions in choosing products; for example, "Lincoln Continental is a high status automobile" (belief) or "I will buy some coffee next time I'm at the supermarket" (intention) or "Toothpaste should be selected on the basis of fluoride content" (choice rule). Not all propositions about products or brands are stored verbally; we assume that they can be stored as visual responses or other sensory responses. But, we suggest that propositions cannot be a communication effect unless they have some sensory manifestation (covert speech, covert seeing, covert tasting, etc.) capable of being "reified" in short-term memory at the time of decision and thereby mediating overt consumer behavior. This does not deny that propositional, abstract, or conceptual storage exists, but rather that because there can be no such thing as an abstract or conceptual "response," it is useless for advertisers to even think about targeting this type of information storage in attempting to create or modify communication effects. At a broader level, the present debate about the "ultimate" form of information representation in memory (Anderson, 1978, 1979; Hayes-Roth, 1979; Kosslyn, 1981; Pylyshyn, 1979, 1981) strikes us as an esoteric and rather fruitless issue. The viewpoint of Bugelski (1977) is much more compatible with our approach, which argues for a very concrete theory of communication mechanisms.

Most advertisements attempt to establish verbal propositions about brands in the form of beliefs (see, for example, a content analysis in Wright & Barbour, 1975). Typically the brand is linked to some attribute or set of attributes in the advertisement which are thought to be or known to be appealing to consumers. Other advertisements, notably retail newspaper ads, attempt to establish verbal propositions about brands in the form of intentions; for example, "I should buy this at that store, now." (Johnson, 1979). Still other advertisements, although at a low incidence according to the Wright and Barbour (1975) survey, attempt to establish verbal propositions about entire product categories in the form of choice rules; for example, "When buying aspirin, buy the cheapest brand."

To the extent that advertising is effective in establishing or maintaining these verbal propositions, it serves a *reinforcing* function. Hence we derive the term verbal propositional reinforcement to describe this particular communication mechanism. The mechanism requires that the consumer engage in elaborative encoding of the advertising content, in effect covertly vocalizing the various propositions. Active participation of this type is likely to be characteristic of "high involvement" learning. It assumes a motivated consumer, for example, a consumer who is "in the market" for the product when exposed to the advertising, and, as noted previously, in conjunction with the voluntary nature of elaborative encoding, motivation is one of the conditions under which elaborative encoding is likely to occur. Extant "cognitive response" research in which cognitive responses are defined and measured verbally, is essentially tapping the verbal propositional reinforcement mechanism.

D. Visual Propositional Reinforcement

As intimated in our discussion of propositional communication effects above, we hypothesize that propositions may be stored visually and indeed in other nonverbal sensory modalities. Visual propositions are implied in the type of pictorial advertising exemplified at the outset of this chapter with the FTC spokesman's contention about the cigarette advertisement. Actually the contention was that pictorial content may produce a verbal proposition. Although this is quite possible, because people readily label pictures, it does not seem necessary to assume that the proposition is verbal or verbalizable. Here we must appeal to intuition or subjective anecdotal evidence. It is our contention that people often experience or even deliberately generate visual imagery scenarios in conscious or short-term memory which help them decide about their consumer behavior. For example, the consumer may picture a rugged character smoking Camel cigarettes without ever putting into words the proposition (belief) that "Camels are for rugged people." Or the consumer may flash a visual image or sequence of images about heavy traffic conditions likely on the way to the local department store which may affect plans (intentions) relating to motor actions such as whether to drive there at that time. The other communication effect postulated for verbal propositions (choice rules) however, does not seem as readily visualized; the act of choice, yes, but not the rule itself, which would seem to be verbal, that is, a self-instruction.

The point to note about visual propositions is that they need never be translated into covert verbal responses. In fact, translation of this type would seem to be an onerous activity as well as an unparsimonious assumption. Yet this is basically the assumption that is made by abstract, conceptual storage models. Remember, one does not act on an abstraction or a concept but rather on some short-term memory representation of the abstraction or concept. A person's actions can be guided by imagery, especially visual imagery, without having to covertly "say" what the image portrays before acting. In short, we can postulate visual propositions linking products or brands to attributes or consequences as mediators of consumer behaviors. Once again, to the extent that advertising establishes or maintains these visual propositions, the term reinforcement can be applied to describe this process. Thus we have visual propositional reinforcement as a fourth mechanism of communication in advertising. This mechanism, aside from the originating external stimulus which may occur in any modality, is entirely visual.

SUMMARY

Visual communication in advertising has been an "obvious" but little understood process. We have attempted in this chapter to explicate this process or, more correctly, this set of processes. We have seen that any type of stimulus employed in advertising—visual or auditory—is capable of communicating visually through visual imagery formation. Advertising stimuli vary in their capacity to elicit visual imagery, however, and a hierarchy based on this capacity was proposed for further research. In short-term memory, where initial responses to advertising presumably occur, visual imagery is hypothesized to be the basis of automatic denotative registration of visual stimuli and potentially to play a role in elaborative encoding of all types of stimuli. Elaborative encoding through visual imagery is proposed as a major complementary alternative to verbal encoding in "cognitive responses" to advertising. In long-term memory, where product and brand-based responses presumably are stored for later retrieval during consumer decisionmaking, visual imagery is hypothesized to be the basis for visual awareness responses, as in product or brand recognition at the point-of-purchase, and to be an alternative mode of storing beliefs and intentions. We also suggested four mechanisms that encompass the entire sequence of stimulus input, short-term information processing, and long-term communication effects and provide a functional account of how visual communication may operate to mediate consumer behavior: iconic rote learning, classical affective conditioning, verbal propositional reinforcement, and visual propositional reinforcement. The first two mechanisms were hypothesized to be characteristic of low-involvement consumer learning and the latter two to be characteristic of high-involvement consumer learning. The comprehensive analysis, although hypothetical in many instances, demonstrates the ubiquity and importance of visual communication in advertising.

ACKNOWLEDGMENTS

The authors are indebted to Richard J. Harris, Kansas State University; Morris B. Holbrook, Columbia University; and Max Sutherland, Caulfield Institute of Technology, for their comments on an earlier version of this chapter. The first author is now at the New South Wales Institute of Technology, Sydney, Australia.

REFERENCES

Abelson, R. P. Script processing in attitude formation and decision making. In J. S. Carroll & J. W. Payne (Eds.), *Cognition and social behavior*. Hillsdale, N.J.: Lawrence Erlbaum Associates, 1976.

Abrams, K. Identifying perceptual structures in sales messages. Paper presented at the third annual Boston Advertising/Marketing Research Day, Boston, March 1981.

Anderson, J. R. Arguments concerning representations for mental imagery. *Psychological Review*, 1978, *85*, 249–277.

Anderson, J. R. Further arguments concerning representations for mental imagery. *Psychological Review*, 1979, *86*, 395–406.

Anderson, J. R., & Bower, G. H. *Human associative memory*. Washington, D.C.: Hemisphere, 1974.

Anderson, P. A., Garrison, J. P., & Anderson, J. F. Implications of a neuropsychological approach for the study of a nonverbal communication. *Human Communication Research*, 1979, *6*, 74–89.

Bandura, A. *Social learning theory*. Englewood Cliffs, N.J.: Prentice-Hall, 1977.

Beard, A. D. *Judgments of visual aesthetic stimuli: The end of the linear additive model's ubiquitous application?* Working paper, Central Michigan University, March 1980.

Begg, I., & Clark, J. M. Contextual imagery in meaning and memory. *Memory and Cognition*, 1975, *3*, 117–122.

Berger, S. M., & Lambert, W. W. Stimulus-response theory in contemporary social psychology. In G. Lindzey, & E. Aronson (Eds.), *The handbook of social psychology, Vol. I*. Reading, Mass.: Addison-Wesley, 1968.

Berrian, R. W., Metzler, D. P., Kroll, N. E. A., & Clark-Meyers, G. M. Estimates of imagery, ease of definition, and animateness for 328 adjectives. *Journal of Experimental Psychology: Human Learning and Memory*, 1979, *5*, 435–447.

Broadbent, D. E. *Perception and communication*. London,: Pergamon, 1958.

Bugelski, B. R. Imagery and verbal behavior. *Journal of Mental Imagery*, 1977, *1*, 39–52.

Cacioppo, J. T., & Petty, R. E. Effects of message repetition and position on cognitive response, recall, and persuasion. *Journal of Personality and Psychology*, 1979, *37*, 97–109. (a)

Cacioppo, J. T., & Petty, R. E. Attitudes and cognitive response: An electro-physiological approach. *Journal of Personality and Social Psychology*, 1979, *37*, 2181–2199. (b)

Calder, B. J. Cognitive response, imagery, and scripts: What is the cognitive basis of attitude? In H. K. Hunt (Ed.), *Advances in consumer research: Vol. V*. Ann Arbor, Michigan: Association for Consumer Research, 1978.

Calder, B. J., Robertson, T. S., & Rossiter, J. R. Children's consumer information processing. *Communication Research*, 1975, *2*, 307–316.

Chapman, R. M., McCrary, J. W., Chapman, J. A., & Bragdon, H. R. Brain responses related to semantic meaning. *Brain and Language*, 1978, *5*, 195–205.

Corballis, M. C. Laterality and myth. *American Psychologist*, 1980, *35*, 284–295.

Crock, S. FTC is seeking way to decide if pictures in advertising convey false impressions. *The Wall Street Journal*, August 11, 1978, 6.

Day, J. Right-hemisphere language processing in normal right-handers. *Journal of Experimental Psychology: Human Perception and Performance*, 1977, *3*, 518–528.

Engel, J. F., Blackwell, R. D., & Kollat, D. T. *Consumer Behavior*. Hinsdale, Ill.: Dryden, 1978.

Estes, W. K. Memory and conditioning. In F. J. McGuigan & D. B. Lumsden (Eds.), *Contemporary approaches to conditioning and learning*. Washington, D.C.: Winston, 1973.

Evans, G. W. Environmental cognition. *Psychological Bulletin*, 1980, *88*, 259–287.

Eysenck, M. W. *Human memory: Theory, research and individual differences*. Oxford: Pergamon, 1977.

Federal Trade Commission. *Consumer information remedies*. Washington, D.C.: U.S. Government Printing Office, 1979.

Finke, R. A. Levels of equivalence in imagery and perception. *Psychological Review*, 1980, *87*, 113–132.

Fishbein, M., & Ajzen, I. *Belief attitude, intention, and behavior*. Reading, Mass.: Addison-Wesley, 1975.

Fleming, M. L., & Sheikhian, M. Influence of pictorial attributes on recognition memory. *AV Communication Review*, 1972, *20*, 423–441.

French, P. L. Nonverbal measurement of affect: The graphic differential. *Journal of Psycholinguistic Research*, 1977, *6*, 337–347.

Geschwind, N. Specializations of the human brain. *Scientific American*, 1979, *241*, 180–199.

Glanzer, M., & Clark, W. H. Accuracy of perceptual recall: An analysis of organization. *Journal of Verbal Learning and Verbal Behavior*, 1962, *5*, 289–299.

Glass, A. L., Eddy, J. K., & Schwanenflugel, P. J. The verification of high and low imagery sentences. *Journal of Experimental Psychology: Human Learning and Memory*, 1980, *6*, 692–704.

Goldberg, E., Vaughan, H. G., & Gerstman, L. J. Nonverbal descriptive systems and hemispheric asymmetry: Shape versus texture discrimination. *Brain and Language*, 1978, *5*, 249–257.

Graefe, T. M., & Watkins, M. J. Picture rehearsal: An effect of selectively attending to pictures no longer in view. *Journal of Experimental Psychology: Human Learning and Memory*, 1980, *6*, 156–162.

Grass, R. C., & Wallace, W. H. Advertising communication: Print vs. TV. *Journal of Advertising Research*, 1974, *14*, 19–23.

Greenwald, A. G. Cognitive learning, cognitive response to persuasion, and attitude change. In A. G. Greenwald, T. C. Brock, & T. M. Ostrom (Eds.), *Psychological foundations of attitudes*. New York: Academic Press, 1968. (a)

Greenwald, A. G. On defining attitude and attitude theory. In A. G. Greenwald, T. C. Brock, & T. M. Ostrom (Eds.), *Psychological foundations of attitudes*. New York: Academic Press, 1968. (b)

Hayes-Roth, B. Evolution of cognitive structures and processes. *Psychological Review*, 1977, *94*, 260–278.

Hayes-Roth, F. Distinguishing theories of representation. A critique of Anderson's "Arguments concerning mental imagery." *Psychological Review*, 1979, *86*, 376–382.

Hendon, D. W. How mechanical factors affect ad perception. *Journal of Advertising Research*, 1973, *13*, 39–45.

Holbrook, M. B., & Lehmann, D. R. The role of message content versus mechanical features in predicting recognition of print advertisements. *Journal of Advertising Research*, 1980, *20*, 53–62.

Holbrook, M. B., & Moore, W. L. Feature interactions in consumer judgments of verbal versus pictorial presentations. *Journal of Consumer Research*, 1981, *8*, 103–113.

Hollander, S. W., & Jacoby, J. Recall of crazy, mixed-up TV commercials. *Journal of Advertising Research*, 1973, *13*, 39–42.

Holyoak, K. The role of imagery in the evaluation of sentences: Imagery or semantic relatedness? *Journal of Verbal Learning and Verbal Behavior*, 1974, *13*, 163–166.

Howard, J. A. *Marketing management: Analysis and planning*. Homewood, Ill.: Irwin, 1963.

Howard, J. A. *Consumer behavior: Application of theory*. New York: McGraw-Hill, 1977.

Howard, J. A., & Sheth, J. N. *The theory of buyer behavior*. New York: Wiley, 1969.

Hull, C. L. *A behavior system*. New Haven: Yale University Press. 1952.

Intraub, H. The role of implicit naming in pictorial encoding. *Journal of Experimental Psychology: Human Learning and Memory*, 1979, *5*, 78–87.

Intraub, H. Presentation rate and the representation of briefly glimpsed pictures in memory. *Journal of Experimental Psychology: Human Learning and Memory*, 1980, *6*, 1–12.

Johnson, J. D. *Advertising today*. Chicago: Science Research Associates, 1979.

Jorgensen, C. C., & Kintsch, W. The role of imagery in the evaluation of sentences. *Cognitive Psychology*, 1973, *4*, 110–116.

Kellogg, R. T. Is conscious attention necessary for long-term storage? *Journal of Experimental Psychology: Human Learning and Memory*, 1980, *6*, 379–390.

Kerrick, J. S. The influence of captions on picture interpretation. *Journalism Quarterly*, 1955, *32*, 177–182.

Key, W. B. *Subliminal seduction.* Englewood Cliffs, N.J.: Prentice-Hall, 1973.

Kieras, D. Beyond pictures and words: Alternative information-processing models for imagery effects in verbal memory. *Psychological Bulletin*, 1978, *85*, 532–554.

Klee, H., & Legge, D. Estimates of concreteness and other indices for 200 transitive verbs. *Journal of Experimental Psychology: Human Learning and Memory*, 1976, *2*, 497–507.

Koen, F. *Verbal and nonverbal mediators in recognition memory for complex visual stimuli.* Washington, D.C.: U.S. Office of Education Report, 1969.

Kosslyn, S. M. The medium and the message in mental imagery: A theory. *Psychological Review*, 1981, *88*, 46–66.

Kosslyn, S. M., & Alper, S. N. On the pictorial properties of visual images: Effects of image size on memory for words. *Canadian Journal of Psychology*, 1977, *31*, 32–40.

Krugman, H. E. The measurement of advertising involvement. *Public Opinion Quarterly*, 1966-67, *30*, 583–596.

Krugman, H. E. Memory without recall, exposure without perception. *Journal of Advertising Research*, 1977, *17*, 7–12.

Kunen, S., Green, D., & Waterman, D. Spread of encoding effects within the nonverbal visual domain. *Journal of Experimental Psychology: Human Learning and Memory*, 1979, *5*, 574–584.

Leuba, C. Images as conditioned sensations. *Journal of Experimental Psychology*, 1940, *26*, 345–351.

Levy, E. *Comparative print advertising.* Unpublished M.S. dissertation, Annenberg School of Communication, University of Pennsylvania, 1979.

Lewis, D. J. Psychobiology of active and inactive memory. *Psychological Bulletin*, 1979, *86*, 1054–1083.

Loftus, G. R., & Kallman, H. J. Encoding and use of detail information in picture recognition. *Journal of Experimental Psychology: Human Learning and Memory*, 1979, *5*, 197–211.

Lutz, K. A., & Lutz, R. J. Effects of interactive imagery on learning: Application to advertising. *Journal of Applied Psychology*, 1977, *62*, 493–498.

Lutz, K. A., & Lutz, R. J. Imagery-eliciting strategies: Review and implications of research. In H. K. Hunt (Ed.). *Advances in consumer research, Vol. V.* Ann Arbor, Mich.: Association for Consumer Research, 1978.

Lutz, R. J. Changing brand attitudes through modification of cognitive structure. *Journal of Consumer Research*, 1975, *1*, 49–59.

Mariani, J. Can advertisers read—and control—our emotions? *TV Guide*, 1979, *27*, 4–6, 8.

McGee, M. G. Human spatial abilities: Psychometric studies and environmental, genetic, hormonal and neurological influences. *Psychological Bulletin*, 1979, *86*, 889–918.

McKelvie, S. J., & Demers, E. G. Individual differences in reported visual imagery and memory performance. *British Journal of Psychology*, 1979, *70*, 51–57.

Metallinos, N., & Tiemens, R. K. Asymmetry of the screen: The effect of left vs. right placement of television images. *Journal of Broadcasting*, 1977, *21* 21–33.

Mitchell, A. A., & Olson, J. C. Cognitive effects of advertising repetition. In W. D. Perrault (Ed.), *Advances in consumer research, Vol. IV.* Atlanta: Association for Consumer Research, 1977.

Mowrer, O. H. *Learning theory and the symbolic processes.* New York: Wiley, 1960.

Mowrer, O. H. Mental imagery: An indispensable psychological concept. *Journal of Mental Imagery*, 1977, *1*, 303–326.

Nelson, K. E. Memory development in children: Evidence from nonverbal tasks. *Psychnomic Science*, 1971, *25*, 346–348.

Newsweek. *Eyes on television 1980.* Report of a study conducted by Audits & Surveys, Inc., available from *Newsweek*, New York.

Nguy, T. V. H., Allard, F. A., & Bryden, M. P. Laterality effects for Chinese characters: A multidimensional approach. *Canadian Journal of Psychology*, 1980, *34*, 91–96.

Nickerson, R. S. A note on long-term recognition memory for pictorial material. *Psychonomic Science*, 1968, *11*, 58.

O'Barr, W. M. Language and advertising. In *Proceedings of the Round Table on Language and Linguistics*. Washington, D.C.: Georgetown University Press, 1979.

Olson, J. C. Inferential belief formation in the cue utilization process. In H. K. Hunt (Ed.), *Advances in consumer research, Vol. V*. Ann Arbor, Mich.: Association for Consumer Research, 1978.

Olson, J. C., Toy, D. R., & Dover, P. A. Mediating effects of cognitive responses to advertising on cognitive structure. In H. K. Hunt (Ed.), *Advances in consumer research, Vol. V*. Ann Arbor, Mich.: Association For Consumer Research, 1978.

Osgood, C. E. Exploration in semantic space: A personal diary. *Journal of Social Issues*, 1971, *27*, 5–64.

Osgood, C. E., Suci, G. J., & Tannenbaum, P. H. *The measurement of meaning*. Urbana, Ill.: University of Illinois Press, 1957.

Paivio, A. *Imagery and verbal processes*. New York: Holt, Rinehart & Winston, 1971.

Paivio, A. Imagery and synchronic thinking. *Canadian Psychological Review*, 1975, *16*, 147–163.

Paivio, A. A dual coding approach to perception and cognition. In H. I. Pick & E. Saltzman (Eds.), *Modes of perceiving and processing information*. Hillsdale, N.J.: Lawrence Erlbaum Associates, 1978.

Paivio, A., Yuille, J. C., & Madigan, S. Concreteness, imagery, and meaningfulness values for 925 nouns. *Journal of Experimental Psychology Monograph*, 1968, *76*, part 2.

Percy, L., & Rossiter, J. R. *Advertising strategy: A communication theory approach*, New York: Praeger, 1980.

Petty, R. E. The importance of cognitive responses in persuasion. In W. D. Perrault (Ed.), *Advances in consumer research, Vol. IV*. Atlanta: Association for Consumer Research, 1977.

Pezdek, K., & Evans, G. W. Visual and verbal memory for objects and their spatial locations. *Journal of Experimental Psychology: Human Learning and Memory*, 1979, *5*, 360–373.

Porac, C., Cohen, S., Steiger, J. H., & Duncan, P. Human laterality: A multi-dimensional approach. *Canadian Journal of Psychology*, 1980, *34*, 91–96.

Potter, M. C., & Levy, E. I. Recognition memory for a rapid sequence of pictures. *Journal of Experimental Psychology*, 1969, *81*, 10–15.

Pylyshyn, Z. W. What the mind's eye tells the mind's brain: A critique of mental imagery. *Psychological Bulletin*, 1973, *80*, 1–24.

Pylyshyn, Z. W. Validating computational models: A critique of Anderson's indeterminacy of representation claim. *Psychological Review*, 1979, 383–394.

Pylyshyn, Z. W. The imagery debate: Analogue media versus tacit knowledge. *Psychological Review*, 1981, *88*, 16–45.

Richardson, J. T. E. Concreteness and imageability. *Quarterly Journal of Experimental Psychology*, 1975, 27, 235–249.

Robinson, J. S. Familiar patterns are no easier to see than novel ones. *American Journal of Psychology*, 1969, *82*, 513–522.

Rossiter, J. R. *Cognitive phenomena in contemporary advertising*. Paper presented at the 1975 Conference on Culture and Communication, Temple University, Philadelphia, 1975.

Rossiter, J. R. Visual and verbal memory in children's product information utilization. In B. B. Anderson (Ed.), *Advances in consumer research, Vol III*. Chicago: Association for Consumer Research, 1976.

Rossiter, J. R. Point of view: Brain hemisphere activity. *Journal of Advertising Research*, 1980, *20*, 75–76.

Rossiter, J. R. Predicting Starch scores. *Journal of Advertising Research*, 1981, *21*, 63–68.

Rossiter, J. R., & Percy, L. Visual imaging ability as a mediator of advertising response. In H. K. Hunt (Ed.), *Advances in consumer research, Vol. V.* Ann Arbor, Mich.: Association for Consumer Research, 1978.

Rossiter, J. R., & Percy, L. Attitude change through visual imagery in advertising. *Journal of Advertising,* 1980, *9,* 10–16.

Rossiter, J. R., & Percy, L. *Advertising and sales promotion management,* in press.

Sang, D. L., & Ross, J. The verbal-loop hypothesis (VLH): A within subject study with a perceptual recognition task. *Psychonomic Science,* 1970, *18,* 345–347.

Shepard, R. N. Recognition memory for words, sentences and pictures. *Journal of Verbal Learning and Verbal Behavior,* 1967, *6,* 156–163.

Slee, J. The consistency of different manipulations of visual imagery: A methodological study. *Australian Journal of Psychology,* 1978, *30,* 7–20.

Smith, C. D. Recognition memory for sentences as a function of concreteness/abstractness and affirmation/negation. *British Journal of Psychology,* 1981, *72,* 125–129.

Standing, L. Learning 10,000 pictures. *Quarterly Journal of Experimental Psychology,* 1973, *25,* 207–222.

Stoessl, S., & Clemens, J. Unpublished data reported in *Marketing News,* May 4, 1979, *12,* 7, 11.

Takeda, M. Visual imagery and eye movements: Effects of projective size of image on eye movements. *Japanese Journal of Psychology,* 1977, *48,* 281–288.

Tannenbaum, P. H., & Kerrick, J. S. Unpublished study reported in C. E. Osgood, G. J. Suci, & P. H. Tannenbaum. *The measurement of meaning.* Urbana, Ill.: University of Illinois Press, 1957.

Toglia, M. P., & Battig, W. F. *Handbook of semantic word norms.* Hillsdale, N.J.: Lawrence Erlbaum Associates, 1978.

Tucker, D. M. Lateral brain function, emotion, and conceptualization. *Psychological Bulletin,* 1981, *89,* 19–46.

Weinstein, S. Brain wave analyses for evaluation of TV commercials and print ads are no longer science fiction. *Marketing Review,* 1979, *34,* 17–20.

Weinstein, S. Brain wave analysis in attitude research. *Marketing Review,* 1980, *35,* 23–26.

Wells, W. D. Communicating with children. *Journal of Advertising Research,* 1965, *5,* 2–14.

Williams, R. L. Imagery and linguistic factors affecting the solution of linear syllogisms. *Journal of Psycholinguistic Research,* 1979, *8,* 123–140.

Wright, P. L. Conditional consumer choice processes and advertising strategy. In Y. Wind & M. G. Greenberg (Eds.), *Moving a head with attitude research.* Chicago: American Marketing Association, 1977.

Wright, P. Concrete action plans in TV messages to increase reading of drug warnings. *Journal of Consumer Research,* 1979, *6,* 256–269.

Wright, P. L., & Barbour, F. The relevance of decision process models in structuring persuasive messages. *Communication Research,* 1975, *2,* 232–245.

Wyer, R. S. *Cognitive organization and change: An information processing approach.* Hillsdale, N.J.: Lawrence Erlbaum Associates, 1974.

Wysocki, B. Sight, smell, sound: They're all arms in retailers' arsenal. *The Wall Street Journal,* April 17, 1979, pp. 1, 35.

5

Advertising Situations: The Implications of Differential Involvement and Accompanying Affect Responses

Rajeev Batra
Michael L. Ray
Stanford University

> *To generalize is to be an idiot. To particularize is the alone distinction of merit. General knowledges are those knowledges that idiots possess.*
>
> —William Blake (1808)

> *You may well reply that we have known for a precious long time that communication effects are contingent on a variety of circumstances. What I am advancing is a statement of faith that we are advancing from a stage in which we had to shrug our shoulders and say "it depends," to the stage where we can be quite specific as to what "it depends," on, that we are developing a set of interlocking propositions that are moving us to a coherent and complex model.*
>
> —Raymond A. Bauer (1968, p. 5)

INTRODUCTION

Advertising has much to offer cognitive psychologists. Not only is it a relatively unexplored site for research, but there is a type and variety of situations in advertising information processing which can be understood by applying cognitive theories and can, if studied properly, provide new insights for the development of psychological theory itself.

The great poet and artist William Blake is invoked above as a warning to those psychologists who would attempt to take generalities from one area of psychology and apply them to another. The main thrust of this chapter is a situational or contingency approach that, in the first instance, recommends that advertising processing be looked at clearly for what it is, rather than something theories would want it to be.

Thus advertising processing should be considered specifically, not in terms of generalities. And further, as the title of this chapter and the late psychologist Raymond Bauer point out, information processing research in advertising should be even more specific in determining the key dimensions of advertising situations.

A number of these situational dimensions are reviewed in this chapter. Even though a considerable amount of direct and related research supports the importance of these dimensions, their potential effects are offered as interaction prediction hypotheses, which are called "microtheoretical notions" (Ray, 1978). This term is used to indicate, à la Blake and Bauer, that the hypotheses are specific to a certain type of situation and are merely notional, ready for further development.

This chapter concentrates on the initial processing of advertising information rather than memory, storage, and use in choices, although the latter three issues are considered. The focus here is largely an applied one, touching upon how the findings can be used for advertising decision making, most prominently in the areas of goal-setting and effect measurement, message strategy, and media strategy. It is suggested that if research implications are used, they will be tested in far more ways than would be possible in just the psychological laboratory.

Finally, before getting into details, it should be pointed out that a rather radical view of the *affect* construct underlies much of the thinking of this chapter. Until quite recently, cognitive psychologists have eshewed affect. Now it can be seen that many of the findings of advertising information-processing research can be explained by a two-dimensional conception of affect that is being embraced by cognitive psychologists, advertising and consumer researchers, as well as psychophysiologists.

Thus, whereas a number of situational dimensions are discussed in this chapter, emphasis is given to the affect and involvement constructs. These variables are seen as having important interactions with all the situational determinants of advertising information processing.

The Nature of Advertising Information Processing

This chapter deals with a type of information processing that is quite different from that found in the majority of cognitive psychology laboratories. Yet it is one that virtually everyone knows—the exposure, perception, comprehension, memory, forgetting, and use of advertising stimuli. A brief bit of introspection reveals that this processing occurs, if at all, under conditions that: are (1) not involving; (2) rushed (approximately four seconds are spent on the average magazine advertising page, broadcast commercials average around thirty seconds in length, billboard writers dare not use more than ten words); (3) "noisy," in the jargon of information theory (the cluttered, overadvertised nature of newspapers, magazines and television is clear to anyone exposed to them); (4) unorganized (advertisements do not appear in a way that would allow ordered information retrieval and use of any kind); and (5) offer little opportunity for immediate or even current information use.

Much learning that occurs as a result of advertising exposure is incidental learning. It is limited in nature. Consider the following findings, primarily from cognitive psychology, which should apply to many advertising processing situations:

1. Only a small proportion of advertising messages receive attention. With the typical family being exposed to well over 1000 advertising messages a day (Britt, Adams, & Miller, 1972), only those that are stronger (louder, brighter, larger, etc.) than others, different (but not too different so as not to be rejected as strange) and of interest or value—have potential for receiving attention (Berlyne, 1967; Kahneman, 1973; Ray, 1973a).

2. Limits of information-processing ability sharply reduce the processing that occurs even after there is attention. Short-term memory capacity is estimated to be four to seven information bits (Miller, 1956, Simon, 1974). And because it appears to be necessary for 5- to 10-second rehearsal of an information bit to occur within short-term memory within 30 seconds of receipt in order for that idea to be put into long-term memory (Bugelski, 1962; Newell & Simon, 1972; Norman, 1969), it is easy to see why only the most outstanding thirty-second television commercial can be accurately recalled by as much as 25 percent of a television audience a day after exposure.

3. There appear to be limits to what consumers will take out of a given advertisement, even if it is repetitively exposed. For instance, Krugman (1972), suggests that there are effectively only three exposures of any television commercial. The first exposure would produce simply a recognition of something new but no processing beyond that. The second exposure would produce all the processing that would ever take place for that individual for that commercial. The third and subsequent exposures are reminders of that information processed. Later in this chapter the situational determinants of these three stages (which might each occur at other than one, two or three exposures) are discussed. Suffice to say at this point that for much of advertising processing, repetition has limited effect in terms of creating a depth of processing that might be desired by advertisers and assumed by some researchers.

Advertising Information-Processing Research: Methods Issues

The type of processing situation outlined above suggests particular methods for studying advertising information processing. If advertising is typically received under low involvement, rushed, noisy, uncontrolled-disorganized, and nondecision-oriented conditions, then adequate research methods to study processing under these conditions should in some way mirror those conditions.

Research purported to tap advertising processing, including some of that reviewed in this chapter, usually fails to simulate one or many of the characteristics listed above. Messages sometimes are not real advertising but instead are long essays or live presentations. Subjects, instead of being exposed to advertising material incidentally, have it forced upon them, are somehow motivated to attend to it and are given all the time and exposure they want for learning. None of the noise of the typical media environment is simulated. In fact, very often the advertising is presented alone with no competition, not even other advertising. Messages are presented in a pattern that allows logical and deep processing, and response measures are taken immediately in a reactive, test-taking atmosphere.

Perhaps one of the most distinctive aspects of this chapter is that most of the advertising research reviewed comes from a research program at Stanford that attempts to simulate actual advertising conditions (Ray, 1973b; Ray & Sawyer, 1971). Usually something similar to the free recall paradigm of verbal learning research is utilized, with advertisements instead of nonsense syllables as the stimuli. Cover stories are used to produce as close to the natural incidental learning situation as possible. The normal noisy advertising situation is simulated by embedding advertising in media contexts and including other and competing advertising. In addition, typical distractions are included in the advertising exposure situation. Although measurement occurs quite soon after exposure, there is usually an intervening task between exposure and measurement, and often, delayed and unobtrusive measures are utilized.

It is probably because of these steps in research method that findings related well to what might be expected from the general description of the nature of advertising information processing discussed above. Specifically, the deep, detailed processing and effects that might be expected from some theories of cognitive social psychology, particularly attitude change theories, were found in only a minority of instances. Instead, a low-involvement pattern of effects caused a reassessment of many aspects of information processing theory as they apply to advertising effects.

Plan of This Chapter

Each of the following sections concentrates on a particular set of advertising situations and outlines the effects of key situational variables, particularly involvement and affect, on advertising information processing. The main source for the situational hypotheses or microtheoretical notions is the Stanford research, but major support is derived from basic research in cognitive and cognitive social psychology.

The chapter sections are, in order: "Initial Processing Effects and Advertising Goals Hierarchies," "Two Processes Underlying Initial Processing Effects,"

"Message Strategy Implications: The Limited Situational Validity of Belief-Based Attitude Change Theories in Advertising," "Media Strategy Implications: Repetition Minimization Opportunities and Scheduling Situations," and "Future Directions for Measurement, Theory Development and Application."

INITIAL PROCESSING EFFECTS AND ADVERTISING GOALS HIERARCHIES

One of the most critical applied decisions in advertising is to determine what goals are to be effected by the campaign. In the past, a learning hierarchy of effects was assumed in order to make this planning decision (e.g., Colley, 1961). It was assumed that an audience had to learn something first, then, on the basis of belief change, their attitudes would change and this would lead to a change in intention and, if other conditions were optimal, the recommended behavior would occur.

This type of hierarchy was proposed both in advertising and in psychology. For instance, the advertising researchers Lavidge and Steiner (1961) proposed a model of advertising effect with the levels being: awareness, knowledge, liking, preference, convictions, and purchase. Management consultant Russell Colley (1961) labeled the learning hierarchy levels: awareness, comprehension, conviction, and action. Psychologist William McGuire's "information processing model" of advertising effect (1978) had the six stages: presentation of message, attention to message, comprehension of conclusion, yielding to conclusion, retention of the belief, and behaving on the basis of the new belief. Even the Fishbein and Ajzen (1975; Ajzen and Fishbein, 1980) tricomponent, expectancy value theory of attitude formation and change posits that beliefs change, first then attitudes, then intentions, and finally, behavior.

Predominance of the Low-Involvement Hierarchy

The advertising information processing research method outlined above (Ray, 1973b, 1976; Ray & Sawyer, 1971; Rothschild & Ray, 1974; Swinyard & Coney, 1978; Webb & Ray, 1979) has found that the ordered learning hierarchy does *not* occur in a majority of advertising situations. In fact the most predominant finding was for a "low-involvement" hierarchy first suggested by Krugman (1965). In this hierarchy, repetitive advertising seemed to have its main effect on the cognitive measure of ad awareness and to a lesser degree on purchase. Attitude measures were not significantly affected in these low involvement findings.

This order of results—with cognitive measures affected most, followed by conative (intention or action), followed by affective (attitude)—is exactly the order that would be predicted by Krugman's hypothesis for television advertising effect. Basically he suggested that consumers watching television were not truly in a deep information-processing mode. Their perceptual defenses were down, and it was possible for repetitive exposures to cause a "shift in the cognitive structure," which might be followed by actual purchase action due to heightened awareness of the advertised brand—*even though no attitude change had occurred.*

This is precisely what was found most often in the Stanford research. In both laboratory and field studies in which subjects saw advertising repetitively exposed under simulated natural conditions, measures of gross awareness were most affected, followed by purchase intention, which was simply indicated by respondents' choices among alternatives on the questionnaire at the end of each study, with respondents assuming they were "in the market for this product."

In addition to showing the low-involvement hierarchy, Fig. 5.1 also shows the standard high-involvement, learning hierarchy (cognitive-affect-conative order of effect) within one study done on political advertising by Rothschild and Ray (1974) and Ray (1976). Respondents were recruited in shopping malls for a study of "shopping of the future." They were shown a large number of print advertisements on a futuristic-looking slide projector. During the presentation they saw up to six ten-second exposures of various political campaign ads as well as those for various products. Following exposure to the future shopping demonstration, they were asked questions about it (an intervening task) and then, in order, questions on unaided recall of ads, cognitive response ("What thoughts went through your mind when you saw that message?"), and purchase or voting intent.

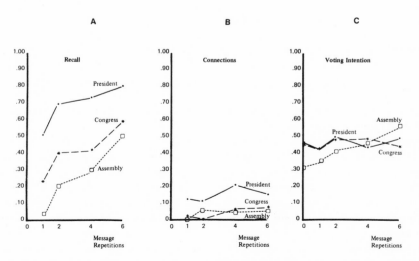

FIG. 5.1.   Hierarchy effects across various political contests. N per message-exposure condition ranged from 25–31 (reprinted from Ray, 1976).

It was expected that the presidential race advertising would be more involving than the congressional, and that the state assembly race ads would be least involving. Rothschild's measure of involvement was the "connections" (statements indicating conscious bridging experiences between the message and the viewer) type of cognitive response. Krugman (1966) indicated that connections can be used to show involvement. As can be seen in Fig. 5.1b, the connections responses, although low, were in the exact order from the president (average of 15 percent per response group) to state assembly (average of about 4 percent per response group).

The results for the three races were also in that order. The presidential race produced some slope in recall, a moderate slope in connections (also an attitudinal affect measure, see Greenwald, 1968 and Wright, 1973) and almost a flat voting intention curve—a good representation of the high-involvement, learning hierarchy. The state assembly race produced dramatic recall and intention curves and minimal effects in intentions after two exposures—a good low-involvement hierarchy sort of response. The congressional race ad response results fell between the other two.

Quite similar results were reported by Swinyard and Coney (1978) even though their ads were for U.S. senator (high involvement) and county treasurer (low involvement), and the study was done in the field with direct mail advertisements and telephone survey measurement. And, importantly, Swinyard and Coney's attitude measure was not connections but instead a five-point "very satisfactory to very unsatisfactory" scale.

Three Advertising Hierarchy Effect Situations

In addition to the low-involvement and high-involvement learning hierarchy, the Stanford research found one other high-involvement hierarchy of advertising effects—called the Dissonance-Attribution hierarchy. This hierarchy is one in which some behavior or behavioral response occurs first, followed by a dissonance or attributional shift in attitude, followed by cognitive shifts in information to support the attitude change.

The high-involvement Dissonance-Attribution hierarchy was found in the Stanford research only in field studies where subjects were able to make some behavioral choice before exposure to advertising. For instance, in studies of "labeling" and "foot-in-the-door" manipulations (Swinyard & Ray, 1977, 1979), subjects were exposed to a personal sales call on behalf of the Red Cross before receiving multiple direct mail advertising appeals.

The three hierarchies appear to occur in three different types of situations defined not only by involvement but also by perceived differences between alternatives, primary information source, and consumer experience with the decision (Ray, 1973b, 1976; 1982). By knowing the effects of these situational variables, psychologists can better plan information processing research on advertising.

The high involvement learning hierarchy has been found in situations with high involvement, clearly perceived differences between advertised alternatives, detailed print messages as the primary information source, and little consumer experience with the choice. The best examples would be consumer information processing for new innovative durable products.

The low-involvement hierarchy has been found in situations with low involvement, a perceived sameness between alternatives, broadcast advertising as the primary information source, and a great deal of experience with the choice. The best examples would be consumer information processing for mature convenience goods such as canned goods and proprietary drugs (e.g., aspirin, toothpaste).

The Dissonance-Attribution hierarchy has been found to occur in situations in which involvement is high, few surface differences can be perceived between alternatives by consumers (although hidden differences are suspected), the primary information source is personal contact, and there is moderate experience with mature products. The best examples would be in consumer information processing for mature and relatively expensive durable goods such as automobiles. Mature products are in the third or maturity stage of what is called the "product life cycle." Following introduction and growth, maturity is a period of relatively high, stable sales, reflecting consumer acceptance, if not enthusiasm, for the product.

Need for an Information-Processing Operationalization

The involvement-differentiation-information source-experience situational identification has been supported by a great deal of research both in the Stanford program and elsewhere. In addition it is a useful categorization for managers setting goals and planning advertising strategy, as well as for psychologists planning research.

But there has been a need to determine, more specifically, exactly what responses and processes are involved in high involvement (either Learning or Dissonance-Attribution) and low-involvement advertising information processing situations. It is to a precise conceptualization of these responses and processes that we turn to next.

TWO PROCESSES UNDERLYING INITIAL PROCESSING EFFECTS

There is a growing body of findings and theory from all types of information-processing research which supports the idea of two types of processing similar to the low- and high-involvement ones suggested above. Cialdini, Petty, and

Cacioppo (1981) call these two types central and peripheral processing and also refer to the deep versus shallow processing concept of Craik and Lockhart (1972), the controlled versus automatic processing concept of Schneider and Shiffrin (1977), the systematic versus heuristic processing concept of Chaiken (1980), and the thoughtful versus mindless or scripted processing concept of Abelson (1976; Langer, Blank, & Chanswitz, 1978).

In advertising research, the contrast was introduced by Krugman in 1965 with his low-involvement television advertising idea. But until quite recently, cognitive psychologists working in the advertising area have more often assumed a high-involvement sort of processing for advertising. Thus a key question for researchers attempting to examine the initial processing of advertising is, What are the key differences between these two types of processing?

Our answer—other than to point out the two different orders of effect outlined in the last section—is that *the most critical difference between low- and high-involvement initial processing of advertising is in the two types of affect invoked.*

The High-Involvement Affective Response

All of the high-involvement hierarchies of effect mentioned in the earlier section—those suggested by Lavidge and Steiner, Colley, McGuire, and Fishbein and Ajzen—assume that awareness leads to comprehension or belief change, which then leads to attitude change and then to the rest of the process or hierarchy. Most important here is that the affect concept is an attitudinal one composed of a great deal of structure and detail. This attitude or affect occurs only after there has been extensive cognitive activity.

Some clue as to the nature of this cognitive activity is suggested by theories and findings related to cognitive response (Greenwald, 1968; Petty, Ostrom, & Brock, 1981; Wright, 1973, 1974).

The basic idea of cognitive-response theory as it would relate to advertising initial processing is that only when people actively use the message (cognitively respond to it) does that message have the potential of changing attitudes. This is, then, an affect concept that is quite detailed and can only be altered by a message that causes quite active, involved, central, deep, controlled, systematic, or thoughtful processing—to use the various terminology of the field.

Low-Involvement Initial Processing: The Role of Affect

The models of message reception processes discussed above either deal explicitly with just a high-involvement mode of initial processing, or fail to come to grips with the consequences of low-involvement processing. In his process model, for instance, McGuire (1978) seems to explicitly deal with just highly involved, "problem solving" learning. He writes:

> This analysis views the recipient of the persuasive communication as an informa-
> tion-processing machine or a *problem-solver* (emphasis added), rather than a re-
> calcitrant resistor or artful evader in the service of needs that have nothing to do
> with the campaign . . . (but) what I am proposing as the information-processing
> approach is not one that views the recipient of the communication necessarily
> taking this avidly interested stance, but rather one that views the advertising cam-
> paign or any other communication as likely to be effective insofar as it succeeds in
> casting him in such a role and keeps him playing the part [McGuire, 1978, p. 157].

McGuire thus does not discuss what the initial processing would be if the communication was, in fact, received only in a "passive," low-involvement, mode.
Similarly, whereas Wright (1973, 1974) argues and shows that in low-involvement situations fewer cognitive responses are generated, and tend to be more
counter-argumentative than support-argumentative, the implications of these
conclusions have not really been explored in the literature. If advertising communications received under low-involvement conditions are not processed in a
deeply cognitive, supportive mode, how then are they received and processed,
and with what implications?

We have already summarized research (above) to show that under typical low-
involvement conditions, the operative hierarchy of effects seems to be such that
behavior seems to be related more to gross positive awareness measures than to
measures of attitude, which in fact follow, rather than precede, action. The
absence of attitude effects as preliminary effects in low-involvement message
reception situations is consistent with the literature on the absence of cognitive
response under such low-involvement conditions; the key conclusion of the
cognitive response literature is that cognitive responses to messages, rather than
message factors themselves, create and modify attitudes, since such cognitive
responses involve the active rehearsal of attitude-relevant cognitions (Greenwald, 1968; Wright, 1973). In other words, low-involvement message reception
creates few cognitive responses but does create awareness; because the absence
of cognitive responses means that attitudes are not strongly created or modified,
any action effects from such low-involving messages are a consequence only of
the effect on awareness levels.

When this process view is merged, however, with the literature on "mere
exposure effects" (Harrison, 1977; Zajonc, 1968), we gain further insight into
the affect-action link just discussed. This research links frequency of exposure to
affective (liking) reactions; under a wide range of conditions, repeated exposure
to some stimulus leads to liking for that stimulus. Three variables limiting this
effect are low stimulus complexity, low stimulus heterogeneity, and low stimulus exposure sequence variability. Explanations for the effect are varied and
competing; they include theories of "response competition," "expectancy
arousal," "opponent process theory," and others. Although the applicability of
these findings has not been shown in the advertising context, support for this
position may be found in Sawyer (1977), who concludes that "mere familiarity

with a brand compared to less familiar brands may be an important attribute per se. . . . Krugman's subtle, delayed influence process may simply be the effect of mere exposure . . . with uninvolving, low-priced convenience goods, there may be little active retention of beliefs about attributes. Even recognizing a familiar brand may be a criterion to try that brand'' (p. 242).

What this suggests is that brand preferences in low-involvement situations are the outcome of a confounded affect-awareness process; the "affect" being talked about here is not, however, the post-cognitive, attitude-affect of the Fishbein and Ajzen (1975, 1980) model, but a precognitive, mere-exposure-based affect.

Thus, in high-involvement situations, messages generate many cognitive responses, modify attitudes, and influence action through such attitude-affect. In low-involvement situations, on the other hand, messages leave attitudes unchanged, but do create awareness and mere-exposure-affect, which then influence action.

Psychobiological Support for the Affect Concept

Such a view, which argues that the appropriate process model for low-involvement message initial processing is noncognitive and largely one of the creation of awareness and precognitive affect, is further supported by a psychobiological perspective on low-involvement message reception. Krugman (1980) has argued that TV watching, the archetypal low-involvement message situation, is predominantly a right brain activity. The role of the right brain hemisphere in generating noncognitive affect is well documented (Hansen, 1981; Sperry, 1973) recent confirmation can be found in Schwartz, Davidson & Maer (1975), Dimond, Farrington & Johnson (1976), and Galin (1976).

We note, however, that the identification of such affect with the right hemisphere of the neocortex may well be incomplete. Another view of the origin and location of affect and emotion in the human brain would "locate" such affect in the "limbic" brain (below the neocortex); this view, popularly known as the "triune brain" model of MacLean, is reviewed in Livingston (1976). Presented with the evidence of both limbic affect and right brain affect, it seems appropriate to ask if we are, in fact, dealing with two different kinds of affect. Limbic affect deals with binary, approach-avoidance, flight-fight, survival responses, which go with a great deal of autonomic arousal and are, in an evolutionary sense, primary. Right brain affect, on the other hand, should not involve autonomic arousal and should depend for its activation, instead, on the aesthetic pleasure that comes from complex and spatially or chronologically pleasing form. It is difficult, at this stage, to specify which of these two (if not both) is involved in the low-involvement affective responses discussed so far.

In advertising, Weinstein et al. (Weinstein, 1980; Weinstein, Appel, & Weinstein, 1980; Appel, Weinstein, & Weinstein, 1979) have shown in numerous studies that different media (e.g., magazines vs. TV) have differential impacts on the levels and nature (hemispheric balances) of brain wave activity, and that such differences can be related to brand recall. Our proposition, then, that the low-involvement message reception process operates primarily via right brain, noncognitive affect (and via differential awareness) seems to be supported. Interestingly, Zajonc (1980) stresses the primacy of such affective judgments over cognitive responses. He argues that human affective judgments are independent of, and precede in time, perceptual and cognitive processes that supposedly form the basis of such affect. Part of his evidence comes from experiments to validate his earlier (1968) ''mere exposure'' hypothesis; he argues that, whereas the earlier explanations involved the factor of stimulus recognition, recent experiments eliminate the recognition factor and still prove a precognitive affective impact.

In sum then, we believe that existing models of the process of message reception deal largely with high-involvement situations; for low-involvement situations, an alternative process model, which deals primarily with exposure-based awareness and affect, is needed (e.g., Greenwald, Leavitt, and Obermiller, 1980). Some of the implications of our (admittedly extreme) ''dichotomization'' of advertising effect-hierarchies and process-models are now explored.

MESSAGE STRATEGY IMPLICATIONS: THE LIMITED SITUATIONAL VALIDITY OF BELIEF-BASED ATTITUDE CHANGE THEORIES IN ADVERTISING

The most important decision in advertising is probably the choice of the advertising message through which the message recipient's attitude to the advertised brand or service may be made more favorable. In the literature, this concern is reflected in the burgeoning research on attitudes and attitude change. Advertising communications can be better designed and more effective if we understand the basis and dynamics of attitude formation and change and use this understanding in both the choice of the advertising message as well as its creative execution.

A full review of alternative attitude models is outside the scope of this paper; such a review may be found in McGuire (1969). The models currently in favor in marketing and advertising are the expectancy-value models (Wilkie & Pessemier, 1973); these include Rosenberg's Instrumentality-Value model, and the Fishbein-Ajzen attitude change formulation. The crucial (for our purposes) concept in these models is their view of the attitude object as a bundle of attributes. Expectancy-value models thus define a person's attitude to an object (or person, issue, etc.) to be the sum of the multiplicative products of expectancies (beliefs about attributes) about the object times the value one places on those attributes.

In the Rosenberg model, the more a given object is instrumental to obtaining positively valued goals and to blocking negatively valued goals, the more favorable the person's attitude toward the object.

A similar unidimensionalist view was urged by Fishbein and Ajzen (1975, 1980), who argued that beliefs (cognitions) were antecedent to attitudes (affect only) which led to intentions (conation). According to the Fishbein-Ajzen view, attitude change can therefore only begin by changing the relevant beliefs, and they develop a model in which attitude change is a function of belief discrepancy (between beliefs held and urged) and facilitating message factors, with the mathematical relationship between discrepancy and attitude change being contingent on the level of facilitation provided by the message/source factors (Fishbein & Ajzen, 1975). Based on their formulation, Fishbein and Ajzen argue that in order to change the attitudes held by a subject one must first change the underlying beliefs, because the attitudes are based on the beliefs; they then proceed to develop a complex algebra of proximal beliefs, dependent beliefs, and so on. Given this theoretical perspective, it is not surprising that most advertising messages tend to be attribute-based, with the objective of modifying the recipient's attitude to the advertised brand by convincing him that it is competitively superior on the advertised attributes.

Note the implicit assumption in the Fishbein-Ajzen formulation, however, that the underlying beliefs about these attributes are "available" for change in the message reception situation. This is a far from trivial assumption. It is quite possible that the attitude *formation* episode is such—as in most low-involvement situations—that the underlying beliefs are not retained after the global attitude (if any) has been formed. The dependence of information storage and recall on the processing task has been demonstrated by Johnson and Russo (1981) and on the "vivid" nature of such information by Borgida and Nisbett (1977). Such reasoning is also in consonance with the literature on message-induced cognitive responses (Greenwald, 1968). It seems reasonable to argue that if in low-involvement situations consumers do not attend to messages with detailed cognitive processing (Bettman, 1979, p. 179), then their cognitive responses are such that fewer cognitions and beliefs are stored, because they are not deeply processed (Craik & Lockhart, 1972).

Affect-referral, the decision-strategy where consumers choose between brands based on overall affect and not component attributes (Wright & Barbour, 1976), may thus sometimes be not only a voluntarily chosen decision *simplifier,* but also a decision heuristic *forced* upon situations, because the subject's first exposure to the message stimulus was such that the underlying beliefs are not available later for an attribute-based comparison, and a brand-based comparison therefore has to take place. Given the literature on availability effects (Reyes, Thompson, & Bower, 1980; Tversky & Kahneman, 1973) it would seem wrong strategy in such low-involvement situations, then, to attempt attitude change through changes in underlying beliefs. What is needed, clearly, is a strategy of "affect as input": brand-based (overall, "halo") comparisons instead of attribute-based ones.

This involvement-based perspective may throw some light on the well-documented failure of many belief-based attitude change programs (Hovland, 1959; McGuire, 1969). As Zajonc (1980) writes in connection with the "perseverence effect" in experiments, "in debriefing, when the experimenter tells the subjects that their success (or failure) was rigged, this new information may no longer be capable of making contact with the original input (which by then has been recoded and discarded) and may therefore have little effect on its original affective consequences."

The advertising implications of this low-involvement "affect as input" hypothesis are also clear. In his experiment on the causal relations among cognitions, affect and behavior, Lutz (1977) was forced to conclude from the low belief-change attitude-change correlation that "from a managerial perspective, the weakness of the relationship between cognitive change and attitude change is disturbing. It is difficult to justify the construction of promotional strategies based on findings of this magnitude." Not only may it be necessary in such low-involvement situations to not attempt belief-based message strategies, therefore, it may also make sense for market leader brands to "inoculate" their "attitude franchises" by deliberately following a "halo communications" strategy, such that competitive belief-based messages fail to create impact. Alternatively, a message that for some reason has to be belief-based must first attempt to get the recipient to receive it in a high-involvement mode, because a low-involvement mode of message reception would involve minimal cognitive response.

This perspective also helps us to understand the situational determinants of the use of emotional versus rational arguments in executing message strategies. A popular rule-of-thumb in the advertising business seems to be "If you have nothing to say, sing it." A charitable (and theoretically more defensible) interpretation is to argue that mature markets where product differences are minimal happen to be low-involvement product-markets, where the level of "natural" drive in the situation is low. As Ray has pointed out (1982, Ch. 10), such situations need the injection of drive via the use of emotional, affective creative execution, to enhance the level of learning. The arguments above for an "affect as input" strategy in low-involvement situations provide a different rationale for the same recommendation: affective creative execution in such situations not only promotes learning but also is more appropriate from the availability-of-beliefs framework.

In sum, then, the dichotomization of situations along the degree of involvement can help us understand the differential role of beliefs and affect in attitude change, such that advertising messages can be more sharply tailored to the attitude change mechanisms operative in that particular situation. While belief-based messages are more appropriate in high-involvement, attribute-processing situations, in low-involvement situations processing is more likely to be on the basis of overall affect, with underlying beliefs being less salient and less available, so that advertising messages might more profitably stress overall affect rather than component beliefs.

MEDIA STRATEGY IMPLICATIONS: REPETITION MINIMIZATION OPPORTUNITIES AND SCHEDULING SITUATIONS

Whereas most academic research in the advertising media planning area has tended to be at the tactical level of the choice between different media vehicles, the involvement-based perspective developed in this chapter is of immense help in two different areas of media strategy: the decisions on the appropriate frequency level and the appropriate scheduling pattern.

Frequency and Repetition Minimization Opportunities

The choice of the appropriate frequency level is important to advertising theory and practice because the continuous escalation of media costs (a prime time network TV minute cost over $100,000 in early 1981) makes the habitual and unthinking use of repetition an expensive and potentially very wasteful strategy. Fortunately, this chapter's development of an involvement-based typology of situations enables us to identify those situations where ad repetition is useful, as well as suggest techniques to minimize the frequency of repetition for those situations where repetition is appropriate. Surprisingly, prior studies and reviews on this question (e.g., Naples, 1979) have made no attempt to determine *situationally* "appropriate" levels of frequency, and have instead tried to find "globally" optimal truths.

This problem is best approached by the use of this chapter's situational typology to answer the following sequence of questions: What kind of consumer "learning" takes place through advertising? How does repetition, in particular, assist advertisers in achieving these "learning" objectives? What does this tell us about situations where repetition may be an appropriate media strategy, and where it may not? What does this tell us about ways in which we may reduce the need for repetition, even where it is an appropriate strategy?

As has been shown in the earlier sections of this chapter, the Colley (1961) hierarchy of communication effects, which works sequentially from the cognitive through the affective to the conative levels, is now seen as being operative only in high-involvement, "true learning" situations. In low-involvement situations, attitude change is not a prerequisite for action, with the direction of communication effects being instead cognitive-conative-affective. (The third hierarchy, following the Dissonance-Attribution conative-affective-cognitive route, is more relevant to situations of personal contact.) What these hierarchies show is that while the effects of advertising begin with attitude change in high-involvement situations, in low-involvement situations all that is necessary is the creation of brand preferences based not on attitudes but merely on greater awareness (see, for instance, Krugman, 1965; Ray, 1973b; Kassarjian & Kassarjian, 1979; Lastovicka, 1979). We have also argued above that in fact such low-involvement preferences may be based not just on gross awareness but on a confounded (à la Zajonc, 1968) affect-awareness basis, the differential awareness having created greater "mere exposure" affect. It would thus seem that the task of advertising is to change belief-based attitudes in high-involvement situations, and to create differential awareness and affect in low-involvement situations. It is against these "learning" objectives that the appropriateness and relative efficiency of repetition strategies must be measured.

The major conclusion of the research on repetition effects in advertising, meanwhile, seems to indicate that repetition has its greatest effects on measures of recall, some effects on brand mention, with the least impact on measures of attitudes and brand preference; specific effects vary with the other situational factors of appeal used, product type, format variables, etc. (Ray, Sawyer, & Strong, 1971). Repetition therefore does not seem to change attitudes by itself; this is not surprising because cognitive responses, which are the stuff of which learning is made (Greenwald, 1968; Wright, 1973) are not a repetition response *per se*.

Repetition thus has only minor effects in high-involvement situations. In low-involvement situations, however, where advertising works through differentially high awareness and positive affect, repetition can be effective because it serves to maintain high awareness (through tackling the "forgetting" of learned material) and create affect (through mere exposure effects). The other roles of repetition mentioned in the literature are to serve as reminders (Krugman, 1972) and to create gradual perceptual shifts (Krugman, 1965).

This differential situational utility of repetition is also confirmed by recent research on advertising "clutter" on television which found high-involvement ads (which generated more cognitive responses than did low-involvement ads in a pilot study) less subject to order effects and clutter, whereas low-involvement ads were so affected, implying that low-involvement ads would benefit more from repetition than would high-involvement ones (Ray & Webb, 1976).

The suggested differential situational utility of repetition is also compatible with learning theory (Ray, 1973a). In high-involvement situations where, for instance, product differences exist between alternatives in the early stages of the life cycle and a high level of drive already exists, consumers approach messages in a problem-solving mode. Thus, in high-involvement situations, all-or-nothing learning is more likely, and repetition by itself is almost meaningless or even negative in effect.

It would thus seem that message repetition, or high levels of frequency, are appropriate only in situations characterized by low consumer involvement in the product and/or media. Even though repetition may be necessary in most low-involvement situations, however, the frequency of such repetition may still be reduced by our knowledge of *why* repetition works in such situations and our success in being able to achieve those same effects through cheaper, nonrepetition strategies, such as the manipulation of message format and media delivery variables.

We have argued above that repetition works in low-involvement situations by tackling the ''forgetting'' of learned material and by creating exposure-based affect. Both these are also achievable by other, cheaper, means. Ads can be made more memorable by the addition of ''structure'' (Silk & Vavra, 1974); by the use of techniques to increase processing by immediate (short-term) memory, such as order effects; and the use of techniques to maximize transferral from immediate to long-term memory, such as enforced sub-vocal rehearsal, in-commercial repetition, and the like. Further, the building-in of affective values into the commercial will not only improve memorability (Bower, 1981; Dutta & Kanungo, 1975) but will also replace the ''indirectly created'' (mere exposure based) affect due to repetition.

Attempts could also be made to ''convert'' low-involvement situations to pseudo high-involvement ones by the addition of ''borrowed interest'' techniques which ''artificially'' increase the level of ''natural'' drive in the situation, such as the use of humor, affect, and so on (Ray, 1982). Of course, borrowed interest techniques must be used quite carefully lest they draw attention from the product or object of the message and thus do nothing to increase its affect-awareness. Another way to ''artificially'' increase involvement is to engineer the messages so more relevant cognitive responses, of the sort found to indicate high involvement in the clutter research reported above (Ray & Webb, 1976), are produced from the advertising.

Finally, repetition can be used more effectively if repeated ads use soft-sell techniques (Krugman, 1962), vary the message within a familiar context (Leavitt, 1966; Weiss, 1966), stay short but familiar to facilitate easy recognition, and use spaced (rather than massed) scheduling to keep recall high (Sawyer, 1974). This last question of appropriate scheduling patterns is far more complex, however, and we turn now to a fuller discussion of this area.

Scheduling Patterns

Once the total frequency of exposures per target consumer has been determined, using criteria such as those developed above, the problem remains of deciding how the weight of the campaign will be applied to the selected media and vehicles across the year. The scheduling decision is thus concerned with the pattern of exposure to the advertising that will be effected against target segments by various expenditure patterns, and how such exposure patterns ''fit'' the advertising response and decay (forgetting) functions operative in that specific advertising situation.

The specific response and decay functions operating in a situation are a function of many factors. One important factor is the level of involvement and therefore the hierarchy and the appropriate measure of effect and response.

The two major kinds of scheduling patterns correspond to massed versus distributed practice. These are seen as endpoints on a continuum of possible "wave" or "continuity" strategies. At one end of this continuum is a wave strategy in which the advertiser spends very little in some periods and more than average in others. At the extreme, the advertiser goes in and out of the media, jolting and fading completely. The time periods when the "waves" peak or trough could be based on seasonality, competitive patterns, media dominance objectives, and so on. The basic assumptions in such strategies are that only by concentrating efforts in certain periods will it be possible to develop sufficient frequency to have impact against key segments, and that during the non-advertising periods the impact will not decay to dangerously low levels.

In the other, "continuity" strategy, the level of advertising is kept essentially constant, regardless of the time period. Such a constant level, no-burst campaign stresses reach and continuity rather than frequency and dominance; the assumptions being made are that target levels of communication response are easy to reach and maintain.

Corresponding to these two generic strategies, then, are two generic sets of assumptions regarding the response and decay functions that operate in given situations. The "wave/dominance" strategies are typically used in what we call the "difficult" response and decay function situations, where it takes a number of responses before there is any response at all, and even if substantial response is achieved with repetition, forgetting can be very quick. (Of course, the ideal situation for a wave/dominance strategy would be one with slow response and slow decay.)

In contrast, the "continuity" strategies are typically used in response and decay function situations, where it is easy to have an effect on target segments with advertising and easy to maintain that effect. In response function terms, this means that each additional exposure after zero exposures produces some significant increase in the target response. In addition, forgetting occurs slowly or almost not at all; decay functions are not steep. (Again, the *ideal* situation for continuity strategies is one with both quick response and quick decay.)

The question now becomes one of deciding which of these two sets of functions (or variants thereof) operates in a given situation, and of developing a scheduling strategy that corresponds to these functions. Ray (1982, Ch. 16) has identified seven situational factors that influence the shapes of the response and decay functions operating in that situation. We first briefly mention six of these seven, and then turn to the seventh (and probably the most important) one, the level of involvement. For all seven, the conclusions presented here are based on the results of the Stanford research project (Ray & Sawyer, 1971; Sawyer, 1973; Strong, 1974, Ray, Ward, & Reed, 1976; Webb & Ray, 1979).

These six operate as follows:

1. Target segment brand and product usage: the more the target segment is already in favor of the brand or market offering being advertised, the more the scheduling situation is likely to be "easy."

2. Product type: to the extent that other information sources are used by consumers, the advertising media scheduling situation becomes "difficult": if advertising is the main source of information, "easy" scheduling tends to prevail.

3. Brand position: the stronger the brand position in terms of share of market and share of consumer mind, the greater the probability that the situation will be "easy."

4. Communication environment and competition: to the extent that the communication environment is cluttered with other advertising and program or editorial material which is not supportive or is conflicting, there is the chance of slipping into the "difficult" situation, regardless of brand position.

5. Advertising appeal and tone: depending on the nature of the target audience, different appeals and tones produce "easy" or "difficult" functions; for example, refutational messages produce an "easy" response in antagonistic audiences, while supportive appeals produce an "easy" response in already-favorable audiences.

6. Advertising format: arresting, unusual and "grabber" formats yield "easy" response and decay situations for lower level measures such as recall and recognition, but not for comprehension, attitude or intention measures.

Although all the six factors above are important, the most important situational factor affecting response and forgetting and, ultimately, scheduling strategy, is the measure of effect and response. What the "appropriate" measure of response should be is largely a function of the degree of involvement (and therefore the appropriate effects hierarchy) in the situation. In general, if the response is on the lower levels of the response hierarchy (such as awareness and simple recall), it is "easy" to raise and "difficult" to maintain, whereas the "difficult" response and slow decay is more likely for measures of detailed comprehension, attitude and intention. This dichotomy has been found repeatedly in the Stanford research although Krugman (1972), points out that recognition seems impervious to forgetting.

Both Zielske (1959) and Strong (1974) found very rapid forgetting for simple ad recall measures, whereas Strong also found that for well-known brands difficult measures like attitude did not seem to decay at all during nonadvertised periods. Interactions therefore certainly exist. But if communications objectives in low-involvement situations are "lower" measures of awareness and recall, "easy" response and "difficult" decay functions are likely, whereas "difficult" response and slow decay are likely for the high-involvement objectives of attitude and intention measures. Appropriate scheduling patterns may thus be developed based on such a situational analysis.

FUTURE DIRECTIONS FOR MEASUREMENT, THEORY DEVELOPMENT, AND APPLICATION

Table 5.1 summarizes much of this chapter and provides some guidelines as to what needs to be done in the future.

Basically this chapter presented a microtheoretical notion or series of such notions in the form of a dichotomy of situations. The high-involvement type of situation is what many researchers, policy-makers and managers seem to assume about the information processing of advertising. It is increasingly becoming more apparent, however, that a large part of advertising effect occurs in a low-involvement type of situation.

The implications of this dichotomy are dramatic and important. Research and application are misled if they assume, for instance, that in all situations, behavior is a function of attitudes. In the low-involvement situation, it is affect-awareness that propels behavior.

TABLE 5.1
Two Situations in Information Processing of Advertising

Characteristics	High-Involvement Situation	Low-Involvement Situation
Degree of Involvement	High	Low
Behavior = f(?)	Attitudes	Affect-Awareness
Degree of Cognitive Responding	High	Low
Subsequent Availability of Beliefs	High	Low
Decision Mode	Compensatory (Cognitive/Belief-Based)	Non-Compensatory (Affect-Based)
Attitude Change Strategy Required	Beliefs-Rational-Attributes	Overall Affect
Degree of Repetition Necessary	Low	High
Media Scheduling Situation	Difficult Response, Easy Decay	Easy Response, Difficult Decay
Appropriate Measures	Obtrusive, Paper and Pencil	Unobtrusive, Physiological

Similarly there is little cognitive responding or later availability of beliefs as a result of advertising in low-involvement situations. Thus measurement must be done on an overall affect basis. In fact, there is some suggestion that physiological measures might tap the gross arousal responses of low involvement more effectively.

Applications in the message area should be done with the differential decision modes and attitude strategies of the two types of situations. Detailed information on attributes is not appropriate for low-involvement types of situations. The media scheduling situation for the low-involvement type tends to be an easy response and difficult (quick) decay one, in contrast to the difficult response and easy (slow) decay situation under high-involvement type.

But we could arguably be classified with the overgeneralizing "idiots" of Blake's quote at the beginning of this chapter if the reader was left with just the dichotomy of Table 5.1. Involvement is a critical variable as this and other chapters in this volume attest. Used alone, however, it does not sufficiently describe advertising information-processing situations. In this chapter, for instance, research was reviewed that indicated that the nature of the hierarchy of effects situation is determined by three other variables (perceived differences between alternatives, primary information source and consumer experience with the decision). Six other variables (consumer favorability and product usage, product type, brand position, communication environment and competition, advertising appeal and tone, and advertising format), in addition to involvement, have been found to affect the nature of the scheduling situation.

In fact, the "media scheduling situation" line in Table 5.1 is actually an overgeneralization of sorts in that high-involvement situations could be "easy" in response if the consumer audience for the advertising is initially favorably biased toward the message. Only if the audience is initially opposed as well as being highly involved, would the situation be "difficult" or slow in response.

The ultimate message of this chapter, then, is similar to Blake's. Information-processing researchers should reach for the *specific* variables that importantly affect response in enduring advertising situations.

REFERENCES

Abelson, R. P. Script processing in attitude formation and decision making. In J. S. Carroll and J. W. Payne (Eds.), *Cognition and social behavior*. Hillsdale, N.J.: Lawrence Erlbaum Associates, 1976.

Ajzen, I., & Fishbein, M. *Understanding attitudes and predicting social behavior*. Englewood Cliffs, N.J.: Prentice-Hall, 1980.

Appel, V., Weinstein, S., & Weinstein, C. Brain activity and recall of TV advertising. *Journal of Advertising Research*, 1979, *19*, 7–15.

Bauer, R. A. Does attitude change take place before or after behavior change? In L. Adler & I. Crespi (Eds.), *Attitude research on the rocks*. Chicago: American Marketing Association, 1968.

Berlyne, D. E. Arousal and reinforcement. In D. Levine (Ed.), *Nebraska symposium on motivation*. Lincoln: University of Nebraska Press, 1967.

Bettman, J. R. *An information processing theory of consumer choice*. Reading, Mass.: Addison-Wesley, 1979.

Blake, W. *Annotations to Sir Joshua Reynolds discourses*, 1808.

Borgida, E., & Nisbett, R. E. The differential impact of abstract vs. concrete information on decisions. *Journal of Abnormal and Social Psychology*, 1977, *7*, 258–271.

Bower, G. H. Mood and memory. *American Psychologist*, 1981, *36*, 129–148.

Britt, S. H., Adams, S. C., & Miller, A. S. How many advertising exposures per day. *Journal of Advertising Research*, 1972, *12*, 3–9.

Bugelski, B. R. Presentation time, total time, and mediation of paired-associate learning. *Journal of Experimental Psychology*, 1962, *63*, 409–412.

Chaiken, S. Heuristic versus systematic information processing and the use of source versus message cues in persuasion. *Journal of Personality and Social Psychology*, 1980, *39*, 752–766.

Cialdini, R. B., Petty, R. E., & Cacioppo, J. T. Attitude and attitude change. *Annual Review of Psychology*, 1981, *32*, 357–404.

Colley, R. *Defining advertising goals for measured advertising results*. New York: Association of National Advertisers, 1961.

Craik, F. M., & Lockhart, R. S. Levels of processing: A framework for memory research. *Journal of Verbal Learning and Verbal Behavior*, 1972, *11*, 156–163.

Dimond, S., Farrington, L., & Johnson, P. Differing emotional responses from right and left hemispheres. *Nature*, 1976, *261*, 690–692.

Dutta, S., & Kanungo, R. N. *Affect and memory: A reformulation*. Oxford: Pergamon Press, 1975.

Fishbein, M., & Ajzen, I. *Belief, attitude, intention and behavior: An introduction to theory and research*. Reading, Mass.: Addison-Wesley, 1975.

Galin, D. Hemispheric specialization: Implications for psychiatry. In R. G. Grenell & S. Gabay (Eds.), *Biological foundations of psychiatry, Vol. 1*. New York: Raven Press, 1976.

Greenwald, A. G. Cognitive learning, cognitive response to persuasion, and attitude change. In A. G. Greenwald, T. C. Brock, & T. M. Ostrom (Eds.), *Psychological foundations of attitudes*. New York: Academic Press, 1968.

Greenwald, A. G., Leavitt, C., & Obermiller, C. What is low consumer involvement? In G. J. Gorn & M. E. Goldberg (Eds.), *Proceedings of the division 23 program*. 88th Annual Convention, American Psychological Association, 1980.

Hansen, F. Hemispheric lateralization: Implications for understanding consumer behavior. *Journal of Consumer Research*, 1981, *8*, 23–35.

Harrison, A. A. Mere Exposure. In L. Berkowitz (Ed.), *Advances in experimental social psychology, Vol. 10*. New York: Academic Press, 1977.

Hovland, C. I. Reconciling conflicting results derived from experimental and survey studies of attitude change. *American Psychologist*, 1959, *14*, 8–17.

Johnson, E. J., & Russo, J. E. Product familiarity and learning new information. In K. Monroe (Ed.), *Advances in consumer research, Vol. 8*. Ann Arbor, Mich.: Association for Consumer Research, 1981.

Kahneman, D. *Attention and effort*. Englewood Cliffs, N.J.: Prentice-Hall, 1973.

Kassarjian, H. H., & Kassarjian, W. M. Attitudes under low commitment conditions. In J. Maloney & B. Silverman (Eds.), *Attitude research plays for high stakes*. Chicago: American Marketing Association, 1979.

Krugman, H. E. An application of learning theory to TV copy testing. *Public Opinion Quarterly*, 1962, *26*, 621–634.

Krugman, H. E. The impact of TV advertising: Learning without involvement. *Public Opinion Quarterly*, 1965, *29*, 349–356.

Krugman, H. E. An answer to one of the unanswered questions. *Proceedings of the 12th Annual Meeting of the Advertising Research Foundation.* New York: Advertising Research Foundation, 1966.

Krugman, H. E. Why three exposures may be enough. *Journal of Advertising Research,* 1972, *12,* 11–14.

Krugman, H. E. Point of view: Sustained viewing of Television. *Journal of Advertising Research,* 1980, *20,* 65–68.

Langer, E., Blank, A., & Chanswitz, B. The mindlessness of ostensibly thoughtful action: The role of placebic information in interpersonal interaction. *Journal of Personality and Social Psychology.,* 1978, *36,* 635–642.

Lastovicka, J. L. Are attitude models appropriate for mass TV advertising? In J. Eighmey (Ed.), *Attitude research under the sun.* Chicago: American Marketing Association, 1979.

Lavidge, R., & Steiner, G. A. A model for predictive measurements of advertising effectiveness. *Journal of Marketing,* 1961, *25,* 59–62.

Leavitt, C. The communication response. In L. Bogart (Ed.), *Psychology in media strategy.* Chicago: American Marketing Association, 1966.

Livingston, R. B. Sensory processing, perception and behavior. In R. G. Grenell & S. Gabay (Eds.), *Biological foundations of psychiatry, Vol. I.* New York: Raven Press, 1976.

Lutz, R. J. An experimental investigation of causal relations among cognitions, affect, and behavioral intentions. *Journal of Consumer Research,* 1977, *3,* 197–208.

McGuire, W. J. The nature of attitudes and attitude change. In G. Lindzey & E. Aronson (Eds.), *The handbook of social psychology, Vol. III.* Reading, Mass.: Addison-Wesley, 1969.

McGuire, W. J. An information processing model of advertising effectiveness. In H. L. Davis & A. J. Silk (Eds.), *Behavioral and management science in marketing.* New York: Ronald Press, 1978.

Miller, G. A. The magical number seven, plus or minus two: Some limits on our capacity for processing information. *Psychological Review,* 1956, *63.*

Naples, M. J. *Effective frequency: The relationship between frequency and advertising effectiveness.* New York: Association of National Advertisers, 1979.

Newell, A., & Simon, H. A. *Human problem solving.* Englewood Cliffs, N.J.: Prentice-Hall, 1972.

Norman, D. A. *Memory and attention: An introduction to human information processing.* New York: Wiley, 1969.

Petty, R. E., Ostrom, T. M., & Brock, T. C. *Cognitive responses in persuasion.* Hillsdale, N.J.: Lawrence Erlbaum Associates, 1981.

Ray, M. L. Psychological theories and interpretations of learning. In S. Ward and T. S. Robertson (Eds.), *Consumer behavior: Theoretical sources.* Englewood Cliffs, N.J.: Prentice-Hall, 1973. (a)

Ray, M. L. Marketing communication and the hierarchy of effects. In *Sage Annual Review of Communication Research.* Beverly Hills, Ca.: Sage Publications, 1973. (b)

Ray, M. L. Attitude as communication response. In D. Johnson & W. D. Wells (Eds.), *Attitude research at bay.* Chicago: American Marketing Association, 1976.

Ray, M. L. The present and potential linkages between the microtheoretical notions of behavioral science and the problems of advertising: A proposal for a research system. In H. L. Davis & A. J. Silk (Eds.), *Behavioral and management science in marketing.* New York: Ronald Press, 1978.

Ray, M. L. *Advertising and communication management.* Englewood Cliffs, N.J.: Prentice-Hall, 1982.

Ray, M. L., & Sawyer, A. G. Repetition in media models: A laboratory technique. *Journal of Marketing Research,* 1971, *8,* 20–30.

Ray, M. L., Sawyer, A. G., & Strong, E. C. Frequency effects revisited. *Journal of Advertising Research,* 1971, *11,* 14–20.

Ray, M. L., Ward, S., & Reed, J. B. Pretesting of anti-drug abuse and education and information campaigns. In R. Ostman (Ed.), *Communication research and drug education.* Beverly Hills, Ca.: Sage Publishing, 1976.

Ray, M. L., & Webb, P. *Experimental research on the effects of TV clutter: Dealing with a difficult media environment.* Cambridge: Marketing Science Institute, Report No. 76-102, 1976.

Reyes, R. M., Thompson, W. C., & Bower, G. H. Judgmental biases resulting from different availabilities of arguments. *Journal of Personality and Social Psychology.* 1980, *39,* 2–12.

Rothschild, M. L., & Ray, M. L. Involvement and political advertising effect: An exploratory experiment. *Communication Research,* 1974, *1,* 291–308.

Sawyer, A. G. The effects of repetition of refutational and supportive advertising appeals. *Journal of Marketing Research,* 1973, *10,* 28–33.

Sawyer, A. G. The effects of repetition: Conclusions and suggestions about experimental laboratory research. In G. D. Hughes & M. L. Ray (Eds.), *Buyer/Consumer information processing.* Chapel Hill: University of North Carolina Press, 1974.

Sawyer, A. G. Repetition and affect: Recent empirical and theoretical developments. In A. G. Woodside, J. N. Sheth, & P. D. Bennett (Eds.), *Consumer and industrial buying behavior.* New York: North-Holland, 1977.

Schneider, W., & Shiffrin, R. M. Controlled and automatic human information processing. I: Detection, search and attention. *Psychological Review,* 1977, *84,* 1–66.

Schwartz, G. E., Davidson, R. J., & Maer, F. Right hemisphere lateralization for emotion in the human brain: Interactions with cognition. *Science,* 1975, *190,* 286–288.

Silk, A. J., Vavra, T. G. The influence of advertising's affective qualities on consumer response. In G. D. Hughes & M. L. Ray (Eds.), *Buyer/Consumer information processing.* Chapel Hill: University of North Carolina Press, 1974.

Simon, H. A. How big is a chunk? *Science,* 1974, *183,* 482–488.

Sperry, R. W. Lateral specialization of cerebral function in the surgically seperated hemispheres. In F. J. Mcguigan & R. A. Schoonorer (Eds.), *The psychophysiology of thinking.* New York: Academic Press, 1973.

Strong, E. C. The use of field experimental observations in estimating advertising recall. *Journal of Marketing Research,* 1974, *11,* 369–378.

Swinyard, W. R., & Coney, K. A. Promotional effects on a high- versus low-involvement electorate. *Journal of Consumer Research,* 1978, *5,* 41–48.

Swinyard, W. R., & Ray, M. L. Advertising-selling interactions. *Journal of Marketing Research,* 1977, *14,* 508–516.

Swinyard, W. R., & Ray, M. L. Effects of praise and small requests on receptivity to direct mail appeals. *Journal of Social Psychology,* 1979, *108,* 177–184.

Tversky, A., & Kahneman, D. Availability: A heuristic for judging frequency and probability. *Cognitive Psychology,* 1973, *5,* 207–232.

Webb, P., & Ray, M. L. Effects of TV clutter. *Journal of Advertising Research,* 1979, *19,* 7–12.

Weinstein, S. Brain wave analysis in attitude research: Past, present and future. In R. W. Olshavsky (Ed.), *Attitude research enters the '80s.* Chicago: American Marketing Association, 1980.

Weinstein, S., Appel, V., & Weinstein, C. Brain activity responses to magazine and TV advertising. *Journal of Advertising Research,* 1980, *20,* 57–63.

Weiss, W. Repetition in advertising. In L. Bogart (Ed.), *Psychology in media strategy.* Chicago: American Marketing Association, 1966, 59–65.

Wilkie, W. L., & Pessemier, E. A. Issues in marketing's use of multi-attribute attitude models. *Journal of Marketing Research,* 1973, *10,* 428–441.

Wright, P. The cognitive processes mediating acceptance of advertising. *Journal of Marketing Research,* 1973, *10,* 53–62.

Wright, P. On the direct monitoring of cognitive response to advertising. In D. G. Hughes & M. L. Ray (Eds.), *Buyer/Consumer information processing.* Chapel Hill: University of North Carolina Press, 1974.

Wright, P., & Barbour, F. The relevance of decision process models in structuring persuasive messages. In M. L. Ray & S. Ward (Eds.), *Communicating with consumers: The information processing approach*. Beverly Hills, Ca.: Sage Publications, 1976.

Zajonc, R. B. Attitudinal effects of mere exposure. *Journal of Personality and Social Psychology, Monograph*, 1968, *9*, 1–28.

Zajonc, R. B. Feeling and thinking: Preferences need no inferences. *American Psychologist*, 1980, *35*, 151–175.

Zielske, H. The remembering and forgetting of advertising. *Journal of Marketing*, 1959, *23*, 239–243.

6 Cognitive Psychology Looks at Advertising: Commentary on a Hobbit's Adventure

James Shanteau
Kansas State University

Reading these chapters on the application of cognitive psychology to advertising is like taking an adventurous trip. We find ourselves leaving all the old familiar landmarks behind, such as traditional laboratory paradigms. Instead, we are faced with a new set of problems and paradigms which are quite different from what we may be used to. Nonetheless, I have considerable optimism that this adventure of a cognitive psychologist looking at advertising will turn out well.

This initial reaction reminds me of J. R. R. Tolkien's (1966) description of Bilbo Baggins' adventure in "The Hobbit." Among Hobbits, the Baggins family was considered to be very respectable "not only because most of them were rich, but also because they never had any adventures or did anything unexpected: You could tell what a Baggins would say on any question without the bother of asking him [p. 17].'' Moreover, when given the opportunity to go on an adventure, Bilbo replies "We are plain quiet folk and have no use for adventures. Nasty disturbing uncomfortable things! Makes you late for dinner! [p. 18].''

Despite these misgivings, he is persuaded to go on a quest by Gandalf, who is also Bilbo's guide and sometimes savior. Despite numerous adventures and misadventures, Bilbo turns out in the end to be quite successful. When he finally returns home, he is much the richer and wiser. "But, he was no longer quite respectable. He was in fact held by all the hobbits of the neighbourhood to be 'queer' . . . (Nevertheless) he did not mind. He was quite content; and . . . he remained very happy to the end of his days, and those were extraordinarily long [p. 285].''

The story of Bilbo Baggins very much reflects my reactions to reading through the five chapters in this section. Cognitive psychology is certainly one of the most respectable areas of experimental psychology—and also one of the least adventurous. By following the traditional paths, one can become (if not rich) at least respectable. In contrast, to use cognitive psychology to study a topic such as the effects of advertising is, to say the least, unpredictable and risky.

However, my reaction is that these chapters demonstrate that there can indeed be considerable profit from taking such risks. Cognitive psychology has, in my opinion, remained satisfied too long with the investigation of a few narrow content areas. Although research into topics such as memory for verbal material has provided numerous insights, the absence of realism is notable. Thus, until cognitive psychology moves outside the laboratory, its contributions will remain suspect.

The previous chapters not only move beyond traditional research areas, but also demonstrate that cognitive psychology does have a great deal to contribute to the understanding of complex real-world issues and problems. In this commentary, I begin by reviewing what I feel are some of the most important contributions of the first five chapters. I then comment on what I see as some of the common characteristics of the present research approaches in terms of both their advantages and disadvantages. Finally, I attempt to offer some suggestions for future research directions.

THE GUIDES FOR OUR JOURNEY

Let me begin our journey by commenting on the contributions of the various authors as they guide us (much as Gandalf guided Bilbo) through the world of cognitive research on advertising. In reaction to the introductory comments by Harris, I think his description of humans as active symbol manipulators deserves particular emphasis. If there is any one general conclusion that can be drawn from past research on information processing, it is that people are actively perceiving, interpreting, and trying to make sense of the world around them. This is no less true for advertising information than it is for any other type of information. Harris also credits the computer metaphor as a model for instigating much of the development of information processing research. Although this is undoubtably true in an historical sense, I wonder whether this metaphor is as helpful today as it was a few years ago. I anticipate that future developments in cognitive psychology will probably come from efforts which break away from the computer metaphor. As an example, the research by Bower (1981) and his colleagues on the influence of emotional states on learning and memory would seem to be particularly important. My guess is that the greatest contributions in advertising research will come from investigators who are similarly innovative.

The chapter by Mitchell illustrates very nicely the necessary interplay between cognitive psychology and social psychology in the study of advertising. There are some very interesting questions asked about the interrelation between memory and attitudes, and the role that both play in processing strategies for advertising. This was also one of the few chapters to have anything to say about individual differences in cognitive processes; as I will comment later, individual differences are likely to be very important in studying the effects of advertising. More questionably, Mitchell seems in some situations to be generalizing a little too readily from the laboratory environment to the advertising environment. Although I have maintained elsewhere that too much is frequently made of the difference between basic and applied research (Shanteau & Phelps, 1977), one cannot on the other hand be insensitive to the differences. Instead, I would argue that the advertising environment has both common and unique elements relative to laboratory research. We should certainly borrow from these common elements, such as the verbal nature of the stimuli. At the same time, it is also important to look for those elements which are unique, e.g., the persuasive nature of advertising stimuli.

The chapter by Burnkrant and Sawyer very appropriately emphasizes the vital part that degree of consumer involvement plays in understanding the effects of advertising. Indeed, it is surprising that the concept of involvement has not received a closer look by cognitive researchers interested in studying attention. Although this concept has been the focus of considerable research emphasis from those interested in advertising, there has been little corresponding interest by more traditional investigators. Another strength of this chapter was the clear awareness of the importance of attitudinal components in the processing of information. As will be noted, the joint emphasis on both cognitive and social psychology is a refreshing feature of advertising research. With this in mind, it was somewhat surprising that no mention is made in this chapter (or in any other chapter) of the vast literature on the social psychology of impression formation. A great many issues of potential importance to advertising researchers have been studied extensively in the context of impression formation. For instance, the issues of information redundancy and inconsistency (Anderson & Jacobson, 1965), serial position effects (Stewart, 1965), and source credibility effects (Birnbaum & Stegner, 1979) have all been looked at in detail in the impression formation literature. One particularly noteworthy study was conducted by Anderson and Hubert (1963). They found evidence for different serial position effects for words and for impressions based on those words; this implies that separate memory processes may be involved for these two different operations. Such findings would seem to be clearly relevant for advertising researchers interested in memory.

The Alesandrini chapter makes a very strong case for the importance of visual as well as verbal information in advertising. Moreover, the interaction between these two types of information is appropriately stressed. For instance, while it has become a cliche to say that one picture is worth a thousand words, it is also the case that one word can completely change the impact or meaning of a picture. This clearly illustrates the importance of considering the interaction between verbal and visual information in advertising. Among a number of interesting research ideas to come out of this chapter is the notion that a visual mnemonic can act an involuntary device for remembering brand names. Although the use of nonverbal mnemonics has been frequently advocated as a voluntary memory aid (Higbee, 1977), the involuntary use of mnemonics would appear to be a fascinating topic for future investigation by researchers in advertising. Another possible research direction not mentioned by Alesandrini would be to look at how blind (or deaf) consumers react to ads. Besides being a relatively unstudied segment of the population, such consumers might lead researchers to some interesting insights into the importance of combined visual-verbal information. Because congenitally blind consumers would presumably only be receptive to verbal messages on television, they would provide an interesting group to compare to sighted consumers who would be sensitive to both verbal and visual information.

The emphasis on the visual aspects of advertising was also at the heart of the chapter by Rossiter and Percy. There were any number of interesting research ideas in this chapter, including the suggestion to look at the imagery value of various parts of advertising messages. Another fascinating possibility would be to compare the images created by various units of information, such as specific words versus sentences or paragraphs. As the authors note, this topic has been little studied either by cognitive researchers or by advertising researchers. (This is just one of several examples, incidentally, where issues that originally arose from research into advertising may in fact influence future basic research in the laboratory. The flow of ideas is clearly a two-way street: from basic to applied, and from applied to basic.) Another intriguing idea to come out of the chapter is the suggestion that highly imageable verbal messages may interfere with visual materials. Such a possibility is certainly worth additional investigation. One of the less understandable aspects of this chapter was its emphasis on classical conditioning. The authors introduce discussions of conditioning at several places, e.g., as a means of learning evaluative (affective) connotative responses. As this would appear to be a tautology, I would have liked to see a more detailed consideration of how such ideas could be empirically validated.

The final chapter by Batra and Ray summarized and systematized many of the points made in the previous chapters. For instance, the issue of consumer involvement plays a key role in this chapter. In addition, Batra and Ray also consider several traditional variables found to be important in consumer research, e.g., the difference between durable and nondurable products. Similarly, this chapter provides the only discussion (albeit quite brief) of the crucial topic of new product introduction, and the differences between new and old products in advertising. Given the concern with mainstream marketing issues in this chapter, it was rather surprising that there was no mention here (or elsewhere) of the role of price in consumer perceptions. It is widely accepted by marketing researchers that one of the most important, if not *the* most important, determinants of consumer choice is price. If this is so, then a parallel interest in the role of price in advertising research would seem appropriate. Also, I found the authors' discussion of potential hemispheric differences in the brain to be worthy of further consideration. However, my experience has been that attempts to find neurological explanations for complex human behavior have often proved elusive. I would therefore urge some caution in the pursuit of psychobiological explanations of advertising behavior.

With this overview of the various chapters, I now turn to providing more general reactions to the set of chapters as a whole.

LOOKING FOR LANDMARKS

As with any venture, there are certain landmarks along the way that are worth noting. In the case of the previous chapters, some of the common research landmarks (or features) will be familiar to any cognitive psychologist, but many will not be. For instance, in a traditional S-R-O breakdown of an experimental paradigm (Woodworth & Schlosberg, 1954), we would look at the features of Stimulus, Response, and Organism (Subject). As an additional feature, we might also consider the general Context in which the research is being conducted. Thus, there are four landmarks we might look for and we will consider each in turn.

In typical cognitive research, the Stimulus generally takes the form of relatively simple verbal or perceptual material. Although there has been an increasing amount of work using complex prose passages, the majority of research in cognitive psychology has relied on simple stimuli, e.g., individual words presented visually. In the research described here, in contrast, the typical advertising stimuli are quite complex and generally multidimensional. Moreover, the total duration of the stimuli (advertisements typically run 30 or 60 sec) is much longer than normally presented in the laboratory. Even in cases where pictorial information is presented alone in advertising research (see the chapters by Alesandrini, and Rossiter and Percy), the stimuli are much more complex than considered in usual cognitive research. Thus, one major landmark that sets these chapters apart is the complexity, multidimensionality, and duration of the stimulus material.

As far as the Response is concerned, a subject in traditional cognitive research is asked to recall, recognize, or identify what he or she is presented. This then leads to dependent measures such as percent correct, reaction time, etc. With advertising research, however, these traditional measures are deemphasized. Although there is some use of dependent measures involving recognition scores and the like, the primary concern in advertising research is with subjects' subjective reactions. That is, the tendency in the present chapters was to evaluate the affective or emotional response to the advertisements. Thus, we see in advertising research little use of the dependent measures which have characterized traditional cognitive psychological research. Instead, there is greater use of response measures which have typically appeared in social psychology studies.

The Subjects in the usual laboratory research project can be described as being at least moderately attentive and fairly highly motivated to do well in the task at hand. That is, subjects will generally try to make high scores, perform the task quickly, and avoid mistakes. In short, the subjects can be said to be highly involved in the research. In comparison, subjects in real-world advertising situations are inattentive, unmotivated, and little concerned about errors. The subjects, in short, have a low level of involvement. As clearly argued in the Batra and Ray chapter, subjects in this condition are likely to be quite different from the high-involvement subjects typically studied in cognitive research studies. This should, if for no other reason, make it obvious that results obtained in the traditional research environment cannot be simply generalized to the advertising situation. Therefore, any attempts to extend the results of laboratory research to the world of advertising must be approached with appropriate caution.

The Context in which cognitive research is normally conducted is highly controlled, contains few distractions, and is methodologically clean. In addition, experiments are generally conducted in a neutral and unbiased environment. Of course, such a context is usually prescribed as the appropriate framework in which to conduct experimental research. Although the research described in the previous chapters for the most part follows this traditional approach to the design and execution of research, the advertising context is notable on two grounds. First, advertisements in the real world are presented in a terribly noisy environment with many distractions. Although no one would purposely set up such a chaotic situation in a research laboratory, this is precisely the context that advertising research must generalize to. Second, the intent of advertisers, unlike experimental psychologists, is far from neutral. In fact, advertisers are extremely careful to create stimulus situations that are most favorable to their particular product. Thus, the environmental context for advertising is quite different than the usual cognitive psychology investigation.

In total, we can see for these four crucial landmarks that advertising research is notably different from traditional cognitive research. Yet despite the apparent discrepancies, these chapters convincingly demonstrate that cognitive psychology does have something to say about the effects of advertising. In the next section, we explore some of the reasons behind this success in the face of so many incongruities.

NEW PATHS, OLD GOALS

Although the major landmarks of advertising research point in different directions from what normally would be expected in information processing analyses, I believe that cognitive psychology can nevertheless make a major contribution to understanding advertising. That contribution comes not so much from generalizing the findings of cognitive research as it does from borrowing the approach used to study cognitive processes. That is, because of differences such as those discussed in the previous section, we should not necessarily expect the findings of cognitive research conducted in a laboratory setting to generalize to the advertising situation. Instead, the value of cognitive psychology for advertising is in the way that problems are conceptualized and in the way that research methods and analyses are designed to investigate information processing. In short, what cognitive research has to offer is a new pathway to the old traditional goal of trying to better understand the effects of advertising.

Based on this observation, there are three questions that deserve consideration. First, what aspects of the approach taken by cognitive psychology are likely to be of most value in advertising research? As I see it, the two most relevant aspects of cognitive research are (1) the emphasis on psychological processes in theory and methodology, and (2) the study of these processes through a divide-and-conquer strategy. The key notion is that the human cognitive system is made up of a series of separable systems that can be studied more-or-less independently. Although there are any number of ways in which information processing might be studied, the approach that has become most popular is to use a functional breakdown based on perception, attention, memory, etc. The success of this approach can be attested to by the contributions made by cognitive researchers in a variety of areas (e.g., see Anderson, 1980). Therefore, what cognitive psychology brings to advertising research is an emphasis on separable psychological processes.

The second question is can the cognitive processing approach work as well in understanding advertising as it has worked in other areas of research? After all, just because an approach works well in a laboratory setting does not mean that the same approach will work as well in the study of complex phenomena. In particular, the divide-and-conquer strategy might be called into question. Perhaps situations as complex as advertising should only be studied in a representative or natural environment (for a more complete development of this line of argument, see Brunswik, 1956). The answer to this question is of course largely empirical; if the divide-and-conquer approach to studying processes helps us better understand the effects of advertising, then that should be reason enough for using the approach. The present set of chapters provide, I believe, just such a positive set of demonstrations. I conclude, therefore, that the separation-of-processes strategy has considerable potential for studying the effects of advertising.

The last question is whether the cognitive approach is sufficient to understand the effects of advertising. The answer from the previous chapters is clearly no; other areas of psychology must also be looked to for contributions. For instance, these chapters place a great deal of emphasis on research related to attitudes and social psychology. There seems to be far more concern, than would normally be expected in cognitive research, with the social/personality approaches to psychology. (As a rough index, I counted the number of citations made to social and personality journals in the chapters; I found over 40 citations to research articles in social/personality journals. This is certainly a higher number than would normally be expected in any typical set of papers on cognitive psychology.) Thus, the previous five chapters demonstrate that the processing approach can and must be expanded to include issues outside of the traditional cognitive framework.

A ROADBLOCK

Despite the general optimism with which I view the potential of the cognitive processing approach to advertising research, I am concerned about the lack of theoretical perspective in most of the chapters. With some exceptions, there is very little in the way of testable theory presented in any of the material. That's not to say that these particular authors have overlooked theory in developing their chapters; rather, this comment is a reflection on the lack of theory in advertising research (and consumer psychology) as a whole. The problem is that while cognitive psychology, as argued earlier, can provide many useful tools for answering questions about advertising, it does not necessarily suggest what questions to ask. Useful questions come from testable theories and precise hypotheses. Unfortunately, such theory-based questions are in short supply in the current advertising/consumer literature.

One source of this problem, which I see in the form of a roadblock, lies in the content specific nature of advertising research. Unlike cognitive psychology, advertising has a highly focused area of substantive concern. An investigator interested in verbal memory can potentially make use of any of a wide variety of stimulus materials and tasks to study a particular research problem. In contrast, advertising research by its very nature is much more restricted in regard to stimuli and tasks. (This is a reflection of the fact that the reason for studying advertising is to answer questions about advertising, not about cognitive processes.)

Although the five chapters contain numerous examples of how a cognitive processing orientation can lead to sound research methodology and analyses, there are fewer examples of new theoretical insights. Yet, additional advances in advertising and consumer research are most likely to come when these areas have developed their own theoretical and conceptual frameworks (see Troutman & Shanteau, 1976). Presently, there are plenty of borrowed concepts in these areas, but little in the way of original theories.

Of course, there are numerous examples of global "theories" of advertising/consumer behavior which often take the form of complex diagrams to describe the potential effects of every mechanism known to influence consumers (e.g., see Engel, Blackwell, & Kollat, 1978). Although such global frameworks may provide useful expositional devices, they do not constitute proper scientific theories in the sense of providing testable hypotheses. That is, these frameworks do not lead to specific researchable questions and they cannot be disproved in any meaningful way. Thus, what are generally viewed as theories in the advertising/consumer research area are not really theories at all.

The lack of a theoretical orientation is not only troubling at a scientific level, but it may also be limiting in a purely practical sense. No less than the basic researcher, the practicing advertiser or marketer wants to know what makes a consumer "tick." These practitioners also want answers to theoretically-based questions such as what factors are important in controlling consumer reactions to advertising? Yet, as argued by Foxall (1980) "it is probably fair to say that the majority of models (i.e., theories) mean little to the businessman who requires a general understanding of how his (sic) customers act and react [p. 22]" (also see Jacoby, 1978). Therefore, the lack of insightful theories is restrictive at both a scientific and a practical level.

SOME POSSIBLE AVENUES TO SUCCESS

Although the advertising/consumer research area as a whole can be faulted for its lack of theory, the present chapters do suggest some possible direction for further theorizing. These ideas, while not necessarily providing the entire basis for a theory, may at least point to some elements and concerns that any theories in this area must reflect. I next discuss what I feel may be four of the most important of these elements.

First, as emphasized in the chapter by Mitchell, the role that attention plays is particularly vital in understanding the effects of advertising. Although there has been a great deal of research on attention from an information processing perspective (e.g., Norman, 1976), most of this work was conducted in situations that are far different than found in advertising. Among other differences, it is worth reiterating the low-involvement role of the subject and the persuasive intent of the messages (see the chapters by Burnkrant and Sawyer, and Batra and Ray for detailed discussions of these issues). Such situations have not been adequately addressed in the traditional approaches to attention. A great deal of consideration, at both the theoretical and empirical levels, is therefore needed into the operation of attention in advertising (see Bettman, 1979, for an initial attempt to incorporate attention into a theory of consumer behavior).

Second, a related concept that undoubtedly deserves detailed consideration in advertising research is that of level-of-processing (Craik, 1979). This concept has, of course, been much discussed in the cognitive literature (e.g., Rumelhart, 1977), but has not yet received much emphasis in advertising/consumer research.

However, the level-of-processing concept raises a number of potentially interesting questions that might be addressed by advertising investigators. For instance, what are the relevant levels for processing advertising information? Also, what would a theory of processing levels look like when applied to advertising?

Third, the nonverbal aspects of advertising are likely to be quite crucial. As extensively discussed in both the Alesandrini and the Rossiter and Percy chapters, the purely visual aspects of advertising are clearly very important. For instance, although there has been a great deal of traditional research on topics related to imagery, there has been little theoretical consideration of imagery in the context of complex stimulus materials, such as found in advertising. Also, there is a need for theoretical analyses of the interaction between visual and verbal information. Although cognitive researchers have tended to compartmentalize visual and verbal cognitive processes, advertising researchers may well profit by examining the joint effect of these two processes.

Fourth, the theoretical relationship between cognitive processes and social processes such as attitudes, beliefs, and motivations must be made clear. Although cognitive psychology has generally been little concerned with these social processes, they are essential to any understanding of consumer reactions to advertising. This point was made clear in nearly all of the chapters in section II by their repeated references to the topic of attitudes. For the most part, however, these references were made in passing and did not incorporate social processes in any fundamental way. For instance, the Fishbein and Ajzen (1975) approach to attitude measurement was frequently cited. Yet, this approach has been found to be seriously lacking both by researchers in social psychology (e.g., McGuire, 1976) and in consumer psychology (e.g., Foxall, 1980). As one alternative, the script approach proposed by Abelson (1976) may provide an avenue with more potential. In any case, it seems apparent that a more thorough understanding is needed of the relationship between attitudes and cognition.

WHAT'S MISSING?

Aside from the preceeding concerns, there are three other issues that I feel are of major importance for theory, but which were overlooked in almost all of the previous chapters. The first of these omissions concerns the part that decision and choice processes play in consumer response to advertisements. Product choice behavior seemingly lies at the center of what advertising is all about (also, see Bettman, 1979). Yet despite this central importance, there is almost nothing mentioned in any of the chapters about how the cognitive processes studied interact with choice mechanisms. This is an oversight which must be corrected before there can be any complete account of the effects of advertising.

The lack of concern for decision making shown in these chapters is not unique. Indeed, there is a similar oversight in most other current work on cognitive processes (Estes, 1980). Part of the problem is a lack of familiarity with current perspectives on judgment and choice research. As Estes (1980) noted, many cognitive researchers still view decision making in terms of a signal detection approach. This is an approach which was introduced into psychology shortly after World War II as an alternative to classic psychophysics. Although the contributions of signal detection research have been extensive (e.g., see Green & Swets, 1966), this is far from the latest word on what is known about judgment and choice processes. As a researcher who has studied decision processes in a variety of settings (e.g., Shanteau & Phelps, 1977), I find it particularly unfortunate that cognitive researchers should be so little aware of the current research in decision making. Decision research is, in fact, becoming increasingly cognitive in its concern with "predecisional processes" (Einhorn & Hogarth, 1981). Thus, I believe that there is a great deal to be gained from a closer attention to judgment and decision making mechanisms.

The second area of serious oversight concerns the importance of what Simon (1957) termed "bounded rationality." This concept states that cognitive limitations leave humans with little option but to construct simplified models of the world and to act on those models. As Simon (1957) argues, a person "behaves rationally with respect to this model . . . (although) such behavior is not even approximately optimal with respect to the real world [p. 198]." Simon (1957) goes on to add that "to predict his behavior, we must understand the way in which this simplified model is constructed, and its construction will certainly be related to his psychological properties as a perceiving, thinking, and learning animal [p. 198]." In short, Simon provides a persuasive argument as to the inevitability of bounded rationality in cognitive psychology.

Although decision researchers have devoted considerable energy to studying the role of bounded rationality (Kahneman & Tversky, 1973; Slovic, Fischhoff, & Lichtenstein, 1977), there seems to have been little corresponding attention from other researchers. Yet, the importance of the concept seems clear in information processing generally and advertising processes specifically. Such questions come to mind as what models do people construct of the world of advertisements, and how do cognitive limitations influence peoples' behavior as consumers? While the present chapters do contain some suggestive indications as to some of the cognitive limitations facing consumers, more emphasis in this direction would be useful.

The third area in which I see serious omissions is the study of individual differences in the cognitive processes of consumers. The role of such differences is clearly of importance in studying the effects of advertising. Different people don't all react to ads in the same way. While individual differences of various types were mentioned in several of the present chapters, they received little emphasis. For example, in their extensive list of important variables in advertising, Batra and Ray at the end of their chapter mention only one obvious individual difference variable and that has to do with amount of consumer experience.

As one possible direction for future research, I would suggest that some of the ideas advanced originally by Brunswik (1956) and later by Hammond (see Hammond, McClelland, & Mumpower, 1980) might provide a useful basis for looking at individual differences in response to advertising. In brief, these researchers have proposed that there is a continuum of thinking which ranges from rational/analytic at one extreme to intuitive/emotional at the other, with a middle ground labeled "quasirational" in between. Analysis of consumers with these varying styles of thinking may prove to be quite informative.

There has been, of course, an increasing amount of research effort devoted to individual differences in the cognitive processing literature. While much of this research has focused on individual difference variables which would not be of interest in advertising research, there are some types of cognitive differences which may be of real value. One example would be the work on developmental trends in information processing capabilities (see Piaget, 1954). Other more recent research on individual differences in cognition may also be quite relevant, e.g., Hunt's work (Hunt & Lansman, 1975) on high versus low verbal subjects may be especially appropriate. Such research would seem to be of considerable importance in increasing our understanding of the effects of advertising on different types of consumers.

END OF THE ROAD

As we come to the end of our journey, it may be well to remind ourselves of one important fact—advertising may simply not be all that important to consumers. As related in the Rossiter and Percy chapter, only 22% of television viewers watch commercials in their entirety. In the long run, this indicates that consumers have a lot more (or less?) on their minds then advertising.

A study by Achenbaum (1972) is relevant on this point. As part of a large scale study on the effects of advertising, Achenbaum found that most consumers were willing to try new products as a result of advertising. However, he also found that personal experience with products exerted a very powerful influence on product choice. As Achenbaum (1972) observes, "consumers are choosing brands based on positive product experience regardless of the advertising [p. 10] . . . . people do not rely only on what they hear or see [p. 13]." Based on these findings, Achenbaum concluded: "If advertising affects their attitudes, it hardly mesmerizes them [p. 13]."

Similar sentiments have been voiced by Foxall (1980), who concluded that studies of consumer behavior have shown that advertising is far from being manipulative and all-powerful. This conclusion is supported by research on cognitive processes which has demonstrated that even an inattentive and unmotivated consumer is a very complex and active processor of information. Thus, such a consumer cannot be easily manipulated by simple exposure to advertising.

It is therefore important to emphasize that advertising may not be very important in the larger scheme of things. It would seem appropriate to keep in mind the lesson of Bilbo Baggins following his adventure. As Gandalf, his guide on the quest, tells Bilbo in their final conversation: "You are a very fine person, Mr. Baggins, and I am very fond of you; but you are only quite a little fellow in a wide world after all!" (Tolkien, 1966, pp. 286–287).

ACKNOWLEDGMENT

The preparation of this chapter was supported in part by Contract MDA903-80-C-0209 from the Army Research Institute. The author wishes to convey his gratitude to the patient and helpful guidance of Richard Harris in the preparation of this manuscript.

REFERENCES

Abelson, R. P. Script processing in attitude formation and decision making. In J. Carroll & J. Payne (Eds.), *Cognition and social behavior*. Hillsdale, N.J.: Lawrence Erlbaum Associates, 1976.

Achenbaum, A. A. Advertising doesn't manipulate consumers. *Journal of Advertising Research, 1972, 2,* 3–13.

Anderson, J. R. *Cognitive psychology and its implications*. San Francisco: Freeman, 1980.

Anderson, N. H., & Hubert, S. Effects of concomitant verbal recall on order effects in personality impression formation. *Journal of Verbal Learning and Verbal Behavior, 1963, 2,* 379–391.

Anderson, N. H., & Jacobson, A. Effect of stimulus inconsistency and discounting instructions in personality impression formation. *Journal of Personality and Social Psychology, 1965, 2,* 531–539.

Bettman, J. R. *An information processing theory of consumer choice*. Reading, Mass.: Addison-Wesley, 1979.

Birnbaum, M. H., & Stegner, S. E. Source credibility: Expertise, bias, and the judge's point of view. *Journal of Personality and Social Psychology, 1979, 37,* 48–74.

Bower, G. H. Mood and memory. *American Psychologist, 1981, 36,* 129–148.

Brunswik, E. *Perception and the representative design of psychological experiments*. (2nd ed.). Berkeley: University of California Press, 1956.

Craik, F. I. M. Levels of processing: Overview and closing comments. In L. S. Cermak & F. I. M. Craik (Eds.), *Levels of processing in human memory*. Hillsdale, N.J.: Lawrence Erlbaum Associates, 1979.

Einhorn, H., & Hogarth, R. M. Behavioral decision theory: Processes of judgment and choice. *Annual Review of Psychology, 1981, 32,* 53–88.

Engel, J. G., Blackwell, R. D., & Kollat, D. T. *Consumer behavior*. Hinsdale, Ill.: Dryden, 1978.

Estes, W. K. Comments on directions and limitations of current efforts toward theories of decision making. In T. S. Wallsten (Ed.), *Cognitive processes in choice and decision behavior*. Hillsdale, N.J.: Lawrence Erlbaum Associates, 1980.

Fishbein, M., & Ajzen, I. *Belief, attitude, intention and behavior: An introduction to theory and research*. Reading, Mass: Addison-Wesley, 1975.

Foxall, G. R. *Consumer behavior: A practical guide*. New York: Wiley, 1980.

Green, D. M., & Swets, J. A. *Signal detection theory and psychophysics.* New York: Wiley, 1966.

Hammond, K. R., McClelland, G., & Mumpower, J. *Human judgment and decision making: Theories, methods, and procedures.* New York: Praeger, 1980.

Higbee, K. L. *Your memory: How it works and how to improve it.* Englewood Cliffs, N.J.: Prentice Hall, 1977.

Hunt, E., & Lansman, M. Cognitive theory applied to individual differences. In W. K. Estes (Ed.), *Handbook of cognitive processes: Introduction to concepts and issues.* (Vol. 1). Hillsdale, N.J.: Lawrence Erlbaum Associates, 1975.

Jacoby, J. Consumer research: A state of the art review. *Journal of Marketing,* 1978, *42,* 87–96.

Kahneman, D., & Tversky, A. On the psychology of prediction. *Psychological Review,* 1973, *80,* 237–251.

McGuire, W. J. Some internal psychological factors influencing consumer choice. *Journal of Consumer Research,* 1976, *2,* 302–319.

Piaget, J. *The construction of reality in the child.* New York: Basic Books, 1954.

Norman, D. A. *Memory and attention: An introduction to human information processing.* (2nd ed.). New York: Wiley, 1976.

Rumelhart, D. E. *Introduction to human information processing.* New York: Wiley, 1977.

Shanteau, J., & Phelps, R. H. Judgment and swine: Approaches and issues in applied judgment analysis. In M. F. Kaplan & S. Schwartz (Eds.), *Human judgment and decision processes in applied settings.* New York: Academic Press, 1977.

Simon, H. A. *Models of man.* New York: Wiley, 1957.

Slovic, P., Fischhoff, B., & Lichtenstein, S. Behavioral decision theory. *Annual Review of Psychology,* 1977, *28,* 1–39.

Stewart, R. H. Effect of continuous responding on the order effect in personality impression formation. *Journal of Personality and Social Psychology,* 1965, *1,* 161–165.

Tolkien, J. R. R. *The Hobbit or there and back again.* (Rev. Ed.) New York: Ballantine Books, 1966. (Originally published, 1937).

Troutman, C. M., & Shanteau, J. Do consumers evaluate products by adding or averaging attribute information? *Journal of Consumer Research,* 1976, *3,* 101–106.

Woodworth, R. S., & Schlosberg, H. *Experimental psychology.* New York: Holt, 1954.

III AN INFORMATION-PROCESSING APPROACH TO MISLEADING ADVERTISING

7 Introduction: "What is Misleading?"

Herbert J. Rotfeld
Pennsylvania State University

INTRODUCTION

A local student-run radio station recently called my office, desiring a taped interview for an upcoming documentary on advertising and consumers. As the tape recorder was started, the first question was "Which ads or types of advertising are misleading?" To the interviewer's dismay, the reply was another question, "Do you mean as an individual consumer, or legally as per the concerns of regulatory bodies, or in terms of research findings on consumer responses to various types of ads?" The three areas are interrelated, but each address slightly different areas of primary concern. This section of the book looks at the third, based on issues raised by the first two.

The following section, entitled "An Information-Processing Approach to Misleading Advertising," would intuitively appear to be a rather narrowly defined area of interest. Or so one might think. However, authors for this section represent a broad range of academic backgrounds, such as psychology, linguistics, journalism, and marketing. None are lawyers, yet the topic relates to a clearly legal issue and concern, one often discussed in reference to the regulatory involvement of the Federal Trade Commission. Although almost every reading includes a discussion of the FTC and its activities regulating advertising content, research discussed in relation to those activities goes in several different directions. The individual discussions might appear contradictory if viewed solely in terms of legal activities and guidelines. However, this section's concern is in approaches to information processing research, not legal case history and decision logic. Variations in perspective represent the different values and concepts of the authors' academic backgrounds; the perspectives complement rather than contradict.

The research approaches presented in this section might best be understood in terms of two broad layperson concerns raised by the issue of misleading advertising. First, can (or should) consumers "trust" the variety of claims made in advertised messages? Advertisers desire to inform and persuade various audiences about products, services or ideas, such that consumer trust of message veracity is often seen as important for the advertisements to have their desired impact. On the audiences' side, there are questions of how much they can rely on such messages, especially as advertising is their main source of market information (Rotzoll, 1976; Rotzoll, Haefner, & Sandage, 1976).

Related to the concern of consumer trust, the second concern involves activities of government and business organizations involved in the regulation of certain types of advertised claims. The modern consumerist clime desires that consumers be able to believe advertised claims as true, so the issue is one of what types of advertised claims, production techniques, and message forms should be regulated and/or proscribed. Of the possible ways that consumers can potentially be misled, it still must be decided where regulation is needed, where consumers could be expected to recognize the possible deception without being harmed, and where the deceptive potential is so small, where so few people might be deceived as to to make regualtion of such messages unnecessary. However, this related question of how many people must be deceived for the claim to be proscribed would be seen as a legal question and not a question researchers can decide for bodies such as the FTC (Gellhorn, 1969; Preston, 1976; Rotfeld & Preston, 1981).

This points up the reason that advertising research perspectives were distinguished from those of both consumers and legal–regulatory bodies. To the authors in this anthology, a layperson would be defined as someone who is not a student of either advertising-communications theory or consumer decision processes. Such a definition describes *both consumers and lawyers and Federal Trade Commissioners*. While both groups have certain understandings or assumptions of how people might think, they are not students of research or theories on areas such as information-processing. Although the early 1970s marked a shift toward the Commission using more consumer research data as evidence in deceptive advertising cases (Brandt & Preston, 1977), the FTC's procedures remain jurisprudential in nature. The decision basis is legal, not the academic concerns of research paradigms on information processing, marketing, consumer psychology or other fields that study consumers' mental processes. The legal view (referring to misleading advertising under the heading of deceptive advertising) involves its own set of definitions and is concerned with rules of evidence and procedures, past case findings and guidelines and the logical consistency of definitions, evidence presented, and past decisions (Preston, 1976, 1977). Similarly, the research is not presented as a basis for academic discussion as to its worth or value. Research data can only serve as evidence within this legal framework.

DISCUSSION

It would be a simple task to compile a listing of the past FTC cases and court decisions that have built up the current legal definition of deception. They include (Francois, 1978, p. 393):

1. A statement may be deceptive even though it might be literally or technically interpreted as accurate and true.
2. Ambiguous statements that readily lend themselves to both truthful and misleading interpretations are deceptive.
3. An ad is deceptive if it fails to disclose important facts where such omissions would deceive a substantial segment of the public.
4. The Commission need not establish that there was actual deception (or actual damage to the public), only the capacity or tendency of the ad to deceive.

This is not a comprehensive listing of all factors in the legal definition of deception. However, it should be clear that the legal definition is properly framed in the impression the ad makes on consumers and that the communication intent of the advertiser is irrelevant. Left unstated are research paradigms and/or methodologies that should be utilized to determine exactly which ads are deceptive. Simply speaking, the legal question for research is one of comparing what is communicated to consumers with what is true and what is untrue.

The above list points up another distinction between legal/regulatory concerns and the perspectives discussed in the following readings. Several of the authors frame their discussion in terms of whether or not consumers actually believe certain claims. Although consumer belief is important in determining actual deception, the Commission's main concern involves the *potential* for deception (4 above), and this is a question of advertising communications as distinct from belief. For a claim to be proscribed, the FTC need only find that the ad has a "capacity or tendency to deceive" a substantial portion of the population in that it communicates false claims (Reed & Coalson, 1977). In short, deceptive capacity may exist prior to actual deception—if a false claim is communicated, it is assumed to possess the capacity to be believed and cause actual deception. If the advertiser wishes to assert that such claims are not believed by consumers and will not cause actual deception, that would be her or his defense to charges of deceptive advertising.

To researchers, it might appear more desirable for the FTC to be required to show actual deception, that consumers believed the claims important in their purchase decisions. However, such a change in the legal requirements would entail an increase in the Commission's burden of proof. The present minimal standard is allowable because the regulatory concern is one of controlling the advertising, not punishing the advertisers, such that the advertiser's literal statements and communications intent is irrelevant (Preston, 1975). The Commission desires that advertising communications be truthful, that consumers be able to trust advertising messages—bringing us full circle, back to the first lay concern presented herein.

It should be noted that there exists a legal class of advertising claims called puffery that, based on what the ad literally states and not on communication or information–processing research, are presumed patently unbelievable such that defendant research showing such consumer non-belief has historically been considered unnecessary (Rotfeld & Preston, 1981). Preston (1975) has detailed how this distinction is an illogical anomaly of modern advertising law, and a growing body of literature points out how puffery should not be treated any differently from all other types of advertsed claims (Oliver, 1979; Rotfeld, 1979; Rotfeld & Preston, 1981; Rotfeld & Rotzoll, 1980, 1981; Shimp, 1979).

At the time of this writing, however, puffery remains as a class of literal advertised claims for which a defense that such claims are not believed does not require the support of consumer research. Some of the readings in this text add research insight that should invalidate laws and regulations that treat puffery any different from all other types of advertised claims. Based on such studies, it could logically be asserted that an advertiser's defense that a false communication does not cause actual deception should be based on consumer research, not the ad's literal content (Rotfeld, 1979; Rotfeld & Preston, 1981). However, these are not "changes" in legal definitions of deception, but rather, research based evidence that should influence legal rules and decision guidelines.

So while many critics attack advertising for the ways it might be misleading consumers, and while misleading advertising is a continuing concern in the legal realm under the heading of advertising deception, such perspectives remain as having their basis in the arguments of laypersons, hopefully drawing insight and direction from studies such as those discussed in this section. Readings in this section are not all *directly* relevant to the concerns of advertising's critics or legal evidence needs of the FTC. However, the prime aim is not to "answer" consumerist and/or legal issues, nor are they trying to decide on *the* methodology for use in the legal realm.

Although a lawyer might feel that the following research and background conceptualizations are not directly relevant to certain legal concerns, it does not mean it is not an informative and valuable addition to our understanding of how people think. This text contains a section on misleading advertising not because it wishes to "answer" any legal issues or problems; it is using the research questions raised by this concern as a common thread or starting point for discussion and analysis. The authors use this issue, the two broad layperson concerns stated at the start of this introduction, to point up possible gaps in our knowledge of how consumers process information. This is a pragmatic and important question to which bodies of research and analysis can be meaningfully applied.

From this starting point, the following researchers go in several different "directions" for research. However, because none are presenting *the* legal perspective, there are no real contradictions in their analysis. They all could give evidence related to concerns in the legal realm. Each direction for research represents an application of the authors' academic backgrounds to questions of misleading advertising. Using this as a starting point for inquiry, there are many possible areas for research.

First are the perspectives of linguistics, both looking at how different claim forms are handled and might be "manipulated" by advertisers. Garfinkel looks at the literal claim forms, how consumers might interpret such forms, and where consumer misunderstandings might exist. As such, his analysis has the clearest intuitive relationship with lay perspectives. Coleman takes this perspective a step further, looking at semantic and prosodic elements as factors to provide a general context for a broadcast message and to help insure or reinforce that a message's meaning is clearly conveyed to the intended audience. Taking a rather unique view of the issue, she points out how a misleading message might be hidden from most viewers, or how an overt disclaimer's impact might be blunted by the context of the total message.

A following reading, by a scholar of marketing and business, deals with more directly relevant legal concerns of deceptive advertising. Shimp starts with the fact that a large amount of commercial advertising utilizes nonobjective, evaluative claims rather than concrete and factual, and then illustrates how the former type of claims can be a source of deceiving consumers as readily as the latter. Shimp's discussion can be related to those of Garfinkel and Coleman in that he cites studies finding how nonobjective advertised claims, because of their communications forms and context, are perceived and believed by some consumers as if they were objective facts.

The following two readings, by psychologists, address slightly different perspectives and concerns. Harris, Dubitsky, and Bruno present an innovative and interesting approach for researching the impacts of potentially misleading claims on consumers. Monaco and Kaiser point out how information processing is a continual, ongoing process, and our need for research on misleading advertising (as with other areas of experimental research) also involves questions of research procedures as we desire validity in terms of audiences at home.

A FINAL NOTE

Some of the authors might have initiated their inquiries desiring to directly answer legal questions and issues in this area. Questions of how well they might have succeeded will be deferred to Ivan Preston's concluding section of comments and reactions. The prime contribution of these readings is best summarized in the final paragraph of that by Harris, Dubitsky, and Bruno:

> Misleading advertising is but one area where the methods and findings of experimental cognitive psychology [or linguistics or marketing or communications re-

search] can be brought directly to bear on some applied problem of considerable social interest and importance. The benefits are two-fold: applied results offer insight into real-world issues and serve as converging evidence for psychological [or linguistic or marketing or communications research] theories and models.

In this book's introduction, Harris discusses the problem of how research literature in advertising is fragmented by disciplines and reported in a variety of journals with limited common readerships. Advertising has many facets that can be viewed from several different perspectives. The readers of the different journals often have very limited common basis for discussion other than some type of interest in advertising. Misleading advertising presents a common thread for the following authors' research and discussion—a rare opportunity for people from such intuitively interrelated but pragmatically distinct disciplines to present their differing ideas and learn from the insight of each other.

REFERENCES

Brandt, M. T., & Preston, I. L. The FTC's use of evidence to determine deception. *Journal of Marketing*, 1977, *41*, 54–62.

Francois, W. E. *Mass media law and regulation*. Columbus: Grid, 1978.

Gellhorn, E. Proof of consumer deception before the FTC. *University of Kansas Law Review*, 1969, *17*, 559–572.

Oliver, R. L. An interpretation of the attitudinal and behavior effects of puffery. *Journal of Consumer Affairs*, 1979, *13*, 8–27.

Preston, I. L. *The great American blow-up: Puffery in advertising and selling*. Madison: University of Wisconsin Press, 1975.

Preston, I. L. A Comment on "Defining misleading advertising" and "Deception in advertising." *Journal of Marketing*, 1976, *40*, 54–60.

Preston, I. L. The FTC's handling of puffery and other selling claims made by implication. *Journal of Business Research*, 1977, *5*, 155–81.

Reed, O. L., & Coalson, J. L. Eighteenth-century legal doctrine meets twentieth-century marketing techniques: F.T.C. regulation of emotionally conditioning advertising. *Georgia Law Review*, 1977, *11*, 733–782.

Rotfeld, H. J. *Advertising puffery as deception: Evidence and arguments*. Boston College School of Management working paper 79-50, 1979.

Rotfeld, H. J. & Preston, I. L. The potential impact of research on advertising law. *Journal of Advertising Research*, 1981, *21*, 9–17.

Rotfeld, H. J., & Rotzoll, K. B. Is advertising puffery believed? *Journal of Advertising*, 1980, *9*, 16–20, 45.

Rotfeld, H. J. & Rotzoll, K. B. Puffery vs. fact claims—really different? *Current Issues and Research in Advertising*, 1981, 85–104.

Rotzoll, K. B. Advertising in the large-four institutional views. *Journal of Advertising*, 1976, *5*, 9–15.

Rotzoll, K. B., Haefner, J. E., & Sandage, C. H. *Advertising in contemporary society: Perspectives toward understanding*. Columbus: Grid, 1976.

Shimp, T. A. Social-psychological (mis)representations in television advertising. *Journal of Consumer Affairs*, 1979, *13*, 28–40.

8

A Pragmatic Approach to Truth in Advertising

Andrew Garfinkel
Manufacturers Hanover Trust Company

INTRODUCTION

There are generally two schools of thought about what advertisers have in mind when they advertise their products or services.[1] On the one hand, advertisers have been accused of using illegal and unethical means of persuading the public to buy their various products and services. Packard (1957) claims that a kind of "mass psychoanalysis" has been used by these "professional persuaders" in their attempts to more effectively sell their goods. On the other hand, Lieberman (1979, p. 1) states that "there is nothing new about the notion that advertising should be truthful and advertising claims should be valid. Since the dawn of advertising, claims were supposed to be truthful." In either case, advertising does play a large role in our economic system in providing information so that consumers can decide between the various alternatives in the marketplace. When it happens that that information is misleading or deceptive, then advertising has not lived up to its responsibility in this respect.

There are essentially five different forces at work which oversee advertisers' claims to make sure that they are honest. (1) The Federal Trade Commission is the main governmental agency whose task is to prevent or correct unfair practices in both general commerce and advertising. Insofar as faulty advertising is con-

---

[1]This chapter is drawn from the author's doctoral dissertation, "A Sociolinguistic Analysis of the Language of Advertising," prepared at Georgetown University in Washington, D.C., in 1978. Dr. Garfinkel, who takes sole responsibility for the contents of this article, is currently an Assistant Secretary in the Marketing Research Department for Manufacturers Hanover Trust Company in New York City.

cerned, the commission's activities are largely devoted to eliminating advertising practices that are considered to be unfair, misleading or deceptive. (2) The industry has self-regulatory bodies, like the National Advertising Review Board, which work toward much the same end. (3) Each of the major television networks has a commercial clearance department. (4) Consumer groups, like Action for Children's Television or the Public Interest Research Group, also oversee advertisers' activities. (5) Even competitive advertisers can help to regulate each other. As Lieberman points out, when Pepsi Cola issued the Pepsi taste challenge to Coca Cola, Coca Cola retaliated and demanded to have validated the research upon which Pepsi's claim was based. Yet even with all these deterrents, there is advertising that still manages to get through which some people will inevitably complain about. Because the problem of deceptive advertising is both revealed and hidden by the use of language, it seems obvious that a linguistic analysis will prove fruitful.

The analysis of deception that is undertaken here starts from a neutral point of view and works toward a determination of whether or not certain television commercials can be considered to be misleading or deceptive. It is assumed here that television commercials constitute a kind of communication vehicle whereby advertisers try to convey useful information to consumers about the various alternatives in the marketplace. In any kind of information exchange, a tacit communication pact exists between speaker and hearer that that information will be truthful and relevant. When that pact is breached and the information given in a commercial is false and/or irrelevant, if the consumer is injured either economically or physically, then the advertiser may be guilty of misrepresenting his product. The goal of this study is to show how a linguistic explanation of how meaning arises in any communicative context can help elucidate when and if such misrepresentation is possible. In that vein, a pragmatic approach to truth and meaning is needed.

In *How To Do Things With Words*, J. L. Austin (1962, pp. 143–144) states that "the truth or falsity of statements is affected by what they leave out or put in (and stand for) a general dimension of being a right or proper thing to say as opposed to a wrong thing in these circumstances, to this audience, for these purposes and with these intentions." That is, truth is a pragmatic question. A sentence or discourse can be defective in some way by virtue of its pragmatic inappropriateness to the social context of its utterance.

Such a pragmatic theory of truth is needed to understand the issue of truth and deception in advertising. Various pragmatic assumptions and informational expectations adhere to the advertising context and play a role in what exactly the consumer understands about the product as a result of being exposed to some form of advertising for that product. For example, Garfinkel (1975) showed that consumers make an assumption, unless they explicitly know otherwise, that any product will prove safe in its normal use. When information about possible health hazards is omitted from the advertisement, the advertiser implies that such safety is the case. If that implication turns out to be false, that is, the consumers' assumption of harmlessness is breached, then there may be a case of deception. This would be an appropriate explanation of Cox, Fellmuth, and Schulz's (1969) complaint that any advertising for diet sodas is deceptive if it does not mention that the artificial sweeteners used in the soda may be harmful to internal body organs. Nowhere does the advertiser overtly state that the soda is safe to drink, but it is a belief which is seemingly affirmed by the absence of any denial. What the consumer understands, then, is a function of such pragmatic aspects of the language of advertising.

WHAT IS DECEPTION?

A viable definition of deceptive advertising has two parts: what the audience understands the message to be (1) must differ from the reality of the situation and (2) it must affect the public's buying behavior in a detrimental way.[2] Aaker (1974) points out that both components—a false claim and physical or economic injury to the consumer—are necessary to adequately prove deception. What is false is not necessarily deceptive if no injury results. Lieberman (1979) gives an example that demonstrates this point. He reports that a flea and tick spray manufacturer wanted to use a dog in its television commercial. Instead of infesting the dog with fleas and ticks to show how the spray worked, the advertiser wanted to apply kerosene to the dog, which would only temporarily make him itch and which would cause him no harm. Although technically the flea and tick spray was ridding the dog of the kerosene itch and not of any flea and tick itch, the network clearance people accepted the commercial on the grounds that the visual appearance of the dog's scratching himself was still accurate. The literal falsity of the claim, in that it was not substantiated by the demonstration, was not considered serious enough to cause any injury.

The point is that if a statement is false, then physical and/or economic injury must be proved if one is to claim deception. It is not always the case that the omission of some information will lead to a potentially false implication. Surely the omission from an advertisement of possible health hazards can be deceptive if the consumer suffers bodily harm in the product's normal use. However, Garfinkel (1975) reports that almost 75 percent of his corpus of television commercials made no reference to the fact that the advertised product has a price or that it is necessary to spend money in order to acquire it. In spite of this omission, there

---

[2]The first half of this definition applies to any false statement. See Tarski (1956, p. 155), "a true sentence is one which states that the state of affairs is so and so, and the state of affairs indeed is so and so."

is no implication that the item is available for free because prior knowledge of the nature of general commerce (i.e., you have to spend money to obtain a product) tells us otherwise. That is, when the consumer goes to the store, he will not be surprised that he needs money to get his merchandise (even though this may not have been mentioned in the commercial) because he will not expect that anything else would be the case. Therefore, he will not be injured.

One other example will prove this point sufficiently. Garfinkel (1977) reports on a study of income tax preparation services done by Consumers Union. In that study, Consumers Union states that H&R Block advertises as one of its 17 reasons to come to them that, if necessary, they will accompany the taxpayer to the Internal Revenue Service if he is audited. However, IRS rules *require* that the preparer accompany the taxpayer in such a situation. In that case, Block is just like any other tax preparation service and the consumer obtains no special benefit by using it. The assumption is made that that characteristic of accompanying the taxpayer to the IRS in unique to Block when, in fact, it is not. The consumer may think that he is paying for a service that only Block offers. However, if one is aware of the aforementioned IRS regulation and if no such assumption of uniqueness is made and if all one believes is that Block is reassuring the consumer of expert counsel at what can sometimes be a frightening IRS audit session, then there is no deception in this respect because no such assumption could be breached.

Clearly, it is extremely important to notice the significance of prior knowledge to a treatment of deception. Such knowledge (e.g., whether it is safe to use a product, whether a specific characteristic is unique to a product, that it is necessary to spend money to get that product) will determine whether or not the audience makes a particular deduction that may later on be proven to be true or false. It is necessary to invoke Wolfram and Wolfram's (1977) notion of "obvious information" at this point. When it is "obvious" that a product is potentially dangerous, even in its normal use, then omitting that information from a commercial is not considered to be deceptive.[3] And the obviousness of the need to spend money prevents there being an implication of gratuity, which would, of course, be false.

So it is not always necessary (or possible) for an advertiser to be completely informative (i.e., to provide all the information available about every aspect of his

---

[3]Most people, whether or not they own or use a car, are aware that an automobile is potentially dangerous at any time. This information is omitted from the following commercial for Dodge Colt, but it is certainly not deceptive in that respect.

Joe Garagiola: The crowds are gathering at the Dodge dealers' Colt carnival. They're coming for smart buys on these little Dodge Colts from Japan. This Colt coupe has a low sticker price that includes tinted glass all around, bumper guards, wheel covers, reclining bucket seats, adjustable steering column and lots more. See your Dodge dealer for his low price during the Colt carnival. It's a great time to get a lot of little car.

Voice-Over: See your local Dodge dealer.

product), only to be as informative as required to meet the needs of his target audience. Some popular critics of advertising (e.g., Packard, 1957, and McLuhan, 1951) state that advertisers want only to subvert and manipulate consumers' behavior for their (i.e., the advertisers') own benefits. Packard particularly feels that advertisers engage in a kind of mass psychoanalysis to persuade consumers to make certain buying choices for reasons that they, the consumers, are unaware of and that they might not have made had they known they were being manipulated. Politz (1960), however, claims that the purpose of advertising is to inform the consumer as well as possible about which of several competing brands may be the best to suit his needs. This author tends to agree with Politz, in that advertising is successful only when it correctly communicates those qualities of the product or service which make it attractive in the first place. Rotzoll (1978) shows that not all advertising is as effective as its backers would like. He states (1978, pp. 12–13) that "the extraordinarily well financed effort directed toward changing the skirt preference patterns of American women from 'mini' to 'midi' was not (a successful attempt to alter patterns)." Howard and Hulbert (1973) take a middle-of-the-road approach, stating that one function of advertising is to give accurate and relevant information when it is needed, but that not all advertising for all products requires that all information be divulged. For example, if one purchases a package of chewing gum and his product experience does not match the expectations he had as a result of an advertisement, there is virtually no injury done (a loss of perhaps 40¢). However, if the same kind of situation occurs when one purchases a new refrigerator, the cost is much greater and the injury more severe. Note once again the need to prove economic or physical injury as evidence of deception. So the ultimate decision on how much and what kind of information must be given in order to deceive or not deceive depends on what requirements must be met in order to abide by that speaker/hearer pact which is implicit in all communication (cf. Grice, 1975). We have seen that, to an extent, this will vary from product class to product class. Other communicative assumptions will apply to all advertising in general.

The more there is to know about a product, the omission of which could cause the hearer to be misled, the more there is a need to include in the advertising. For example, in August 1975 the Federal Trade Commission offered the following as a guideline to the advertising of air conditioners. The failure to disclose an air conditioner's Energy Efficiency Ratio (a measure of its energy consumption) was deemed to constitute an unfair and deceptive practice. As Cohen (1974) points out, however, advertising that promotes products which are high energy users and that at one time was completely acceptable may become designated as deceptive when an energy shortage occurs. At this time, a measure of energy consumption becomes critical and its omission may lead to the false conclusion that all air conditioners are equally efficient. The need for this information to be disclosed reflects changing economic and political forces, and so a definition of deception in this respect also needs to be dynamic and to change with the times.

At this point, it is necessary to confront the question of "deceptive to whom?" Moreover, how extensive must the deception be before it is possible to claim that a serious case of deception exists? The Federal Trade Commission has been entrusted with protecting both those with some degree of expertise and "the public—the vast multitude of which includes the ignorant, the unthinking and the credulous." The "fact that a false statement may be obviously false to those who are trained and experienced does not change its character nor take away its power to deceive others less experienced."[4]

A dichotomy between "experts" and "the unthinking" does not appear to be really sufficient for a determination of deception. Different people will have different degrees of knowledge of how a product works. And if just one "credulous" person is deceived, is that enough? What percentage of the population must be deceived before a corrective judgment is made? And who is to constitute that population—everybody and anybody, whether or not they are likely purchasers or users of the product, or the primary target audience? By invoking the court's demand that the unthinking and the ignorant be protected, the FTC has tacitly demanded 0 percent deception. In two cases where the FTC had charged deception, the defendants produced credible marketing surveys which showed that 86 percent and 91 percent, respectively, of their survey samples would not have been deceived in the way that the FTC had charged. But the Commission ruled that the remaining percentages, however small, were sufficient for a determination of deception.[5]

In both the Benrus and Rhodes decisions (discussed in footnote 5), some portion of the sampled population was privy to information that kept them from being deceived and another portion, which did not have that information, was more inclined to be misled. Here again we see the relevance of prior knowledge to whether or not the consumer makes the right or wrong deductions and whether or not he is deceived.

A STUDY OF TELEVISION COMMERCIALS
FOR BREAKFAST CEREALS
AND FAST FOOD RESTAURANTS

This study reports on a content analysis that was done of the television advertising for two product classes: breakfast cereals and fast food restaurants. These classes were chosen because they were the ones for which the greatest number of

---

[4]These quotes are taken from a court decision in *Charles of the Ritz Distributing Corp. vs. Federal Trade Commission.*

[5]In the case of Rhodes Pharmacal Co., Inc., the defendant showed that 91 percent of their sample would not believe that their product, Imdrin, was a treatment and cure for arthritis and rheumatism, as the FTC had charged. But the FTC ruled that the remaining 9 percent had to be protected.

In the case of the Benrus Watch Co., Inc., the FTC questioned the pricing system used to show that a sale was in progress. Benrus showed evidence that 86 percent of the public would not be deceived, mainly because they knew that watch prices varied from store to store even though the manufacturer's list price remained the same. Again the FTC ruled that the remaining 14 percent were susceptible to being deceived.

commercials were collected over a six month period of data collection (breakfast cereals, N = 8; fast food restaurants, N = 9).

During the period of data collection, randomly selected on-air commercials were videotaped as they appeared in their normal broadcast slots. The data collection was done at different times of the year to prevent a very heavy predominance of commercials for seasonally advertised products from occurring in the data base. The only criterion imposed was that the commercials had to appear during the prime time viewing hours (approximately 7:30 P.M. to 10:00 P.M.) to assure that these would be commercials meant primarily for adults.

Primarily using the videotape facilities at the Georgetown University Library and the Center for Applied Linguistics in 1976, I simply turned on a video recorder while watching television to make a copy of each selected commercial. An audiotape was also prepared of each commercial to facilitate transcription of its contents. The 17 commercials to be discussed below are part of a data base containing 299 commercials recorded in this manner.

A qualitative and quantitative examination is done here to determine: (1) what kinds of information are given in television advertising for these two product classes and how that information can be classified into broader information categories; (2) what different linguistic means are used to convey that information (i.e., assertion, presupposition or implication); (3) how much of the information within each category is given by which linguistic principle. This will allow an analysis of the degree of indirectness with which different kinds of information are conveyed.

Three semantic principles have consistently been found in the television commercials for breakfast cereals and fast food restaurants: assertion, presupposition, and implication.[6] The two product classes have different information categories, however, viz.:

---

[6]These terms are used here in the following manner.

Assertion: the meaning asserted by a sentence is true if the sentence itself is true. Likewise, a false sentence has a false meaning. Two equivalent assertions will have equivalent truth conditions. "Mary's father is dead" and "Mary's male parent is dead" assert the same meaning and have the same truth value.

Presupposition: a condition or state of affairs required for a sentence to have any truth value at all is a presupposition of that sentence. The sentence "I love New York" requires that there be some place called "New York" in order to be meaningful.

Implication: a proposition that is consequence of the realities of the discourse context in which other utterances are made is implied by the speaker or speakers of those utterances in that context. An implication is not related in any way to the truth value of the utterance or utterances which give rise to it. The realities refered to above deal with the nature of conversational cooperation. As a result of the maxims of cooperation, when one stranger approaches another and asks "Do you know how get to Carnegie Hall?" the hearer will deduce that the speaker is not testing his knowledge, but is actually asking for directions. In this study, a very special use of the term "implication" is also involved, that is, any information given by pictures in the commercial. The meaning given by these pictures is considered to be implied because of the relevance they take on by virtue of being shown in the advertising context, as opposed to other contexts in which they may have other meanings.

BREAKFAST CEREALS

Crunch
Ingredients
Nutrition
Part of a complete breakfast
Target audience
Taste

FAST FOOD RESTAURANTS

Atmosphere
Convenient
Customer is special
Full meal
Ingredients
Kinds of food available
Leader in the field
Price
Quality of food
Target audience

The data have been analyzed in terms of both the information categories and the semantic principles listed above and a quantified approach is possible. That is, a determination can be made of which information categories occur most often and which semantic principles, that is, assertion, presupposition, or implication, are utilized most often. The resultant impact on the consumer with regard to each information category is also discussed.

Breakfast Cereal Commercials

Commercials for the first product category, breakfast cereals, are dominated by nutrition claims. Within the 8 commercials, there were 27 nutrition claims, of which 22 were given by implication. Nutrition is a relative notion because different people have different nutrition needs. Consumers Union reports that the "recommended daily allowance" (RDA) mentioned in breakfast cereal commercials is composed of averages set up by the National Academy of Sciences/National Research Council for different ages, builds, and sexes. This RDA may be applicable to some people, but understates the nutritional needs of such people as children under four, pregnant women, and adult males. If all of these cereals are consumed along with other foods that provide a nutritive balance, then there should be no problem. The nutrition lacking in the cereal would be compensated for by the nutrition in these other foods. Six of the commercials studied showed the cereal as part of a complete breakfast. The question to be considered is: how strongly is this representation made? In all six commercials, other foods are shown in the picture while other comments about the cereal are being made. For example, in a Post Grape-Nut commercial, while the voice-over is saying "Grape-Nuts is a natural cereal fortified with vitamins. It has the crunchy, nutty taste people like," a pitcher of milk, some toast, and coffee are shown along with a box of Grape-Nuts. Talking about the cereal while it is shown with other foods seems to imply that they all complement each other and should be consumed together. It is not necessary to say anything about having a complete breakfast in order to convey this information. In fact, in only two commercials, one for Wheaties and one for Kellogg's Raisin Bran, is it specifically mentioned that the cereal is part of a larger breakfast (Wheaties—"And I've got her eating the good breakfast she used to feed me. And you better believe Wheaties is a part of it"; Raisin Bran—"They start their complete breakfast with Kellogg's Raisin Bran"). Although these advertisers clearly realize the need to supplement the cereal with other foods, the degree to which this is expressed may vary. The consumer who believes otherwise may not perceive that message in these commercials because the nutrition message is conveyed most often by means of implication. The other foods seen with the cereal may be construed to be desirable additions, but not as necessary supplements. Here the indirectness of the way the information is given could lead to miscommunication.

The primary purchasers of cereals are adult women, particularly mothers. However, anyone can pour a bowlful of cereal for themselves and eat it. Are the people who primarily eat a particular brand of cereal the same people for whom it was designed nutritionally? One way to begin answering this question is to see to whom the cereal is being advertised, that is, who is the target audience and how is that information being conveyed to them? The implication arises in all of the commercials that the cereals are appropriate for *everyone*. For example, in a Cheerios commercial, because the entire family in the commercial is seen playing and enjoying themselves, it must be *all of them* who got their "powerful start" from Cheerios. In a Post Grape-Nuts commercial, since two different women, three different men and one boy all profess to like the cereal, presumably it is good for all of them. Both a little schoolboy and his teacher like Kellogg's Raisin Bran, Wheaties is shown as being good both for athletes and everyday people who are just trying to stay in shape, and Total is said to give "you 100 percent of the recommended allowance of all these important vitamins and iron." Because no mention is made that people of different ages or builds have different requirements, one could assume this "allowance" applies to everyone. At the beginning of a Wheat Chex commercial, the boy's father tells him "They're good for you" (i.e., the boy), but at the end, the generic term "people" is used in "People who don't like Chex cereals have never tried Chex cereals," thereby making it seem appropriate for everyone. Finally, a Nabisco Cream of Wheat commercial implies that that cereal can fulfill the daily requirements for iron of children, women, and men. If, as Consumers Union claims, no cereal can satisfy the nutritional needs for all people, then there may be another possibility for miscommunication in this particular information category.

As for the ingredients of these cereals, by law they must be listed on the package in order of presence by weight. The main ingredients are very often incorporated into the name of the cereal. Including the ingredients in the brand name has been counted here as an example of implication because the relationship of the name to the ingredients is not openly explained anywhere. Because a person must make that particular deduction (e.g., "they wouldn't call it Wheaties if it did not contain wheat") to understand the name/ingredient relationship, this has been counted as informing by means of implication. Sixteen of 21 references to the ingredients come this way; the other five are by presupposition (i.e., in "he loves those *two scoops of raisins* in a package of Kellogg's Raisin Bran," the use of "two scoops of raisins" presupposes their existence, but calling it "Raisin Bran" implies that it contains raisins and bran). There is little chance that a cereal would claim to contain any ingredients that it did not, in fact, contain, no matter how that claim was made. Any such implication would be rather blatantly false. In this information category, there would be little possibility to mislead.

The last two categories, *taste* and *crunch,* are not readily subject to verification and different people might have different perceptions with regard to what is tasty or crunchy. It is not possible to account for different people's tastes and, since the authenticity of these claims is necessarily subjective in nature, it does not even make sense to talk about the truth or falsity of these claims. At any rate, the amount of injury suffered as a result of some disappointment caused by these claims is not likely to be significant.

In sum, the notion of *nutrition* in breakfast cereal advertising is one where the potential exists for miscommunication. Consumers may misunderstand both the notion of "recommended daily allowance" and of how other breakfast foods play into the nutrition provided by the cereal itself. The other information categories that appear in the advertising for this product category are either clearly objectively verifiable (e.g., ingredients) no matter how the information is communicated and would likely not be tampered with or entirely subjective, unverifiable, and not very significant (e.g., crunch).

Fast Food Restaurant Commercials

As for fast food restaurants, the only claims made about the *quality of food* are that it is "good" or "delicious." Of course, the criteria by which to define "good" are nebulous at best, because "good" can refer to taste or nutrition and then to many different characteristics within each of those particular categories. For example, in a Jack-in-the-Box commercial, the voice-over, in referring to all the foods available there, says, "And these are just some of the *good things* you can get at Jack-in-the-Box"; in a Rustler Steak House commercial, one dancer says to another, "Oooohh, we're gonna have *good steak* tonight, honey!"; or, in a Pizza Hut commercial, "There's a lot of *good things* at Pizza Hut." Perhaps the most interesting implication occurs in a Ponderosa Steak House commercial, where a Chinese cook leaves the restaurant where he works and goes to the Ponderosa for dinner. Now a connoisseur of Chinese restaurants knows that Chinese cooks generally eat their own cooking, so the implication exists that Chinese food may be good, but Ponderosa steaks are better. Of course, making that deduction depends on a certain kind of "specialized" knowledge. In any event, the claim is so vague and equally subjective that a finding of miscommunication is hardly likely. In the Jack-in-the-Box, Rustler Steak House, and Pizza Hut commercials mentioned above, the phrases *good things* and *good steak* are only there to generate a positive image for the establishment and are, again, so vague and subjective that no specific verifiable meaning can be attached to them. Furthermore, as Consumers Union reports, many Americans apparently do like the taste of the food at fast food restaurants because they keep going back for more.

The image that most of these restaurants are trying to dispel is one of serving processed food that is prepared prior to the customer's arrival. These restaurants want to show that *the customer is special:* Burger King—"Order up a double treat 'n' have it your way"; McDonald's—"You, you're the one," "We do it all for you." Examination of the texts of the commercials for this category shows that these are the only two advertisers who make that claim because they have to try the hardest to dispel the notion of serving food that is already prepared before the customer enters the restaurant. Because it is so important a point to these two competitors, it is probably not coincidental that 16 of the 21 "customer is special" claims made by them are made by direct assertion. A visit to either of these establishments will show that customers can indeed get service tailored to their desires and that they need not accept food prepared prior to their arrival, so the question of miscommunication is not likely to arise here either, albeit for a different reason than in the quality category.

Because the customer is special, it must also be *convenient* for him to patronize these restaurants. McDonald's says it is "always here, close by, right on your way," and Ponderosa, by visual sequences, implies that that Chinese chef was served quickly. "Convenience," of course, is a subjective matter and there are no real objective criteria by which to measure it. It is difficult to imagine that anyone would be injured if a McDonald's were not really close by or if he had to wait to get served at Ponderosa—maybe annoyed, but not injured. Deception is just not applicable here.

One of the major drawing cards of each institution, of course, is the kind of food it offers. As it happens, the different varieties of food available are most often given by presupposition in a scenario where a potential customer is placing his order or a spokesman is offering one type of food or another: Burger King—"I'll have a double meat hamburger with no pickle," "Two Whoppers and two chocolate shakes"; Pizza Hut—"Try our thick and chewy pizza . . . and then have a teeny oven baked pasta"; McDonald's—"Put your thirst on ice with a triple thick McDonald's shake.'' Mention of the item presupposes its existence and, in this case, presupposition is being used to inform. And telling about each institution's food is what this business' advertising is all about. With that knowledge in hand, we can be fairly sure that the advertiser is being honest.

In that same vein, when the advertiser mentions, whether by implication (Jack-in-the-Box), by presupposition (Ponderosa), or assertion (Rustler) that a *full meal is available,* it is very likely to be true.

Directly related to this is Burger King's *ingredients* claim of using ''100 percent pure beef'' in its hamburgers, which can also include ''double meat.'' More often than not, this ingredients claim is presupposed. Now meat cuts may vary and there may also be different ways of calculating the amount and purity of beef in a meat product. Clearly, the claim is being made so that people will not think of this ''fast'' food as ''junk'' food. It may be a difficult task for Burger King to shake off that image and its method of proof may differ from others. A finding of miscommunication here may have to be based on two concepts—a reliable measure of beef content and a measure of believability of the claim. If a dependable measure showed that there was less than 100 percent pure beef in a Burger King hamburger, but relatively few people believed the claim in the first place, a finding of miscommunication may be questionable since the number of people injured would be minimal.

Who are the people who go to fast food restaurants? Every commercial here is made to appeal to ''everyone.'' Some are depicted as family restaurants: Roy Rogers—''He (Pappy Parker)'s ready and waiting at every one of my family restaurants.'' Most fast food restaurant commercials accomplish giving this information visually and that is counted here as an example of implication. For instance, a McDonald's commercial shows a banker, a mechanic, a bride and her groom, some barbers, and some firemen all going to a McDonald's restaurant and Burger King conveys a family image by showing a mother and son ordering a meal there and Rustler Steak House just shows a large crowd scrambling to get in the front door. And, as noted above, if a Chinese-American likes to eat at Ponderosa Steak House, then any other American certainly should too. This is the kind of information category which has no ready verification. Certainly *everybody* does not eat at McDonald's and, perhaps, not everyone should. Not everyone needs to eat ''fast'' food and save time and money. The message conveyed, however, is that these restaurants are available to all types of people, which is certainly true (provided they are well behaved, etc.). The possibility of miscommunication just does not seem applicable here.

Consumers Union reports that, at the restaurants they surveyed, the food is cheap in price, as restaurant food goes. So we can be fairly sure that a statement like ''it's nice to know that you can get a complete steak dinner at Ponderosa *at a very relaxing price*'' is going to be true (however much a relaxing price amounts to). And when the voice-over says, specifically, ''For the unbelievable sum of about $2.50, you can enjoy a delicious steak at the Rustler Steak House,'' any gross deviation from that amount would clearly be false and injurious. One would therefore expect that claim to be true. The following is an interesting example of the finding that the more previous information one needs to figure out the implied meaning of a statement, the more likely he may be to misunderstand and, perhaps, be misled. Burger King says, "Yup, double the meat, but not double the price." This could imply that a double hamburger, for instance, costs *exactly the same* as a regular hamburger. It is unlikely that that is the case; what this statement probably means is that a double hamburger costs more than one regular hamburger but less than two regular hamburgers. One needs to know about business pricing practices in order to make the correct interpretation. The other interpretation would be false and an advertiser might be taken to task for it.

A category similar to that of target audience in that it is unverifiable, in a sense, is *atmosphere*. Eight of the commercials (all but the one for Jack-in-the-Box) show the customers smiling and enjoying themselves while eating. Presumably these are pleasant places to go, where one can eat comfortably and without being hurried. Yet, what is comfortable to one may be uncomfortable to another. If those who go in expecting to sit in plastic contoured seats or on wooden benches are reasonably satisfied, then the message has done its job. It is unlikely that, after seeing any of these commercials, someone would go into any of these establishments and expect to be served at his table or to sit in a plush seat. That is, few people, if any, are likely to be misled by fast food restaurant commercials into believing that they will get anything but what is delivered in the information category of *atmosphere*.

The notion of being a *leader in the business* arises by implication both times it occurs. Ponderosa says "You don't know how good it is until you eat someplace else" and Jack-in-the-Box says "Watch out McDonald's." The former statement implies that the food at other restaurants is not as good as the food at Ponderosa. This implication arises from the presupposed function of advertising to highlight the product's attributes. It need not have any such implication at all in other contexts (i.e., it could just mean "You do not have the means to judge"). The latter statement is meaningful as a warning to McDonald's only if you already know that McDonald's is a leader. So both of these implications rely on some previous knowledge, but the claim really amounts to "puffery," an advertising term for mild self-aggrandisement. This category, like some of the others examined in this study, is not judged here to fall within the realm of potential miscommunication.

Insofar as advertising for fast food restaurants is concerned, there does not seem to be much room for a determination of miscommunication since the criteria needed to judge the validity of most of the information categories are either completely subjective (e.g., atmosphere) or necessarily objective (e.g., the types of food available). That is, one cannot make a universally acceptable decision on whether the food is "good" or if the restaurant is "convenient" or if the customer really is "special." Conversely, because the advertiser is specifically selling a steak dinner or a thick shake or fried chicken or a double meat hamburger to attract customers to his establishment, failure to fulfill those promises may cost him disappointed customers and sink him into legal problems as well. The only information category we could find where a claim may not be borne out by the facts (i.e., ingredients) is one where it may not be entirely clear what the facts actually are. Based on this study, the opportunity for miscommunication in the commercials for this product class would seem to be limited.

The television commercials under study here have shown a high degree of communication by implication and presupposition. The information content of the commercials for the two product classes has been shown to be nonobjective to a very large extent. In the absence of any objectively verifiable information, even by implication, the ability to determine the truth of a commercial thereby becomes more difficult and "truth" may not even be a concept which is applicable to the given information. Attributes such as "atmosphere," "taste," "convenience," and "crunch" only influence the affective rating of the product but they cannot be measured in any material way. This statement itself should not be construed to mean that advertisers are trying to skirt the truth-in-advertising issue by avoiding factual statements which have "hard and fast" proof. Creating an image for a product is an important function of advertising. These advertisers are indulging in exactly the kind of soft-sell approach that is most likely to successfully attract customers to their product.

RELEVANCE OF INFORMATION IN ADVERTISING

Howard and Hulbert (1974) provide a marketing definition of informational relevance. Information must fall into any of four types of categories to be considered relevant to purchasing decisions. The following diagram is adapted from Howard and Hulbert (1974, p. 35):

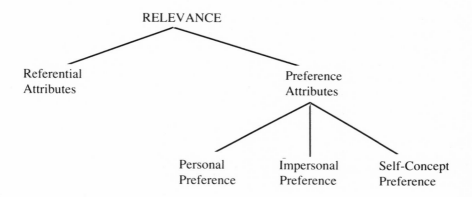

Referential attributes are objective, denotative features which the consumer uses to distinguish between similar brands. The size and color of a box of cereal and the cereal's ingredients could be referential attributes. Preference attributes are the consumer's subjective evaluations of the brand that combine to determine his attitude toward it. A personal preference would be the buyer's evaluation of the physical properties of the item, for example, the crispiness of the fried chicken available at a restaurant. An impersonal preference would be the buyer's evaluation of some contingent property of the item, for example, its price. A consumer may prefer Ponderosa Steak House to Rustler Steak House because a complete meal at Ponderosa is cheaper than at Rustler. A self-concept preference would be a buyer's choice of one brand over another because it would elevate him socially (e.g., one might buy a Lincoln Continental instead of a Ford Pinto for that reason).

Garfinkel (1977) shows that these categories of relevance are arranged in different hierarchies of importance for different product classes. For example, referential attributes (such as strength and absorbability) are more important in paper towel advertising than in automobile advertising (where the impersonal preference of price may be more important) and the self-concept preference of personal beauty is most important in cosmetics advertising.

The information categories previously listed are evaluated as follows:

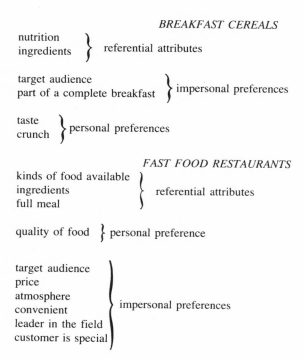

BREAKFAST CEREALS

nutrition
ingredients } referential attributes

target audience
part of a complete breakfast } impersonal preferences

taste
crunch } personal preferences

FAST FOOD RESTAURANTS

kinds of food available
ingredients
full meal } referential attributes

quality of food } personal preference

target audience
price
atmosphere
convenient
leader in the field
customer is special } impersonal preferences

Clearly, in terms of usefulness, referential attributes and impersonal preferences are more important than personal preferences in judging the relevance of the information in breakfast cereal commercials. By presenting these kinds of information, the advertiser is confirming our expectations of useful information.

The information in fast food restaurant commercials does not readily fall into such a hierarchy. All the information may be considered to be of equal value.

Effective advertising for other product classes may show a different tendency. In commercials for other product classes, where a hard-sell approach is used to induce consumers to make a purchase, there may be more objectively verifiable information presented, perhaps by direct assertion. Note the heavy use of direct assertion in the presentation of fast food restaurants' most important point—the customer is special. Both the kinds of informational relevance and the semantic means used to present the information may characterize hard-sell versus soft-sell advertising. Insofar as breakfast cereal and fast food restaurant advertising is concerned, we have seen how they interact to produce a generally low-key advertising vehicle.

As similar as these two product classes are in this respect, let us also note the large difference between them. There was considerably more potential for misunderstanding in breakfast cereal advertising than in fast food restaurant advertising. The notion of "nutrition" is more important in the former than in the latter. An expenditure for food that turns out to be nonnutritional even though it is advertised as being nutritional may constitute injury. Fast food restaurants do not advertise their food as being necessarily nutritional. This does not mean that their food is not nutritional, but that nutrition is not a competitive factor between different companies. An expectation of nutrition must be made by the consumer in order that it be breached and he deceived. This difference in potential misunderstanding may very well be a cognitive distinction between the two product classes—one is expected to be nutritious, the other not (or no assumption is made at all).

CONCLUSIONS

A commercial is designed to be a vehicle that communicates one or several essential sales messages with the intention and desire of interesting a predefined market segment in the product. That is the basic purpose of advertising and advertisers are as likely to believe what they say about their product as anyone else is. Deception, when it occurs, is an unfortunate offspring of this communication process. A very precise definition of deception is needed to be able to effectively measure it. An adequate behavioral definition of deception contains far too many variables to easily bandy that term around. Some of these are described in the following.

First of all, it is necessary to choose the proper vocabulary in describing this problem. "Deception" seems to place the burden of the problem on the shoulders of the advertiser and "misunderstanding" places it on the shoulders of the consumer. Therefore, I have tried to use the more neutral term "miscommunicate" for those instances where consumers may misunderstand and consequently be deceived.

It was stated earlier that, in deception, there must be a misleading claim which injuriously affects buying behavior. That is the bare essential of an operational definition designed to cover as broad a spectrum as possible of misleading advertising. However, certain marketing research questions need also to be addressed in forming this definition: does a particular commercial whose claims are in doubt break through the clutter of other commercials to adequately register the product category and brand name? Are the main ideas recalled to a high degree? Does the commercial cause consumers to actually purchase the brand that is advertised?

Let us briefly deal with each of these questions. If the consumers cannot recall the brand name of the product being advertised either immediately after exposure to the commercial or 24 hours after exposure (both these methods are used in marketing research), could they ever remember it when they go to the market in order to make a purchase decision about it? The likely answer is no. Similarly, if they cannot remember what the claims are, it is equally unlikely that they could be misled by them. It is important that I have chosen brand name and main idea *recall* as criteria here and not just brand name *recognition*. Most marketers would prefer that their commercials establish the ability to recall a brand name so if the consumer does not see it in her store, she could proceed to ask for it. Indeed, in many drugstores and specialty departments in department stores, this is the only way to get a product because it may be kept behind a counter, out of the consumer's line of vision. Recognition of it on the shelf would therefore be impossible. Nor could it occur if the store where the consumer happened to be shopping did not carry that brand. She would have to be able to remember what it was in order to name it, go to another store and try to find it.

Similarly, deception would be unlikely if consumers did not believe the claims that were made in the commercial in question. Furthermore, it would be difficult to accept a finding of deception with regard to a commercial with a high level of brand name recall and main idea recall, but which had little impact on buying decisions and which did not significantly affect the key market segment in question. Finally, it must be the primary target audience which is detrimentally affected, for no one else is even likely to be interested in the advertisement.

This study has been largely concerned with using linguistics to show that neither of the viewpoints outlined in the opening paragraph (i.e., those of Packard and Lieberman) is correct. In between these two extremes—one uniformly condemning advertising as unscrupulous and the other uniformly supporting its truthfulness—is a large gray area where the notion of truthfulness is just not applicable. There is a large amount of completely subjective advertising claims about which it cannot be said that they are either true or false; they cannot be measured in this way. Moreover, some information categories are just not that essential and neither is their truth or falsity—if their truth can even be determined (see the earlier discussion of breakfast cereals' crunchiness). Whether or not it is a problem that it is not always possible to attach a truth value to certain statements in television commercials is a question that the advertisers themselves and the regulatory bodies mentioned at the beginning of this chapter will have to answer.

This attempt to measure potential misunderstanding is only a first step, albeit a very important one, and is restricted to the product classes that are its data base. When a television commercial is called into question, the claim that is under attack must be clearly defined. A linguistic/pragmatic analysis can reveal what the claim is and what form it takes. Form can, in fact, affect what the claim actually is. There must also be a decision as to the material verifiability of the claim, that is, is it a subjective claim that is really difficult to clearly prove or an objective claim that is readily ascertained? If the claim is relevant and objective, is it misleading or not? If a significant segment of the target is injured, then there may be a case of deception at hand. But clearly, many criteria enter into a finding of deception. The linguistic criteria discussed here must be viewed as a part of the pragmatic context in which the information exchange takes place. They must then be integrated with certain legal, consumerist and marketing criteria to create a truly useful notion of deception.

REFERENCES

Aaker, D. Deceptive advertising. In D. Aaker & G. Day (Eds.), *Consumerism*. New York: Free Press, 1974.

Austin, J. L. *How to do things with words*. New York: Oxford University Press, 1962.

Charles of the Ritz Distributing Corp. vs. Federal Trade Commission. 143 F. 2nd 676 (2nd Cir. 1944).

Cohen, D. The concept of unfairness as it relates to advertising legislation. *Journal of Marketing*, 1974, *38*, 8–13.

Cox, E. G., Fellmuth, R. C., & Schulz, J. E. *The Nader report on the Federal Trade Commission*. New York: Baron Publishing Company, 1969.

Garfinkel, A. *Linguistic aspects of truth in advertising*. Paper presented to the Fourth Annual Conference on New Ways of Analyzing Variation. Washington, D.C.: Georgetown University, 1975.

Garfinkel, A. Truths, half-truths and deception in advertising. *Papers in Linguistics*, 1977, *10*, 135–149.

Grice, H. P. Logic and conversation. In P. Cole & J. Morgan (Eds.), *Syntax and semantics: Speech acts*. New York: Academic Press, 1975.

Howard, J., & Hulbert, J. *Advertising and the public interest: A staff report to the Federal Trade Commission*. Chicago: Crain Communications, 1973.

Howard, J., & Hulbert, J. Advertising and the public interest. *Journal of Advertising Research,* 1974, *14,* 33–39.

Lieberman, S. *The new world of claim substantiation and claim substantiation research.* Paper presented to the Seventeenth Annual Advertising Research Conference. New York: American Marketing Association, 1979.

McLuhan, M. *The mechanical bride.* New York: Vanguard Press, 1951.

Packard, V. *The hidden persuaders.* New York: David McKay, 1975.

Politz, A. The dilemma of creative advertising. *Journal of Marketing,* 1960, *25,* 1–6.

Rotzoll, K. *What factors affect response to ads?* Advertising Working Paper No. 5. Urbana, Ill.: University of Illinois, 1978.

Tarski, A. *Logic, semantics and metamathematics.* Oxford: Oxford University Press, 1956.

Wolfram, W., & Wolfram, T. How come you asked how come? In R. Fasold & R. Shuy (Eds.), *Studies in language variation.* Washington, D.C.: Georgetown University Press, 1977.

9

Evaluative Verbal Content and Deception in Advertising: A Review and Critical Analysis

Terence A. Shimp
University of South Carolina

INTRODUCTION

The amount spent in the United States on advertising in 1978 was in excess of $43 billion, and the present growth rate in the industry far exceeds that for the remainder of the economy (Coen, 1979). Though some question whether these vast expenditures are economically sound (e.g., Bogart, 1978), few would deny that advertising is an indispensable component of a free enterprise economy. Nevertheless, the institution of advertising is much maligned. Critics have accused it of everything ranging from partial responsibility for inflationary prices to effusing society with misdirected materialistic and hedonistic value orientations (see Aaker & Myers, 1975, for an in-depth discussion of the criticisms).

Criticism of advertising reached its peak during the consumer movement of the 1960s and early seventies. The fervor and political activity of this period generated major institutional changes in advertising. Perhaps the greatest development was the intensified industry self-regulation and governmental regulation, epitomized by Congress' enactment of the Federal Trade Commission (FTC) Improvement Act of 1975 (Udell & Fischer, 1977). The FTC has vigorously utilized its augmented powers, ostensibly with the intent of improving the quality and quantity of product information available to consumers. The result has been an obvious diminution in the incidence of gross distortions, misrepresentations, and unconscionable lies (Gardner, 1975) used in national advertising.

Some observers (e.g., Armstrong & Russ, 1975; Pollay, Fryer, & Zaichowsky, 1977) believe that an unintended consequence of the increased regulation has been a reduction in the amount of the "hard data" in ads and a trend toward the use of nebulous, evasive, and subjective claims, which may presumably mislead receivers in a subtle manner. Federal Trade Commission officials and some advertising professionals share the view that government regulation has spawned a trend toward less objective advertising. For example, Hooper White (1978), writing in *Advertising Age,* the major publication in the ad industry, offered this explanation for the resurgence of animation and cartoons in TV commercials:

> With government controls tightening, animation allows for hyperbole and visual exaggeration, no longer acceptable in live action (or allowed in copy heard in the sound track). It's the very willingness of the viewer to extract attitudinal information from animation that can give it a unique strength in today's controlled environment [p. 45].

Tracy Westen, past deputy director of the FTC's bureau of consumer protection, claimed that the commission's traditional role of attacking blatantly false and deceptive ads may partially account for the trend away from specific product claims in advertising (Westen raps, 1978). This concern was echoed by Michael Pertschuk, FTC chairman during the Carter administration, who, while complimenting an advertising self-regulatory body for helping the FTC to eliminate blatantly false and deceptive advertising, suggested that the task remaining for the FTC is to curtail the widespread use of "subtle forms of deception, half-truths, unsubstantiated claims and the mine field of psychological manipulation" (Comparative ad's, 1978).

Regulatory pressure is not the only reason why so much contemporary advertising is nonobjective and noninformative. Leo Bogart, a noted advertising authority, offers this explanation:

> Once we accept the principle of competition among firms producing what is essentially the same commodity [so-called parity products], it follows that advertising—perhaps not all, but certainly a good deal of it in that product class—will be noninformational, except for the very fundamental information that the brand exists. When brand image represents the only distinctive feature the advertiser has to sell, he is more likely to use irrelevant and nonrational appeals and to rely on gimmick techniques to capture attention and heighten identity [Bogart, 1978, p. 18].

The fact that nonobjective advertising is widespread has been documented in three content analysis studies. Resnik and Stern (1977), using the entire ad as the analytic unit, found that fewer than one half of a sample of 378 commercials contained *any* objective product information. Another study of TV commercials used the assertion (Osgood, 1959) as the basic coding unit. A total of 1450 assertions were extracted from the 243 analyzed commercials; 58.5 percent of these represented non-objective information (Shimp, 1979). Similar results were obtained by Marquez (1977) in an analysis of 600 magazine ads. Approximately two-thirds were classified as predominantly noninformative.

Purpose of Chapter

An in-depth analysis and review of the widespread use of nonobjective, noninformative advertising is presented in this chapter. The following section explains this advertising genre. Next the deception potential of this advertising is addressed, and the supportive empirical evidence is reviewed. A final section discusses the policy implications and research needs.

THE NATURE OF VERBAL CONTENT
IN ADVERTISING

A basic distinction in verbal content has been emphasized in a wide range of disciplines (Holbrook, 1978). In psycholinguistics, for example, the distinction is between representational versus emotive processes or symbolic versus evocative functions (Rommetveit, 1968) or denotative versus connotative meaning (Osgood, Suci, & Tannenbaum, 1957). Though a variety of labels have been used for roughly the same distinction, many advertising researchers have identified this fundamental dichotomy in the verbal content of ad messages—for example, inherent versus arbitrary (Preston & Bowen, 1971), valid versus invalid (Shimp & Kuehl, 1976), informative versus persuasive (Marquez, 1977), data claims versus puffery claims (Coney & Patti, 1978), factual versus evaluative (Holbrook, 1978), objective versus subjective (Shimp, 1979).

One set of labels is probably as good as the next, but Holbrook's choice of "factual" versus "evaluative" is the convention adopted for this chapter. Following a brief review of the nature of advertising language, a detailed treatment of the distinction between factual and evaluative advertising content is undertaken.

Advertising language, like other linguistic constructions, consists of words and sentences that combine to form claims or representations. In a formal linguistic sense these constitute assertions, where an assertion is "a linguistic construction in which a referent is associated with or dissociated from a complement via a verbal connector" (Osgood, 1959, p. 45). The referent is the advertised brand; a complement is an adjective or adjective phrase that describes the referent or states how the referent's product will benefit the consumer; and the verbal connector is the verb or verb phrase that associates referent and complement. Stated in an alternative fashion, the advertised brand is a sign, and an advertising assertion signifies something about the sign; that which is signified is a significate (Preston, 1967; Preston & Bowen, 1971).

The advertiser's objective in making assertions is to associate the advertised brand with a significate valued highly by consumers. Many options are available. One study (Shimp, 1974) identified twenty distinct types of advertising significates that are used widely in national TV commercials. These 20 significates, though individually unique, group meaningfully into the 2 general categories of factual versus evaluative verbal content.

Factual Versus Evaluative Content

Factual advertising content is different from evaluative content both in terms of word choice and, more importantly, with regard to the perceptual task imposed upon receivers in order to obtain meaning. In a factual advertising assertion, the significate represents a concrete, tangible, physical reality of the advertised product (cf. Holbrook's, 1978, and Shimp's 1979, discussion of objective advertising). Consider these examples by a hypothetical automobile advertiser: "Our model has a diesel engine." "It will get 50 miles per gallon."

In contrast, the significate in an evaluative advertising assertion does not represent a physical property of the advertised product. The product is characterized, instead, with the use of abstract and vague language that is devoid of physical referents. This is illustrated by the automobile advertiser who claims: "You'll have confidence on the road when you drive a . . ." "This new model is incomparably luxurious." From a legal perspective, such advertising is termed puffery, that is, advertising representations "which praise the item to be sold with subjective opinions, superlatives, or exaggerations, vaguely and generally, stating not specific facts" (Preston, 1975).

The process by which receivers extract meaning from evaluative advertising claims is more complicated and more subject to error than is the case with factual advertising. This stems from the fact that perception involves the use of information from memory in addition to the perceptual input itself (Lindsay & Norman, 1972). As a result, evaluative claims are inherently more ambiguous than factual claims; the receiver is required to make more choices in order for meaning to emerge (cf. Berdine, 1974; Foss, Bever, & Silver, 1968).

Consider the difference between the factual claim "Our model has a diesel engine" and the evaluative assertion "This new model is incomparably luxurious." The former claim is clearly less ambiguous. Extracting meaning from it essentially requires only that the receiver possess some rudimentary knowledge about automobiles. All receivers possessing this knowledge would exhibit high consensus in the meaning inferred from the claim. On the other hand, it is likely that receivers would infer multiple, nonequivalent meanings from the vague evaluative claim; "incomparably luxurious" would evoke a variety of interpretations.

DECEPTION POTENTIAL OF EVALUATIVE ADVERTISING

The issue of deception has become more complicated in recent years. Whereas in the past the FTC concentrated on blatantly deceptive advertisements, its focus has turned more recently toward advertisements that are not so clearly deceptive (Armstrong & Russ, 1975). A concomitant development has been the increased academic attention devoted to the topic. The nexus of various writings (e.g., Aaker, 1974; Armstrong, Kendall, & Russ, 1975; Cohen, 1972; Gardner, 1975; Haefner & Permut, 1974) is that deception results from the interaction of the advertisement with the receiver's memory and does not rest solely in the advertising message. Thus, a false advertising claim is not necessarily deceptive if the receiver does not perceive or believe the falsity. Similarly, a literally true claim may be deceptive if it fails to provide necessary qualification so that the receiver will not be misled.

Two major conceptualizations of the nature of deception have been advanced. The more encompassing view holds that deception occurs when either a false advertising claim or a true but unqualified claim is perceived and believed, thereby altering the receiver's cognitive structure in a fashion that a nondeceptive claim would not. A more rigorous conceptualization contends that deception results only if purchase behavior is affected. According to this latter view, an advertisement may deceive consumers into believing that a product will provide a trivial benefit. If, however, this benefit is not salient to consumers in their purchase decisions, it possesses no serious negative behavioral consequences, and thus "real" deception has not occurred.

How Evaluative Advertising Deceives

Based on the rigorous conceptualization of deception, the following sequence must occur in order for a particular evaluative claim to be regarded as deceptive:

1. The consumer *perceives* the claim.
2. The claim (or implication therefrom) is *believed*.
3. The claim (or implication therefrom) is *important*.
4. The important belief (or implication therefrom) becomes represented in *memory*.
5. The claim (or implication therefrom) is *false*.
6. *Behavior* is influenced as a result of either the deceptive claim or the implication derived from the claim.

Perception of Evaluative Claims.   A number of factors determine whether consumers attend an ad; included are such considerations as novelty, how interesting the ad is, and its practical value (Aaker & Myers, 1975). Though most consumers probably regard evaluative claims as having little practical value, it is unlikely that advertisers would spend $10,000-to-$200,000 per minute of broadcast time unless commercials, consisting largely of evaluative claims, were at least getting the attention of consumers. What evaluative claims may lack in practical value is probably compensated for by greater novelty and interest resulting from advertising creativity.

Believability of Evaluative Claims.   An advertising claim, whether factual or evaluative, cannot deceive unless consumers believe it. Two reasons account for why evaluative claims are believable (1) the claim *per se* may be believed or (2) the claim implies something else which is believed. These two concepts, beliefs, and implication, are critical to an understanding of the manner by which evaluative claims may deceive advertising receivers.

According to Fishbein and Ajzen (1975, p. 131) "beliefs refer to a person's subjective probability judgments concerning some discriminable aspect of his world; they deal with the person's understanding of himself and his world." One's beliefs about a given object (e.g., an advertised product) result from direct experience with the object (such as prior ownership), from information received and accepted from external sources (e.g., advertisements), or from drawing inferences from other beliefs (Fishbein & Ajzen, 1975). Though beliefs are resistant to change, research evidence is overwhelming in showing that (1) people will alter their beliefs in light of compelling new information; (2) maintenance of internal consistency is important when revising beliefs; (3) and as a result of this striving for consistency, revisions in one belief may "spillover" to other beliefs such that these related beliefs are revised also (Lutz, 1975; Olson & Dover, 1976). Thus, an evaluative advertising claim may influence a target belief directly or, through an inferential process, it may influence a related belief. In either instance, the impact of an evaluative claim is more likely the result of what is implied than of what is stated directly.

Implication is a fundamental aspect of information processing. Various studies have demonstrated that language comprehension is influenced by implied information (e.g., Just & Clark, 1973; Offir, 1973). In contrast to the directly asserted meaning of a message, implication is a type of meaning derived by logical and heuristic procedures determined by the receiver's memory structure (Harris & Monaco, 1978). Implications are either logical or pragmatic. The former exists when an assertion necessarily implies some information, whereas the latter exists "when an utterance leads the hearer to expect something neither explicitly stated nor necessarily (logically) implied in the sentence" (Harris & Monaco, 1978, pp. 2–3). The following example illustrates this difference; it also points out why evaluative claims may deceive.

Direct Assertion: "Brand X golf ball has a unique new construction."

Logical Implication: No other golf ball is constructed the same way.

Pragmatic Implication: This new golf ball is somehow better than others because of its unique new construction.

Though this claim asserts nothing directly about product quality, the golf enthusiast, a highly motivated information processor (Burnkrant, 1976) when potential ways of lowering the golf score are involved, is likely to "read between the lines" to infer that this is exactly what the claim means. Assuming the pragmatic implication is internalized as a brand-specific belief, it may influence other beliefs, such that the consumer may also believe that the advertised ball is more durable than other brands, will travel farther, and so on.

Evaluative claims are believable because of pragmatic implication and thus potentially deceivable. The likelihood of this happening hinges on whether the implication of fact is believed prior to perceiving the evaluative claim (see Oliver, 1979). For example, if one believes that imported beer is superior to domestic, then upon receipt of an evaluative claim suggesting that the advertised brand is imported, this may imply to the receiver that the beer merits its premium price. This implication would have been improbable had the receiver not believed that imported beers are superior.

For the sake of completeness, it is important to note that implied meaning is not restricted to evaluative advertising claims. Consider the following factual claim:

Direct Assertion: "Brand Y cereal contains 100% natural ingredients."

Logical Implication: It has no preservatives or other chemical substances.

Pragmatic Implication: It is more nutritional (or lower in calories, etc.) than cereals which are not 100% natural.

The direct assertion is a factual advertising claim because the statement is objectively verifiable; the cereal either is or is not 100 percent natural. Nonetheless, the illustrated pragmatic implications point out that consumers may indeed cull meaning from the claim in addition to that which is asserted directly. Advertisers are well aware of this tendency. Research by the Florida Citrus Commission found that "natural" and "nutritious" are near synonymous in meaning to consumers (Rozen, 1978). A survey performed by the Doyle Dane Bernback advertising agency corroborates this by showing that two-thirds of surveyed respondents regarded natural foods as healthier than other foods (Shoppers contradictory, 1978). Alarm over consumers' misunderstanding of the meaning of "natural" and advertisers' exploitation of this prompted the Institute of Food Technologists, an 18,000-member group of food scientists and technologists, to prepare a set of guidelines for food companies and ad agencies discouraging the use of claims that state or imply that natural foods are superior to processed foods (Food group, 1978).

Importance of Evaluative Claims.   A third necessary condition for evaluative claims to be deceptive is that they, or implications therefrom, be salient in the sense of influencing consumers' purchase decisions. Whether evaluative claims are "purchase influential" is entirely contingent on the particular claim. Creative copy writers and account executives are assumed to often succeed in selecting claims that are likely to evoke implications salient to the purchase decision.

Representation of Belief in Memory.   Another condition necessary for evaluative claims to deceive is that they be represented in memory. As noted by Jacoby and Small (1975), the "residual impact" of an ad is of primary concern because behavior is based typically on information residing in long-term memory rather than that restricted to temporary storage. Two areas of research provide evidence that evaluative claims, or, more importantly, the implications therefrom, achieve permanent memory. First, several recent studies have demonstrated that people are more likely to remember the pragmatic implications of a sentence than the direct assertion itself or its logical implication (Brewer & Lichtenstein, 1975; Johnson, Bransford, & Solomon, 1973; Schweller, Brewer, & Dahl, 1976). A second line of research, more directly pertinent to the issue, has shown that meaning inferred from a sentence, though not directly present in it, is indeed represented in memory (Barclay, 1973; Bransford & Franks, 1972).

Falsity of Evaluative Claims.   Another necessary condition to establish the deceptiveness of evaluative advertising is whether such claims are false. This may be no small task compared to determining the falsity of factual claims. These latter claims contain significates which represent physical properties of the advertised product. The claim that a certain automobile model will get 50 miles to the gallon, for example, can be subjected to scientific testing and either accepted or rejected based on test results. The significates in evaluative claims, in contrast, do not represent physical properties. Consequently, physical science testing cannot be employed to assess the veracity of such claims.

Consider the hypothetical claim used previously which stated that "Our model is incomparably luxurious." There obviously is no way of testing this other than by surveying consumers and requesting their opinions, and this would be inconclusive because consumer opinions most certainly would be mixed. However, though an evaluative claim per set cannot be unambiguously judged true or false, the pragmatic implications inferred therefrom can be. For example, if consumers infer from "incomparably luxurious" that the advertised automobile has a certain feature (such as reclining seats or leather upholstery) that it does not have, then the evaluative claim is just as deceptive, though not as blatantly so, as an untrue factual claim.

Behavioral Influence of Evaluative Claims.   The ultimate issue is whether evaluative advertising influences purchase behavior. One study (Shimp &

Yokum, 1981) has examined the issue directly, and two others have studied purchase intentions, the precursor to behavior. Details of these studies are delayed until a subsequent section. Let it suffice to say at this point that a modicum of evidence supports the possibility that deceptive advertising may at least initiate trial purchase behavior.

Summary. Arguments have been advanced showing the potentiality for evaluative advertising claims to satisfy all the necessary conditions for deception. Such claims may be influential in determining purchase; they are likely to be perceived; practical implications inferred from evaluative claims are highly believable; these implications are represented in memory; and they may indeed be false. The discussion turns now to an examination of the specific advertising research that is beginning to offer empirical evidence demonstrating that evaluative claims do mislead and deceive.

ADVERTISING RESEARCH EVIDENCE

The few studies performed so far represent three approaches to the issue: (1) one line of research has examined whether advertising receivers "read into" ad messages and extract meaning additional to that contained in the manifest content (the "information expansion research"); (2) another approach has explored the effects evaluative advertising has on receivers' beliefs (the "attribute-specific belief research"); (3) a third and most direct approach has examined whether evaluative claims influence behavioral intentions (the "direct evidence research").

The Information Expansion Research

Several studies have examined whether advertisements communicate meaning to receivers that transcends the meaning conveyed by the literal, manifest content. The reality of such influence would indicate that advertising is capable of beguiling receivers in an insidious manner. An initial study to examine this possibility was performed by Preston (1967). The guiding research assumption was that ad receivers commit logical fallacies when processing advertising information, that is, there is a tendency for people to draw inferences from ads which are not logically justified by the manifest advertising content. For example, if a cigarette advertiser claimed that its brand has less tar and nicotine than other brands, and consumers interpreted this to mean that smoking this particular brand is nondeleterious, then a logical fallacy would have been committed.

College students were exposed to multiple magazine ads. Five statements relating to each ad's content were constructed: a true statement (i.e., a correct paraphrasing of the ad content), a false statement, a statement entirely independent of the ad content, a logically valid statement, and a logically invalid statement. Each statement was evaluated as to whether it was an accurate or inaccurate representation of the ad content. Of primary interest was whether the logically invalid statement would be perceived as an accurate representation.

The data reflected a strong inclination for respondents to accept the logically invalid statements; nearly two-thirds of all such statements were accepted. This rather remarkable finding suggests that advertising receivers glean information that is not logically contained in ads. Could it be that the public has been conditioned to expect and tolerate advertisers' "license to exaggerate?"

This query was addressed in a follow-up study by Preston and Scharbach (1971). The objective was to assess whether people process ads differently (i.e., less logically) than they process alternative message forms. Twelve ads from the prior study, for which respondents had shown a strong tendency to accept the illogical statements, were selected. The content of each was reconstructed into three additional message forms: a news story, a business memorandum, and a personal letter. Student respondents were exposed to all twelve messages, three from each message form. Each message was accompanied by the five types of statements used in the previous study; respondents evaluated each in terms of whether it reflected accurately the message content.

The logically invalid statements were significantly more likely to be accepted when presented in advertisements than when presented in the other message forms. This suggests that the processing of advertising messages may represent an atypical form of information processing. Perhaps the public is more tolerant of advertising hyperbole and less inclined to counterargue (Greenwald, 1968; Wright, 1973) than is the case with other message forms. This possibility remains, unfortunately, an empirical issue as Preston and Scharbach's (1971) provocative hypothesis has not been further tested. Assuming it does accurately reflect information processing of advertising messages, then it suggests that when processing ads people are more likely to be misled and more persuasible than they are when processing other message forms.

That advertising receivers "read between the lines" to extract meaning from ads was demonstrated vividly in a study by Harris (1977). The basic research issue was whether implied advertising claims are processed as if they were factual assertions. Advertisements for 20 fictional products were constructed. Each product had two ad versions: one in which the critical claim was directly asserted, the other in which it was implied pragmatically.

The 108 participating college students heard tape recordings of the ads. In 10 of the products the critical claims were directly asserted, whereas they were implied in the other 10 ads. Respondents were simply required to evaluate whether a paraphrased version of each ad's critical claim was true, false, or of indeterminate truth value. To examine the effect of memory on these perceptions, three memory conditions were designed into the experiment: (1) one group evaluated the critical claims immediately after hearing each tape recorded ad ("immediate" condition); (2) a second group also evaluated each ad immediately after exposure, but this group also read a written script while listening to the ad ("concurrent" condition); (3) the final group did not evaluate each ad until having listened to all 20 ads; this "delayed" condition group was thus responding from long-term memory. An additional manipulation was used by presenting instructions to one-half of the respondents, prior to exposure to the ads, which explicitly warned them not to interpret implied claims as if they had been directly asserted. Thus, the study involved a 3 (memory conditions) × 2 (instruction conditions) × 2 (claim-type conditions) experimental design.

The finding of relevance to the present discussion involves respondents' tendency to process the implied claims as factual assertions. Over 70 percent of the implied claims were evaluated as true. This statistic is actually attenuated by the "instructions" condition where respondents were forewarned not to be deceived by implied claims. When the "no instructions" group is considered separately (and this group is clearly more characteristic of normal advertising reception), the number of implied claims perceived as true was slightly over 80 percent. Though this statistic is still significantly smaller than the percentage of directly asserted claims which respondents perceived as true, it reinforces Preston's earlier findings (1967; Preston & Scharbach, 1971) showing that receivers are prone to commit "mistakes" when processing advertising messages.

Further demonstration of receivers' tendency to extract "concealed" meaning from ad messages is provided by Shimp (1978). The relatively widespread advertising practice of using claims containing open-ended comparative adjectives (so-called incomplete comparatives) was examined. The guiding research premise was that such claims are potentially deceptive by virtue of being inherently susceptible to multiple interpretations, some of which are likely false. Consider, for example, the statement that "brand X is better." Psycholinguists (e.g., Glucksberg & Danks, 1975) would characterize this claim as being lexically ambiguous. Some receivers would interpret this to mean that X is better than Y with respect to attribute "a," whereas others may infer that X is better than Z with respect to attribute "b." Additional interpretations are clearly possible. Because it is unlikely that all interpretations are correct, some receivers must inevitably be misled.

To test this premise, three TV commercials containing incomplete comparative statements were selected. For illustration purposes, only one of these is discussed. It contained the statement that "Mennen E goes on warmer and drier." The ad did not specifically indicate what Mennen is warmer and drier than. A preliminary study revealed, however, that this statement, in context of the particular ad, evokes three alternative interpretations (closure alternatives): (1) than any other deodorant on the market; (2) than deodorants made with chemicals; (3) than a lot of other spray deodorants. Three separate studies using distinct measurement methods were conducted to assess whether respondents (college students) were inclined to use these closure alternatives in inferring meaning from the open-ended comparative statements. One study randomly assigned 192 students to three equal-sized groups of 64 each. After reading the script version of the commercial, students responded to a series of statements pertaining to the ad content. Likert-type scales were the measuring instrument. The incomplete comparative statement (Mennen E goes on warmer and drier) was embedded in these statements. However, each group received the incomplete comparative augmented with a different closure alternative. For example, one group's test booklet had "Mennen E goes on warmer and drier than any other deodorant on the market."

The results were dramatic in showing that incomplete comparatives evoke multiple interpretations. Over 50 percent of the respondents in each group agreed or strongly agreed that the ad actually claimed what the experimentally augmented incomplete comparative said it claimed. These findings were supported by the other two studies that used different measuring methods. Moreover, similar results, though not so dramatic, were manifest for the other two ads as well. Considered collectively, these results offer strong evidence indicating that receivers do indeed draw inferences beyond the incomplete content of comparative statements.

Rotfeld (1978) also explored the "information expansion" phenomenon. Advertisements for five inexpensive consumer products were used. Each ad contained both factual and evaluative (puffery) content. These were shown to 100 nonstudent adults. After reading each ad, respondents were provided with a list of claims that might have been stated or implied in the ads. Four types of claims were on the list: fact and fact-implied, puffery, and puffery-implied claims. Respondents were required to indicate which of these statements they believed to be true. The most outstanding finding was that the puffery and puffery-implied claims were no less likely to be believed than the fact and fact-implied claims.

The Attribute-Specific Belief Research

Two very creative studies have investigated whether evaluative advertising affects receivers' attribute-specific beliefs, that is, those beliefs involving product characteristics salient to the purchase decision. If evaluative advertising has a demonstrable impact on beliefs, then, in accordance with conventional thinking (e.g., Fishbein, 1967), it may also influence purchase intentions as well as behavior itself.

In an experiment by Olson and Dover (1978), coffee bitterness was selected as the evaluative advertising attribute. This choice was based on a preliminary test that revealed that bitterness is the most salient consideration in consumers' coffee purchase decisions. Fifty-one housewives were divided into control and experimental groups. The experimental group received a series of three exposures to ad-like messages that had been designed to elicit false beliefs about the experimental brand of coffee. All messages emphasized that this new brand contained "no bitterness." Four days after receiving the last message, the house-wives actually tried a sample of the coffee. However, at the trial the coffee was made intentionally bitter by increasing by 50 percent the recommended quantity per serving. The control group also participated in the taste trial but did not receive the pretrial advertisements.

The data demonstrated that the deceptive ads created a strong and false belief in the experimental group concerning the perceived bitterness of the new coffee. Sixty-four percent of the participants believed the deceptive ("no bitterness") claim before they had the opportunity to try the coffee. After trying the bitter coffee, the inflated beliefs declined, but they remained significantly higher than the control group's beliefs. This finding suggests that deceptive beliefs may be at least partially sustained even in light of nonsupportive behavioral information—a finding explainable by cognitive consistency theory (see Oliver, 1979, for a cogent discussion of how cognitive consistency partially explains the effective-ness of advertising puffery).

The relative effectiveness of factual and evaluative advertising in influencing consumers' attribute-specific beliefs was examined in an experiment by Hol-brook (1978). Two distinct ads were constructed for a hypothetical French auto-mobile named the Vendome. One ad consisted entirely of factual information relating to six automobile attributes (e.g., riding and handling characteristics). The other contained only evaluative information on the same six attributes. These were exposed repeatedly to two samples of graduate students, one receiv-ing the factual ad and the other the evaluative ad. After four separate exposures, measures were obtained on respondents' beliefs pertaining to the Vendome's possession of the six attributes.

Data analyses were performed by conducting tests for significant differences between the factual ad group's and evaluative ad group's belief scores. Five separate tests were performed: one for mean differences between the two groups on the most important attribute only, and four others for the mean differences in the sum of the k most important attributes (where k = 2, 3, 4, or 5). The factual ad group's mean scores were higher in all five tests, but statistical significance was achieved only at k = 3. The factual ad did not have a significantly greater impact than the evaluative ad on respondents' beliefs for the two most important attributes.

The study also revealed that the group receiving the factual ad perceived the ad as significantly more credible than did the group exposed to the evaluative ad. This finding, in connection with the pattern of the belief findings, indicates that the factual ad was more effective overall than was the evaluative ad. However, as noted by Holbrook, any implications must be tempered by the possibility that the study was biased in favor of the factual ad. In particular, the respondents were business graduate students who are more analytic and more hard data-oriented than are most consumers. Also, the experimental product is one where technical considerations are more important than is the case in most buying situations. In any event, this study provides an excellent set of procedures that other researchers would be advised to replicate.

The Direct Evidence Research

Only one study (Shimp & Yokum, 1981) has directly examined whether deceptive beliefs resulting from evaluative advertising influences purchase behavior. Two other studies (Harris, 1977; Olson & Dover, 1978) have come close by examining the effect on behavior's immediate precursor, behavioral intentions. The Harris (1977) study, described previously with the information expansion studies, also incorporated a procedure for assessing what effect claim type, whether directly asserted or pragmatically implied, has on purchase intentions. Respondents in this study were exposed to tape recorded ads for 20 hypothetical products; the critical claim in half of the ads was directly asserted, whereas it was implied in the other half. The respondents assigned to the "concurrent" condition (simultaneous exposure to a tape recording and a written script) were given a list of the 20 products and asked to select the 10 they would be most likely to buy. The findings indicated that products advertised with implied claims were just as likely to be selected as those advertised with directly asserted claims.

The Olson and Dover (1978) study, also discussed previously, offers additional evidence concerning the impact of evaluative advertising on purchase intentions. The experimental group received three ad exposures, after which their intentions to purchase the new, "non-bitter" coffee were measured (pretrial intentions). After taste-testing the coffee, made intentionally bitter, respondents were once again measured for intentions to purchase the coffee (posttrial intentions). The control group's intentions were measured only after taste-testing the product (posttrial intentions).

The experimental group's pretrial intentions were significantly greater than the control group's posttrial intentions, suggesting that the deceptive advertising certainly affected purchase inclination. The trial experience, however, resulted in a statistically significant reduction in the experimental group's mean intention. After testing the bitter coffee, respondents were less inclined to want it. Nonetheless, the experimental group's posttrial intentions remained more positive than were the intentions of the control group, which had not received the deceptive advertising. Thus, although intentions were diminished somewhat, the trial experience did not entirely eliminate the deceptive influence.

In the only known study to examine the impact of deceptive advertising on actual purchase behavior, Shimp and Yokum (1981) designed two experiments that manipulated advertising content and then measured the impact advertising had in sustaining repetitive purchasing. Both experiments revealed that evaluatively deceptive advertising was neither more nor less effective than factually deceptive advertising.

POLICY IMPLICATIONS AND RESEARCH NEEDS

The foregoing review has indicated that consumers do indeed read between the lines in processing evaluative advertising information—incomplete comparatives are perceptually completed, logical fallacies are committeed, and implications are processed as if they were assertions of fact. Related more directly to the purchase act itself, the evidence indicates that evaluative advertising does influence attribute-specific beliefs as well as purchase intentions. And, even in light of disconfirming behavioral information, these cognitive elements are largely sustained due to prior exposure to deceptive evaluative claims.

This situation, according to various critics, is lamentable and necessitates fundamental changes in the public policy regulating advertising. The following views are illustrative.

> The viewer is entitled to know that the claim made for a product is true. We [the FTC] want to restore integrity in the marketplace. I think viewers are skeptical now—and in many cases suitably skeptical [Michael Pertschuk, FTC chairman, quoted in Weisman, 1977, p. 11].

> Puffery deceives, and the regulations which have made it legal are thoroughly unjustified. . . . The rules which say [it is] nondeceptive and therefore legal are based on incorrect assumptions about the facts of human behavior and upon incorrect applications of the legal precedents from which they supposedly derive [Preston, 1975, p. 4].

> [It] is a worthy objective of future research . . . to determine exactly what sorts of implications are functionally, that is, psychologically, equivalent to assertions. Upon such clarification, it would certainly be appropriate [for the FTC] to make such false implications in advertising legally equivalent to false assertions [Harris, 1977, p. 608].

> [T]he courts should exercise their prerogative to apply more stringent standards to the use of implied deception while evidence as to its effect is being gathered [Oliver, 1979, p. 24].

A common strain running through these different perspectives is that evaluative, puffery advertising deceives, and, therefore, remedial action is imperative. Implicit in this call for greater regulation is the assumption that this deception is somehow detrimental to consumers. The argument goes like this: evaluative advertising statements, or implications therefrom, create false beliefs; these beliefs, in turn, influence consumers' attitudes toward the advertised product; consumers are influenced ultimately to purchase products and brands that would probably not be purchased if it were not for the deceptive advertising. To this logic, the cynic may retort: ''What real harm results from consumers trying a new product or brand. If they don't like it, they'll just stop buying it and switch to another brand.'' This argument rests on the assumption that consumers are able to discover the falsity of implied deception, and, as a result, experience disconfirmation of prepurchase expectations, leading to dissatisfaction with the chosen alternative and a likely switch to another brand on the next purchase occasion. Were this argument accurate, there would be little cause for concern; the ''cost'' to consumers would be minimal—a one-time outlay for a typically low-priced item.

A compelling counter-argument can be constructed, however. Oliver (1979) contends that recipients of implied deception are not likely to experience disconfirmation of their prepurchase expectations. Two explanations are proposed. On the one hand, it is physically impossible for evaluative claims to be disconfirmed. Consider, first, a factual claim stating that ''Our model will get 50 miles to the gallon.'' Confirmation or disconfirmation of this claim is an obvious possibility. In contrast, no physical basis is available for the consumer to disconfirm the (implied) claim that one will be happier, prettier, or sexier if one uses a certain personal hygiene product. A second explanation of why disconfirmation may be unlikely is the tendency for people to avoid cognitive inconsistency. Even if a discrepancy between prepurchase expectations and product performance is perceived, consumers may be motivated to ignore, suppress, or minimize this inconsistency in order to avoid psychological discomfort. The Olson and Dover (1978) findings from the coffee bitterness experiment probably represent a manifestation of this phenomenon.

Thus, assuming that disconfirmation is unlikely, it can be concluded that the harm resulting from implied deception transcends a one-time purchase experiment. Indeed, upon trying a new product, consumers may continue to purchase it for an extended period. The harm, though perhaps not great in a monetary sense, results from the notion that this type of insidious influence on consumer behavior is at odds with standards of fair play and decency. Moreover, the unscrupulous advertiser achieves an unfair advantage over competitors.

Deception Versus Unfairness

The natural extension from the arguments developed to this point is that the FTC should intensify its efforts to obviate evaluative advertising that deceives. The regulatory trend, in fact, has been in this direction. The FTC has increasingly challenged selling claims made by implication (Preston, 1977). Another trend has been the increased use of external evidence (e.g., consumer surveys) as a basis for supporting cases against firms accused of engaging in deceptive advertising. This development was necessitated by the FTC's efforts to curtail subtle forms of deception (Brandt & Preston, 1977).

However, there very well may be a distinct limitation on the FTC's ability to regulate evaluative advertising using deception as the sole regulatory basis. Reed and Coalson (1977), for example, challenge the view that evaluative advertising is deceptive. The basis for their argument is that such advertising influences consumers' feelings but not their beliefs, and based on conventional interpretations deception is not possible unless beliefs have been affected. Support for this position is provided by the notion of low-involvement learning (Krugman, 1965; Ray, 1973). According to the low-involvement model, consumers are not actively involved in processing advertising information, particularly broadcast advertising, and, therefore, do not have well-formed cognitive structures (beliefs and attitudes) prior to initially trying a new product or new brand.

But whereas deception may not provide sufficient grounds for regulating evaluative advertising, an alternative regulatory basis is provided by the unfairness doctrine (see, e.g., Cohen, 1974). Following is a summary of Reed and Coalson's (1977) explanation for why evaluative advertising is unfair to consumers:

1. Much advertising involves high-context communication, that is, most of the information is not contained in the message per se, but, instead, is contained in the context surrounding the message or is internalized in the receiver.

2. The intent of such advertising is to condition receivers' emotions. (The term "emotionally conditioning advertising" is used to describe this.)

3. Emotional conditioning is accomplished via a classical conditioning process where, through repetitive advertising, the product becomes associated with emotions (e.g., Coca-Cola is happiness).

4. Because of this emotional conditioning, the consumer upon encountering the "conditioned" product/brand in the store is prompted to purchase it, as it is perceived as a means of fulfilling emotional needs, relieving anxieties, and so on.

5. Because it is likely that some (many, most) products are incapable of delivering upon these promised results, the advertising which promotes them is unfair—the "risk" is imposed on consumers that the product might not perform as advertised.

Needed Research

Regardless of whether the regulatory basis is deception or unfairness, additional research is needed to better understand how evaluative advertising affects consumers. A major shortcoming of the deception-related research is that it has not firmly established that evaluative advertising actually influences behavior. It is one thing to show that evaluative advertising creates deceptive beliefs; it is quite another to demonstrate that these beliefs motivate purchase; and an even more stringent requirement is to establish that the deceptively-instigated trial purchase behavior is sustained in light of (potentially) disconfirming evidence. A strong case against evaluative advertising would obtain by demonstrating the plausibility of all links in the "deception chain," that is, evaluative advertising → deceptive beliefs → trial purchase → sustained behavior.

Utilization of the unfairness doctrine against evaluative (or emotionally conditioned) advertising also raises some important research issues. The essence of the unfairness argument is that an ad is unfair if promises of emotional need fulfillment or anxiety relief are made which the advertised product cannot possibly satisfy. Research requirements in support of unfairness are two-fold. First, it must be determined whether a particular ad promises emotional fulfillment or anxiety relief. This is a relatively straightforward requirement that can be satisfied using standard content analytic procedures. The second requirement is exceedingly more complex. It would be necessary to establish whether a product is in fact capable of delivering upon its promises. To illustrate this complexity, consider "typical" beverage commercials that promise receivers camaraderie, joy, reward for a hard days work, and nearly every other pleasure known to mankind. The research to justify an unfairness claim would have to demonstrate that a particular beverage will not provide these pleasures. It does not strain the intellect to appreciate how difficult it would be to generate unambiguous evidence showing that beer, for example, will (or will not) enhance interpersonal relations and/or satisfy intrapersonal needs. Because these consequences depend greatly upon personal and situational factors (i.e., whatever pleasures are obtained from beer consumption depend on the consumption gestalt and not just beer *per se*), research evidence would be highly contingent upon the specific research procedures (sampling plan, statistical context, etc.). Thus, though unfairness is a more encompassing policy tool than deception, the research requirements to support the former are much more difficult to satisfy.

Another area of needed research, with implications for both the deception and unfairness mechanisms, involves the study of nonverbal communication. The research reviewed in this chapter, not to mention the thrust of the chapter itself, has been devoted exclusively to verbal communication. Indeed, the study of nonverbal communication as it relates to marketing and advertising has been limited (Bonoma & Felder, 1977). Advertising, particularly that communicated via TV, has its effects on recipients through nonverbal modes—paralanguage, kinesics, and proxemics (Kess, 1976)—in addition to or in interaction with verbal effects. Limiting the study of deception and unfairness to verbal communication is inadequate. This limitation has been recognized by FTC officials (e.g., Westen raps, 1978). The study of nonverbal communication would enhance understanding of advertising-related information processing and would facilitate more enlightened policy regarding deception and unfairness in advertising.

CONCLUSION

The verbal content in advertising reflects a preponderance of nonobjective, evaluative claims over the factual. At lest two major factors account for this situation. On the one hand, many heavily advertised product categories contain brands that from a physical perspective are essentially equivalent to competitors' brands. In the absence of real differences, advertisers rely on various forms of verbal and nonverbal hyperbole and symbolism as a means of creating perceived differences. Also, increased regulation by self-regulatory bodies as well as by the FTC has perhaps discouraged advertisers from using factual claims, which are more likely to be challenged than are evaluative claims.

It is obvious that evaluative advertising is widely used. Not so obvious, but equally real, is the fact that such advertising is capable of deceiving receivers. The information processing of nonfactual advertising claims appears somewhat different than that associated with other message forms. Receivers of advertising messages have presumably been "conditioned" to be more tolerant of exaggerations and overstatements in advertising than in other message forms. The result is that receivers are prone to "read between the lines" in order to extract meaning from messages that are often vague and laden with symbolism. Specific manifestations of this include committing logical fallacies, processing implied claims as if they were factual assertions, and perceptually completing incomplete advertising statements.

The evidence in support of the deception potential of evaluative advertising is meager but consistent and growing. In addition to studies that have demonstrated the "reading between the lines" tendency, other empirical efforts have shown that evaluative advertising influences attribute-specific beliefs and also purchase intentions. Moreover, evidence suggests that even in view of disconfirming evidence, cognitive elements influenced by deception are somewhat resistant to change.

There is a major remaining gap in the empirical efforts that have examined the deceptive potential of evaluative advertising. In particular, only one study (Shimp & Yokum, 1981) has explored whether deceptively-formed beliefs do indeed influence purchase behavior, and the results are equivocal. Of course, whether purchase behavior resulting from deception is sustained in light of disconfirming evidence has not been studied either.

Research is needed also to examine the argument that the adverse effects of evaluative advertising result from an "unfairness" mechanism rather than from deception. A corollary to this is the need to study the potential deception and/or unfairness that may result from nonverbal modes of advertising communication.

REFERENCES

Aaker, D. A. Deceptive advertising. In D. A. Aaker & G. S. Day (Eds.), *Consumerism*. New York: Free Press, 1974.

Aaker, D. A., & Myers, J. G. *Advertising management*. Englewood Cliffs, N.J.: Prentice-Hall, 1975.

Armstrong, G. M., Kendall, C. L., & Russ, F. A. Application of consumer information processing work to public policy issues. *Communication Research*, 1975, 2, 232–245.

Armstrong, G. M., & Russ, F. A. Detecting deception in advertising. *MSU Business Topics*, 1975, *23*, 21–31.

Barclay, J. R. Comprehension and sentence memory. *Cognitive Psychology*, 1973, *4*, 229–254.

Berdine, W. R. Some relationships between perceived generality and ambiguity in a set of words. *Language and Speech*, 1974, *17*, 305–311.

Bogart, L. Is all this advertising necessary? *Journal of Advertising Research*, 1978, *18*, 17–26.

Bonoma, T. V., & Felder, L. C. Nonverbal communication in marketing: Toward a communicational analysis. *Journal of Marketing Research*, 1977, *14*, 169–180.

Brandt, M. T., & Preston, I. L. The Federal Trade Commission's use of evidence to determine deception. *Journal of Marketing*, 1977, *41*, 54–62.

Bransford, J. D., & Franks, J. J. The abstraction of linguistic ideas. *Cognition*, 1972, *1*, 211–249.

Brewer, W. F., & Lichtenstein, E. H. Recall of logical and pragmatic implications in sentences with dichotomous and continuous antonyms. *Memory and Cognition*, 1975, *3*, 315–318.

Burnkrant, R. E. A motivational model of information processing intensity. *Journal of Consumer Research*, 1976, *3*, 21–30.

Coen, R. J. Ad spending is outmuscling national economy in general. *Advertising Age*, January 8, 1979, S-7, S-8.

Cohen, D. Surrogate indicators and deception in advertising. *Journal of Marketing*, 1972, *36*, 10–15.

Cohen, D. The concept of unfairness as it relates to advertising legislation. *Journal of Marketing*, 1974, *38*, 8–13.

Comparative ads' effect praised by Pertschuk. *Advertising Age*, November 27, 1978, 40.

Coney, K. A., & Patti, C. H. *Can marketers substantiate their claims?* Unpublished manuscript, Arizona State University, 1978.

Fishbein, M. A behavior theory approach to the relations between beliefs about an object and the attitude toward the object. In M. Fishbein (Ed.), *Readings in attitude theory and measurement*. New York: John Wiley, 1967.

Fishbein, M., & Ajzen, I. *Belief, attitude, intention, and behavior: An introduction to theory and research*. Reading, Mass.: Addison-Wesley, 1975.

Food group hits 'natural.' *Advertising Age*, December 4, 1978, 54.

Foss, D. J., Bever, T. G., & Silver, M. The comprehension and verification of ambiguous sentences. *Perception and Psychophysics*, 1968, *4*, 304–306.

Gardner, D. M. Deception in advertising: A conceptual approach. *Journal of Marketing*, 1975, *39*, 40–46.

Glucksberg, S., & Danks, J. *Experimental psycholinguistics: An introduction*. New York: John Wiley, 1975.

Greenwald, A. G. Cognitive learning, cognitive response to persuasion, and attitude change. In A. G. Greenwald, T. C. Brock, & T. M. Ostrum (Eds.), *Psychological foundations of attitudes*. New York: Academic Press, 1968.

Haefner, J. E., & Permut, S. E. An approach to the evaluation of deception in television advertising. *Journal of Advertising*, 1974, *3*, 40–45.

Harris, R. J. Comprehension of pragmatic implications in advertising. *Journal of Applied Psychology*, 1977, *62*, 603–608.

Harris, R. J., & Monaco, G. E. The psychology of pragmatic implication: Information processing between the lines. *Journal of Experimental Psychology: General*, 1978, *107*, 1–22.

Holbrook, M. B. Beyond attitude structure: Toward the informational determinants of attitude. *Journal of Marketing Research*, 1978, *15*, 545–556.

Jacoby, J., & Small, C. The FDA approach to defining misleading advertising. *Journal of Marketing*, 1975, *39*, 65–73.

Johnson, M. K., Bransford, J. D., & Solomon, S. K. Memory for tacit implications of sentences. *Journal of Experimental Psychology*, 1973, *98*, 203–205.

Just, M. A., & Clark, H. H. Drawing inferences from the presuppositions of affirmative and negative sentences. *Journal of Verbal Learning and Verbal Behavior, 1973, 12,* 21–31.

Kess, J. F. *Psycholinguistics: Introductory perspectives.* New York: Academic Press, 1976.

Krugman, H. E. The impact of television advertising: Learning without involvement. *The Public Opinion Quarterly,* 1965, *29,* 349–356.

Lindsay, P. H., & Norman, D. A. *Human information processing: An introduction to psychology.* New York: Academic Press, 1972.

Lutz, R. J. First-order and second-order cognitive effects in attitude change. *Communications Research,* 1975, *2,* 289–299.

Marquez, F. T. Advertising content: persuasion, information, or intimidation? *Journalism Quarterly,* 1977, *54,* 482–491.

Offir, C. Recognition memory for presuppositions of relative clause sentences. *Journal of Verbal Learning and Verbal Behavior,* 1973, *12,* 636–643.

Oliver, R. L. An interpretation of the attitudinal and behavioral effects of puffery. *Journal of Consumer Affairs,* 1979, *13,* 8–27.

Olson, J. C., & Dover, P. A. Effects of expectation creation and disconfirmation on belief elements of cognitive structure. In B. B. Anderson (Ed.), *Advances in consumer research, Vol. 3.* Cincinnati: Association for Consumer Research, 1976.

Olson, J. C., & Dover, P. A. Cognitive effects of deceptive advertising. *Journal of Marketing Research,* 1978, *15,* 29–38.

Osgood, C. E. The representational model and relevant research methods. In I. de Sola Pool (Ed.), *Trends in content analysis.* Urbana, Ill.: University of Illinois Press, 1959.

Osgood, C. E., Suci, G. J., & Tannenbaum, P. H. *The measurement of meaning.* Urbana, Ill.: University of Illinois Press, 1957.

Pollay, R. W., Fryer, C., & Zaichowsky, J. *The information content of television advertising: A longitudinal and cross-sectional study.* Discussion draft of paper presented to the American Institute for Decision Sciences, Chicago, October 1977.

Preston, I. L. Theories of behavior and the concept of rationality in advertising. *Journal of Communication,* 1967, *17,* 211–222.

Preston, I. L. *The great American blow-up: Puffing in advertising and selling.* Madison, Wis.: University of Wisconsin Press, 1975.

Preston, I. L. The FTC's handling of puffery and other selling claims made by implication. *Journal of Business Research,* 1977, *5,* 155–181.

Preston, I. L., & Bowen, L. Perceiving advertisements as emotional, rational and irrational. *Journalism Quarterly,* 1971, *48,* 73–84.

Preston, I. L., & Scharbach, S. E. Advertising: More than meets the eye? *Journal of Advertising Research,* 1971, *11,* 19–24.

Ray, M. L. *Marketing communication and the hierarchy-of-effects* (Rep. P-53-C). Cambridge, Mass.: Marketing Science Institute, 1973.

Reed, O. L., Jr., & Coalson, J. L., Jr. Eighteenth-century legal doctrine meets twentieth-century marketing techniques: F.T.C. regulation of emotionally conditioning advertising. *Georgia Law Review,* 1977, *11,* 733–782.

Resnik, A., & Stern, B. L. An analysis of the information content in television advertising. *Journal of Marketing,* 1977, *41,* 50–53.

Rommetveit, R. *Words, meanings, and messages: Theory and experiments in psycholinguistics.* New York: Academic Press, 1968.

Rotfeld, H. J. *Advertising deception, consumer research puffery: An inquiry into puffery's power and potential to mislead consumers.* Unpublished doctoral dissertation, University of Illinois, 1978.

Rozen, L. Marketers cautious about capitalizing on nutrition. *Advertising Age,* October 30, 1978, 74.

Schweller, K. G., Brewer, W. F., & Dahl, D. A. Memory for illocutionary forces and perlocution-ary effects of utterances. *Journal of Verbal Learning and Verbal Behavior*, 1976, *15*, 325–337.

Shimp, T. A. *An analysis of the structural and content characteristics of national television adver-tising*. Unpublished doctoral dissertation, University of Maryland, 1974.

Shimp, T. A. Do incomplete comparisons mislead? *Journal of Advertising Research*, 1978, *18*, 21–27.

Shimp, T. A. Social-psychological (mis)representations in television advertising. *Journal of Con-sumer Affairs*, 1979, *13*, 28–40.

Shimp, T. A., & Kuehl, P. G. A typology and empirical analysis of commercial message content. In C. D. Schick (Ed.), *The challenge of change to advertising education*. Austin, Texas: American Academy of Advertising, 1976.

Shimp, T. A., & Yokum, J. T. The influence of deceptive advertising on repeat purchase behavior. In K. Bernhardt (Ed.), *The changing marketing environment: New theories and applications*. Chicago: American Marketing Association, 1981.

Shoppers contradictory, frozen food meeting told. *Advertising Age*, November 27, 1978, 38.

Udell, G. G., & Fischer, P. J. The FTC improvement act. *Journal of Marketing*, 1977, *41*, 81–87.

Weisman, J. We will be embarking on a long fight with advertisers. *TV Guide*, November 12–18, 1977, 10–11.

Westen raps lack of 'hard' data in national ads. *Advertising Age*, August 14, 1978, 70.

White, H. Return of the cartoon. *Advertising Age*, November 20, 1978, 45.

Wright, P. L. The cognitive processes mediating acceptance of advertising. *Journal of Marketing Research*, 1973, *10*, 53–62.

Semantic and Prosodic Manipulation in Advertising

Linda Coleman
University of California, Berkeley

INTRODUCTION

Most readers of this book have probably had the experience of coming away from a commercial with the impression that a particular claim was made. Later examination of the transcript, however, reveals no such claim. In some cases, we can see that the claim was suggested by the material that appears in the transcript—the connotations of some of the words, for example, or a line of reasoning we are forced to take in order to make sense of the events in the advertisement. Even so, we may have difficulty showing exactly what caused us to believe that the claim had occurred overtly. In other cases, nothing in the words or grammatical structure appears to support our interpretation. We are left to conclude that it was not *what* was said, but rather *how* it was said that conveyed the message we thought we heard.

Such cases demonstrate that communication involves a great deal more than simply putting words together in a grammatical structure or seeing to it that all and only the necessary information is included. Our processing of an utterance is dependent upon our understanding of the context in which it occurs—who the speaker is, what sorts of things are being talked about, the relationship between the speaker and the addressee, and so on. Much of our understanding of the context comes from our sociocultural background knowledge. Much of it is negotiated on the spot by the participants (or, in the case of advertisements, conveyed to the addressee) in part by the semantics and by how things are said (Gumperz, 1977, 1982).

Linguists refer to the "how things are said" aspect of communication as prosody. Prosody includes those linguistic and paralinguistic features that make up what we normally think of as intonation, emphasis or accentuation, and "tone of voice"—specifically, (1) the overall pitch register (high, medium, or low); (2) changes in pitch; (3) the length of consonants and vowels; (4) loudness; (5) the speed of speech; and (6) the rhythm of speech. (For detailed treatments of these features, see Bolinger, 1978; Crystal, 1975; Ladd, 1980.) Prosodic cues direct our processing of utterances by signalling the relative importance of individual segments and the relationships between various pieces of information conveyed. They thus guide us—if all goes well—in finding the interpretation that the speaker intended within the range of interpretations allowed by the syntax and semantics of the utterance (Gumperz, 1982).

Because semantic cues are also important in setting up the context within which an utterance is to be understood, the first section of this chapter concentrates on some uses of semantics in advertising. The second section examines some of the prosodic features that appear frequently in television commercials and their effect on our processing of the information contained in those commercials. In the third section, two television commercials are examined in depth, tying together the material in the first two sections. Although it would be preferable to be able to spend the semantics section entirely upon semantics and save prosodic analysis for later, real communication simply does not work that way. In many cases it is necessary to appeal to prosodic analysis for a more thorough understanding of the semantics and to introduce semantics into the examination of prosody. For the same reason—and because semantics and prosody play such a large role in contextualization—problems of context are dealt with throughout, rather than in a separate section.

To indicate prosodic features we use an adaptation of Trim's (1975) transcription system. This system divides utterances into major and minor tone groups. Major tone groups are bounded by full pauses and so, for our purposes, can be considered the rough equivalent of sentences as one expects them to be spoken— with a 'full stop' at the end. Minor tone groups are bounded by smaller pauses within the major tone groups. The end of a major tone group is indicated by double slashes (//), of a minor one by a single slash (/). The intonation of stressed syllables will be marked as follows: a line to the left of the syllable or over the vowel indicates the direction the voice takes (e.g., rising or falling), whereas the height of the line indicates the pitch of the voice at the start of the syllable.[1] Thus:

---

[1]These markings are normally reserved for the tonal nucleus, i.e., "the last intonational information point in a tone group" (Trim, 1975, p. 3). As this paper is not intended primarily for linguists, I have, in the interests of simplicity and to avoid confusing readers who are unaccustomed to intonational marking conventions, used them for any syllable in which a significant pitch change occurs.

, = low rise (i.e., rising tone, but at a low pitch)
′ = high rise
ˌ = low fall
ˋ = high fall
⁻ = high pitch (unchanging)

˘ = fall-rise
^ = rise-fall
_ = low pitch (unchanging)

A colon after a vowel (e.g., "adoːre') indicates that the vowel is unusually long and drawn out. Lengthened consonants are indicated by doubling the letter (e.g., 'humm'). Changes in the speed of speech are indicated by subscript *acc* for acceleration, *dec* for deceleration. Voice tone and loudness are indicated, where relevant, in the text.

SEMANTICS

Both television and print advertising contain many examples of manipulation of language to get the message across. The use of the word "manipulation" should not be taken to imply that these cases are necessarily deceptive; many are not even slightly misleading. Puns, invented words (e.g., "gasid indigestion"), and sentences that would be considered anomalous in normal speech are frequently used to startle the audience and get their attention or to serve as mnemonics. A case in which this sort of word-play is carried through an entire commercial is an advertisement for Wilkinson II razor blades. A sultry-looking Englishwoman, lounging in a very plush chair, speaks to the camera in a low, breathy voice:

(1)a American'men are s̄uch ˌbeasts //
   b I adô:re them //
   c But there ˌare times / when they can be írritàting /
      acc
   d s̄uch 'rough nécks //
      dec
   e Thāt's / when ˄ I ˌsay //
   f put a little ^English / on ˄ your ˌTrac Two rázòr //
   g Thêse Wìlkinson Two Cártrìdges / slip right înn //
      acc
   h so móst twin-blade râzors / can have the fāmous /
                                           dec
      Wìlkinson ˌedge //

i   B̄e a smòo:th American //
j   Put a little Ēnglish / on your - Trac Twó ⸴ razor //[2]

The word-play that runs throughout involves the analogy between roughness of personality and roughness of face. When such extended punning occurs in normal conversation, one of its points of interest is to see how long it can be kept up without the equivalences so created falling apart. Likewise, the viewer's interest is presumably held by curiosity as to whether the word-play can be sustained through the entire commercial. It is in fact overtly maintained in (a), (c), (d), and (i) by the double meanings of "beasts," "irritating," "roughnecks," and "smooth." Additional punning occurs in the phrase "put a little English on your razor," where a set phrase from the game of billiards is connected with the Englishness of the product. This is discussed further below.

The difficulty in trying to isolate one specific kind of linguistic behavior for study is well illustrated by this commercial. At least part of the effect of the semantic play hinges on the viewer's understanding of the context which is created within the commercial—what sort of person is speaking, and what sorts of things she is apt to be referring to. This in turn is conveyed, in part, by her voice tone, intonation, English accent, and style of speech. Furthermore, there is some attempt made to draw the viewer into the ad. The speaker uses a low voice tone, which suggests that she and the addressee are close together. The pronouns "I" and "your" are both prominent prosodically, receiving high tones. Additionally, the rising intonation on the word "roughnecks" suggests that a question is being asked, which is, of course, not the case here. It is, however, perfectly normal to use rising intonation on a statement by way of asking whether the addressee understands or is in agreement with what has been said (Lakoff, 1975).[3] This being the mass media, the speaker cannot, of course, get any signal from the addressee, but she immediately proceeds to her next point, which, in a situation where true interaction were possible, would occur only if she had indeed received confirmation of understanding.

The immediate context of the woman's speech, then, is one of some sort of face-to-face interaction. In fact, her appearance, intonation, voice tone, and facial expressions, as well as her surroundings, all of which could be described as sexy, suggest a very specific type of interaction—an old-movies style seduction. As typified by Bogart and Bacall, seductions in such films are frequently preceded by a series of sexual *double entendres* by means of which the seducer

---

[2]Reproduced with Permission of the Copyright Owner, The Wilkinson Company. This advertisement has been analyzed from a slightly different perspective by Gumperz (1982, pp. 100–104).

[3]Bolinger (1978) identifies rising tone as indicating that there is more to come. It occurs frequently as the final tone on questions because, obviously enough, an answer is expected. The same holds for a situation like that in the advertisement, where a statement is transformed into a question by the use of final rising tone.

tries to find out how willing the addressee is without being too overt about it. This makes more sense of the rising intonation on "roughnecks." A simple pun is an end in itself; it is either understood or not understood, and if the latter, then it has failed totally, because a pun loses its whole point if it must be explained. Sexual double entendre of this sort, however, is a means to an entirely different end. The addressee must not merely understand the word play but must also signal willingness to go along with what it suggests. The speaker, then, is signaling, "Do you understand what I'm *really* talking about?" and her continuation as though she had received a signal of agreement covertly puts the viewer in the position of collusion with her. (The word play that actually occurs is quite innocent, of course. The advertiser is merely mimicking the seduction context in the hopes of selling some razor blades.)

The word "roughnecks" is in a sense the interactional pivot of the commercial, as it is the immediate means by which the viewer is put in collusion with the speaker. It is semantically pivotal as well, as it prepares for the introduction of roughness of face as the second element of the dominant word-play in the commercial. In its meaning of "people who behave roughly," it is pronounced as a two-syllable unit with stress on the first syllable. In (d), however, the speaker pronounces it as two separate syllables with nearly equal emphasis and a slight pause between them. Everything that has preceded (d) requires that the word take the meaning "rough people," but the prosody forces the interpretation "necks that are rough," which only makes sense in light of the following reference to shaving.

Another prosodic feature, the lengthened final consonant of "slip right in" in (g), highlights this phrase which carries the sexual double entendre through the two facts about the product which are overtly stated. The first fact is that the product is a razor blade, in (f); the second is that it fits most twin-blade razors, in (h).

By bringing cultural knowledge to bear, we can connect the two sets of apparently unrelated puns—those involving roughness of behavior/face and those involving Englishness and putting a spin on a billiard ball. Putting English on a billiard ball suggests indirectness, in contrast to the excessive directness inherent in rough behavior. The stereotype has it, furthermore, that the English are more refined, less direct in personal interaction, and have better taste than Americans. Thus, the advertisement also carries the implication that an American man who uses the product will thereby render himself worthy even of an Englishwoman's interest.

The entire message of the advertisement, then, barring the two overtly stated facts mentioned above, is carried by the word-play within the context established both by the word-play itself and by the prosodic cues which guide the viewer's interpretation of the word-play.

Semantic manipulation also occurs in advertisements with rather more information content. The use of one word or phrase rather than another can convey information beyond what we take to be the literal meaning of the message. An example is the use of jargon. When both speaker and addressee understand the jargon, it can be used as a linguistic shortcut, either to facilitate communication, or simply because it is the most accurate means available for talking about the subject matter. When jargon is used to an uncomprehending addressee, the speaker violates two maxims of conversation: (a) be as clear as necessary; (b) be as informative as necessary. This does not necessarily imply duplicity on the part of the speaker.[4] The speaker may be trying to be as clear and informative as possible without violating another maxim—that one does not say things one know to be untrue. By using words that are overtly not informative enough, the speaker helpfully provides a clear signal to the addressee that (b) is being violated. The underlying assumption is that the addressee could not understand any more about the subject matter within the limits of the communication. (See Grice, 1975, for the maxims of conversation and a discussion of necessary violations of them.) For this reason, jargon can also be used to convey that the addressee is much less knowledgeable and therefore has no right to argue with the speaker.

The following examples illustrate some of the uses of jargon in advertising. In one case, the informativeness maxim is straightforwardly violated, as described in the preceding paragraph. In another, the advertiser makes an obvious effort to avoid a violation, leading the hearer to somewhat different conclusions about the product and the manufacturer.

Commercials for various kinds of waxes often state that the product contains "special polymers" and sometimes just "polymers." Because it is a technical term not commonly used, "polymer" is probably not well understood by most Americans. Its use suggests that the manufacturer has a great deal more expertise in chemistry than the average consumer, which, of course, is true. When no explanation of the term is given, which is usually the case, it is conveyed that the viewers could not understand any more within the limits of that particular communication. In that case, however, why mention it at all? The implication is that the presence of polymers, or special polymers, in the product is extremely significant—so much so that the advertisers are willing to make their communication somewhat anomalous by violating two maxims that need not have been violated had the jargon term not been introduced in the first place.

---

[4]As Grice (1975) points out, we tend to assume that our coconversationalist is trying to be as cooperative as possible. If two maxims happen to conflict in a particular situation, the speaker must decide which will override the other. Common sense also tends to eliminate duplicity as an explanation in most cases, since if the speaker wishes to conceal something, there is usually the option of staying off the subject entirely. While very few people seem to feel that advertisers are entirely above exaggerating the virtues of their products, the same assumption still holds. It is after all the advertisers who are communicating with us—not we with them—and they are spending a great deal of money to do so. They have entire control of what is dealt with in their advertisements, and if they wish to avoid a subject, it is generally within their power not to bring it up at all.

In the following segment of a magazine ad, the advertisers put their jargon to rather different use by employing the two maxims mentioned above:

(2) . . . The speed at which a toothpaste dissolves is called the "Dispersal Rate." Because Aim is a gel, not a paste, it has an exceptionally fast dispersal rate. This means when a child brushes with Aim, it spreads its good taste faster than paste in the normal brushing time. . . .[5]

Technical jargon frequently uses words available in everyday language, but with a somewhat different meaning. "Disperse" is a verb normally used of groups of discrete objects, such as people, marbles, or particles, not of things that come in a mass, such as toothpaste or gel. In an advertisement for this sort of product, then, the use of this word implies that we are dealing with the substance on the particle level, rather than in the way most of us think of it. "Rate" connotes precision of measurement, associated with scientific research. "Dispersal Rate," emphasized by capitalization and quotation marks, is thus easily identifiable as technical jargon and conjures up images of laboratories and scientific testing.

At first glance, the introduction of the term "dispersal rate" seems totally useless. No sooner do the advertisers introduce it than they explain both what it means and how it applies to the product. It would certainly have been simpler to say something like "because Aim is a gel, not a paste, it dissolves/spreads through the mouth unusually rapidly." However, the companion maxim to the one mentioned above—"be as informative as necessary"—is that one should not give more information than is needed (Grice, 1975). The assumption is that the maxim is observed unless there is some compelling reason for violating it. This assumption, combined with the use of the term in a sentence about the product immediately after it has been defined, suggests that the information could not have been conveyed easily in any other way than by using jargon, even though that required pausing to define the term before it could be used. If something can *only* be talked about with a technical term like "Dispersal Rate," we are apt to assume that it is very modern and based on the latest scientific research. We may also be more likely to trust a company that takes the trouble to give us extra background information about the product. (The readers of the advertisement are presumably aware that the term does not appear in advertisements for other toothpastes or gels.) Finally, of course, as with the use of "polymer," the jargon serves as a linguistic demonstration of the company's expertise.

The converse of the "polymer" situation also occurs in advertising, when a descriptive phrase (periphrasis) is used, whereas the object's name, which would be readily understood by the audience, is avoided. The result is a sort of "anti-

---

[5]Reproduced with Permission of the Copyright Owner, Lever Brothers, Inc.

jargon.''[6] One of the most common kinds of anti-jargon involves references to simple aspirin with phrases like ''pain reliever'' or ''the pain reliever/ingredient most recommended by doctors.'' The use of a more indirect term like a definite description in place of the name ''aspirin'' implies that the ingredient is something very technical which the layperson could not identify or understand. Because aspirin is well known, it makes no sense to refer to it otherwise than by that name. As a result, the addressee could easily conclude that the ''pain reliever'' could not be mere aspirin.

As the above examples show, careful semantic selection can convey information far beyond what appears on the surface as the ''literal meaning'' of an advertisement. We have seen how some of our basic assumptions about how communication works require us to interpret certain uses of semantics in certain ways. In the next section, we observe the function of prosody in guiding us to particular interpretations of semantic and syntactic material in advertisements.

PROSODY

In this section we examine the use of various prosodic features to draw attention to certain segments, to indicate the speaker's attitude toward the product or the viewer, to suggest material that is not present on the surface, and to interpret the grammatical function of particular words.

Product Names

Variation in tempo and pitch can be used to call attention to a product name. For example, the line ''. . . // 'Introdùcing / Chrÿsler Le ˌBaron // . . .'' is an instance of the very frequent practice of giving the product name a tone group of its own for emphasis. It is also common to find the product name spoken with somewhat higher pitch than the surrounding material, or with ''smile-voice'' (i.e., a voice tone which clearly indicates that the speaker is smiling).

In example (3) the prosody of the product name is altered to give it two different connotations:

(3) . . . // 'Now 'people / who've turned awây /
                             acc

from the taste of dìet sòft drinks /
are túrning to Dìet Pèpsi // the ōne-calorie dìet 'cola
             dec   *acc*

---

[6]I am indebted to Paul Kay (personal communication) for suggesting this term.

with the / hónest-tò-Pépsi ˏtaste // D̄iet / Pèpsi Còla //[7]
      dec   *dec*

The announcer speaks the name of the product both times with pitch higher than the rest of the utterance. Interestingly, on the first utterance of the name, it is a unit—"Dìet Pèpsi". (Compare, for instance, the parallel intonation on the subsequent unit, "Pèpsi Còla.") The second utterance of the name adds the word "Cola," and separates the word "Diet" into its own tone group, as well as beginning the unit "Pepsi Cola" with a high falling tone. This gives a reading of "Pepsi Cola" as the product name, with the "Diet" apparently serving as an adjective, indicating a particular kind of Pepsi Cola, not—as the earlier utterance's intonation suggested—a different product name. Of course, the first utterance of the name, with "Diet" as part of the product name, occurs at the end of a sentence introducing it as a diet soft drink. The second utterance, identifying it as a kind of Pepsi Cola, occurs immediately after the point is made that it still tastes like Pepsi, rather than like other diet soft drinks. The product can thus benefit from both identifications within the same advertisement.

In a rather unusual tone grouping, there is no pause after "diet cola." Instead, there is a slight pause after "with the" and before "honest". This is also the start of a deceleration, so that "honest to Pepsi taste" is highlighted. In addition, there is also a slight pause after "honest," so that it is a unit in itself. The announcer slows his speech at each mention of the product name, with the final mention of the name being at the slowest tempo in the commercial.

It is also possible to use the product name as an adjective. This usually involves giving it less significance prosodically, but the inferences that the hearer must make as a result can be useful to the advertiser.

(4) . . . // In ˏminutes / Pōlaroid's Prònto /
    gives you shárp / cleàr / ŚX-sèventy /
    còlors that ˏlast // . . .[8]

The name of the type of Polaroid camera (SX-70) occurs as the third element in a list of adjectives and does not receive the intonation that, as mentioned above, is frequently used for product names. Rather, the rise on the "S" of "SX" and the fall on "seventy" parallel the intonation of the other two adjectives ("sharp" receiving a rising tone, "clear" a falling tone). This suggests, subtly enough, that there are certain kinds of snapshot colors that are "SX-70 colors" and that differ from other kinds of colors, just as sharp colors differ from colors that are not sharp, and clear colors differ from colors that are not clear. In order to do this, the speaker has had to reduce the product name prosodically to an adjective.

---

[7]Reproduced with Permission of the Copyright Owner, PepsiCo, Inc.
[8]Reproduced with Permission of the Copyright Owner, Polaroid, Inc.

"SX" is pronounced like the English place-name "Essex," with the vowel of the second syllable reduced.

Attitude

The use of "smile-voice" to indicate approval or pleasure when uttering the name of a product has already been mentioned. Other attitude indicators occur in advertisements as well. In example (5), a character in a commercial shows his attitude toward the product, and his prosody conveys some additional information about the situation.

In the commercial from which (5) is taken, a wife tricks her husband into using the product, Head & Shoulders shampoo; he believes that he is using her "beauty shampoo" instead of a dandruff shampoo. They make a bet on whether or not his dandruff will return—he says it will, she says it won't. She then shows him the bottle. He says:

(5) //Heád ànd Shoulders!// No ˏfair!//[9]

The combination of semantics and prosody in (5) insure that the viewers will understand that the speaker knows the brand and believes it to be an effective dandruff shampoo. The high falling tone is cited by Crystal (1975, p. 38) as associated with "definite emotional commitment"—he mentions specifically "emphasis" and "surprise." The speaker of (5) feels that his wife has cheated on their bet by introducing as a "beauty shampoo" a shampoo that is intended to control dandruff. This much is apparent from the words alone. The prosody shows strong emotional protest—she has not merely cheated; she has destroyed any chance he had of winning the bet. That is, there is no doubt whatsoever about the product's effectiveness. Interestingly, it was the practice in the company's earlier commercials of the same general plot to have a scene billed as taking place a day or so later to show that the dandruff had not returned. Here, it is simply presupposed that the matter is settled.

Prosodic features indicating attitude have a special use in commercials for medicines.

(6) . . . // Those˟bursting / ˏ Alka-Seltzerˏbubbles / reliê:ve / your ˏacid indiˏgestion
    and ˏaching ˏhead // For ˏacid indigestion alône / 'Alka-Seltzer ˏGold //[10]
                  acc

An announcer is the speaker. The first sentence (major tone group) of (6) is spoken with a low creaky voice and at a slower pace than the material which follows it. The long vowel of "relie:ve" and the series of low rising-falling

---

[9]Reproduced with Permission of the Copyright Owner, Procter and Gamble, Inc.
[10]Reproduced with Permission of the Copyright Owner, Miles Laboratories.

tones, like the low creaky voice tone, are the sort of prosodic features that might be used by someone in pain. The prosody thus shows the announcer's sympathy toward the sufferer—and by association the company's sympathy. The first syllables of "Alka-Seltzer" and "bubbles" are timed to coincide with the dropping of the two tablets into the glass, so that the words are reinforced by the visual and background audio parts of the commercial.

In the second major tone group the announcer drops most of the prosodic features indicating sympathy with a sick person, keeping only the low voice tone. Speed of speech picks up and the rhythm is less regular. The rising-falling tone on "alone" is mostly a rise, with a slight fall on the end, so that it is heard primarily as a rising tone. This word is followed by the product name with a final low falling contour. This intonation pattern, along with the lack of a verb in the second major tone group, are typical of what one finds announcers in commercials doing, but not typical of other kinds of speech. Thus the announcer signals prosodically that he is taking on his "announcer status," which allows him to close the commercial in the way the audience is accustomed to having commercials end—with voice-over mention of the product name.

Contrast

Advertising has long been famous for the incomplete comparative, e.g., "For faster relief, use Brand X," in a commercial where no other product is mentioned. Aaker and Myers (1975), in their book *Advertising Management,* discuss closure, the tendency people have, when faced with an incomplete sequence such as a comparative with no standard, to supply the missing material themselves, and then to perceive the item as having been complete from the start. One of the examples they cite is the old Salem cigarette jingle: "You can take Salem out of the country but // you can't take the country out of Salem" (p. 291). After the jingle had been around for a while, it was possible for the advertisers to supply only the first half and trust the audience to "hear" the entire jingle. (See also the article by Terence A. Shimp, this volume, and Shimp, 1978.) The prosodic equivalent of the incomplete comparative is contrastive accent minus one of the contrasted items.

Contrastive accent is the prosodic signal that one segment is being put in opposition to another. For example: "I said to *report* the trouble, not *broadcast* it" (Bolinger, 1961; for a discussion of various theoretical perspectives on contrastive accent, see Chapter IV of Ladd, 1980).[11] As with the incomplete com-

---

[11]In a broad sense, all accents are contrastive, since there is always another word that could have appeared instead of the accented one. For example, in a sentence like "Jane speaks *French,*" no contrast is necessarily implied between French and any other specific language, although a contrast is

parative, when contrastive accent is used in an advertisement minus one of the contrasted items, the hearers will tend to supply an appropriate completion.

For example, an air freshener in a decorative dispenser claims to be:

(7) . . . // The aīr freshener / you dòn't have to ˎhide //[12]

implying that all the others are too unattractive to be left out in the open. The sentence is repeated twice in the commercial, both times with the same contrastive accent on "don't."

The contrast implied in the following segment is somewhat more complex than the simple positive-negative opposition in (7).

(8) . . // A mōuthwash só effèctive /
    it fights stròng mouth odors // . . .[13]

Contrastive accent occurs on "strong." This makes the word more prominent and also implies a contrast with "weak mouth odors," which, presumably, the product also fights. Recall the conversational maxim mentioned above that one does not give unnecessary information. If all mouthwashes were effective against strong mouth odors, claiming that one particular mouthwash had this property would be as unnecessary as claiming that it is a liquid. An additional contrast is thus implied between the advertised product, which fights "strong mouth odors," and at least some rival products, which fight only the "weak mouth odors" implied by the contrastive accent. (As no other products are mentioned in the commercial from which (8) was taken, the hearers must fill in the identity of the weaker rivals for themselves.)

In commercials for over-the-counter drugs such as pain relievers or colds medications, comparisons are often made overtly between the advertised product and its competitors in terms of amount of medication, number of symptoms relieved, and so on. After a listing of the competitors' qualities, it is sometimes claimed that, on the other hand, the advertised product "contains *stròng* pain

---

certainly implied between French and other languages in general. The more narrow the range of alternatives, the more justified we are in identifying the accent as contrastive (Bolinger 1961, p. 87). The limitation of alternatives can be a matter of the immediate context of the utterance; that is, we could identify the accent on "French" as contrastive if the sentence were said to someone who had just tried to converse with Jane in German. It can also be dependent on the meanings of the words involved. Accented negatives, for example, are contrastive because the alternative to a negative is its absence, giving a positive sentence. Similarly, if the accent in the example mentioned above had been on "speaks," a contrast would have been implied (Jane *speaks* French, but she can't *read* it) because there are a limited number of things one can do with a language, and therefore only one or two alternatives to the accented word.

[12]Reproduced with Permission of the Copyright Owner, American Home Products, Inc.

[13]Reproduced with Permission of the Copyright Owner, Lever Brothers, Inc.

relievers" or "is a *pòwerful* medicine."[14] As in example (8), the contrastive accent on these words implies an opposition with something that is "weak," presumably the medicine in the competing products or the products themselves. In those cases where the overt message of the commercial is that the advertised product relieves *more* specific problems than its competitors, there is usually no overt statement that it is *better* at relieving a particular symptom. However, the contrast implied by the heavy accentuation of words like "strong," "powerful," etc., can lead hearers to draw that inference.

We can see, then, that closure works on more subtle material than incomplete comparatives. Given a case of contrastive accent with no contrasted element within earshot, the hearer might reasonably be supposed to fill in the missing material. The matter could be put more strongly. Unless the advertisers intend the hearer to fill in the missing material, there is no conceivable reason why segments should be accented in this way.

A somewhat different use of contrastive accent occurs in the following segments of a beer commercial, spoken by a voice-over announcer:

(9)a Trìumph // 'Some mēn / are content with nóthing ˏless //
   b 'They never ˏgo / for ˏbro:nze or ˏsilver //
                      dec
     'They gò / for the gôld // . . .
   c . . . // Sháre with yòur ˏfriends /
     the plēasure of wôrld-fàmous ˏTuborg // . . .[15]
     dec

Accentuation which can be identified as contrastive occurs here in (b), where "they," referring to the "some men" of (a), is contrasted by implication with "other men" who do not have the qualities mentioned in these two lines. On the words "bronze" and "silver," the announcer's voice tone is also lower and slightly nasal, indicating disparagement of those metals (or medals) in contrast with gold. Another contrastive accent occurs in (c), on the word "your." Because it makes no sense to have to be told to share the beer with your own friends instead of with everyone else's, the purpose of the accent may be to draw the viewer into the advertisement, as in example (1)f and j, "put a little English on *your* Trac II razor." Alternatively, the implication may be that other people are already sharing Tuborg with *their* friends, and the addressee is invited to follow their example. If this is the case, the utterance carries the additional implication that Tuborg has been accepted as a good beer by a number of other people, which presumably means that it is a good beer.

---

[14]These examples are fictional, in that they do not represent the exact wording of any particular commercial; rather, they are composites of several different phrases to be found in commercials for various products.

[15]Reproduced with Permission of the Copyright Owner, Carling National Brewery.

ANALYSIS OF TWO COMMERCIALS

So far we have, for the most part, dealt with small segments of advertisements. In this section we look at two commercials, combining the material in the preceding two sections to produce a general analysis of each of them. The reader should be aware, however, that a great deal of work remains to be done before linguists will be able to produce anything like a complete analysis of even the simplest and most common everyday utterances. As we are dealing here with sophisticated and carefully planned pieces of communication, our analysis will do no more than scratch the surface.

The first commercial is primarily of prosodic interest, the second primarily of semantic interest. We are paying special attention as well to the line of reasoning created in each case and how the prosodic cues guide the hearer in making sense of the text.

The main point of the following commercial is the contrast between the Contac time capsule, which is taken only once every twelve hours, and a liquid cold medicine that is taken every four hours. The latter also contains a pain reliever and a cough suppressant, both of which are lacking in Contac. Both products contain decongestants. The television audience is accustomed to commercials for cold medications which make a point of the number of different symptoms relieved by the advertised product, so that, at first glance, this distribution of ingredients looks like a poor selling point for Contac. This commercial manages to turn it around nicely, however. It is set in a bedroom at night; the husband evidently has a bad cold and awakens his wife with his sneezing:

(10)a Wife: One more ˄ sneeze / and Î'm ˄ leaving //
    b Husband: I can't ˄ breathe // congéstion //
    c Wife: Ȳou dìdn't take Contàc //
    d Whàt dìd you take? // 'I'll ˌfind it //
    e Ahâ! // Dòn't you 'know / this only works
                        dec
       fóur / hours / per dŏse? //
    f 'Contac / works up to twêlve //
    g That's eight hours / móre relìef from Contàc //
    h And thís / has thìngs for cóughs and âches /
       acc
       Còntac / chose nôt to ûse //
    i Dò me a ˌfavor // 'I don't want to ˌleave you //
       dec
    j Gìve your còld to ˌContac //
       And lèt's get some sléep //[16]

Lines (a) and (b) set up the situation. (c) is spoken with high pitch and accent on "you" and "Contac." The fact that the wife immediately concludes from his discomfort that he did not take Contac requires the viewers to make the assumption that Contac is very effective and that, had he taken it, he would not now be congested. The emphasis on "did" with mid-to-high falling tone in (d) tells us that she presupposes that he took *something*. (d) itself suggests a peculiar situation. Instead of waiting for an answer, she volunteers to find whatever it is he took, as though she did not expect him to be able to identify it. He must therefore be very careless about medicines. Alternatively, (d) suggests that he is in no condition to find or identify what he took. This implies that the alternative to Contac has unpleasant side effects, such as reducing mental alertness. The medicine that the wife finds is in fact a liquid that does have this effect.

The advertisers neatly avoid a potential anomaly in this situation. The commercial is set at night, when the participants are supposed to be asleep. The side effect of decreased mental alertness is not very harmful when one is sleeping—indeed, it is difficult to imagine a situation when it would even be relevant to a man who is home in bed in the middle of the night. The commercial creates just such a situation, however, with the question in (d). We learn from the visual material that the man has contrived to lose his medicine in the drawer of his nightstand. From his failure to respond to the question in (d) we learn that he is apparently incapable of either looking for it or identifying it verbally. Additionally, the very fact that he woke his wife up with his sneezing, coupled with the fact that the commercial closes with her urging him to take another medicine, indicates that his four-hour dose has expired; he evidently was not alert enough to know to take another dose.

In (e), "four hours per dose" has an unusual pattern of emphasis (one rising tone and two falling-rising tones) on three of the four words—only "per" is reduced. The working time is emphasized again in (f), with high rising-falling tone on "twelve." The hedge "up to" is spoken more rapidly than the surrounding material, and with lower voice tone and no accent.

In (g) the wife gives the result of a simple subtraction. (g) itself is an obvious statement, such as one might make to a small child. Throughout the commercial she uses high pitch register and, within that pitch register, frequent changes in relative pitch. This is also typical of speech to a small child. Similarly, she enunciates more clearly and carefully than people normally do, even in commercials. In combination, these features suggest strongly that she views her husband as a careless, irresponsible, somewhat childlike person who needs guidance at every step.

In addition, (g) serves to drive home the point that Contac works appreciably longer than the competitor. The period of time over which each product is effective has already been stated once. In both cases, intonation contours were used which called attention to the numbers. Here, the point is repeated in the form of the difference between them.

Let us return for a moment to the context within which these utterances take place. The man has awakened after his four-hour medicine has run its course. Because the medicine is for night-time use, we may assume that he took it before going to bed. As his wife urges him to take Contac in (j), we may also assume that four hours have passed—she is presumably not urging him to mix medicines, and there is no evidence that the rival medicine has stopped working early. If all this is so, however, he could just as well take another dose of the liquid, because if he has been asleep for four hours, he will have to get up in four more hours anyway. In real life, the only reason for taking Contac at this point would be if it worked appreciably better than the other medicine during the same four-hour time span. In a commercial, of course, we expect that the characters will end up using the advertised product, regardless, so that this line of reasoning does not in itself constitute a claim that Contac works better than the competitor.

The notion that Contac works better is hinted at, in fact, but not until (j), where it is implied that to ''give your cold to Contac'' will result in getting some sleep, entirely outside of the question of how long each of the medicines works. This inference is readily available to the audience because they are aware that it would be a selling point for the product, and so they may well perceive it as being present in the commercial (see Preston & Scharbach, 1971).

Returning to the text, the initial ''and'' of (h) indicates that what follows will be in harmony with expectations based on what has gone before (Lakoff, 1971). Lines (e)–(g) gave reasons why Contac is superior to the other medicine, so the ''and'' signals that (h) will be an additional reason. The woman's adult-to-child prosody and the obviousness of (h) indicate that she will probably overexplain anything that needs explaining. Her failure to state what is wrong with cough suppressant and aspirin substitute, combined with the audience's awareness that some medications can have unfortunate side effects, implies that it is so obvious as to need no explanations.

Line (h) contains the one piece of information that could be interpreted as a point against Contac. The prosody of this line defuses this negative reading, however. In other commercials for this product, the sentence containing this information is generally spoken at lower pitch and more softly and rapidly than the rest of the commercial, e.g.,

(11)a . . . // ‚This ‚also has ‚cough supprèssant /
     acc
   and áspirìn súbsti ‚tute //
  b Wè chŏse / not to p̄ut them in ‚Contac // . . .

(11)a begins with two low falling tones—normally the sort of thing one expects to find at the end of a major tone group. Every word in (a) receives strong accent, except for ''has,'' which receives less emphasis, and ''and,'' which receives none. Crystal (1975, p. 38) associates a non-final falling tone with insistence, abruptness, and irritation, among other things. The speaker in (11), a voice-over announcer, does in fact sound both grim and annoyed. In (11)b, however, pitch and loudness return to normal—that is, to what is found elsewhere in the commercial—with mid-to-high falling-rising tone and a following minor tone group boundary emphasizing "chose." The implication is that the information in (a) is unpleasant.

In (10)h as well, the volume is lower and speed is increased. Instead of low falling tones, the speaker uses a series of rise-falls. She does not sound grim or annoyed, but she does sound concerned. In both cases, the inference is readily available to the hearer that the speaker is issuing a warning of sorts. This is supported by the use of "chose" in the immediately following clause in both cases.

Line (i) relates the conversation back to the situation set up in (a) and (b). The first half of (j) is the Contac slogan. Like many slogans, it makes little sense, but the image of handing one's cold over for treatment, that is, divorcing it from oneself, is a much more powerful one than that of merely treating one's cold while one still has it. By the juxtaposition of the material in the two major tone groups in (j), it is implied that taking Contac will result in getting to sleep.

Line (j) is also prosodically interesting. The material in the second major tone group is spoken with "smile-voice." The speaker also uses a lower pitch register for (j). Pitch change occurs relatively gradually in these two tone groups, in contrast to the sudden and frequent variations in relative pitch that have marked the rest of her speech. The point at which she urges her husband to take the product is the first time she has spoken to him as an adult. It is also, for what it is worth, the first time she expresses any solidarity with him. This occurs in the first person plural reference in "let's" and contrasts with the heavy emphasis she has been putting on the pronoun "I" in the rest of the commercial.

Example (10) is primarily an informative commercial. The main piece of information—the length of time the product is effective—is overtly stated in (e)–(g). Another claim—that the product is an effective medication—is presupposed in (c) and implied in (j). In addition, the information that the advertised product does not contain some medications found in other products is overtly stated, but in such a way that the prosody defuses a potentially negative interpretation of the material for the product.

In contrast, the main point of example (12) is not to convey any sort of objective information about the product, a wine. Rather, the commercial concentrates on conveying information about the speaker, who is presented as a role model for viewers who feel insecure about their choice of wine. He is presented as independent, successful, and unconcerned about what anyone else thinks of his taste in wine. He is a youngish man, casually dressed, and he addresses the

camera throughout. As with example (1), the commercial mimics a casual interpersonal interaction between the speaker and the viewer.

(12)a   Man: I had a good reâson /
                  for starting my ‚own ‚travel ‚agency //
                                      dec
   b   I was fî:red / by my óld 'one //
                     dec
   c   And ‚now I'm ‚brea:thing ‚down their ‚necks //
   d   ‚Look / there are 'plenty of 'bo:sses around /
                               acc
   e   wílling to 'tell you / how to ˎlive //
   f   right down to . . what wîne to drink //
   g   But Cólony Rùby Caber‚net / is my ōwn ‚choice //
                     dec
   h   and I'd rather �⸗live / with ‚that //
   i   It's from Itálian Swīss Còlony / and it's de‚licious //
                                dec
   j   Ann (VO): Còlony // Be‚cau:se / tāste is the ónly ‚way /
                  to ‚choose a ˎwine //[17]

The speaker's individuality beings with his accent, which is that of the South-
western United States. Most people in television commercials have no identifiable regional accent; the exceptions are usually accents associated with strong
stereotypes, such as those of New York or the Deep South. This speaker's
accent, however, has no such stereotypes, and so makes him distinctive while
allowing him to be characterized by what he says rather than by preconceived
associations held by the audience.

In (a)–(c) the speaker gives a brief autobiography: he was fired, started his
own business, and is now nearly as successful as those who fired him. "Fired"
in (b) is highlighted prosodically by accentuation and by the lengthened vowel.
The vowel is also nasalized, suggesting sarcasm or contempt. In (c) he describes
his success, not in absolute terms, but in terms of competition with his former
employers. The line is very clearly enunciated; the first syllable of "breathing"
has a lengthened vowel and the "k" and "s" of "necks" are clearly articulated.
This kind of clear enunciation can suggest restrained aggression toward the
people the speaker is talking about.

The speaker is the subject of the first three sentences. This is accomplished by
putting the second sentence, (b), the only one where he was acted on rather than
the actor, in the passive voice. This alone would mean very little, but in combination with the rest of the speaker's characterization in the commercial it
implies self-confidence—that is, he is quite willing to talk about himself. It

---

[17]Reproduced with Permission of the Copyright Owner, United Vintners, Inc.

further serves to signal that the first three lines of the commercial are to be taken as a unit.

In the next three lines, (d)–(f), the speaker generalizes what he has been talking about and applies it to the audience. Line (d) begins with a low falling tone on "look." This intonation, suggesting definiteness (Crystal, 1975, p. 38), occurs on a word normally used to call the addressee's attention to something. This use of "look" is normal for superior-to-inferior speech, but not inferior-to-superior or equal-to-equal. It also indicates that more explanation or a specific example will follow.

"Bosses" also has a lengthened and nasalized vowel suggesting sarcasm or contempt. That is, the speaker does not think the people so referred to are really or properly bosses, or he acknowledges their status but has no respect for them. "Plenty" has a rising tone, which is followed by a falling tone on "bosses," and in (e) the same pattern occurs with a rise on "willing" followed by a fall on "tell you." The overall effect is of a slight sing-song pattern, which supports the inference that the speaker is contemptuous of the "bosses."

The speaker's attitude is also indicated by the semantics of (d) and (e). "Plenty" has a different connotation from other terms indicating amount, such as "many" or "a lot." Specifically, it refers to "a lot" or "enough" in terms of some desired amount. For example, five envelopes are not "many," but if all one wants to do is send out two letters, one can say that one has "plenty of envelopes." The speaker, then, is suggesting that if one wants "bosses," there are more than enough of them. The bosses are, furthermore, "willing," rather than, for example, "determined" or "trying" to tell one how to live. That is, they are acceding to the demands of those who listen to them, with the implication that one has a choice in whether or not one will pay attention to them.

In (f), the speaker continues his commentary on the "bosses" by giving a specific example. The pause after "to" suggests that his utterance is unplanned—he does not have an example ready and must pause to think of one. This is common enough in commercials. However, this speaker's pronunciation adds some additional support to the illusion of spontaneity. "To" has a number of possible pronunciations. One is the "citation form," the form we use when we pronounce the word all by itself. This form has a long "ū" as the vowel and is phonetically represented as [tu]. In more casual speech, however, the vowel is often not pronounced in this way. Instead, the word is pronounced in a way that is sometimes spelled "tuh," represented phonetically as [tə]. In (f) the speaker uses the latter pronunciation, typical of casual speech. However, the word following the pause, "what," begins with the same sound that the citation form of "to" ends with—a "w" is merely a "u" which is acting as a consonant. Even in casual speech, we tend to anticipate sounds. A speaker who knows that his next word is going to begin with a "w" will probably pronounce an immediately preceding "to" with a long "ū". A speaker who pronounces the word as "tuh," however, clearly does not know that his next word is going to begin with "w", so that the impression is given that this speaker is really speaking spontaneously.

Lines (g)–(h) form another unit, in which the main topic is the product itself. Oddly the product name in (g) occurs in abbreviated form. This happens again in (j), where the announcer, normally the one person in a commercial who gives the fullest form of the product name, also uses the abbreviated form. In fact, in 1976, when this commercial was run, the winery was beginning a shift in identification from "Italian Swiss Colony" to "Colony." Aside from contributing to this shift, the abbreviation of the product name carries some implications which are useful to the advertiser. A product with a reasonably lengthy name can be reduced to a single salient syllable or word. It is usually so reduced by people who are sufficiently familiar with it that full identification is not necessary, and who refer to it often enough that a reduced form of the name is desirable as a linguistic shortcut. In the case of some products that are essentially institutions, the familiarity is nearly universal: almost everyone is able to identify a "Rolls" as a Rolls Royce automobile, for example, or "Rémy" as Rémy-Martin Cognac.

There is a deceleration on the product name, and it receives a tone group of its own. In addition, the pitch is slightly higher than in the rest of the utterance. Each word of the product name is equally stressed. This gives the name more prominence, but also signals a new topic. There is rather an abrupt shift from lines (a)–(f), where the speaker is talking about life in general, to (g)–(i), where he is discussing the product. With the first tone group of (g), the viewers must shift their interpretation that the speaker has been discussing his views about things in general to the realization that all of the preceding material has merely been leading up to talking about his choice of product. This apparent break in the discourse is smoothed over by the prominence given to the product name, and is aided by the audience's awareness that this is, after all, a commercial, and that mention of a specific product is by now long overdue.

Line (h) contains material which is semantically anomalous. "Would rather" indicates preference for something; "live with" is synonymous with "put up with," witness the fact that it occurs frequently in phrases like "(just) have to live with . . . ," and indicates that the subject's preference is against the object of "live with." There is some danger that the audience may understand this line as meaning something like, "I'd rather put up with this product than go along with what the 'bosses' suggest." This negative reading is defused by what the audience knows of the speaker's character and by the tone group placement in the line. In the rest of the commercial, the audience has seen that the speaker is aware that he does not hold the standard point of view, and that he is quite capable of being sarcastic. The use of "live with" can therefore be interpreted as his ironic way of phrasing how the "bosses" view his choice of wines. (In case the audience has any doubts, he states in the next line that the product has the one characteristic good wine is supposed to have—it tastes good.) There is a minor tone group boundary after "live," which breaks up the formulaic phrase. This vitiates the negative reading the phrase would certainly have if it were spoken in a single tone group, and also allows the hearer to connect the occurrence of "live" in line (e), where the speaker is being told "how to live," with line (h), where he states that he would prefer to "live with" something else.

In (i) the speaker gives the winery's full name for the first time, making the connection between the "new" Colony and the "old" Italian Swiss Colony. Once again, the name is spoken with pitch slightly higher than normal and at slower speed. Another anomalous feature occurs in this line. "Delicious" receives heavy stress and a low falling tone, showing certainty (Crystal, 1975, p. 38). The low tone is particularly noticeable because of the high pitch on the product name in the previous tone group. "Delicious," however, is an unlikely candidate for this kind of intonation, because it is one of a set of adjectives which convey the speaker's attitude rather than objective fact.[18] What we would expect from what we already know about this speaker, however, is that he would deliver his opinions as though they were absolute and incontrovertible fact, so that what appears to be anomalous is very much in character for him.

Another peculiarity of "delicious" is that it is not a word one frequently hears in connection with wine. The use of a nonstandard term suggests that the speaker is not very concerned with what the standard terminology is; again, this is in character. Although most people do not use "delicious" for wine, it is an appropriate adjective for describing something that tastes good. The speaker wants to say that the wine tastes good. Therefore, nonstandard or not, he will call it "delicious" if he wants to. The term may also have some value for viewers who know little about wine, and for whom more standard descriptive terminology might be intimidating or, worse from the advertiser's point of view, incomprehensible. "Delicious" is easily interpretable, and has the advantage of being a common word that these viewers can associate easily with their own experience.

In (j) the announcer repeats the product name, again in its abbreviated form. It is, as usual, given higher-than-normal pitch and a tone group of its own. The rest of (j) is an overt statement which summarizes the message that has been implied throughout the commercial.

This commercial is unusual in that the product is not mentioned until the commercial is more than half over. Comparatively little is said about the product itself, except what can be learned from the speaker's reaction to it. However, the point of the commercial is precisely that the viewers should emulate the speaker in being independent and selecting their wine on the basis of taste. There is good

---

[18]Lakoff (1975, pp. 11–13) provides a number of examples of adjectives of this sort. One of their characteristics is that they cannot occur with negatives, except in statements which echo previous statements. For example, one cannot, upon taking a bite of cake, remark, "This cake isn't delicious," unless one is echoing and contradicting a previous statement, "This cake is delicious." Similarly, one doesn't hear sentences like "That dress isn't lovely" or "That isn't a terrific car."

reason, then, for not talking much about the product. The advertisers cannot very well combine the message to be independent and make one's own decisions with an injunction to buy their product rather than any other. Rather, the idea that the wine is good is conveyed through the speaker's attitude towards it, aided by the assumption that a company which urges selection of a product on the basis of taste must be confident that they can pass their own test.

CONCLUSIONS

There is a great deal more to communication than the mere stating of certain propositions. Like all communications, advertisements take place within specific contexts that are supported by the semantics and prosody used. The choice of particular words conveys certain things about how we are to view the objects so referred to—whether, for example, they are technologically sophisticated or commonplace and simple. Specific contexts can be evoked by using the sort of semantic behavior that is typical of those contexts, for example, puns, casual speech, jargon, and so on.

The prosody of a sequence works along with the semantic elements to create and maintain the context of an utterance. Prosodic cues also direct our processing of the information presented in the utterance. Cues such as voice tone, pitch, tempo, and duration are used to draw attention to certain segments, to de-emphasize others, to convey the speaker's attitude toward the subject matter, and to indicate the function of a particular segment within an utterance. The importance of prosodic cues is demonstrated by the fact that the hearer of a commercial can arrive at very different conclusions about what is being said than will the reader of a transcript not analyzed for intonation.

Prosody and semantics combine with cultural knowledge to provide an understanding of what is going on in the context created in a commercial. This allows additional information to be conveyed by the creation of a line of reasoning using linguistic signals against the background of what we already know about such contexts in real life. The material implicit in such a line of reasoning can be conveyed without being overtly stated or logically presupposed.

In some cases, it may seem that the conclusions drawn are too distant from the literal meaning of the material. However, in no case have we been led to a conclusion that does not fit in quite well with what the advertiser is interested in doing—praising the product. If the inferences we have drawn were merely a matter of reading too much into the choice of words or the tone of voice, or of expecting an intentionally unrealistic situation in a commercial to follow real-world expectations too closely, then some of our conclusions ought to have been in the other direction.

SUMMARY

In advertising, as in other forms of communication, a variety of linguistic and paralinguistic signals are used to guide the hearer in processing the information presented. In this chapter, techniques used in the linguistic analysis of interaction are applied to the understanding of advertisements.

Semantic selection assists the hearer in understanding the context within which the speaker is operating, as demonstrated in the analysis of a commercial that mimics a stereotyped interaction. An examination of the functions of jargon in advertisements illustrates the use of semantic elements to communicate additional information about the subject matter.

Prosodic features such as pitch variation, voice tone, volume and tempo guide the hearer's processing of utterances. Examples are given of the use of prosodic cues to direct the hearer's attention to segments that are in focus, to signal the omission of material, to indicate the speaker's attitude, and, with semantics, to establish and maintain a context for the communication.

The material dealt with in the sections on semantics and prosody is combined in the analysis of two commercials. Linguistic signals are further shown to operate with cultural knowledge to create lines of reasoning that can convey information in addition to that which is overtly stated.

ACKNOWLEDGMENTS

This study was supported in part by Grant #USPH-GM-01207, administered through the Institute of Human Learning, University of California, Berkeley. I am indebted to Charles J. Fillmore, John J. Gumperz, Paul Kay, Robin T. Lakoff, and Catherine O'Connor for their comments and suggestions.

REFERENCES

Aaker, D. A., & Myers, J. G. *Advertising management.* Englewood Cliffs, N.J.: Prentice-Hall, 1975.

Bolinger, D. L. Contrastive accent and contrastive stress. *Language,* 1961, *37,* 83–96.

Bolinger, D. L. Intonation across languages. In J. H. Greenberg (Ed.), *Universals of human language, Volume 2: Phonology.* Stanford, Calif.: Stanford University Press, 1978.

Crystal, D. *The English tone of voice.* London: Edward Arnold, 1975.

Grice, H. P. Logic and conversation. In P. Cole & J. Morgan (Eds.), *Syntax and semantics: Speech acts, Vol. 3.* New York: Academic Press, 1975.

Gumperz, J. J. Sociocultural knowledge in conversational inference. In M. Saville-Troike (Ed.), *Georgetown University round table on languages and linguistics 1977: Linguistics and anthropology.* Washington, D.C.: Georgetown University Press, 1977.

Gumperz, J. J. *Discourse strategies.* Cambridge: Cambridge University Press, 1982.

Ladd, D. R., Jr. *The structure of intonational meaning.* Bloomington, Ind.: Indiana University Press, 1980.

Lakoff, R. T. Ifs, ands, and buts about conjunction. In C. Fillmore & T. Langendoen (Eds.), *Studies in Linguistic semantics.* New York: Holt, Rinehart & Winston, 1971.

Lakoff, R. T. *Language and woman's place.* New York: Harper & Row, 1975.

Preston, I. L., & Scharbach, S. E. Advertising: More than meets the eye? *Journal of Advertising Research,* 1971, *11,* 19–24.

Shimp, T. A. Do incomplete comparisons mislead? *Journal of Advertising Research,* 1978, *18,* 21–27.

Trim, J. *English intonation.* Unpublished manuscript, 1975.

11 Psycholinguistic Studies of Misleading Advertising

Richard Jackson Harris
Tony M. Dubitsky
Kristin Jo Bruno
Kansas State University

In examining the issue of misleading advertising, a central question is "What does an ad mean?" Whereas at first that might seem a trivially simple question to answer, in fact it is not. In line with current thinking in cognitive information-processing psychology, meaning is considered here not as a static property of the stimulus (e.g., ad), but rather as an emergent property growing out of the interaction of the stimulus and the hearers' or readers' knowledge already stored in their memories. For this reason the same ad may mean different things to different people and it may mean more than what it says directly. This chapter gives an account of our research project studying what advertisements mean, using this interactionist assumption and the research framework and methodology of experimental cognitive psychology.

RESEARCH IN PROSE PROCESSING

Basic psychological research in semantic information processing, beginning with Bartlett (1932), has shown that memory is constructive in nature (e.g., Bransford, Barclay, & Franks, 1972; Bransford & Johnson, 1973; Brewer, 1975, 1977; Dooling & Christiaansen, 1977; Graesser, 1981; Johnson, Bransford, & Solomon, 1973; Loftus, Miller, & Burns, 1978; Sanford & Garrod, 1981; Spiro, 1980a, 1980b; Sulin & Dooling, 1974). People do not store and retrieve input literally, but instead they modify it on the basis of the context and their stored knowledge and beliefs. Such alteration means that people do not remember input verbatim but rather a more or less distorted version based largely on inferences that they constructed during comprehension.

241

Recent studies have shown that even very subtle implications can invite people to make inferences and subsequently remember these inferences as explicitly stated (see Harris, 1981, and Harris & Monaco, 1978, for reviews). For example, subjects in Brewer's (1977) study tended to recall (2) when they had actually heard (1). Whereas (2) is strongly implied by (1), it may be the case that (3) and not (2) is true. Although most people in most contexts may infer (2) upon

1. The hungry python caught the mouse.
2. The hungry python ate the mouse.
3. The hungry python caught the mouse but did not eat it.

hearing (1), the implication is only probabilistic, and for some situations in which (1) could be said, (3) could be true instead of (2). It has been found consistently with a wide variety of tasks and materials that subjects readily make such inferences in comprehension and in a later memory task are unable to distinguish this inferred information from directly asserted facts. This has been shown with simple sentences (Brewer, 1977), complex sentences (Harris, 1974), negated continuous adjectives (Brewer & Lichtenstein, 1975), very brief stories (Johnson et al., 1973), historical-biographical material (Sulin & Dooling, 1974), courtroom testimony (Harris, 1978; Harris, Teske, & Ginns, 1975), leading questions (Harris, 1973; Loftus, 1975; Loftus, Miller & Burns, 1978; Loftus & Palmer, 1974), and advertisements (Bruno, 1980; Bruno & Harris, 1980; Harris, 1977; Harris, Dubitsky, & Thompson, 1979; Harris, Dubitsky, Perch, Ellerman, & Larson, 1980; Harris, Dubitsky, Connizzo, Letcher, & Ellerman, 1981; Preston, 1967). Such pragmatic inference drawing has also been shown to occur at least as pervasively in children as in adults (Brown, 1976; Bruno, 1980; Glenn, 1978; Harris, 1975; Hildyard, 1979; Paris & Carter, 1973; Paris & Upton, 1976; Stein & Glenn, 1979). In fact, educators teach inferring to children as a reading skill to help them integrate discourse (e.g., Robinson, Monroe, Artley, Huck, Jenkins, & Aaron, 1967). This aids in understanding written and oral communication throughout life. Although such inferring is usually helpful in accurately and completely interpreting stimulus input, there are some situations, such as eyewitness memory, juror memory, and consumer information processing of advertisements, where it is crucial to discriminate asserted from implied information.

IMPLICATIONS IN ADVERTISING

The focal point of the present research project is the investigation of the way in which the inference-drawing nature of human information processing is important in advertising, especially when a question of deceptive advertising is being considered. Taking the interactionist approach, this chapter examines how the consumer constructs the meaning of an advertisement through its interaction with his or her knowledge already in memory. It is this interpretation that presumably will affect a subsequent purchase or other behavior. This crucial step in understanding the effects of advertising involves a psychological question of information-processing. The focus of this chapter is to bring the research tools and methodology of experimental psychology to bear on this important social, legal, and economic issue. The relevant legal background and cases are discussed by Preston (1975, 1977; Brandt & Preston, 1977; Rotfeld & Preston, 1981).

Previous studies of memory for commercials have used rather gross measures, such as overall amount of information recalled, which has often been surprisingly low. Our present research, however, has focused on specific claims in advertising, rather than on more general effects of global affective reactions or name-recognition. Although product claims may be directly asserted, they are often only implied. The basic research finding that implied information is often remembered as fact has important ramifications for advertising.

There are many ways in which an advertisement can imply a false claim without asserting it directly (Preston, 1975; Schrank, 1975). One method is through the use of hedge words, which weaken an assertion but may leave a strong implication (e.g., *Zap Pills may help relieve pain* does not guarantee relief). Also, comparative adjectives may be used without ever specifying the subject of the deleted clause in the underlying syntactic structure (e.g., *Chore gives you a whiter wash* would not be false if the deleted clause were *than washing with coal dust*). Imperatives may be perniciously juxtaposed in such a way as to imply a spurious causal connection between two activities (e.g., *Get through a whole winter without colds; take Eradicold Pills* does not insure that taking the pills will produce the healthful effect). The negative question is a useful device for implying an affirmative answer that may not be true (e.g., *Isn't quality the most important thing to consider in buying aspirin?*).

Inappropriate, incomplete, or inadequate reporting of survey or test results may also easily mislead the consumer. Reporting only the number of respondents answering a given way and not the percentage or sample size, or vice versa, can be highly misleading. Inappropriate sampling techniques or incomplete specification of the competition in comparative tests are similar flaws, as is reporting only the number responding to a survey, when the number questioned may have been much larger. The reporting of piecemeal results to imply an unwarranted general conclusion is also a misuse of test results (e.g., using *a Leprechaun has more front seat headroom than a Toyota Tercel, more rear-seat hiproom than a Chevette, and a larger trunk than a Ford Escort* to imply that the car has more interior room by all measures than the three competitors).

Objective truth or falsity should not be confused with misleadingness (cf. Preston, 1975). An advertisement may be false without being misleading, as in the case of an outlandish spoof never taken seriously (*Our crackers are made by elves*). Alternatively, it may be misleading without actually being false, as in the examples discussed above. Whereas truth may be a legal and/or linguistic question, misleadingness is a psychological question of information processing, because it involves the consumer's interpretation. Recently there has been an increasing recognition in both the research and legal communities of the importance of the consumer's interpretation of such claims.

In a review of the Federal Trade Commission's (FTC) decisions in misleading advertising cases, Brandt and Preston (1977) found that, until the 1970s, the commission relied mainly on the personal intuitions of the commissioners to determine whether or not an ad was misleading. However, during the 1970's the FTC gradually took a more consumer-oriented approach to misleading ads (Brandt & Preston, 1977; Cohen, 1980; Isaacs, 1972; Preston, 1975, 1977; Rotfeld & Preston, 1981; Russo, 1976), in which the impression that the consumer has as a result of the ad was evaluated to determine misleadingness, rather than evaluating the advertiser's intent to deceive. This more cognitive approach took into account the fact that the consumer's world knowledge could interact with the ad to produce a false belief, whether or not it was so intended by the advertiser. Furthermore, the FTC now often uses consumer testimony and external behavioral research to build its case. Not only does it disallow blatant false claims, but it has also at times proscribed a variety of implications (Preston, 1975, 1977). Clearly, there is a need for behavioral research on consumers' comprehension of implications, to be used as input in ruling on misleading advertising cases. To this end, Preston (1977) has called for researchers to actively investigate implications in advertising to aid the FTC in defining and preventing misleading advertising. There is some evidence that such implementation is starting to occur (Glassman & Pieper, 1980; Rotfeld & Preston, 1981; Rotfeld & Rotzoll, 1980).

What follows is a discussion of our methodology for testing consumers' comprehension of potentially misleading claims and applications of this methodology to various research issues.

THE PARADIGMATIC EXPERIMENT

In order to facilitate discussion of the present research, the methodology for a typical study is described in detail. Extensions and variations of this paradigmatic study are examined later.

Materials

Twenty-four brief advertisements of between 25 and 100 words were written for fictitious products of the type frequently advertised on radio and television. Each commercial had two versions, one in which a critical claim about the product was directly asserted and the other where the same claim was merely implied. Also, for each advertisement two test statements were written. The first was a paraphrase or restatement of the information asserted or implied in the critical claim of the commercial. The second statement was a control item of either false (for 12 items) or clearly indeterminate (for 12 items) truth value. These false and indeterminate control items were included in materials in all of the present research. They were necessary to guard against an otherwise overwhelming number of "true" items, from the subject's point of view. Sample advertisements and test sentences appear in Table 11.1.

There were thus two lists of stimulus items, each with 12 implication and 12 assertion commercials, in random order, with any given item appearing in one form or the other on each list. There was one list of 48 test sentences, 24 testing the critical material either asserted or implied to be true in the ad, 12 sentences always false, and 12 always of indeterminate truth value. Unless otherwise indicated, these same types of materials were used in all of the studies. Counterbalancing of assertion-implication versions and the construction of lists was as described above.

Design and Procedure

All of the subjects were told initially that this was a study in how well they understood and evaluated commercials. Then they heard an audio tape recording of the 24 experimental ads, half of which contained directly asserted claims and

TABLE 11.1
Sample Experimental Materials (Harris, 1977)

---

1. *Assertion Commercial:* Aren't you tired of the sniffles and runny noses all winter? Tired of always feeling less than your best? Taking Eradicold Pills as directed will get you through a whole winter without colds.
   Implication Commercial: Aren't you tired of sniffles and runny noses all winter? Tired of always feeling less than your best? Get through a whole winter without colds. Take Eradicold Pills as directed.
   Test Sentence (critical): If you take Eradicold Pills as directed, you will not have any colds this winter.
   Test Sentence (indeterminate filler): Eradicold Pills have been proven more effective in laboratory tests than Anacin or Bayer.

2. *Assertion Commercial:* Do you have tired, aching feet at the end of a long day? You should be wearing the Moon Shoe, with its revolutionary new cushion sole. Be kind to your sore feet. Moon Shoes will relieve tired, aching feet.
   Implication Commercial: Do you have tired, aching feet at the end of a long day? You should be wearing the Moon Shoe, with its revolutionary new cushion sole. Be kind to your sore feet. Moon Shoes are just right for you.
   Test Sentence (critical): Moon Shoes will make your tired aching feet feel better.
   Test Sentence (false filler): Moon Shoes have a solid wooden sole for better support for weak arches.

Note: Copyright (1977) by the American Psychological Association. Reprinted by permission.

half implied claims. This was immediately followed by their responding to the 48 test sentences; they judged each sentence on a 1–5 scale as 1 (false), 2 (probably false), 3 (indeterminate), 4 (probably true), or 5 (true). They were also allowed the option of indicating if they did not remember anything about the product mentioned. Half of the subjects heard the first list, whereas the remainder heard list 2; however, all subjects received the same list of sentences in the same order on the response task.

Subjects

Unless otherwise specified, all subjects were native English-speaking college students in introductory psychology courses at Kansas State University. They had chosen the research option of earning extra course points by participating in experiments.

Statistical Analyses

Unless indicated otherwise, all experiments were either simple one-way or completely crossed factorial designs, with varying numbers of within-subjects and between-subjects factors, in addition to the basic independent variable of claim type (asserted or implied). The major dependent variable analyzed was the mean response to assertion and implication items, with higher numbers indicating higher probabilities of interpreting claims as facts. The basic null hypothesis predicts no difference between the interpretation of asserted and implied claims, with both mean ratings being high (true). Our program of research has systematically tested several variables to see if they can improve the discrimination of asserted and implied claims. Responses to false and indeterminate control items were also analyzed to insure they were answered correctly, that is, responding with "1" to the former and "3" to the latter.

Demonstration of the Phenomenon

The basic and consistent finding of our work is that subjects draw inferences from the claims in the ads and remember those inferences as facts. Although there is often a claim-type main effect, with lower truth-value ratings to implied than asserted claims, the difference is typically only moderate and within the range of strongly true responses. Often in conditions with no special instructions or training about implied claims there is no difference at all between asserted and implied claims, with both identified as probably true or true 80–85 percent of the time. In almost no case has any manipulation brought the majority of the responses out of the true side of the scale, although some manipulations, notably the use of a training session and reduction of memory load by immediate testing, have significantly lowered it.

The rest of this chapter examines the ways that we have used this basic paradigm to investigate several specific variables and issues in studying misleading advertising. These include: (1) development of procedures for training people to discriminate asserted and implied claims; (2) use of a wide variety of dependent measures; (3) studies of ads in real and laboratory situations; (4) subject variations in knowledge and experience; (5) differences of advertisements and other types of prose; and (6) developmental differences.

TRAINING TO AVOID INTERPRETING
IMPLIED CLAIMS AS FACTS

One of the major variables examined is that of training subjects not to infer the truth of implied claims in ads. Findings from such research may be eventually used to develop consumer education programs that could be implemented in public schools and other settings.

The basic design of these training studies was a 2×2 factorial, with the within-subjects variable of claim type (asserted or implied) and the between-subjects variable of a training versus a control condition. The major hypothesis has been that there will be a significant interaction of training and claim type, with the training reducing the mean truth-value rating to implied, but not to asserted, test claims.

Instructional Training

The earliest training manipulation we used involved merely a lengthy set of verbal instructions cautioning subjects not to interpret implied claims as asserted facts. The instructions used by Harris (1977) appear below:

As you listen to these commercials, be careful that you do not interpret implied information as fact. Sometimes people, including advertisers trying to sell products, will not state a claim directly as asserted fact but rather will only strongly imply that the particular claim is true. You may infer that the advertiser has said something about his product which in fact he has only suggested, but he has suggested it in such a way that it is very easy for you to naturally, obviously, and normally expect the claim to be true.

For example, consider the commercial "Moo Moo Milk tastes great. Keep your family feeling healthy. Buy Moo Moo Milk." What claim does this commercial imply about the product but not definitely state as fact? Write this down on the bottom of your informed consent sheet. The commercial did not directly state that Moo Moo Milk keeps your family healthy; it only implied that. Does everybody understand that? Sometimes, however, a commercial or other piece of information *does* directly assert a fact without uncertainty. Consider this example: "Moo Moo Milk tastes great and it keeps your family feeling healthy. Buy Moo Moo Milk." In this case it directly states that Moo Moo Milk keeps your family healthy; it is more than merely implied. Any questions?

The experimental group of subjects heard these instructions, whereas the control group of subjects heard only the initial instructions to listen carefully to the ads because afterward they would be asked some questions about them.

In this experiment the instructions had only a very modest (and nonsignificant) effect. However, in another condition the memory load was decreased by allowing subjects to evaluate the truth of each test claim immediately after hearing each ad instead of at the end of the entire list of commercials. In this condition, instructions significantly reduced the mean truth-value rating of implied claims. Still, however, a majority of the judgments of implied claims were close to the true end of the scale under every condition.

Small Group Interactive Training

Although the subjects who heard the special instructions in Harris (1977) did show some ability to discriminate asserted and implied claims if tested immediately after hearing the ad, our primary goal was to develop an instructional task that would be effective in long-term memory. Such a condition does, after all, most closely approximate the situation of a real consumer trying to remember product information at some time after hearing the original ad. Thus, the initial instructions used in Harris (1977) were extended and developed into small-group training sessions, involving subjects' active participation and experimenter-subject interaction.

In these studies with a small-group training session (Bruno, 1980, 1981; Bruno & Harris, 1980; Harris et al., 1978, 1979, 1981) the experimenter interacted with a group of 2–6 subjects for 15 minutes, discussing exercises designed to identify implied claims in ads. The control group had a similar session, except that no mention was made of implied claims in ads, and subjects either performed a totally unrelated activity or focused on aspects of the ads other than implications (e.g., rating informativeness, drawing packaging, or reading slogans aloud.) Care was taken to insure that the experimental and control sessions both lasted exactly 15 minutes and that the same amount of group interaction occurred.

In the studies using a control session involving advertising materials (Bruno & Harris, 1980; Harris et al., 1979, 1981), the same list of sample commercial slogans was used in both the training and control groups. All subjects received a sample list of slogans such as (4) and (5).

4. Scruff Mouthwash attacks germs that cause bad breath.
5. Save yourself a bundle on groceries. Buy Pennywise canned vegetables.

In the control session the subjects first rated the slogans for informativeness (1–5 scale); next both the subjects and the experimenter took turns reading the slogans aloud with as much dramatic expression as possible, pretending to be radio announcers recording the commercial. For the second part of the control session for each product in each slogan, subjects either drew a picture of the product in actual use, the type of person who might use the product, or the type of package the product might appear in.

On the other hand, subjects in the training group were told that "When you are listening to the commercials . . . do not interpret implied information as directly asserted fact. Sometimes advertisers will strongly imply that a particular claim about a product is true but will not directly state that claim." The experimenter then worked through as many of the examples from the sample list of commercial slogans with the subjects as the 15-minute session permitted, calling specific attention to the following types of potentially deceptive implications: (1) hedges; (2) juxtaposed imperatives implying a causative relation; (3) incomplete statistical reporting; and (4) overly general statements. Individual subjects were asked to identify the implication and reword the ad to state the claim directly. Care was taken to insure that all subjects in the group actively contributed during the training session.

In some early studies (e.g., Harris et al., 1979, experiment 1) there was a consistent global effect of training on judgments of both implied and asserted claims. To attenuate what may have been undue skepticism in subjects receiving training, examples of asserted as well as implied claims in advertisements were included in later training studies so that implied claims were not overemphasized. What follows is a typical interaction from one of the later training sessions:

> Of course, sometimes information is directly asserted as fact in commercials. Consider these pairs of examples. What is merely implied in the first slogan is expressed directly as fact in the second slogan:
> Keep your family feeling healthy. Buy Moo Moo Milk.
> Moo-Moo Milk will keep your family feeling healthy.
>
> Do you want the best hot dog that modern technology can offer? Buy Frank's Hot Dogs today!
> Frank's Hot Dogs are the best hot dogs that modern technology can offer, so buy them today!
>
> Here are some final examples of commercial slogans that directly assert facts without any uncertainty:
> Poly-color TV is half the price of every other color set.
> Stapey's Car Wax has protective powers that will defend your auto exterior against any grease, grime, and sap!

The most enduringly effective demonstration of such training in long-term memory was that of Bruno and Harris (1980) and Bruno (1981, Experiment 1).

Subjects in Bruno and Harris' study received either a training or control session of the sort described above and then performed the response task. There was a main effect of training, indicating that the experimental group had rated all responses as less true, perhaps because the training had made them generally skeptical of ads. However, the same subjects were brought back two, seven, and nine days later. On each of these three subsequent occasions they heard the same list of ads again and performed the same response task. In addition, the training group was given a brief reminder not to interpret implied claims as facts, but they did not receive another training exercise. In each of the three subsequent sessions subjects judged implied claims as less true than they had the previous time, whereas the judged truth of asserted claims did not change. The control group judged both asserted and implied claims more true from the first to the second session but did not change their ratings thereafter. Bruno (1981) replicated this effect using a different response measure. In addition, she found some discrimination of asserted and implied claims by the experimental group initially rather than the general skepticism found by Bruno and Harris. These results suggest that the greatest effect of such training may not be observable until after repeated presentation and testing.

THE DEPENDENT MEASURES QUESTION

The Discrete Choice Problem

Realizing that a binary true-false scale was clearly inadequate to use in a verification task involving implications, our earliest advertising studies (Harris, 1977; Harris et al., 1980, experiment 2; Bruno, 1980; Harris et al., 1979) employed a discrete three-choice scale, that is, true, false, or indeterminate in truth value. With this type of response task, the major dependent measure analyzed was the number of true responses to asserted and implied claims. The logic was that if subjects inferred that an implied claim was true, they should have answered the test sentence true; if they recognized the probabilistic nature of the implied item, they should have responded indeterminate. Naturally, the use of such a scale requires the inclusion of filler sentences that are clearly false or indeterminate, a practice followed in all of the studies. The large majority of responses to both asserted and implied critical items are true; thus these responses have been analyzed. However, an analysis of only the number of true responses does not discriminate between the responses answered as false and those answered indeterminate. Although the number of indeterminate responses was examined as well, the total number of such responses was usually too low for a fully meaningful statistical test.

Alternative approaches and analyses have been considered. For example, Bruno (1980) performed a signal detection analysis on her data. Whereas this is possible to do and may be useful, it is not completely appropriate for such three-choice data. Assuming a true response to an assertion is clearly a hit, then a true response to an implication is clearly a false alarm. However, misses and correct rejections are not so clearly defined. For example, should a miss be defined as a false or indeterminate response to an asserted claim, or both? More critical is the problem of how to label false and indeterminate responses to implied claims. Whereas an indeterminate response may constitute a correct rejection, a false response does not. In addition, due to the probabilistic nature of an implication, a "correct" answer cannot be clearly defined. That is, a true response is "correct" if the inference is drawn, whereas an indeterminate response is "correct" if the inference is not drawn. Whether or not it would be "correct" to draw such an inference in a real-world situation would depend entirely on the context. Clearly, then, a signal detection analysis is not particularly useful for this response measure.

Most of our recent studies have used the five-point scale described earlier in the paradigmatic experiment. This scale ranges from false to true. Thus, every person's score on each critical item is included in the analysis, and it allows finer discriminations to be made than is possible with only three responses. However, there is some question as to whether or not the "indeterminate" response belongs at the midpoint of the scale.

Thus, Bruno (1981) developed and tested a two-stage response task. First, subjects had to respond yes or no to whether or not there was enough information given to judge the truth value of the test statement. If the response was no, no further response was made on that test item. If the response was yes, however, subjects then rated the truth of that test statement on a four-point scale ($1 =$ false, $2 =$ probably false, $3 =$ probably true, $4 =$ true). This two-part task had several advantages over previous measures. First of all, it removed the potential ambiguity of a response category or scale midpoint called "indeterminate." Instead, a "no" response on the first part of the task (i.e., there was not enough information to rate the truth value of the test item) can be unambiguously interpreted as an indeterminate response. Second, the two dependent measures allowed a more sensitive analysis of the subjects' inferential processes. The number of yes responses to implication items on the first part of the task could be considered as the number of inferences drawn, whereas the responses to implication items on the second stage may be interpreted as a measure of inference strength.

Results from Bruno (1981) using this measure in advertising training studies generally replicated or were consistent with earlier work, except that the training effect was consistently more effective in producing discrimination of assertions and implications than most of the previous work. Thus, it was concluded that the two-part response task was the most useful measure so far devised for this type of work. However, a number of other measures have been examined.

Alternative Response Measures

In an unpublished study, Harris, Bruno, and Dubitsky (1978) used four different response tasks to assess the effects of training on the ability to discriminate between implied and asserted claims in commercials. Whereas all of the subjects had heard the same list of ads, one-quarter performed each task. The four different measures were administered to equal numbers of subjects within each training and control group. The first measure was the standard three-choice task used by Harris (1977) and described earlier.

Subjects tested using the second measure were told to assign each statement a number from 0 (0 percent probability of being true) to 100 (100 percent probability of being true), with 50 indicating a 50-50 chance of being true, based on the commercial they had heard.

The third task used the cloze procedure and presented the entire written text of each advertisement but without the critical claims for either assertion or implication versions. Subjects were told to ''write as close to the exact words as possible but do not hesitate to guess if you only remember the general meaning.'' Whether subjects had drawn the critical inference and remembered it as fact could be assessed by noting how they had completed the critical deleted phrase, for example, what they inserted in the test item Crust _____ cavities.

The cloze task contains the simplicity of a free-recall response task while eliminating the tendency for subjects to respond with information from the ad, which, though correctly remembered, was not relevant to the critical claim. It also substantially reduces the ambiguity and uncertainty experienced by raters in assigning recall protocol material to response categories.

The fourth task was a multiple-choice test with each item consisting of four alternatives which appeared in random order: The first and second were paraphrases of critical claims from the assertion and implication versions, while the final two were false and indeterminate distractors. A sample item was

''Crust Fluoride: a. prevents cavities, b. fights cavities, c. eliminates bad breath, d. is orange-flavored.'' The subjects were instructed to choose one of the answers, but to also indicate any other choices they thought were also correct. Results in terms of main effects and interactions were not consistent across the various response tasks, although for the majority of the measures, the cell means were in the predicted directions.

Recognition and Recall Measures

More traditional memory measures have been more useful. Harris, Dubitsky, and Thompson (1979, experiment 2) presented subjects with the tape-recorded ads followed by a binary forced-choice recognition-memory task. This demonstrated that subjects could in fact recognize asserted (69 percent correct) and implied (77 percent correct) claims if presented with both to identify. This answers a possible objection to our work that the basic discrimination is too difficult to expect people to make. Beyond this, however, forced-choice recognition is really only useful to test memory for wording changes, because it bears little resemblance to cognitive tasks a consumer would perform. In fact, Harris et al. (1979) found some evidence of a task artifact of selecting the implied rather than the asserted version when guessing, perhaps due to a desire to show that one was not "tricked" by the wording.

Recall may also be examined. Harris et al. (1979, experiment 3) tested the effects of a training session on the ability to discriminate asserted and implied claims. The dependent measure was a cued-recall task, where subjects were given the name of the product and asked to "write down the most important thing that was said about the product in the commercial that you heard." A major drawback of this procedure is that the prose materials are too long to even attempt to recall verbatim. Thus, the chance is high that the critical part of the ad will be completely omitted in the recall protocols and thus contribute nothing to testing the hypothesis of interest. Establishing response categories and reliably assigning responses to them may also be a difficult task. In the above study the following categories were used:

1. Assertion recall—"a verbatim or paraphrased version of the claim as stated in the assertion version of the commercial."
2. Implication recall—"a verbatim or paraphrased version of the claim as stated in the implication version of the commercial."
3. Correct irrelevant recall—"some portion of the commercial other than the critical claim is recalled in verbatim or paraphrased form."
4. Intrusions, omission, and other unclassifiable errors.

Analyses of variance were performed on the number of assertion recalls for both asserted and implied claims. The critical prediction was an interaction of claim type and training on the assertion recalls, with fewer assertion recalls in the implication-training cell than the corresponding control cell or either assertion cell. This interaction was significant. Many of the total responses, however, were classified "correct irrelevant" and thus were not usable in testing relevant hypotheses.

Confidence Ratings

Some of our studies have asked subjects to indicate a confidence rating along with their responses. For example, experiment 1 in Harris et al. (1979) had subjects evaluate claims as true, false, or indeterminate in truth value, along with a degree of confidence in their response on a 1–5 scale. The data were then analyzed in three ways: (1) number of true responses for assertion and implication items; (2) confidence in true judgments for both types of items; and (3) a combination score obtained from turning the three-choice response task and the confidence data into an 11-point linear scale. To do this, the five false responses were scored 1–5, in decreasing sureness of judgment. The five true responses were scored 7–11, in increasing order of sureness of judgment. All of the indeterminate responses, regardless of confidence rating, were scored 6, the midpoint of the scale. Simple analyses of variance of the numbers of true responses and combination score analyses generally replicated each other, with the confidence ratings higher for asserted than implied claims. From these and similar results it was concluded that confidence ratings really do not add much in terms of meaningful data.

Noncognitive Measures

In spite of the variety of dependent measures used, all of our studies have concentrated on informational, as opposed to attitudinal or behavioral, measures. The interest has been in what the subjects believed, which may or may not be reflected in how they felt or what they bought.

As Shimp (this volume) has pointed out, there has been very little research on potentially misleading advertising using behavioral measures, that is, examining if being misled really affects purchase behavior. Our paradigm does allow examination of purchase intention, even if not actual buying behavior. Harris (1977) asked the subjects at the conclusion of the experiment to check the ten out of the 20 products advertised that they thought they would be most likely to buy after hearing the experimental ads. There was no effect of either claim type or instructions. This suggests that implied claims are equally as convincing as asserted claims on intention to purchase and that positive effects of training on evaluation of truth value of claims does not carry over to the purchase intention. This supports Olson and Dover (1978), who found that cognitive awareness of misleadingness is easier to produce experimentally than attitudinal or behavioral ramifications of it. Further research is needed on such dependent measures.

INCREASING THE ECOLOGICAL VALIDITY

Whereas our studies discussed so far were all conducted in the laboratory with specially constructed stimuli, the research to be discussed next consists of closer approximations to the situation facing the actual consumer attending to ads while listening to the radio or watching television.

Real Versus Fictitious Ads

Our method is adaptable for use with either fictitious or real ads. Each has its own advantages and disadvantages. Real ads, of course, more closely approximate the marketplace situation, but their use is inevitably confounded by the unknown amount and nature of the subject's prior information and attitudes about that product. On the other hand, although fictitious ads can largely control for effects of prior information (except in cases where the simulated ad reminds subjects of a real one), this approach takes away something from the reality of the situation, in that subjects typically understand the products are not real ones. This unreality argument may be a more cogent criticism in studies measuring purchase intention or actual behavior than it is in studies of memory and comprehension.

In deciding to use fictitious products, a further question arises as to whether or not they should sound realistic. For example, it is possible to construct outlandish product names in order to keep the subjects entertained (and thus presumably better motivated) during the experiment. However, one argument that has been advanced post hoc to account for the relatively weak effects of the training sessions in our early studies links humor to interference with the training session. Either subjects listening to funny ads do not take the training session seriously or they focus on the brand name itself rather than the content of the sample slogan. This "interference" argument would support the use of "serious" or "realistic" fictitious product names in experimental ads. What this type of fictitious brand name might be, however, remains open to question.

The brand names we have constructed are probably as humorous as real product names. On several occasions we had to discard ostensibly "silly" brand names (e.g., "Udder Delight" for a cow-milking machine, "Cornies" for a breakfast cereal) because they turned out to be real products. Our experimental product names may appear to be sillier than real product names only due to their novelty. For example, the Armadillo car may at first sound more humorous than the Rabbit, but this impression is probably an artifact of the familiarity of the latter brand name.

Although all of the studies discussed so far have used fictitious product names, Harris et al. (1980, experiment 1) examined memory for asserted and implied claims in lists of experimental ads using real product names and attributes. This study used the claim type variable and two conditions differing in memory load, that is, whether subjects evaluated the test sentences immediately after each commercial or at the end of the entire list. In addition, subjects evaluated each product on the dimensions of trustworthiness before hearing the ads and completing the standard 5-point truth-rating tests. The most important finding was that there was a global effect of trust ratings on the judged truth values of both implied and asserted claims. Trust ratings were significantly positively correlated with truth ratings of implied and asserted claims in both immediate and delayed memory conditions. Thus, subjects were more likely to rate claims about products they trusted as true than claims about products they had less trust in.

The Contextual Question

All of our research cited above examined the memory and comprehension of simulated radio commercials in isolation. In a different approach to increasing ecological validity, Harris et al. (1980, experiment 2) used an instructional training manipulation to examine the effects of training on memory for claims in fictitious ads embedded in the context of a real program. A total of 16 experimental fictitious ads were spliced into four naturally occurring breaks of a "Face the Nation" radio broadcast. Although the predicted critical interaction of claim type by training group was not significant, the means were in the expected direction, with fewer true responses to implications in the training group than to implications in the control group, thus replicating the delayed condition of Harris (1977). It is not surprising that identification of implied claims would be even more difficult in the context of a program, because more time elapsed between stimulus and test and because subjects' attention was probably directed primarily at the program, not the commercials, as it is in real life.

Extension to Natural Television Viewing

Finally, Harris et al. (1980, experiments 3 and 4) examined memory for implied and asserted claims for real products in real ads in a real TV broadcast. Subjects who had watched either "The CBS Evening News" or "Happy Days" at home the night before judged that claims implied in the commercials were as true as those directly asserted. Although there was no way to carefully control for the a priori difficulty of the asserted and implied claims by using asserted and implied versions of each claim, this study demonstrated the feasibility of using the present methodology with real broadcast programs and commercials.

SUBJECT VARIABLES

This research methodology can also be used to investigate ads for different types of products with different subject populations. It may be, for example, that subjects can discriminate asserted and implied claims better for products in which they have a personal interest. Although our research has generally used products that most people are at least familiar with and probably have used themselves, an exception occurred in a pair of studies by Harris et al. (1981). In this study half of the ads were for products familiar and useful only to farmers but of little use to other people, whereas products in the other ads would be useful and familiar to all. Additionally, half of the college-students subjects had rural backgrounds and half did not. The urban-rural dichotomy is a potentially useful one, in that readily available college students are easily divisible into two samples with different knowledge and interest on one issue (agriculture), although they are presumably equivalent in other ways. Similarly, two kinds of ads (farm and nonfarm) are readily usable.

Two lists of 24 ads each were constructed. Each list contained 12 ads for farm products and 12 for nonfarm products. The nonfarm products would be of interest and use to anyone, but the farm products (e.g., herbicide, pig starter, silos, tractors, irrigation systems, implements) would be of no use to nonfarmers. Six of the commercials of each type contained an implied claim and six contained an asserted claim.

After completing the 5-point truth-rating task, all subjects were handed a brief questionnaire in which they were to indicate whether they lived on a farm or ranch now or formerly and, if so, for how long; whether they had ever spent considerable time on a farm besides living there (e.g., summer job, extended visits); and how knowledgeable they considered themselves about agriculture. This information was used to select "farmers" and "nonfarmers" from the entire sample of subjects tested.

Results of the first study, however, were disappointing, in that there was only a main effect of training, with the specially instructed subjects responding true less often than control subjects across four sessions over nine days. Although the means were in the predicted direction of farmers being able to discriminate asserted and implied claims better for farm products than nonfarmers could, the difference was not significant. However, in a second study where subjects performed the response task while reading the ads, farmers judged claims about farm products as more true than claims for nonfarm ads, whereas the nonfarmers showed no such difference. This suggests that familiarity or commitment to the product makes people less critical. This is consistent with the finding of Harris et al. (1980, experiment 1), where claims about real products that were more highly trusted were rated more true than claims about less-trusted products.

Familiarity has also been manipulated experimentally by varying the number of presentations of an ad. On the last day of the four-session study by Harris et al. (1981), subjects heard a second set of ads, half of which had been repeated four times in the previous sessions and half of which were new. The training from the experimental group transferred to the new set of materials, although the effect was generalized, with all critical test claims, not just implications, being rated less true than by the control group.

ADS VERSUS OTHER TYPES OF PROSE

Although it is difficult to test directly, there is some evidence that it is more difficult to discriminate asserted from implied claims in ads than it is in other types of prose. One of the few studies to examine this directly was Preston and Scharbach (1971), who embedded the same information in the form of an ad or one of three other types of discourse; they found subjects were most likely to make unwarranted inferences from the ad form. In our own research, Bruno (1980) found consistently in her studies using both ads and brief stories that both adult and junior high subjects had more difficulty learning not to infer implied claims in ads than they did in stories.

Similarly, Harris et al. (1980, experiment 3) tested subjects' drawing of inferences from both the commercials and the content of a television news program. They found that subjects consistently rated implications of the ads as being more true than implications of the news stories. Of course, these conclusions, like those of Bruno (1980), must be tempered by the fact that the ad and non-ad materials were necessarily different. Preston and Scharbach's design avoids this methodological problem, but their material may have often been a bit bizarre, because a given piece of information often does not convincingly fit into an ad as well as other types of discourse. Further work needs to be done on this issue.

DEVELOPMENTAL STUDIES

Although most of our work has been with adults, we have also obtained some interesting developmental results. Bruno (1980) found a marginally significant training effect in which adults drew fewer inferences from ads than seventh- or ninth-graders after training. Thus, adults profited more from training than did seventh- or ninth-graders. The fact that adults profit more from training indicates that consumer education may be most valuable at the high school level.

Harris (1975), using the same type of response with simple sentence, nonad materials, found a developmental change from ages 4–11 in the ability to identify implied claims as "can't tell" rather than true, although the eleven-year-olds were still significantly poorer than the adults at this ability. Such results suggest that the ability to "turn off" this inferring process is a late-developing metalinguistic ability.

GENERAL DISCUSSION

Although falsity is a linguistic property of the message, and fraudulent intent a legal question, misleadingness is a property of the receiver (consumer) and is the most promising area for psychological study. Whether somebody is in fact misled is at heart an information-processing question amenable to empirical investigation. Results from our program of research have demonstrated the efficacy of a technique for studying misleadingness in advertising and a method of reducing this misleadingness through the use of various training procedures. Not only can the methodology presented here be used with different types of response tasks and allow stimuli to be presented in several different modes but it is also an objective assessment instrument.

Results from this program of research suggest that the tendency to hear an ad, infer information implied about the product to be too strongly true, and remember the information that way is a very strong cognitive tendency and one that is altered only with great difficulty. It is probably a part of the more general information-processing tendency to impose structure and interpretation on incoming sensory information and experience. The mind is not passively tape-recording but rather is constantly constructing interpretations, which are then encoded into long-term memory. When effort is made to retrieve them, such as in hearing the commercial again, answering a question about the product, or making a decision about whether to purchase it, the constructed interpretation is retrieved and used.

Every time stored information is retrieved, it is subject to at least slight change that emerges from interaction with new and related stimulus material. For example, in Bruno and Harris's (1980) study, each subsequent presentation of the experimental ads slightly modified the stored memory representation. The reason that subjects correctly identified more and more implied claims on each trial is because in every session some percentage of the subjects, upon hearing the ad again, apparently noticed the implication and thus revised their stored memory representation about what that product did, in many cases revising it from asserted to implied form.

One reason it may be so difficult to train people to discriminate asserted and implied claims is that the skill being trained is essentially a metalinguistic ability that works against a strong psychological and linguistic tendency. To draw inferences and assume them to be true is a natural, and normally useful, function of the human information processor. Subjects in the training studies are essentially being asked to stop doing what is normal. Thus they must approach the task in a very conscious problem-solving and metalinguistic way, that is, learning what words, constructions, and so on to monitor in order to stop the normal language processing activity from occurring.

Research like this project can have fairly direct applications in consumer education programs (e.g., Logan & Moody, 1979; Schrank, 1977), which are currently of considerable interest to school, church, and community groups, as well as to others developing curriculum materials. Certainly more work needs to be done in improving training sessions and assessing development of the skill at different levels, however.

As noted in the introduction, the FTC is increasingly responsive to consumer data to help determine whether an ad is misleading. Research such as this project should be valuable for the FTC, the NAB (National Association of Broadcasters), and other government and industry agencies overseeing advertising. To do so usefully requires that there be some scientifically appropriate way of gathering and interpreting these data. Our research offers one such methodology.

Misleading advertising is but one area where the methods and findings of experimental cognitive psychology can be brought directly to bear on an applied problem of considerable social interest and importance. The benefits are twofold: applied results offer insights into real-world issues and also serve as converging evidence for psychological theories and models. Certainly many other problems must be amenable to such an approach as well.

REFERENCES

Bartlett, F. C. *Remembering*. London: Cambridge University Press, 1932.

Brandt, M. T., & Preston, I. L. The Federal Trade Commission's use of evidence to determine deception. *Journal of Marketing, 1977, 41,* 54–62.

Bransford, J. D., Barclay, J. R., & Franks, J. J. Sentence memory: A constructive versus interpretive approach. *Cognitive Psychology, 1972, 3,* 193–209.

Bransford, J. D., & Johnson, M. K. Considerations of some problems of comprehension. In W. Chase (Ed.), *Visual information processing*. New York: Academic Press, 1973.

Brewer, W. F. Memory for ideas: Synonym substitution. *Memory & Cognition, 1975, 3,* 458–464.

Brewer, W. F. Memory for the pragmatic implications of sentences. *Memory & Cognition, 1977, 5,* 673–678.

Brewer, W. F., & Lichtenstein, E. H. Recall of logical and pragmatic implications in sentences with dichotomous and continuous antonyms. *Memory & Cognition, 1975, 3,* 315–318.

Brown, A. Semantic integration in children's reconstruction of narrative sequences. *Cognitive Psychology, 1976, 8,* 247–262.

Bruno, K. J. Discrimination of assertions and implications: A training procedure for adults and adolescents. *Journal of Educational Psychology, 1980, 72,* 850–860.

Bruno, K. J. *An investigation of cognitive processes that mediate inferring in persuasive texts*. Unpublished doctoral dissertation, Kansas State University, 1981.

Bruno, K. J., & Harris, R. J. The effect of repetition on the discrimination of asserted and implied claims in advertising. *Applied Psycholinguistics, 1980, 1,* 307–321.

Cohen, D. The FTC's advertising substantiation program. *Journal of Marketing, 1980, 44,* 26–35.

Dooling, D. J., & Christiaansen, R. E. Levels of encoding and retention of prose. In G. H. Bower (Ed.), *The psychology of learning and motivation, Vol. 11*. New York: Academic Press, 1977.

Glassman, M., & Pieper, W. J. Processing advertising information: Deception, salience, and inferential belief formation. *Journal of Advertising, 1980, 9,* 3–10.

Glenn, C. G. The role of episodic structure and of story length in children's recall of simple stories. *Journal of Verbal Learning and Verbal Behavior, 1978, 17,* 229–247.

Graesser, A. C. *Prose comprehension beyond the word*. New York: Springer-Verlag, 1981.

Harris, R. J. Answering questions containing marked and unmarked adjectives and adverbs. *Journal of Experimental Psychology, 1973, 97,* 399–401.

Harris, R. J. Memory and comprehension of implications and inferences of complex sentences. *Journal of Verbal Learning and Verbal Behavior, 1974, 13,* 626–637.

Harris, R. J. Children's comprehension of complex sentences. *Journal of Experimental Child Psychology, 1975, 19,* 420–433.

Harris, R. J. The comprehension of pragmatic implications in advertising. *Journal of Applied Psychology, 1977, 62,* 603–608. (Reprinted by permission.)

Harris, R. J. The effect of jury size and judge's instructions on memory for pragmatic implications from courtroom testimony. *Bulletin of the Psychonomic Society, 1978, 11,* 129–132.

Harris, R. J. Inferences in information processing. In G. H. Bower (Ed.), *The psychology of learning and motivation, Vol. 15*. New York: Academic Press, 1981.

Harris, R. J., Bruno, K. J., & Dubitsky, T. M. *Measuring deceptive advertising: A methodological study*. Unpublished study, Kansas State University, 1978.

Harris, R. J., Dubitsky, T. M., Connizzo, J. F., Letcher, L. E., & Ellerman, C. S. Training consumers about misleading advertising: Transfer of training and effects of specialized knowledge. *Current issues and research in advertising 1981*. Ann Arbor: University of Michigan Graduate School of Business Administration Division of Research, 1981.

Harris, R. J., Dubitsky, T. M., Perch, K. L., Ellerman, C. S., & Larson, M. W. Remembering implied advertising claims as facts: Extensions to the "real world." *Bulletin of the Psychonomic Society, 1980, 16,* 317–320.

Harris, R. J., Dubitsky, T. M., & Thompson, S. Learning to identify deceptive truth in advertising. In J. H. Leigh & C. R. Martin, Jr. (Eds.), *Current issues and research in advertising 1979*. Ann Arbor: University of Michigan Graduate School of Business Administration Division of Research, 1979.

Harris, R. J., & Monaco, G. E. The psychology of pragmatic implication: Information processing between the lines. *Journal of Experimental Psychology: General*, 1978, *107*, 1–22.

Harris, R. J., Teske, R. R., & Ginns, M. J. Memory for pragmatic implications from courtroom testimony. *Bulletin of the Psychonomic Society*, 1975, *6*, 494–496.

Hildyard, A. Children's production of inferences from oral texts. *Discourse Processes*, 1979, *2*, 33–56.

Isaacs, L. R. Psychological advertising: A new area of FTC regulation. *Wisconsin Law Review*, 1972, 1097–1124.

Johnson, M. K., Bransford, J. D., & Solomon, S. K. Memory for tacit implications of sentences. *Journal of Experimental Psychology*, 1973, *98*, 203–205.

Loftus, E. F. Leading questions and the eyewitness report. *Cognitive Psychology*, 1975, *7*, 560–572.

Loftus, E. F., Miller, D. G., & Burns, H. J. Semantic integration of verbal information into a visual memory. *Journal of Experimental Psychology: Human Learning and Memory*, 1978, *4*, 19–31.

Loftus, E. F., & Palmer, J. C. Reconstruction of automobile destruction: An example of the interaction between language and memory. *Journal of Verbal Learning and Verbal Behavior*, 1974, *13*, 585–589.

Logan, B., & Moody, K. (Eds.). *Television awareness training*. New York: Media Action Research Center, 1979.

Olson, J. C., & Dover, P. A. Cognitive effects of deceptive advertising. *Journal of Marketing Research*, 1978, *15*, 29–38.

Paris, S. G., & Carter, A. Y. Semantic and constructive aspects of sentence memory in children. *Developmental Psychology*, 1973, *9*, 109–113.

Paris, S. G., & Upton, L. R. Children's memory for inferential relationships in prose. *Child Development*, 1976, *47*, 660–668.

Preston, I. L. Logic and illogic in the advertising process. *Journalism Quarterly*, 1967, *44*, 231–239.

Preston, I. L. *The great American blow-up: Puffery in advertising and selling*. Madison: University of Wisconsin Press, 1975.

Preston, I. L. The FTC's use of puffery and other selling claims made "by implication." *Journal of Business Research*, 1977, *5*, 155–181.

Preston, I. L., & Scharbach, S. E. Advertising: More than meets the eye. *Journal of Advertising Research*, 1971, *11*, 19–24.

Robinson, H. M., Monroe, M., Artley, A. S., Huck, C. S., Jenkins, W. A., & Aaron, I. E. *Open highways book 7*. Glenview, IL: Scott Foresman, 1967.

Rotfeld, H. J., & Preston, I. L. The potential impact of research on advertising law. *Journal of Advertising Research*, 1981, *21*, 9–18.

Rotfeld, H. J., & Rotzoll, K. B. Is advertising puffery believed? *Journal of Advertising*, 1980, *9*, 16–20.

Russo, J. E. When do advertisements mislead the consumer? An answer from experimental psychology. In B. B. Anderson (Ed.), *Advances in Consumer Research, Volume 3*. Cincinnati: Association for Consumer Research, 1976.

Sanford, A. C., & Garrod, S. C. *Understanding written language: Explorations of comprehension beyond the sentence*. New York: Wiley, 1981.

Schrank, J. *Deception detection*. Boston: Beacon Press, 1975.

Schrank, J. *Analyzing advertising claims*. Palatine, IL: Learning Seed Company, 1977.

Spiro, R. J. Accommodative reconstruction in prose recall. *Journal of Verbal Learning and Verbal Behavior*, 1980, *19*, 84–95. (a)

Spiro, R. J. Constructive processes in prose comprehension and recall. In R. J. Spiro, B. C. Bruce, & W. F. Brewer (Eds.), *Theoretical issues in reading comprehension*. Hillsdale, N.J.: Lawrence Erlbaum Associates, 1980. (b)

Stein, N. L., & Glenn, C. G. Analysis of story comprehension in elementary school children. In R. O. Freedle (Ed.), *New directions in discourse processing*. Norwood, N.J.: Ablex, 1979.

Sulin, R. A., & Dooling, D. J. Intrusion of a thematic idea in retention of prose. *Journal of Experimental Psychology*, 1974, *103*, 255–262.

12

Effects of Prior Preference, Inferences, and Believability in Consumer Advertising

Gregory E. Monaco
University of Kansas
and
Kansas Neurological Institute
Donn Kaiser
Southwest Missouri State University

INTRODUCTION

Advertising research, reported in this volume and elsewhere indicates that subjects perceive unsubstantiated, implied claims of advertisements as if they had been directly asserted as fact (Harris, 1977; Harris, Dubitsky, & Bruno, this volume; Preston, 1967; Preston & Scharbach, 1971; Shimp, 1978). Because the FTC (Federal Trade Commission) may often demand substantiation for only the directly asserted claims of advertisers (see Preston, 1977, 1980), it would seem that advertisers can victimize the unwary consumer by *implying* unreliable or patently false information which the consumer will remember as fact—*as if* it had been directly asserted. Harris (1977), for example, demonstrated that subjects who heard the commercial

1. Aren't you tired of sniffles and runny noses all winter? Get through a whole winter without colds. Take Eradicold pills as directed.

recognized

2. If you take Eradicold pills as directed, you will not have any colds this winter.

as having been directly asserted. Harris and Monaco (1978) have termed statements, like (2), *pragmatic inferences*. Pragmatic inferences, like (2), are highly probable, but not necessary, interpretations of their messages, like (1). It becomes obvious that (2) is not a necessary interpretation of (1) when one considers that the statement

3. Taking Eradicold pills, as directed, will not affect the frequency with which you have colds this winter.

is not inconsistent with commercial (1), although the consumer is much less likely to remember (1) as (3).

Pioneering advertising-inference research by experimental psychologists has focused upon variations in the text of the commercial in order to demonstrate that subjects remember implied claims as if they had been directly asserted. On the basis of purchase decisions made by subjects who hear implied and asserted claims for various products, Harris (1977) concluded that "Thus there is no reason to reject the null hypothesis that a product is just as likely to be selected for purchase if the advertising claim is implied as if it is asserted" (p. 607). Our research has attempted to focus on the *consumer*, rather than the commercial, in order to determine whether individual characteristics—for example, sex and attitude—predispose him/her toward making particular inferences. The first part of this chapter deals primarily with subject variables and their influence on what the subject remembers about a commercial. We feel that this focus on the consumer has permitted us to make some subtle observations concerning the interaction between the commercial message and the listener or reader. And these observations have induced a mild scepticism in us regarding the results of early advertising-inference research. The second part of our chapter discusses this issue in more detail and presents the results of a methodological study that we undertook as a result of this scepticism.

PART I: THEORETICAL BACKGROUND

A large body of research has demonstrated that when subjects process sentences, paragraphs, and passages, they make pragmatic inferences (see Harris & Monaco, 1978, and Harris, 1981, for a review). For the most part, the tasks employed in these experiments were designed to determine whether the subjects would make certain critical inferences, like (2), after presentation of a stimulus message, (1). The tasks were not designed to determine whether some subjects would make different inferences than other subjects. This is not a fault of these experiments because they were designed to demonstrate that making inferences from natural language stimuli is a widespread behavior. We know intuitively, however, that people are different in terms of what they know about and how much they know, for example. We might then ask if there are not individual differences among us regarding what we are likely to infer from a message.

Bartlett (1932) demonstrated that subjects *construct* different inferences from the same message when they have different *world knowledge*—that is, know different things. The recall protocols of his subjects were simplified versions of the story they were asked to remember. The recall protocols were somewhat consistent among subjects from the same culture. For example, British subjects made similar inferences about presupposed events occurring between episodes. This provided evidence that the original story was simplified to fit the subjects' world knowledge. Thus, Bartlett concluded that his subjects constructed individual representations of the original story by making certain simplifying inferences that made the story consistent with what they knew.

Kintsch and van Dijk (1975) demonstrated that differences in world knowledge affect how much information is recalled and the way in which it is recalled—and, perhaps, stored in memory. They asked a group of AngloAmerican students and a group of native American Indians to read and then recall an American Indian narrative story. This story did not conform to traditional Western narrative structure—exposition, complication, and resolution—but conformed to the American Indian narrative structure of ''fours.'' The students, of course, were only familiar with traditional Western narrative structure whereas the American Indians were at least somewhat familiar with traditional American Indian narrative structure. Thus the world knowledge of the two groups differed. Analysis of the recall protocols demonstrated that the AngloAmerican students recalled less information from the original story than the American Indians. Additionally, the recall protocols of the students demonstrated that they attempted to recall, if not process, the story using traditional Western narrative structure. They simplified the original story to fit their world knowledge of narratives. Thus, differences in world knowledge between the two groups affected both the amount of information recalled and the way in which it was recalled.

It seems, then, that in any attempt to describe how information is processed we must take into account the contribution of each subject's world knowledge. Most cognitive psychologists may see this as an idealized goal of information-processing research. A few researchers, however, have gone as far as abandoning traditional information-processing models (e.g., Atkinson & Shiffrin's, 1968, duplex model of memory), that do not account for the contribution of the different world knowledge of each individual, in favor of more holistic approaches. Neisser's (1976) approach, for example, begins with the assumption that stimulus information interacts with a subject's schemata (i.e., world knowledge) in order to determine how that information will be processed. Consequently, each subject may process the same stimulus information differently.

One model which is capable of handling Neisser's assumptions is the Craik and Lockhart (1972) levels-of-processing model. Craik and Lockhart demonstrated that more meaningful information is processed more deeply and is therefore better remembered. We would expect meaninfulness to vary across individuals as a function of their world knowledge. Thus, two subjects may read or hear the same message about electronics, but one may recall more information about the message because he/she has more world knowledge about electrical engineering and, hence, the message is more meaningful. More to the point, two people may hear the identical commercial about Eradicold pills, (1): If one of them is an M.D., he/she may be less likely to make the critical inference, (2), because of his/her world knowledge of the complexity of colds.

This last example suggests an alternate interpretation—apparent differences in processing may only be differences in attention. The M.D. may just not attend to the commercial. Nonetheless, the reason he/she does not attend to it has to do with his/her particular world knowledge. (See the concept of *involvement* in advertising literature, e.g., Burnkrant & Sawyer, Ch. 2, this volume.)

It may be that the processing of the same stimulus information is different for each individual. The point is that what the subject remembers is clearly a function of the interaction between his/her unique world knowledge and the stimulus input. With respect to inferences, we have adopted Bartlett's metaphor of construction and assume that inferences are constructed from the message by a hearer/reader so they will conform with his or her unique knowledge of the world—his/her *world view*. We therefore approach our research expecting that each subject will listen to the stimulus message and construct inferences based on this world view.

If we expect each individual to construct different inferences, however, how can we conduct our research? The fact is that, with regard to some topics, we should be able to group individuals on the basis of their world views and therefore make some reasonably accurate and interesting predictions regarding their inference behavior.

THE CONSUMER'S WORLD VIEW

Fritz Heider (1958) distinguished between two types of psychology: *naive psychology* is the knowledge of behavior that has accumulated over the past two thousand or more years and has been recorded, informally, in our literature—it is the psychology which all of us use, daily, in our interpersonal relations; *scientific psychology*, on the other hand, is the knowledge of behavior that has accumulated in research laboratories for over one hundred years and has been formally recorded in research journals—it is the psychology which few of us ever use outside of the laboratory. Heider's opinion was that if all the accumulated wisdom of scientific psychology had never been accumulated, the world would be no worse off. Perhaps Heider's observations are also applicable to the advertising industry: one shrewd ad writer's guess may be worth a hundred research studies. But psychologists often use naive psychology to develop hypotheses. So, let's try to use some naive psychology to "psyche out" the consumer.

Most of us are biased. With regard to commercial products, "biased" means that most of us have consistent preferences—what's called "brand loyalty." We prefer different brands of cigarettes, for example, and for different reasons (world knowledge). This is in spite of the fact that most smokers can't distinguish between brands. Some people have strong preferences for cars—there are those who "swear by" Chevrolet and others who "swear by" Fords. Often brand loyalty is accompanied by a tangled web of faulty reasoning. For example, when a friend surveyed local farmers' attitudes before purchasing any particular make of pickup truck, he found that the farmers were in apparent unanimity over the superiority of Fords to Chevrolets. So he bought a Ford. Unfortunately, he forgot to ask his "subjects" whether or not they had ever actually owned a Chevrolet. Nonetheless, he now agrees that Fords are superior to Chevrolets— although he has never owned one of the latter.

What do preferences mean, in terms of advertising and inferences? Well, let's consider our friend, again, and imagine that he hears a commercial five years from now about Ford pickups—he should be ready to buy a new one then. He will probably listen very closely because, from what we have already ascertained, his world view is that Ford manufactures a really fine truck. If, by chance, the commercial message is that

4. Ford pick-ups have more front seat leg-room than Chevrolet pick-ups and more storage-space than Dodge pick-ups.

he is quite likely to infer that

5. Ford pick-ups have more room than any other pick-up.

although that may not be the case at all. Harris (1977) has demonstrated that subjects make inferences like (5) when a fictitious car manufacturer's name is used. The point, however, is that our friend is probably more likely to infer (5) after hearing (4), than he is to infer (7) after hearing (6):

6. Chevrolet pick-ups have more front seat leg-room than Ford pick-ups and more storage space than Dodge pick-ups.
7. Chevrolet pick-ups have more room than any other pick-up.

This is because we know that his *prior preference* is for Fords—one aspect of his world view—and we expect him to construct only those inferences like (5), which are consistent with his world view. In fact, he may not attend to commercial (6) because of his preference for Fords. Ehrlich, Guttman, Schonbach, and Mills (1957) found that, consistent with predictions based on Festinger's (1957) theory of cognitive dissonance, new car owners chose to read significantly more advertisements about the cars they recently purchased than advertisements about other cars they had considered for purchase or cars not involved in the choice. Old car owners (those who purchased cars at least one year prior to the study) showed a similar, but not statistically significant, bias. Interestingly, few of the old car owners recalled that any other make of car was even considered prior to their purchase decision. Festinger (1957) suggests that "over a period of time, old car owners tended to forget or deny that they even seriously considered other makes (Festinger, 1957, p. 54). Purchasers appear to selectively filter new information that pertains to their purchase decision, based upon prior purchase decisions.

Let's go a little bit further in our naive analysis of the consumer. Our friend knows a lot of people with pick-up trucks (veterinarians, farriers, people who use their pick-ups to pull horse trailers or carry campers, etc.), not just farmers. Yet he sought the opinion of *farmers* in order to make a decision about which pick-up to purchase. Why? Some farmers use their pick-ups only to drive to the store and back—so they're not the most reliable judges. Veterinarians, on the other hand, carry a minilaboratory in their pickups across poor terrain; and farriers haul heavy forges (for making horseshoes) and other equipment in their pickups— usually, until the trucks need to be hauled away themselves. This would seem to qualify them more highly than farmers. Nonetheless, our friend seems to consider that farmers have the required knowledge and expertise to make them qualified judges of pickup trucks, even for a nonfarmer's use.

Once again, we get an inkling of this consumer's world view. We would predict, then, that if our friend heard the commercial

8. An independent survey showed that 8 out of 10 farmers think that Ford makes a better truck.

he would not hesitate to infer that

9. Farmers think that Fords are the best trucks made.

or

10. Farmers think that Ford pickups are the best pickups made.

or even

11. Ford makes the best pickup.

even though these are not necessary conclusions from (8) and are somewhat improbable. We would certainly not expect everyone who hears (8) to infer (9)–(11). It is just that we know enough about this one individual's world view— that Ford makes great trucks and that farmers are reliable judges of a truck's quality—to make strong predictions about what inferences he would construct: We know that he will process the information in (8) so that his inferences will conform to his world view. Because we have a pretty good idea of what that world view is, we can make these predictions with confidence.

So far we've been analyzing the world view of one consumer. We know that he has a *prior preference* for Fords and his *attitude* toward farmers is that they are reliable sources of information about trucks. Suppose we present him with the commercial

12. An independent survey showed that 8 out of 10 farmers think that Good-year makes a better tire.

The only differences between commericals (8) and (12) are the brand and type of product being advertised. And we only know that our friend thinks farmers are reliable sources of information about pickup trucks. Nonetheless, we might predict that he would infer

13. Farmers think that Goodyear tires are the best tires made.

knowing what we do about his attitude toward farmers—that they are, at some level, reliable sources of information. Harris, Monaco, and Perch (1977) demonstrated that subjects construct more inferences from messages that originate from more credible sources.

Commercials, of course, are frequently designed to appeal to our world view—in this case, spokespeople are often "credible" sources such as doctors, dentists, presidents of companies, etc. Commercials like

14. An independent survey showed that 8 out of 10 denstists recommend Crest.

or

15. I'm a dentist and I use Crest.

are obviously designed to lead us to infer

16. Dentists think that Crest is best.

by appealing to our world view that dentists are credible sources of information about toothpaste. And if our world view *is* that dentists are experts about toothpaste, we will likely infer (16) after hearing (14) or (15).

We can summarize by stating that each consumer has a unique world view and that this world view is best evidenced as *prior preference*. We should be able to find groups of consumers who have similar preferences about a product. We expect that prior preference (world view about a product) interacts with a commercial message in order to determine what inferences are constructed about the product being advertised in the commercial. Therefore, we predict that a group of subjects who have similar product preferences will construct inferences from a commercial that will be consistent with their world view: If they like the product or spokesperson, they will be more likely to construct favorable inferences about the product after hearing the commercial.

FEAR AND LOATHING ON
THE CAMPAIGN TRAIL: 1976[1]

In our first endeavor into the area of consumer preference, advertising, and inferences we wanted to find two products that would polarize our subject population, on the basis of their prior preferences, for one or the other product. In September of 1976, when we initiated this research, the two hottest products around were the presidential candidates, Gerald Ford and Jimmy Carter. Because feelings run rather high during a presidential campaign, we expected to find a sufficient number of subjects who were pro-Ford and pro-Carter.

In general, candidates for elected political office rely on radio and television advertising in their pursuit of consumer votes, rather than consumer dollars; Carter and Ford were no exceptions (Lelyveld, 1976; Smith, 1976). To get elected, of course, the candidate must be appealing to the widest range of voters. The voters, themselves, differ in their world views—some favor the Equal Rights Amendment, others do not; some favor detente, others oppose it. Neither candidate can take a stand with regard to such sensitive issues without running the risk of alienating those voters who disagree with that stand. Thus the candidate often makes ambiguous statements (see Stanley, 1976, for a discussion and additional examples) about these issues from which listeners, with different world views, might infer opposite conclusions. For example, 14 lines into his speech before the Democratic National Committee, in which he accepted their nomination for president, Carter said that

17. We have been shaken by a tragic war.

Apparently that statement referred to the "Viet Nam war," although Carter was not explicit. Statement (17) is consistent with

---

[1]We stole this title from Hunter Thompson.

18. The war was tragic because it was a mistake to enter the conflict in the first place.

and

19. The war was tragic because the U.S. pulled out too soon.

Statement (17) implies *both* (18) and (19). If Carter was lucky, opponents of the Viet Nam war inferred (18) and concluded that he was on their side, whereas proponents of the war inferred (19) and concluded that Carter sympathized with them. (Because Carter did not specify which war he was talking about, he could always claim that he was talking about the Revolutionary war—it was the Bicentennial—and only worry about alienating Tories.)

Our hypothesis is that prior preference for a candidate significantly influences the number of inferences one constructs from information contained in commercials about the candidate. In the present study, our objective was to determine whether prior preference for either Gerald Ford or Jimmy Carter would significantly influence the number of inferences a subject would construct from information contained in Ford and Carter commercials (euphemistically called "paid political announcements"). Two of the variables manipulated were (prior) Preference (of the subject for either Ford or Carter) and Commercial (for Ford or Carter). At the start of the experiment, each subject indicated his/her preference by responding to the following question:

20. If the Presidential election were held tomorrow, for whom would you vote: Ford or Carter? _____

Each subject then heard two prerecorded commercials—one for Ford and one for Carter. We expected subjects to construct more inferences from the information contained in the commercial about the favored candidate (e.g., Ford) than from the information contained in the commercial about the unfavored one (e.g., Carter) as measured on a subsequent recognition test. Thus a significant Preference × Commercial interaction would indicate that a subject's prior preference—one aspect of his/her world view—determined the number of inferences he/she constructed from a commercial.

Two other variables were also manipulated in order to determine whether the sex of the subject and/or the sex of the spokesperson for a candidate would affect the number of inferences constructed by the subjects. Although we had no firm hypotheses about the effects of these two variables, we did consider that they should be important, particularly with regard to the processing of information about politics. Because U.S. politics is dominated by males, subjects might find a male spokesperson more credible than a female spokesperson and thus construct fewer inferences about the information in commercials with a female spokesperson. Another possibility is that subjects who prefer Ford ("conservative Republicans") might find a female less credible than a male spokesperson whereas subjects who prefer Carter ("liberal Democrats") might find a male and female spokesperson equally credible.

Method

Subjects. The subjects were 36 male and 36 female undergraduate students at Kansas State University who participated in the experiment as part of a course requirement. They were run in small groups.

Materials. Experimental materials consisted of a cassette tape for presentation of Ford and Carter commercials and an eight-page booklet consisting of a questionnaire, a distractor task, and a recognition-of-information test for each commercial.

The cassette tape contained four recorded commercial pairs. Each pair consisted of a commercial for Gerald Ford and a commercial for Jimmy Carter. The four commercial pairs differed only in sex of spokesperson for Ford and Carter and order of commercial presentation. In the first pair there was a male spokesperson for Ford and a female spokesperson for Carter; the Ford commercial preceded the Carter commercial. In the second pair, sex of spokesperson was the same but order of the commercials was reversed—the Carter commercial preceded the Ford commercial. In the other two pairs sex of spokesperson was reversed: there was a female spokesperson for Ford and a male spokesperson for Carter. The Ford commercial preceded the Carter commercial in one pair and followed the Carter commercial in the other.

The content of the Ford commercial was written to conform with statements Ford made during his election campaign. The content of the Carter commercial was written to conform with statements Carter made when he accepted the nomination for the presidency before the Democratic National Committee.

The eight-page booklet, in which subjects recorded their responses, contained: (1) a blank page; (2) a questionnaire that contained question (20) embedded among other questions pertaining to the subject's sex, political affiliations (if any), religious attitudes, and attitudes toward the E.R.A. and abortion; (3) another blank page; (4) and (5) two pages containing a distractor task; (6) a recognition-of-information test about the information contained in the first commercial that the subject heard; (7) a recognition-of-information test about the information contained in the second commercial that the subject heard; (8) a statement about the purpose of the experiment in order to debrief the subject.

Each recognition-of-information test contained 20 statements. The statements in one test (Ford test) were based on information in the Ford commercial and the statements in the other test (Carter test) were based on information contained in the Carter commercial. The statements for each test were chosen such that 5 were true, 5 were false, and 10 were of indeterminate truth value (i.e., implied) with respect to the commercial on which they were based. For example, the Carter spokesperson asserted that "the Democratic party has made mistakes—but Carter admits it." Statement (21) was contained in the Carter test and was true with respect to the content of the Carter commercial. The Ford spokesperson asserted that "Ford won't ignore the agricultural problems." Statement (22) was contained in the Ford test and was false with respect to the content of the Ford commercial. The Carter spokesperson also asserted that "he (Carter) realizes that it's time for a complete overhaul of the tax system," which may imply, but does not directly assert, statement (23). Statement (23) was contained on the Carter test and is of indeterminate truth value with respect to the Carter commercial.

21. Carter admits the Democratic Party has made mistakes.
22. Ford will ignore agricultural problems.
23. Carter wants to lower taxes.

An individual test consisted of the 20 statements based on the Ford or Carter commercial in a random order. Each statement was followed by the letters "T," "F," and "I." At the top of each test was an explanation of these response categories and the instructions to "PLEASE CIRCLE THE CORRECT ANSWER."

Design and Procedure. A 2^4 factorial design was employed. There were three between-subjects factors—Subject Preference (either pro-Ford or pro-Carter), Subject Sex (male or female), Spokesperson Sex (either a male spokesperson for Ford and a female spokesperson for Carter or a female spokesperson for Ford and a male spokesperson for Carter)—and one within-subjects factor—Commercial (either a Ford or a Carter commercial).

At the start of the experiment, each subject was given a booklet and asked to fill out the questionnaire on the second page. Subjects were then asked to turn to the third (blank) page and were told; "You will hear two speakers express their differing opinions on an issue of current controversy, the Presidential election." Subjects then heard one of the four recorded commercial pairs. One half of the subjects heard the Carter commercial first. The other half heard the Ford commercial first. After hearing the commercials, subjects were instructed to turn to the next page of their booklet and begin the (distractor) task. Subjects were allowed to pace themselves. After a subject finished the distractor task, he/she was allowed to immediately proceed to the recognition-of-information tests for the two commercials. Subjects were again allowed to pace themselves.

Results

The questionnaires were first examined to determine each subject's Preference and Sex; Spokesperson Sex was determined by the commercial pair which the subject heard. Because each subject heard both Ford and Carter commercials, responses to the implied items in the Ford test and the Carter test were treated separately. This permitted a four-factor (Preference × Subject Sex × Spokesperson Sex × Commercial) analysis of variance on the number of "I" ("indeterminate") responses a subject made to the implied items on the Ford test and Carter test. The "indeterminate" category was chosen for analysis because an "indeterminate" response to an item indicates that the subject *did not* construct a pragmatic inference, that is, recognized that the implied statement would not have to be true. Either a "true" or "false" response to an implied test item would indicate that the subject has made a pragmatic inference. For example, the spokesperson for Carter said (17). As discussed above, either a "true" or "false" response to the test item:

24. Carter realizes that the Viet Nam war was a mistake.

would indicate that the subject has made an inference: A "true" response is consistent with the pragmatic inference (18), and a "false" response is consistent with the pragmatic inference (19). Only an indeterminate response to a statement like (24) would indicate that the subject has not constructed either inference. (Because all subjects responded to all implied items on the two tests, the number of "true" and "false" responses to implied items on either test is merely the total number of implied items per test—10—minus the number of indeterminate responses to those items.)

The analysis revealed two significant interactions. The first was the predicted Preference × Commercial interaction, $F(1,64) = 33.98$, $p < .05$. Inspection of the means presented in Table 12.1 suggests that subjects with different prefer-

TABLE 12.1
Mean Number of Implied Test Items (Out of 10) Correctly Identified
as "Indeterminate" and Broken Down by Preference and
Commercial[a]

	Commercial	
Preference	Ford	Carter
Ford	2.69	3.78
Carter	3.39	2.17

[a]Larger cell means indicate that a group constructed fewer pragmatic inferences. Smaller cell means indicate that the group constructed more pragmatic inferences.

ences responded differently to the two commercials. Specifically, subjects who preferred Ford constructed more inferences about the Ford commercial than about the Carter commercial (i.e., marked fewer implied items "indeterminate" on the Ford test than on the Carter test), and subjects who preferred Carter constructed more inferences about the Carter commercial than about the Ford commercial (i.e., marked fewer implied items "indeterminate" on the Carter test than on the Ford test). Simple main effects analyses confirmed this (using an adjusted experimenter-wise error rate of .025 for both comparisons) for subjects who preferred Ford, $F(1,64) = 21.13$, $p < .025$, and for subjects who preferred Carter, $F(1,64) = 26.88$, $p < .025$.

The analysis also revealed a significant Preference $\times$ Subject Sex $\times$ Spokesperson Sex interaction $F(1,64) = 4.35$, $p < .05$. The cell means are presented in Table 12.2. Although not defying interpretation, the presence of this interaction was difficult to analyze in terms of either simple interaction or simple, simple main effects. Since analysis of this interaction was primarily a "fishing expedition," the experimenter-wise error rate was appropriately adjusted to the .01 level. None of the simple interaction effects were significant at this level and only one—the Preference $\times$ Experimenter Sex for male subjects—was significant at the .05 level, $F(1,64) = 4.05$. Further analysis of the simple, simple main effects of the triple interaction revealed that male subjects who preferred Ford constructed fewer inferences when there was a male spokesperson (regardless of commercial) than did male subjects who preferred Carter. This difference, however, was not significant at an appropriately adjusted error rate. Rather, it was significant only at the .05 level, $F(1,64) = 4.21$. Nonetheless, it appears that male subjects who preferred Ford constructed fewer inferences (i.e., identified more statements as "indeterminate") when there was a male spokesperson

TABLE 12.2
Mean Number of Implied Test Items (Out of 10) Correctly Identified
as "Indeterminate" and Broken Down by Experimenter Sex,
Preference, Subject Sex[a]

Preference	Spokesperson Sex	
	Male	Female
	Male Subjects	
Ford	3.61	2.50
Carter	1.89	3.17
	Female Subjects	
Ford	3.11	3.72
Carter	3.28	2.78

[a]Larger cell means indicate that a group constructed fewer pragmatic inferences. Smaller cell means indicate that the group constructed more pragmatic inferences.

than did male subjects who preferred Carter and that this difference was responsible for the presence of the significant triple interaction.

DISCUSSION

The results of this experiment are consistent with the hypothesis we proposed:
that preference for one product (in this case a presidential candidate) would affect
the number of inferences an individual constructs about a commercial for that
product or about a rival product. We feel that these results are best interpreted
within a more general framework of memory as a constructive process. The
constructive theory of memory, discussed earlier, assumes that an individual's
representation of a message is a product of the interaction between the speaker–
writer's message and the individual's world view. The constructive theory thus
predicts that an individual will construct a representation of a commercial message in light of his/her preference—one aspect of his/her world view.

It is important for the researcher to keep in mind that information is not
processed in a vacuum. That is, individuals carry with them knowledge that will
affect the manner in which they process new information. Models of the informa-
tion-processer that do not take this fact into account cannot hope to explain how
nonnaive individuals, like consumers, process information, like commercials,
which is directly relevant to their daily lives. We feel that the constructive theory
of memory is flexible enough to account for different processing of the same
information by different individuals and to also suffice as a meaningful model of
memory.

Much advertising research which has examined subjects' inference behavior
has used commercials about fictitious products as stimuli. These experiments
may permit one to generalize to the class of commercials that advertise *new
products* with which consumers have no familiarity but do not allow one to
generalize to the class of commercials which advertise *old products* (with which
consumers have some familiarity through other commercials and/or through first-
hand experience) in new ways. By using commercials about real products—the
presidential candidates—and by assessing subjects' preferences at the start of the
experiment, we were able to make meaningful predictions about their inference
behavior which is generalizable to the second class of commercials described
above. We feel that this demonstrates the feasibility of using commercials about
real products as experimental stimuli and supplements previous advertising-
inference research.

To end this section we would like to shift focus away from the experiment and
direct it towards ourselves as experimenters. Our pre-experimental hypothesis
represented our world view. The hypothesis was arrived at somewhat naively.
Suppose that we had not obtained the significant Preference × Commercial
interaction. How would this have affected our experimental conclusions? We

probably would have constructed certain inferences regarding the experiment. For example, we might have inferred that our "commercials" were inadequate, or that the experiment was poorly designed. Notice that one inference is missing: namely, that prior preference *does not* affect the inferences we construct. It is unlikely that we would have constructed this last inference because it conflicts with our world view, as stated originally. The fact that we seldom abandon our naive hypotheses quite likely leads to selective forgetting about experiments which produce null results. Let the researcher beware!

PART II

It is not at all clear that the laboratory is the best place for conducting research— particularly commercial advertising research. The requirement of "controlled conditions" in the laboratory may impose too severe restrictions upon us, as experimenters; and we may simulate, rather than reproduce, the phenomenon intended for study. For example, the laboratory offers the potential for examining how consumers process information contained in commercial messages under controlled conditions. But how faithful a representation of the average consumer is the subject in an experiment? Can we generalize to the average consumer from our experimental results? If not, how can we design laboratory experiments that will permit such generalizations? We feel that these are important questions which must be discussed by researchers. This section is an attempt to deal, by example, with some of them.

A BRIEF LOOK AT TASK DEMANDS

For some time we have been concerned about the ecological validity of laboratory research designed to examine how consumers process information contained in commercials. In real life, the shift from television or radio program to commercial interlude is often a signal to direct attention elsewhere. For some of us this shift is a signal to re-enter into conversation—or argument—with our viewing partners. For others, the shift from program to commercial is a signal to leave the room, for one reason or another. It's not hard to understand why—we don't turn on the television or radio to watch/listen to commercials.

We might say, then, that the shift from program to commercial is a discriminative stimulus to direct attention *away* from the T.V.; and anything we remember about the commercial should be attributed to incidental learning. The start of an experiment, however, is a signal to the subject to direct attention *toward* the commercial. And even if the subject is not specifically directed to do so, he/she probably has a stronger inclination to try to remember the content of the commercial than does the consumer, at home. Moreover, in the laboratory situation listening to a commercial is probably an outstanding event in the day for the subject when we consider that most subjects are participating in the experiment between or after classes.

The typical advertising-inference experiment is conducted by allowing the subject to hear one or more stimulus commercials about fictitious products, followed by a recognition-of-information test for facts implied by or asserted in the commercial. Immediately preceding the test, the subject is often given "truth instructions," which indicate that the information heard in the commercial should be considered true. Truth instructions is an example of a procedural variable which tends to reduce rather than increase the similarity between the experimental subject's situation and that of the consumer, at home. The consumer in the marketplace is not given truth instructions but may choose to believe or disbelieve the advertisers' claims.

Harris, Monaco, and Perch (1977, experiment 3) reported an experiment that was designed to determine whether favorability of information about a store, presented to subjects before hearing the commercials for products sold in that store, would affect the number of inferences they would construct. Each subject heard stimulus commercials advertised by the "Cheapermarket store." Preceding the commercials the subjects heard either highly favorable or highly unfavorable information about the store. After hearing the commercials, the subjects were told to "accept everything said in the advertisement as true" and were then allowed to answer recognition-of-information test questions. Harris, Monaco, and Perch found a significant interaction between favorability (high versus low) and type of test item (pragmatically implied by or directly asserted in the commercials). Specifically, subjects were more likely to construct a pragmatic inference if they heard highly *un*favorable information about the store. Favorability had no effect upon subjects' responses to directly asserted test items. This remarkably unintuitive result may have been an artifact of the procedure— specifically, the truth instructions.

In an unpublished study, Harris and Monaco tested this latter hypothesis by replicating the earlier experiment but leaving out the truth instructions (as in the experiment reported above). This procedure was expected to more closely approximate real-world conditions where consumers can choose to believe or disbelieve any claims presented in an advertisement. Table 12.3 presents the means obtained in both experiments. Harris and Monaco failed to replicate the previous results when truth instructions were omitted from the procedure. No significant main effects or interactions were present. When both sets of data were analyzed together, a significant interaction between favorability, type of test item, and instructions emerged, $F(1,64) = 4.17$, $p < .05$, indicating that the favorability by test item interaction reported by Harris, Monaco, and Perch was probably an artifact of the truth instructions they used.

The use of truth instructions in advertising-inference experiments is clearly a questionable procedure. The ecological validity of the task is doubtful and the

TABLE 12.3
Mean Numbers of "True" Responses (Out of 8) from Harris,
Monaco, and Perch (1977)—in Parentheses—and Harris and Monaco
(1978)

	Claim Type	
Source Information	Assertion	Implication
Favorable	6.27(6.79)	6.33(5.58)
Unfavorable	6.47(6.75)	6.43(6.58)

results become highly suspect. Further, if such "minor" matters of procedure can be responsible for such gross differences in subject behavior, we must certainly take precautions not to accidently demand our subjects to behave peculiarly by overlooking the procedural demands we impose.

One way to avoid procedural problems is to leave the laboratory, altogether. Harris, Dubitsky, Perch, Ellerman, and Larson (1980) have made a preliminary attempt to avoid the artificiality of the laboratory as a setting for commercial advertising research by having a group of subjects watch a news program at home. The following day subjects returned to the laboratory to be tested on their recognition memory for information in news show and commercials. Harris et al. found no effect of type of test item (i.e., implied vs. asserted test items), giving support to the Harris and Monaco replication of Harris, Monaco, and Perch (1977). Although Harris et al. had to give up the "experimental control" obtained by having subjects attend to commercials in the laboratory, the experiment seems more ecologically valid in the sense that laboratory-imposed task demands during commercial viewing were eliminated.

Not all hypotheses can be readily examined outside the laboratory, however. And if a variable like instructions can have such a drastic effect upon subject behavior in the laboratory, these variables must be systematically examined prior to generalization of experimental results to the consumer in the real world. In planning our next experiment, we attempted to examine the effect of truth instructions in the context of our overall research objective: the study of the interactive effects of prior preference and commercial message upon subject-consumers' construction of inferences.

FEAR AND LOATHING IN
THE LABORATORY: 1978

In the next experiment we were again interested in the effects of our experimental consumer-subjects' world views (prior preferences) upon their construction of inferences about a commercial message. We asked all experimental subjects to respond to test statements implied by a stimulus commercial, first, under conditions of truth instructions (where they were told to accept everything stated in the commercial as true and to answer test statements based on the commercial information, only) and, then, under conditions of "belief" instructions (where subjects were told to answer test statements on the basis of their belief and opinions). Rather than presidential candidates, we chose more typical products— Chevrolet and Ford cars—as the subject matter of stimulus commercials.

Instead of having all subjects hear commercials for Ford and Chevrolet cars, we ran equal numbers of subjects, having either a Ford or Chevrolet preference or no preference for either car manufacturer, in two commercial groups (one for Ford and one for Chevrolet) and two control groups (where subjects did not hear the commercials but responded to test statements for Ford or Chevrolet under conditions of belief instructions). This permitted us to keep the Ford and Chevrolet commercial texts and test statements identical, offering more control over materials than could have been obtained in the last experiment. Inclusion of the control groups permitted an analysis of the effects of hearing versus not hearing the commercial itself.

Instead of asking our subjects to circle either *True, False,* or *Indeterminate* in response to each test statement, we asked them to rate the statements on a seven-point scale (1 = Certainly False to 7 = Certainly True). In this way, subjects could be given an overall score for their responses to the 15 implied test statements. These scores would indicate the direction of subjects' inferences—low scores would indicate that subjects inferred that the items were false whereas high scores would indicate that subjects inferred that the majority of items were true. For example, we would expect subjects who preferred Ford cars to score

25. You'll feel good if you own a Ford.

somewhat higher than subjects who were either indifferent to Ford and Chevrolet cars or who prefer Chevrolet cars. (We must note that although one group of subjects had no preference for either Ford or Chevrolet cars, they do not constitute a homogeneous group that falls between the Ford-preference and Chevrolet-preference groups. Many of the subjects labeled "indifferent" may have had strong preferences for another automobile manufacturer. Thus, we could not have expected them to score a test *statement about Ford cars*, like (25) any differently than subjects who preferred Chevrolet cars. However, we could expect them to score that statement differently than subjects with a strong Ford preference.)

The design of the experiment *should* lead us to anticipate commercial-group subjects' data to reveal a strong Preference (for Ford, Chevrolet, or neither) by Commercial (for Ford or Chevrolet) interaction when analyzing their responses to implied test statements. This result would be most consistent with the results of our earlier experiment. However, we expected an analysis of experimental subjects' responses to test statements under conditions of *truth instructions to reveal no such interaction*. We expected an analysis of their responses under conditions of belief instructions, however, to clearly reveal such an interaction between subjects' prior preferences and the inferences that they constructed from commercial messages. Such disparate results are to be expected if subjects actually follow the truth instructions and respond purely on the basis of commercial information without introducing the "bias" of their preference. These results would further confirm our hypothesis that the presence of truth instructions in the commercial task destroys the validity of generalization between the experimental population given truth instructions and the real-world consumer population. In comparing control and commercial-group subjects, we expected analyses of the tests presented under conditions of belief instructions to reveal an effect of commercial presentation, indicating that commercial-group subjects had, in fact, been influenced by hearing the commercial.

Method

Subjects.   The subjects were 80 Kansas State University and Southwest Missouri State University undergraduates who participated in the experiment in order to fulfill a course requirement or for extra course credit. Equal numbers of subjects from each university participated in each experimental and control condition permitting analysis of university as an independent variable.

Materials.   For this experiment, the materials consisted of a questionnaire, a commercial, in which the names of Ford and Chevrolet could be substituted, a set of 25 statements about the commercial in which the product names could also be substituted, and two response sheets.

The questionnaire was composed of 50 pairs of 1978 model cars and instructions to the subjects to circle the one car from each pair that he/she preferred. Twenty-five of these 50 pairs constituted all possible combinations of Chevrolet's Nova, Chevelle, Monza, Impala, and Vega with Ford's Mustang, Granada, LTD, LTD II, and Pinto. These 25 critical pairs were used to determine subjects' preferences for Ford cars and Chevrolet cars, or indifference toward (equal preference for) the two car manufacturers. The particular models of Ford and Chevrolet cars for the 25 critical pairs were chosen after interviews with both Ford and Chevrolet car salesmen to determine competitive models. The remaining 25 pairs were combinations of other makes and models of cars and primarily served as distractor items to obscure the purpose of the task—determination of Ford versus Chevrolet preference.

The stimulus commercial was composed of highly favorable statements about Ford and Chevrolet cars from brochures obtained from dealers. These statements were arranged into a 3-minute skeleton commercial. The following paragraph is an excerpt from the commercial:

26. The new _____ was conceived as a highly individual, very personal automobile that would appeal to a particularly discriminating buyer. What sets _____ apart from most other cars is a wonderful combination of subtle touches on the outside and in. It's a very complete car. One that we believe is now at the pinnacle of excellence. The _____ is more impressive to look at. Its lean, low lines have an elegant look. They are similar in design to those found in European sports sedans costing many times more.

Ford and Chevrolet commercials were obtained by substituting the names Ford and Chevrolet, respectively, for the blanks. Each commercial was then recorded onto a cassette tape for presentation to the subjects.

The 25 test statements were written such that 15 of them were pragmatically implied by the commercials, and were, thus, extremely favorable (e.g., statement 25). Five were directly asserted in the commercial, and five were false with respect to the information contained in the commercial. A test consisted of the 25 test statements in a random order. The two tests differed only in that the name Ford was substituted for the name Chevrolet in the Ford test.

Each response sheet contained 25 spaces for subjects to mark their responses to test statements and the scale, (27).

27. 7. CERTAINLY TRUE
     6. MOSTLY TRUE
     5. MORE TRUE THAN FALSE
     4. NEITHER TRUE NOR FALSE
     3. MORE FALSE THAN TRUE
     2. MOSTLY FALSE
     1. CERTAINLY FALSE.

One response sheet contained instructions to the subjects to rate the test statements, using scale (27), "according to how true or false they are based on the commercial you just heard" (truth instructions). The other contained instructions to "rate the statements according to how true or false they are based on your own opinions and beliefs" (belief instructions).

Procedure. All subjects filled out the questionnaire first. The Ford commercial group then heard the Ford commercial. The Chevrolet group heard the Chevrolet commercial. After hearing the commercial, they were given the appropriate set of test statements and turned to the first response sheet (truth instructions) to rate each test statement. Upon completion, the subject turned to the next response sheet (belief instructions) to rate each statement again. The control groups filled out the questionnaire and then responded to either the Chevrolet or Ford test statements on the response sheet containing belief instructions, the scale, and blanks to rate each statement. All subjects were permitted to pace themselves when responding to test statements.

Results

Questionnaires. Subjects were classified as having a Ford-preference, Chevrolet-preference, or no-preference for either Ford or Chevrolet on the basis of their responses to the 25 critical Ford-Chevrolet pairs. Subjects who chose a Ford car over a Chevrolet car on 18 or more of the critical pairs were classified as having a Ford-preference; those who chose Ford cars over Chevrolet cars on 11 to 15 of the pairs were classified as having no-preference for either Ford or Chevrolet cars; those who chose Ford cars over Chevrolet cars on fewer than eight pairs (i.e., chose Chevrolet cars over Ford cars on 18 or more of the pairs) were classified as having a Chevrolet-preference. There were five subjects having each of the three preferences in the two commercial and two control groups.

Commercial Subjects. The design of the experiment permitted analysis of experimental subject data in a variety of ways. We chose to analyze truth-instruction responses to the 15 implied test statements independently of belief-instruction responses. Typically, subjects would have only been given truth instructions and therefore only this analysis would be conducted. The designs for the two analyses are identical $2 \times 2 \times 3$ factorials, completely between. Commercial represents the Ford versus Chevrolet car commercials; the second factor, University, represents Kansas State University versus Southwest Missouri State University; and the third factor, Preference, represents either Chevrolet-preference, Ford-preference, or no-preference for either car manufacturer.

The dependent variable for both analyses was the sum of a subject's responses to the 15 implied test items under conditions of either truth or belief instructions. Large sums for implied items indicate that, on the average, subjects rated them as true, whereas small sums for implied items indicate that subjects rated them as false.

An analysis of responses to implied items under conditions of truth instructions revealed no significant main effects or interactions. An analysis of subjects' responses to the identical items, under conditions of belief instructions, revealed a significant Commercial $\times$ Preference interaction, $F(2,48) = 4.54$, $p < .05$. Means are presented for both instruction conditions in Table 12.4. First, under both conditions of instructions, subjects who preferred the car manufacturer being advertised, on the average, rated the implied-test statements higher (i.e., more true) than subjects who preferred the other car manufacturer or who were indifferent to either. The effect was more pronounced, however, when subjects were given belief instructions. Second, mean sums of responses to the implied-test statements were higher for all groups when asked to rate the statements based upon the commercial (truth instructions). An analysis of variance revealed that

TABLE 12.4
Mean Sums of Responses to 15 Implied Test Items Broken Down by
Car Preference, Commercial, and Instruction Condition

	Commercial	
Preference	Ford	Chevrolet
	Truth Instructions	
Ford	83.0	85.7
Chevrolet	80.6	90.0
Neither	80.4	81.9
	Belief Instructions	
Ford	69.0	66.0
Chevrolet	57.4	74.1
Neither	62.4	62.9

the effect of instructions was significant when all experimental data were ana-
lysed together, $F(1,48) = 163.35$, $p < .05$. Cell means are 83.6 and 65.3 for
truth and belief instructions, respectively. The higher mean for the truth-instruc-
tions condition indicates that, when asked to rate test items based upon the
commercial message, subjects tend to rate implied test items as truer than they
would have rated them based upon their own beliefs and opinions.

Commercial Versus Control Groups.   The fact that subjects judged implied
test items as less true (i.e., constructed fewer inferences) when asked to rate
them according to their own opinions and beliefs does not necessarily indicate
that they would have constructed fewer inferences if they had heard the same
commercial at home. Furthermore, under conditions of belief instructions commercial-group subjects may have ignored the commercial content and responded
purely on the basis of their prior beliefs, just as they appeared to have ignored
their prior beliefs and to have responded purely on the basis of commercial
content under conditions of truth instructions. To determine whether the commercial message interacted with the experimental subjects' world-views (prior
preference) when they responded to the statements under belief instructions, a
comparison of Commercial-group and control-group data was conducted. Control subjects responded to the same test statements as Commercial-group subjects
under conditions of belief instructions. However, because control subjects did
not hear either commercial, significant effects involving the presence versus
absence of the commercial would indicate that the presence of the commercial
significantly affected commercial-group subjects' responses under conditions of
belief instructions.

A $2 \times 2 \times 2 \times 3$ analysis of variance, completely between, was conducted on
the sums of each subject's response to the 15 implied test statements under
conditions of belief instructions. The factors were the same as in the preceding

analyses with the exception that one factor, Commercial Presence, was added to account for the presence or absence of the commercial for commercial or control groups, respectively.

The analysis of implied items revealed only a significant Commercial × Preference interaction, $F(2,96) = 7.72$, $p < .05$. Means are presented in Table 12.5. Because control subjects did not hear a commercial, this interaction may best be termed a "Test × Preference" interaction where Test indicates either the Ford or Chevrolet test.

Post-hoc tests of Kansas State University data, alone, and Southwest Missouri State University data, alone, (undertaken because of significant differences in variability between control groups from the two universities, $F(29,29) = 1.98$, $p < .05$), again revealed significant Commercial × Preference interactions. Only the analysis of Kansas State University subjects' data, however, revealed a significant effect of Commercial Presence, $F(1,48) = 4.89$, $p < .05$. For the Kansas State University subjects, at least, we can assume that the commercial did affect their responses under conditions of belief instructions. For the Southwest Missouri State University subjects, however, we cannot.

DISCUSSION

The results of this experiment indicate that, when asked to respond to implied test statements about a commercial on the basis of that commercial (truth instructions), subjects responded as if they had no prior preference. When asked to respond on the basis of their beliefs (belief instructions), however, subjects responded to the same statements as if they had never heard the commercial (as the initial comparison of control and commercial group data seemed to indicate).

With regard to the effect of truth instructions, we feel that the interpretation is clear—truth instructions produce a response bias in subjects. Our subjects, in particular, responded to statements implied by commercials as if they had no particular preference for the product advertised, for an alternative product, or for

TABLE 12.5
Mean Sums of Responses to 15 Implied Test Items Broken Down by
Commercial and Car Preference for Combined Commercial and
Control Groups

| Preference | Commercial | |
	Ford	Chevrolet
Ford	71.8	65.9
Chevrolet	59.7	71.1
Neither	63.4	66.1

neither. In fact, they subsequently responded to the statements on the basis of those preferences when given different instructions. Even if the only effect of truth instructions is to induce subjects to use the favorable end of the response scale, systematic bias destroys the ecological validity of the experiment—in no case can we generalize our results to the consumer, at home.

Similarly, belief instructions appear to have biased commercial-group subjects to respond to the implied test statements as if they had not heard the commercial. For these items there was no evidence of an effect of hearing the commercial when commercial and control-group data was first analyzed together. (Subsequent analyses revealed a significant effect of hearing the commercial for the Kansas State University subjects, only.) Subjects were clearly responding to the subject matter of the tests on the basis of their preferences. Hearing the commercial seems to have barely affected their pattern of response. Our conclusion is that belief instructions (which have been reported in advertising-inference experiments) should also be avoided. Our suggestion, at this point, is that no instructions—either belief or truth—be used prior to time of test (as in our first experiment).

SUMMARY

Information processing is an ongoing behavior that does not begin and end with presentation of a stimulus message in the laboratory. We demonstrated that the person's world-view, specifically prior product preference, plays a significant role in the determination of what inferences will be constructed from a commercial message. Similarly, we demonstrated that instructions to subjects play a significant role in the determination of how they will respond to statements about the commercial message. We feel that the study of the subject's prior preference as it interacts with a commercial message will continue to be an interesting area of research as long as researchers are careful to insure that their experimental results are ecologically valid in terms of the consumer at home.

ACKNOWLEDGMENTS

Preparation of this manuscript was supported under Grant #00870 from the National Institute of Child Health and Human Development (NICHHD) to the University of Kansas. The authors wish to thank Warren Buster, Lori Childs, Connie Mangrum, and Terry Werner for their assistance in data collection; Richard J. Harris, Carla Cantrell, and Jeanne Tomiser for their helpful comments on, suggestions for, and frequent criticisms of the manuscript.

REFERENCES

Atkinson, R. C., & Shiffrin, R. M. Human memory: A proposed system and its control processes. In K. W. Spence and J. T. Spence (Eds.), *The psychology of learning and motivation: Advances in research and theory Volume 2.* New York: Academic Press, 1968.

Bartlett, F. C. *Remembering.* London: Cambridge University Press, 1932.

Craik, F. I. M., & Lockhart, R. S. Levels of processing: A framework for memory research. *Journal of Verbal Learning and Verbal Behavior,* 1972, *11,* 671–684.

Ehrlich, D., Guttman, I., Schonbach, P., & Mills, J. Post-decision exposure to relevant information. *Journal of Abnormal and Social Psychology,* 1957, *54,* 94–102.

Festinger, L. *A theory of cognitive dissonance.* New York: Harper & Row, 1957.

Harris, R. J. Comprehension of pragmatic implications in advertising. *Journal of Applied Psychology,* 1977, *62,* 603–608.

Harris, R. J. Inferences in information processing. In G. H. Bower (Ed.), *The psychology of learning and motivation, Volume 15.* New York: Academic Press, 1981.

Harris, R. J., Dubitsky, T. M., Perch, K. L., Ellerman, C. S., & Larson, M. W. Remembering implied advertising claims as facts: Extensions to the "real world." *Bulletin of the Psychonomic Society,* 1980, *16,* 317–320.

Harris, R. J., & Monaco, G. E. The psychology of pragmatic implication: Information processing between the lines. *Journal of Experimental Psychology: General,* 1978, *107,* 1–22.

Harris, R. J., Monaco, G. E., & Perch, K. L. *The effect of source credibility on drawing inferences from history, advertising, and courtroom testimony.* Kansas State University, Human Information Processing Institute (KSU-HIPI) Report #77-9, October 1977.

Heider, F. *The psychology of interpersonal relations.* New York: Wiley, 1958.

Kintsch, W., & van Dijk, T. Recalling and summarizing stories. *Language,* 1975, *40,* 98–116.

Lelyveld, J. The selling of a candidate. *The New York Times Magazine,* March 28, 1976.

Neisser, U. *Cognition and reality.* San Francisco: W. H. Freeman, 1976.

Preston, I. L. Logic and illogic in the advertising process. *Journalism Quarterly,* 1967, *44,* 231–239.

Preston, I. L. The FTC's use of puffery and other selling claims made by implication. *Journal of Business Research,* 1977, *5,* 155–181.

Preston, I. L. Researchers at the Federal Trade Commission: Peril and promise. In J. H. Leigh & C. R. Martin, Jr. (Eds.), *Current issues and research in advertising 1980.* Ann Arbor: University of Michigan Graduate School of Business Administration Division of Research, 1980.

Preston, I. L., & Scharbach, S. E. Advertising: More than meets the eye. *Journal of Advertising Research,* 1971, *11,* 19–24.

Shimp, T. A. Do incomplete comparisons mislead? *Journal of Advertising Research,* 1978, *18,* 21–27.

Smith, P. The man who sold Jimmy Carter. *Dun's Review,* August, 1976.

Stanley, J. P. The stylistics of belief. In D. Dieterich (Ed.), *Teaching about Doublespeak.* Urbana, Ill.: National Council of Teachers of English, 1976.

13

Research on
Deceptive Advertising:
Commentary

Ivan L. Preston
University of Wisconsin

Although coming from diverse sources, the articles of Section II are readily treatable as one unified topic. Their thrust is that the consumer's encounter with an advertisement often results in the conveyance and belief of representations about the product over and beyond the verbal propositions the ad literally states. This fact has consequences for the field of information processing and also for the regulation of advertising, the latter because a potential for producing extra-literal beliefs often means a potential for being deceptive and so violating the law.

In the following I will discuss in turn (1) the ways in which the various authors show that what is communicated goes beyond literal verbal content, (2) the fact that such a result can made an ad deceptive, (3) the impact of these phenomena on the advertising industry, and (4) their impact on the field of information processing.

WHAT IS COMMUNICATED GOES BEYOND LITERAL
VERBAL CONTENT

This proposition is approached in four different ways by the five papers, since the articles by Harris, Dubitsky and Bruno and by Monaco and Kaiser represent the same research program; these latter two will frequently be referred to as "the Harris group." Three of the sources, Garfinkel, Shimp, and the Harris group, stress the notion that literal verbal content leads to the perception of additional implied verbal content and that consumer response will be determined in signifi-cant part by the latter. Garfinkel asserts this on the basis merely of finding that implications exist, whereas the others discuss empirical evidence that research subjects have seen and/or believed such implied content and/or made purchase decisions on the basis of it. Shimp stresses the additional notion that literal content consisting of evaluative claims will lead to the assumption by implication of factual claims not literally stated.

The Coleman article does something different, stressing that what we should identify as a broadcast ad's literal verbal content consists not merely of the words but of the way the words are spoken. Thus, while the other authors treat the literal verbal content as consisting of the ad's words as written (often basing their discussion on print ads), Coleman urges that the literal content should be regarded as being much more. Because of this distinction, the Coleman article will be discussed separately in the analysis that follows.

Garfinkel, Shimp, and the Harris Group

Garfinkel's discussion is in both theory and analysis the least detailed of the set of articles. His "pragmatic truth" amounts to an assumption that what a consumer gets from a message depends on more than just the message. He appears to believe that this viewpoint is newer than it is; in fact, it has been in vogue at the FTC for some time (see Preston, 1977), and is often supported by consumer response data (Rotfeld & Preston, 1981). Garfinkel offers no empirical support, but asserts by an unidentified method of content analysis that the ads he examines make numerous claims by implication and therefore have a degree of "indirectness" that carries a potential for deceiving the consumer. Given the evidence available in the other articles in this section and from sources elsewhere, we can confidently assume that he is correct.

The primary focus of Shimp is on a number of studies of consumer response to evaluative claims, often involving differential response to such claims as compared to factual ones. Although Shimp has done some of the experimental work, his method here is integrative; he establishes a conceptual framework for studying evaluative claims, and incorporates the various studies therein. The critical distinction he stresses is that the evaluative claim explicitly presents no information about the product, i.e., nothing about its tangible, physical properties. His general conclusion is that people derive such information anyway, presumably by implication.

Shimp's discussion raises the question of what we mean by information in the term "information processing." To those for whom factual claims are informative while evaluative ones are not, the conclusion must be that more things than just information are being processed. A way out of this definitional problem would be to define information as anything and everything about the product that the ad conveys. It would mean the inclusion of some strange types of content that could scarcely be regarded as truly informative.

If that is not satisfactory, the solution perhaps is to conclude that we are dealing not narrowly with information processing but more generically with "message" or "claim" or "stimulus" processing or just plain "advertisement processing." In any event, whoever invented the term "information processing" probably was not thinking of advertising solely, and therefore did not sufficiently consider that what we are given by ads and what we process from ads often consists of more than just "information" narrowly construed.

One of the pieces of evidence Shimp uses is the original research of Harris on implications, whose extended efforts are summarized by the Harris group. The method compares level of belief of literal vs. implied claims, and the main finding is that the level of belief of implied claims is high on an absolute basis. On a comparative basis it is sometimes just as high as for literal claims, and sometimes only slightly less high.

A considerable strength of the Harris group's efforts is its ongoing nature, which has resulted in many useful variations in test conditions, measurement instruments, and types of products, as detailed by Harris, Dubitsky, and Bruno. The numerous replications of the paradigmatic experiment definitely strengthen the validity of the overall findings.

These researchers have also varied their instructions to subjects, most notably in offering training aimed at encouraging people to judge implied claims as "indeterminate" rather than "true." This training shows some success.

The focus of the Monaco and Kaiser report is on how the general findings reported by Harris, Dubitsky, and Bruno may differ from person to person. First they examine prior preference among two competing topics, and find that we tend to see more implications in the message favoring the one we prefer. Monaco and Kaiser use this result to stress the notion of individual differences; however, we might also note that it suggests that some implications are more likely to occur than others, apparently because they make more sense in terms of what people prefer a message to say or what they expect it to say. That is, the study subjects may have been individually different in that some preferred one political candidate and some the other, but in terms of information processing they were the same in the tendency they showed to see the implications they would most like to see.

This suggests that two or more implications with the same degree of logical connection to the asserted statement will not necessarily be conveyed to the same degree. People do not respond to implications solely on their probability as predicted on a strict logical, objective basis. Instead, they respond to what they want to see conveyed, or as with Preston and Scharbach (1971), to what they think it would be reasonable to expect that the communicator is trying to say. This appears to be a ripe area for further study.

Monaco and Kaiser also examine the relative impact of using "truth" instructions, "belief" instructions, or neither. They conclude that both types are biasing and should not be used. From the viewpoint of determining what beliefs people derive from ads, this seems correct. The truth instructions propel people toward blanket acceptance of what the advertiser urges, whereas belief instructions push them toward reliance on their prior beliefs. There is another viewpoint, however, from which to view the question of instructions; I will take it up in the later discussion of how evidence about implications constitutes evidence of deceptiveness.

Coleman

The germ of Coleman's article may be found in her statement, "The importance of prosodic cues is illustrated by the fact that the hearer of a commercial will arrive at very different conclusions about what is being said than will the reader of a transcript not analyzed for intonation [p. 238]." In other words, the literal content of a broadcast ad is not what we think it is if we think it consists only of the words as written on storyboard or script. Rather, it consists of all the aspects of form presented by the advertiser just as much as it includes the aspects of content presented (and surely the choice of form is every bit as deliberate as the choice of content).

Coleman discusses the use of semantics, including puns, double meanings, jargon, and even "anti-jargon." She discusses prosodic features, which involve voice characteristics produced by varying and manipulating such things as pitch level, duration of sounds, loudness, speed, and rhythm. There are other curious features such as hedges and "smile voice." I am persuaded to suggest the additional concept of "laughing voice," which occurred upon watching a TV pitchman in my hometown—he's called Crazy Lennie because, you see, his prices are so low that you'll be laughing, too!

Coleman presents a theoretical analysis that is eminently testable. Although she herself does not deal with actual behavioral responses, there seems no reason to doubt that her suppositions would be borne out by empirical work. Her clear message is that if you examine form as well as content you can better predict what a hearer's response will be.

The relationship of Coleman to the other authors is that elements of form will lead to the conveyance of different implications than would otherwise happen. Sometimes, too, elements of form will aid the advertiser by discouraging the acquisition of implications not favorable to the product. In this way Coleman's paper is quite related to the others in its conclusions. Its significant difference is in stressing that we should identify an ad's literal content accurately before moving along to discuss what that content implies.

Summary

All of the articles in this section converge on the conclusion that ads communicate more than their literal verbal content. In general the studies are stronger in showing that this happens than in explaining why. Probably the main reason it happens is that consumers find it reasonable and normal to conclude that the advertiser is saying certain favorable things about the product that were not literally said. Although this explanation may be applied to all sorts of human assertions, there is reason to believe that people see more implications in ads than in other sorts of messages because they recognize them as things the advertiser would *want* to say.

This suggests a follow-up experiment, which would compare implications advertisers *would* want to have conveyed with implications they *would not* want to have conveyed. It would involve implications that are reasonable to derive from the literal content but which if accepted by the consumer would result in *decreased* desire for the product. For example, an ad might say "Women love such-and-such," which might lead, via the enabling belief that "Men are different from women," to the implication that "Men will not love such-and-such." Such a negative conclusion might be as equally reasonable an implication as many positive conclusions, but the hypothesis is that consumers would not tend as strongly to see it conveyed. Confirming that expectation would strengthen the principle that people see favorable implications in ads because they tend to see ads saying things it would be natural for ads to say.

The above is supported by Monaco and Kaiser's candidate experiment in that both suggest that people act consistently with their world knowledge. Also consistent is the result described by Monaco and Kaiser as unintuitive in which people recognized more implications as true after hearing unfavorable information about a store than when they heard favorable information. The explanation would appear to be that it goes against one's world knowledge to hear an ad saying unfavorable things, and that the consumer is motivated to resolve this inconsistency. One solution might be simply to reject the unfavorable information; however, some subjects were given truth instructions which apparently blocked them from that solution. Therefore they resolved their inconsistency through a greater tendency to draw favorable implications so as to interpret the message more in terms of their standard expectations about ads.

A final observation about the five articles is that they do not exhaust the ways by which consumers draw implications from literal verbal content. From the Coleman piece we might interpolate the possibility of examining how form accompanies verbal content in print advertising. Verbal materials are presented, for example, in different types faces or by lines divided in certain ways or isolated from other copy in certain ways. In addition there is a whole range of nonverbal elements that undoubtedly produce verbal implications, sometimes by themselves and sometimes by interacting with the literal verbal elements. The range of effects has only begun to be recognized.

For the purpose of assessing the present articles, however, we need not insist that all possibilities be covered. The assessment this reviewer feels is appropriate is that demonstration of many aspects of the implication process has been offered, and that the conclusion is solidly drawn that many more advertising claims reach the eyes, ears, and minds of consumers than those that exist merely in the words literally conveyed.

WHAT IS COMMUNICATED OFTEN PRODUCES A POTENTIAL FOR DECEPTION

The previous comments were restricted to the phenomenon of understanding more from an ad than it literally contains. The significance of this process for present purposes lies in a presumed tendency to create advertising deceptiveness. But we must avoid thinking that such a result follows automatically; rather, not all implied meanings of ads are involved. Consequently, I am treating as a separate step the contributions of our five articles toward illuminating the process of creating a potential for advertising to deceive.

The Legal Difference Between Deception and Deceptiveness

I want first to discuss something I regard as a stumbling block in the literature in this area. When I see discussions of deceptive advertising, I habitually apply what I consider to be a reasonable expectation that the writers are referring to the legal standard for that topic. To discuss whether an ad is deceptive, I assume, is to discuss whether it is deceptive by law. I do not know of any other practical reason for discussing deceptiveness; I don't understand what you can do with the topic when you fail to consider the legal concept.

Deceptive advertising is very much an applied rather than basic matter. Its essential meaning is that it affects consumers' behavior, presumably negatively, which will thereby affect the government's behavior, which will in turn affect the advertiser's future behavior as well as penalize him/her for past actions. If the part played by the government were eliminated, the above scenario would not apply and there would be much less reason for discussing the topic of deceptiveness.

Consequently I have been puzzled that a number of writers, including two in the present group, have chosen to bypass the legal standard in favor of discussing a concept that is related but not the same. The result is a nagging problem of definition which I want to sort out before examining what these articles contribute to the area. It is a matter of practical consequence, because sliding from one concept to another will result in a variance of conclusions about the relevance of the research we are discussing.

What Garfinkel and Shimp do is to speak of deception rather than deceptiveness, the latter implying a potential for deception. If there is deception there must be someone deceived, whereas with a potential there is not necessarily anyone actually deceived. To deal with the concept of deception when one is presumably discussing the legal standard is to imply that there must be deception in order to violate the law. That is not correct.

An ad doesn't have to deceive to be legally deceptive. The FTC (with the states generally following) is empowered to act against "deceptive acts or practices," and this phrase apparently has been difficult for scholars of behavior to interpret. Armstrong, Gurol, and Russ (1980) state that "In the law literature there is no 'general' statutory definition of deceptive advertising" but their statement is correct only if we construe it narrowly to mean that the FTC Act itself makes no elaboration of "deceptive acts or practices." Taken any more broadly, the statement is incorrect because FTC law as developed in its administrative cases and court reviews clearly establishes an operational definition for its legal standard. It is that an ad is legally deceptive when a majority of the five commissioners votes its opinion that the ad has the "capacity to deceive."

To assert existence of such capacity, the FTC need not show that deception has actually occurred but need only offer evidence that the ad *may* deceive some significant number or proportion of consumers. The evidence may of course consist of incidents of actual deception, which would be a most conclusive type of evidence. But that is not necessary; the required evidence need consist of nothing more than the content of the ad when the commissioners feel that such content on its face implies existence of the legal standard of capacity to deceive.

Consequently, Garfinkel errs when he says that deceptive advertising involves affecting the public's buying behavior in a detrimental way (p. 177). Deception involves that, but the legal standard does not. Similarly, Jacoby and Small (1975), discussing the parallel term "misleading" as used by the Food and Drug Administration, define a misleading ad as one which causes "a common impression or belief . . . which is incorrect or not justified." To match the legal standard they would have to say that the ad "has the capacity to cause people to have a common impression or belief . . . which is incorrect or not justified."

A different type of error is made by Armstrong, Gurol, and Russ (1980) when they say that "In finding deception, the FTC depends on discovering that consumers (1) have perceived false claims and (2) believed them." That is a useful definition of deception, but it is not what the FTC tries to find. The Commission doesn't have to look for deception and often doesn't.

The most subtle confusion occurs when writers say they are defining deception, and do so accurately, and do not explicitly attribute the term or its definition to the FTC. Gardner (1975) states, "If an advertisement . . . leaves the consumer with an impression(s) and/or belief(s) . . . factually untrue or potentially misleading, then deception is said to exist." Olson and Dover (1978) say that "deception is considered to occur when consumers acquire demonstrably false beliefs as a function of exposure to an advertisement." Armstrong and Russ (1975) say that "For deception to occur it is not sufficient that the claims are false. They must also be believed." And in this book, Shimp says there are two ways to define deception, one centering on effects on belief and the other centering on effects on buying behavior.

These four writers are discussing a meaningful concept and are doing so usefully. The problem is that readers are likely to derive the impression that by discussing deception they are discussing the requirements for what is legally violative. The surrounding contexts suggest that the authors indeed think that is the case.

How have such problems happened? A search for possible sources of the confusion shows that Aaker (1974) is cited by several of the above authors, that Aaker cites no earlier source, and that no earlier source appears to exist. Aaker's article is entitled "Deceptive Advertising," and within it there is a subheading entitled "What is Deceptive Advertising?" under which he says that "deception is found when an advertisement is the input into the perceptual process of some audience and the output of that perceptual process (a) differs from the reality of the situation and (b) affects buying behavior to the detriment of the consumer."

It is another useful definition of deception. But Aaker has intertwined "deceptive" and "deception" so thoroughly that they appear to be no different, and he has set the definition of "deception" within a context of comments about the FTC so as to convey the impression that the legal standard is being described.

Another, and minor, source of definitional difficulty is shown by Armstrong, Gurol, and Russ's (1980) comment that ". . . the FTC has commissioned its own research to measure the residual effects of the deception that the Listerine corrective advertising campaign has sought to eliminate. This research appears to be the first study commissioned by the FTC that uses belief-based measures to judge the level of deception [p. 28]." Within the context of their article these authors seem to be implying that it was the first time the FTC had researched a case of deceptive advertising properly. Such suggestion is wrong if it implies that deception must be shown to prove deceptiveness.

The reason such research was done in the Listerine case (Warner-Lambert, 1975) was that the case involved corrective advertising, which does require proof of actual deception rather than just capacity. The rationale for the corrective remedy is elimination of false beliefs that consumers hold, thus the necessity to show first that they actually hold them. But that is a separate part of an FTC case; even though the Commission had to show evidence of actual beliefs about Listerine in order to pursue the corrective remedy, it still had to show only a capacity to deceive in order to demonstrate that Listerine committed a deceptive act. The commissioners might have rejected the belief-based measures as valid evidence and so refused to sanction corrective advertising, yet still have ruled that a deceptive act occurred.

The significance of the definitional confusions described here is that readers of this literature may acquire an incorrect appreciation of the relationship to legal proceedings of certain kinds of research findings. Data on consumers' acquisitions of false beliefs or of deception-produced behavior may be erroneously assumed to play a role in the legal determination of deceptiveness that they do not in fact play.

I want at this time, however, to shift gears and acknowledge what I feel is a distinctly good side of this confusion. I have pondered the question, ''Why do these people want so much to talk about deception rather than the potential or capacity for it?'' I have concluded that they want to talk about deception for the absolutely excellent reason that the concept is more fundamental than is deceptiveness. Capacity per se produces no harm to consumers and thus has no social significance; only the resulting deception does. Therefore the capacity to deceive is important only if the potential becomes the real in a significant number of instances.

Potentials that result in no concrete manifestations get very little press. It is possible to speak of unicorns, and there is some fascinating literature on the topic, but society doesn't discuss unicorns very much because they never happen. Deception does happen.

And so, aren't these writers implicitly saying: ''Let's discuss what really matters!

Further, these writers may well be reflecting the fact that the only really convincing evidence of the existence of the capacity to deceive, despite the FTC's nonrequirement of it, is deception itself. If we never saw actual deception, we would eventually cease to belief in such a thing as the capacity for it. The FTC's use of ad content as per se evidence of capacity would become regarded as silly if there were not, somewhere in the background, some evidence of the real thing.

Thus, aren't these writers implicitly saying: Let's discuss the real evidence!

Even further, if a comparison of deception and deceptiveness brings a conclusion that deception is more important, is it possible that our writers may be questioning the FTC's means and methods for conducting its affairs?

Aren't they implicitly saying: Let's change the legal standard!

I believe they are saying these things, even when they do not seem to be consciously aware of doing so. They are saying there is something wrong with the way the law works, something the behavioral researchers know that the lawyers don't know. It is evident in Gardner's (1975) statement that Aaker's definition is commendable for focusing on buying behavior, which the FTC ignores. Similarly, Shimp in this book calls it a ''major shortcoming'' of research about deception that it has not firmly established that evaluative advertising actually influences behavior. Shimp says further that of the two ways of defining deception, one involving effects on belief and the other involving effects on buying behavior, the latter is more rigorous and thus preferable. What he surely would subscribe to in addition is that either method is more rigorous and preferable than relying simply on an examination of the ad.

To say all these favorable things about using the concept of deception is not to say that the FTC has been inept in ignoring it. Perhaps from a behavioral researcher's viewpoint, it has; however, there is a significant legal rationale that cannot be casually dismissed. One part of it is that the goal of regulation has been established as being preventive, which means that FTC policy is to prohibit deception before it happens. An ad that looks as though it *may* cause deception therefore must be legally actionable prior to the potential's realization. It is true enough that there frequently is failure in preventing deception before it happens—in fact, it is ironic that the very concept of corrective advertising involves the FTC's self-acknowledgment that the goal of prevention was not achieved. Still, to block deception in advance of its occurrence is the ideal, and the law must function so as to make that possible.

A related aspect is that the FTC functions on behalf of all the public at once rather than, as with the common law of the tort of fraud, on behalf of one or a small number of persons specified by name. The common law requires the prosecution to show that deception, and resulting damages, have occurred for each of those specified persons. If this had to be done for millions of members of the American public, nothing would ever be accomplished. Use of the concept of capacity thereby relieves the law from having to make a case that simply cannot be made.

A further legal necessity is that evidence of a company's misdoing must be tied specifically to the act or practice which is to declared violative. Evidence that consumers have acquired certain false beliefs may demonstrate that they have been deceived yet be inconclusive as to the source. It is untypical to find that an identified deception can be attributed to no cause other than the advertising. The capacity concept, meanwhile, is always tied specifically to the ad in question.

These reasons suggest that the legal standard will not be readily changed. The challenge for behavioral researchers, therefore, is to develop evidence that is satisfactory by their standards but also satisfactory for the legal process. The contributors to this book undoubtedly will be helpful in achieving such a goal.

Garfinkel, Shimp, and the Harris Group

Turning to those contributions, the findings of Garfinkel, Shimp, and the Harris group all imply the existence of a deceptive capacity and/or actual deception. They find the conveyance to consumers by implication of favorable claims which seem unlikely to be true and which, if believed, will therefore cause harmful purchasing decisions.

Garfinkel's data are of the content analysis sort, from which he argues that ads which convey content that extends beyond literal content are likely to have a capacity to deceive. The Shimp and Harris group data involve several sorts of consumer response which indicate the existence of deception and therefore capacity to deceive. Shimp discusses deception specifically, whereas the Harris group generally is content to draw the broader conclusion that people will be disadvantaged when they derive from ads a belief of claims the ad didn't really make. It is not hard to infer, however, that the Harris results imply evidence of deceptiveness.

Whether or not these experimental results can be applied to actual legal cases is affected by the difference between experimental and real life situations. Beliefs and purchasing decisions in, for example, the Olson and Dover research, could easily be attributed to the coffee ads they used. Nothing else could have been the source. With real ads the product is on the market and various sources are available for learning about it. Attributing the results solely to a given ad is difficult.

The way around this, in my opinion, is to encourage researchers to focus on identifying *types* of deceptive claims in experimental studies, following which the regulators can use the research in prosecutions involving ads of the same types. The regulators can argue that, although the research did not examine the prosecuted ads, it examined ads containing assertions with similar structure, thus the same conclusions should apply.

In terms of our critical concepts, if you study deception on an experimental basis for a given type of content, then in a future case involving ads of the same type you can switch to an examination merely of capacity to deceive based on content analysis. Proof of deception for a certain type of ad today would imply proof of capacity to deceive for an ad of the same type tomorrow. Content analysis, which might seem unreasonable for an initial study of a certain type of content, will thus be entirely reasonable for subsequent studies.

In this scenario the researchers are appeased because evidence of actual deception is introduced as a criterion, but the lawyers also are appeased because they are enabled to retain capacity to deceive as the legal standard.

The important linkage in this strategy is that tomorrow's ad must be shown convincingly to be of the same structure as today's. Elsewhere I have shown (Preston, 1977) that an analysis of recurring structure of types of implications can be done on existing FTC cases; however, the Commission has not shown much tendency to take official notice of such categorizing.

It appears to me that the contributors to this book have gone a long way toward enabling advertising regulators to identify types of past advertisements which can be used in identifying future ones. The principles that Shimp has identified about evaluative claims ought to be applicable to similar claims that appear in the future, for example the tendency for consumers to treat such claims as though they were factual claims. Shimp also asserts that evaluative claims involve more chance for error and less for consensus than do factual claims. The Harris group's study of implications contributes in the same way, suggesting that certain types of literal content will produce the same implications in subsequent ads as they have in those ads examined in the current research.

Coleman

Coleman also has contributed, very much, in this direction. Her general conclusion is that information processing and subsequent buying behavior will be affected by the speech forms she discusses. She makes almost no explicit mention of deceptiveness, yet her article quite loudly implies that matters of form frequently produce a deceptive potential, and in fact that the creators of ads know exactly how to produce such potential and are prone to do so deliberately.

Coleman's discussion of hedges is instructive on this point. The hedge is a way for the advertiser to have his cake and eat it, too. It is presented so that it will be little noticed. That is just what the advertiser wants because he is only saying it to mollify the FTC and doesn't want anyone else such as a consumer to hear it. Such result of course can happen only if the FTC hears differently than consumers do—which indeed will be the case if the FTC deals with ads on the basis of transcripts alone while consumers deal with them as transmitted over the air.

Is that what happens? My personal observation from working at the FTC is that its people certainly know that a TV storyboard or radio script does not convey the message as consumers see it. Yet, the very nature of activity at the Commission creates a strong tendency for attorneys and judges to consider ads as they appear on paper. The judge reviewing a case record may indeed reexamine an actual television film as often as desired, but isn't it convenient to think of it sometimes by looking at the written record? And isn't it difficult to keep in mind these strange sorts of things that Coleman discusses.

Aspects of prosody may be taken seriously in the abstract, but will not be fully applicable in practice until such time as the symbol system gets recorded routinely onto written scripts and people are able to comprehend it as readily as they comprehend English. The odds against it all happening very soon must be immense.

A Methodological Issue Involving Truth Instructions

Before leaving this topic of showing deceptive capacity, I want to mention a methodological issue prompted by the discussion of Monaco and Kaiser about the relative value of truth instructions, belief instructions, or no instructions. In the research of the Harris group, the experimental subject is asked to state what he/she believes about a given statement—whether it is true or false. If, as said earlier, the legal standard is one of capacity rather than of actual deception, it would follow that the appropriate research question would be "Does the ad convey this statement?" rather than "Do you believe this statement?" This is because the matter of conveyance can be attributed to the ad, whereas the matter of belief cannot necessarily be attributed to any one of the various sources of information about the product.

That is why the experiments of Preston (1967) and Preston and Scharbach (1971) asked about what was conveyed, i.e., not whether a statement was true or false but whether it was an accurate or inaccurate restatement or paraphrase of what was stated in the ad. A similar method was used by Preston in an FTC case, Sunoco (1974), in which subjects' tendencies to specify "accurate," which they might do without necessarily believing the claim, were used as corroborating evidence by the judge for his decision that a capacity for deception existed.

The Harris group, however, has gone the route of inquiring about belief, which on the surface appears to be a distinctly different procedure. However, I suspect that asking about truth or falsity while using truth instructions is very similar to asking what the ad conveyed. If the subject is instructed to accept what the ad says as true, without questioning on the basis of his/her own experience, then responses of "true" are simply indications of what the ad conveys rather than of what he thinks about the topic. This may not be exactly equivalent functionally to the Preston procedure, but my point is that when the Harris experimenters have used truth instructions they have been closer to the legal standard than when they have not. Monaco and Kaiser say that truth instructions are biasing in that they pull the results away from measuring belief, which in turn measures deception. The direction they are pulled, however, is toward measuring deceptiveness!

To use neither truth nor belief instructions, as Monaco and Kaiser recommend, is to use a method similar to that of Jacoby, Hoyer, and Sheluga (1980), who spoke of modeling their measures after Preston and Scharbach (1971) but instead used true-false questions. Their research was funded by the American Association of Advertising Agencies for purposes of being used as evidence in legal matters, yet this change moved their work away from the legal standard. The law doesn't want to know what the consumer thinks is true; it wants to know what the consumer thinks the ad claimed. An ad doesn't have to deceive in order to be deceptive.

IMPACT ON THE ADVERTISING INDUSTRY

What is at stake in our five articles from the viewpoint of the advertising industry is the possibility, in fact the fear, that the FTC may acquire the ability to identify deceptiveness even more readily than in the past. The tendency to find deceptiveness is of course a function of political considerations as well as factual evidence, and readers may feel that the current tapering off of FTC activity for political reasons will assure industry that in the future it has nothing to worry about.

That can be disputed, on the ground that the pendulum has always taken wide swings and that we will inevitably see a return someday to the proregulatory attitudes of the past decade. When it happens, the regulation of deceptiveness will be based on a great deal more knowledge of human behavior than was available to the FTC in 1970.

Further, one might argue that FTC activity concerning deceptive acts will not taper off as much as in other FTC areas. Much of the recent publicity about the Commission has spoken of the cancelling of antitrust cases involving questions of competition: oil, breakfast cereal, automobiles. Moreover, the publicized setbacks involving advertising have centered on unfairness (a legal standard apart from deceptiveness) and the issuing of rules (a procedure apart from individual cases). No attacks have been made specifically on the Commission's privilege to use the criterion of deceptiveness within the traditional case procedure. Thus, although political pressure may dampen its use for awhile, the legal vehicle most significant for present purposes remains intact.

Let us then assume that the theory and data of our five articles will eventually be brought to bear in regulatory proceedings. When this happens, the significance for the advertising industry is that there could be revealed far more capacity for deception in American advertising than the FTC has so far even dreamed about. Elsewhere (Preston, 1980) I have written that research on consumer behavior tends naturally to be proregulation because it reveals human limitations, and therefore most new data takes us farther and farther from the concept of the fully rational human who makes all the right decisions and needs no outside assistance. Our five articles bear out this point very well. The Coleman piece, for example, with its discussion of such terms as "polymers" and "dispersal rate," suggests there are many types of ad content which consumers have trouble handling.

Any discussion of prosody is anathema for the industry; the same for talk of implications and evaluative claims. And how about puffery! I emphasize the term "discussion," because it is not these phenomena per se but rather the *talk about them that industry dislikes. The phenomena themselves actually have served the advertisers exceedingly well—so long as they are not discussed!* Use them quietly and they work marvelously, but start to talk about them—get the FTC and consumers looking and asking questions—and somehow the magic disappears.

Probably we ought to have more recognition of the fact that successful communicating in advertising often succeeds through miscommunicating. In many cases, as advertisers well know, ideas can be conveyed through implication that cannot be conveyed in any other way. The study by Jacoby, Hoyer, and Sheluga (1980) on miscomprehension defines that term as the evocation of a meaning not contained in nor logically derivable from the message. They do not seem to realize that in advertising such a result may not be miscomprehension at all but rather fulfillment of the advertiser's conscious goal.

From all of this discussion we may confidently conclude that the advertising industry will not care to support or participate in research on extraliteral content. It is to industry's advantage to argue that consumers generally are very intelligent, and then feign innocence when there appears an instance in which they are not. If there is no prior documentation, industry can claim it couldn't have known in advance that such a thing could happen. But if a lot of research shows consumers prone to commit errors, then industry cannot pretend it didn't know. The research in this book goes a long way toward establishing the limited processing ability of consumers as a known social fact.

There is one angle in our articles that industry will appreciate. If what you advocate is that consumers are as bright as the legendary rational human, then as a matter of social policy you urge the advantages of education in place of regulation. By coincidence, the Harris program is devoted in considerable part to training people to recognize implications and reject them.

But why, one might ask, would the advertising industry advocate education if the result were to be that no one would be affected by implications anymore? Would that not deprive advertisers of certain traditional advantages? The answer probably is that industry wants to *advocate* education, but doesn't so enthusiastically want actually to *have* that education. It is entirely feasible to advocate education, which has the result of lobbying against regulation, yet at the same time be far less solicitous toward actual implementation. For those who find this cynical, it was the precise tack taken by industry in the famous children's advertising case.

Should industry fail to show interest in research on consumers, an opportunity will probably never arise to supply something that is severely needed in FTC deceptive advertising proceedings. It is the development of a standardized method for determining deceptiveness. Typical operating procedure at the Commission has been to conduct things pretty much from scratch in each new case, but the realization is growing that there would be much advantage in standardizing the procedure for obtaining evidence.

A problem, however, is that such standardization probably cannot be achieved without industry participation and agreement. If FTC unilaterally developed a method and offered it in hearings as being *the* method, lawyers for industry could simply argue that there was no consensus on the matter in the research community as a whole. Many members of the advertising and marketing research community, after all, are employed by industry. The prognosis for cooperation, therefore, is not good.

IMPACT ON THE FIELD OF INFORMATION PROCESSING

The fact that the contents of our five articles can affect the ad industry means that the field of information processing is by no means restricted to matters that are abstract, arcane, ethereal, and academic. Further, the articles suggest that a new dimension be added to the ways in which information processing has been focused thus far in its literature. Much of the field is involved with whether some given information gets to the consumer accurately, inaccurately, or not at all.

The assumption is that the communicator wants to transmit a certain statement—let's call it X—and the researcher studies the relative tendency of consumers either to get X, or some part of X, or mistakenly get something else, or get nothing at all. The assumption behind the study is that the communicator wants the consumer to get all of X and nothing else.

What we see in the contributions of this book is not quite that situation. Rather, when the consumer is given X and gets another message, Y, it is likely that Y is no mistake nor inaccuracy from the viewpoint of the communicator. The communicator likely is quite conscious of the fact that Y, which is favorable to him/her, is exactly what the consumer is expected to get from the message. Further, Y may be something the communicator wants to avoid stating literally because of the social disapprobation that would ensue. Therefore, it becomes an attractive aspect of information processing to discover that one may convey Y by saying X.

This of course makes a difference in the way we define the success of information processing. Probably we should define it in terms of the communicator's goals for consumer belief rather than in terms of the mere copying of the message. Put another way, we should identify the communicator's goals independently of the message content rather than simply inferring them from that content.

None of this of course will be news to advertising practitioners; it will appear as a novel approach only to those who regard information processing as a purely theoretical matter. As I have written elsewhere (Preston, 1982), following the lead of Wilkie and Farris (1976), research on advertising should not be allowed to fall too completely under the spell of that kind of information processing research that concentrates only on the consumer's behavior and not at all on the advertiser's. Advertising exists to sell goods, not to effect good information processing, and it will gladly do so with the help of good, bad, or no processing. It will be a useful development if research turns toward a great concentration on this sort of paradigm.

The study of deceptiveness and deception should of course be included in the paradigm. In a simple sense we might equate deceptiveness simply with inaccurate conveying of content. That is, the consumer either gets the message accurately or else gets deceived. It's not quite that elementary, however, because only certain inaccuracies amount to deception. Further, there is the issue of the advertiser's intent to produce given inaccuracies. In legal proceedings a finding of deceptiveness can be made without having to show that the advertiser intended such result; completely innocent effects can be just as violative as purposeful ones. Despite this legal viewpoint, the scholar of information processing might meaningfully examine the difference between intended and unintended effects.

Another impact of information processing, as exemplified by the Shimp article, is the matter discussed earlier of the nature of "information" as a significant variable. Information processing research generally treats consumer information as amounting to assertions of relevant fact about a product. We should recognize, however, that much of advertising content, and thus much of the "information" that consumers find available to process, consists of something other than information as so defined. The field therefore should get into the issues of identifying the nature of different kinds of "information," of doing content analyses of the relative presence of these kinds in advertising as contrasted to elsewhere, and of pointing research toward studying the differential processing of these different kinds.

An appropriate concluding observation is that our articles suggest that advertising has characteristics that other sorts of consumer messages do not. Researchers should identify and study *advertising processing* as a distinct subset of information processing.

REFERENCES

Aaker, D. A. Deceptive advertising. In D. A. Aaker & G. S. Day (Eds.), *Consumerism: Search for the consumer interest.* New York: The Free Press, 1974.

Armstrong, G. M., Gurol, M. N., & Russ, F. A. Defining and measuring deception in advertising: A review and evaluation. In J. H. Leigh & C. R. Martin, Jr. (Eds.), *Current issues and research in advertising 1980.* Ann Arbor: The University of Michigan, 1980.

Armstrong, G. M., & Russ, R. A. Detecting deception in advertising. *MSU Business Topics,* 1975, *23,* 21–32.

Gardner, D. M. Deception in advertising: A conceptual approach. *Journal of Marketing,* 1975, *39,* 40–46.

Jacoby, J., Hoyer, W. D., & Sheluga, D. A. *Miscomprehension of televised communications.* New York: American Association of Advertising Agencies, 1980.

Jacoby, J., & Small, C. The FDA approach to defining misleading advertising. *Journal of Marketing,* 1975, *39,* 65–68.

Olson, J. C., & Dover, P. A. Cognitive effects of deceptive advertising. *Journal of Marketing Research,* 1978, *15,* 29–38.

Preston, I. L. Logic and illogic in the advertising process. *Journalism Quarterly,* 1967, *44,* 231–239.

Preston, I. L. The FTC's handling of puffery and other selling claims made "by implication." *Journal of Business Research,* 1977, *5,* 155–181.

Preston, I. L. Researchers at the Federal Trade Commission: Peril and promise. In J. H. Leigh & C. R. Martin, Jr. (Eds.), *Current issues and research in advertising 1980.* Ann Arbor: The University of Michigan, 1980.

Preston, I. L. The association model of the advertising communication process. *Journal of Advertising,* 1982, *11(2),* 3–15.

Preston, I. L., & Scharbach, S. E. Advertising: More than meets the eye? *Journal of Advertising Research,* 1971, *11,* 19–24.

Rotfeld, H. J., & Preston, I. L. The potential impact of research on advertising law. *Journal of Advertising Research,* 1981, *21,* 9–17.

Sun Oil. *FTC Decision,* 1974, *84,* 247.

Warner-Lambert. *FTC Decisions,* 1975, *86,* 1398.

Wilkie, W. L., & Farris, P. W. *Consumer information processing: Perspective and implications for advertising.* Cambridge: Marketing Science Institute, 1976.

Biographical Section
(in alphabetical order)

KATHRYN LUTZ ALESANDRINI did her undergraduate and masters-level work at the University of Illinois at Urbana-Champaign and completed a Ph.D. in Learning and Instruction at the University of California, Los Angeles. She is currently an Assistant Professor in the Instructional Design and Technology Program of the College of Education at The University of Iowa. Her interests focus on the role of the visual in human thinking, learning, and communication and on identifying strategies to facilitate those three areas.

RAJEEV BATRA is a doctoral student at the Graduate School of Business, Stanford University. He has an M.B.A. from the Indian Institute of Management, Ahmedabad, India, and an M.S. (Advertising) degree from the University of Illinois. He worked as a Brand Manager for over two years with Chesebrough-Pond's Inc. in India. His research interests are in the areas of consumer information processing and advertising management.

KRISTIN JO BRUNO has a B.S. from California State University, Long Beach, two M.S. degrees in psychology and computer science from Kansas State University, and a Ph.D. in psychology from Kansas State University. She now works for Hewlett-Packard in Los Angeles.

ROBERT E. BURNKRANT has a B.S. degree from University of Wisconsin at Madison and an M.B.A. from the University of Colorado. He has a Ph.D. in Business from the University of Illinois at Urbana-Champaign. He is currently Associate Professor of Marketing, College of Administrative Science, The Ohio State University. His research interests include consumer information processing, attitude structure and the attitude-behavior relationship and attribution theory. His research includes publications in *Journal of Business Research, Journal of Consumer Research* and *Journal of Personality and Social Psychology*.

LINDA COLEMAN is a native of Washington, D.C. She has an A.B. and M.A. in linguistics from the University of Michigan and a Ph.D. in linguistics at the University of California, Berkeley. While her main interest is in the use of various linguistic features in persuasive discourse, she is also involved in work on the language of Evangelical Christianity, conversational interaction, and grade-school reading comprehension tests. Currently she is Assistant Professor of English at the University of Maryland.

TONY M. DUBITSKY is an Assistant Professor of Psychology at Lamar University in Beaumont, Texas. He has a B.S. from the State University of New York College at Oswego and an M.S. and Ph.D. in Experimental Psychology from Kansas State University. His current research interests are in the areas of consumer information processing and prose comprehension.

ANDREW GARFINKEL has a B.A. in French from the State University of New York at Stony Brook, an M.A. in linguistics from the University of Rochester, and a Ph.D. in linguistics from Georgetown University. He has been working in the field of marketing research since 1977 and is currently a Senior Marketing Analyst in the Marketing Research Department at Manufacturers Hanover Trust Company in New York City.

RICHARD JACKSON HARRIS has a B.A. from the College of Wooster and an M.A. and Ph.D. in Experimental Psychology from the University of Illinois at Urbana-Champaign. He is currently an Associate Professor of Psychology at Kansas State University. In addition to studying deceptive advertising, he is involved in other psycholinguistic research on inference drawing, discourse, and the use of metaphor in advertising and psychotherapy.

DONN L. KAISER has a B.A. from Kansas State University and an M.A. from Wichita State University. His Ph.D. in Psychology from Kansas State University is in the area of social psychology and personality. He teaches in the Psychology Department at Southwest Missouri State University, Springfield, Missouri. Current research interests include the study of attributions of responsibility and the effects of censorship.

ANDREW A. MITCHELL is an Associate Professor of Marketing in the Graduate School of Industrial Administration, Carnegie-Mellon University. He received his Ph.D. from the University of California, Berkeley and has recently published articles in the *Journal of Marketing Research, Journal of Consumer Research, Management Science* and the *Journal of Marketing*. In addition to his research on advertising effects, he is also studying the content and organization of consumer memory and consumer decision making.

GREGORY E. MONACO received his B.S. from Northwestern University, and his M.S. and Ph.D. degrees, in experimental psychology, from Kansas State University. Currently he is a research associate with the Bureau of Child Research, University of Kansas and a Courtesy Assistant Professor with the Department of Human Development and Family Life. Areas of current research include cognitive processes in reading and the development of educational programs for teaching reading skills to exceptional children.

LARRY PERCY is Vice President and Corporate Research Director of Creamer, Inc., and has extensive experience in the practical application of communication and information processing theory to strategic marketing and advertising decisions. Prior to joining Creamer Inc. in 1978, he spent over 14 years with three other advertising agencies: Gardner Advertising, Ketchum MacLeod & Grove, and Young and Rubicam. Publications of Mr. Percy have appeared in many journals. He is principal author of *Advertising Strategy: A Communication Theory Approach* and has contributed chapters to several marketing and communication textbooks. He also serves on the Editorial Board of the *Journal of Marketing Research* and the *Journal of Business* and the Editorial Review Board of *Current Issues and Research in Advertising*. Percy received a B.S. in mathematics from Marietta College in 1965.

IVAN L. PRESTON is Professor in the School of Journalism and Mass Communication at the University of Wisconsin. He obtained the Ph.D. from the College of Communication Arts of Michigan State University in 1964, and was on the faculty of the School of Journalism at Pennsylvania State University from 1963–68. He has also worked as a newspaper reporter and photographer, a university news service editor, and an account executive in advertising and public relations. Preston is the author of *The Great American Blow-Up: Puffery in Advertising and Selling,* and of numerous articles in scholarly journals. Preston has been a consultant in matters of deceptive advertising for the Federal Trade Commission, participating in cases several times and working fulltime at the Division of Advertising Practices in Washington, D.C., during 1979.

MICHAEL L. RAY is Professor of Marketing and Communication at Stanford University's Graduate School of Business. His M.A. and Ph.D. in Social Psychology are from Northwestern University. He is a specialist in marketing communication, advertising and the behavioral science approach to marketing problems. He has published over 70 articles including four state-of-the-art chapters for handbooks. He edited two of the first books on the field of consumer information processing and is author of *Advertising and Communication Management* (Prentice-Hall, 1982).

JOHN R. ROSSITER is principal lecturer in marketing at the New South Wales Institute of Technology in Sydney, Australia. He has taught previously at the Wharton School, University of Pennsylvania and at the Graduate School of Business, Columbia University. Publications by Rossiter have appeared in many business and behavioral science journals. He is coauthor of two books on television advertising and children, as well as *Advertising Strategy: A Communication Theory Approach*. He has delivered management seminars in the U.S. and Australia on communication theory applied to advertising and promotion. Rossiter received his Ph.D. in communications from the University of Pennsylvania in 1974, after spending a number of years in the marketing research industry. He has an M.S. in marketing from UCLA and an undergraduate honors degree in psychology from the University of Western Australia.

HERBERT J. ROTFELD is Assistant Professor of Advertising at the Pennsylvania State University School of Journalism. He has a B.S. in Communications, M.S. in Advertising and Ph.D. in Communications, all from the University of Illinois at Urbana-Champaign. His main teaching interest is in "Advertising and Consumerism," and his articles on the theoretical, legal and empirical aspects of advertising regulation and public criticism of advertising practice have appeared in various journals and conference proceedings.

ALAN G. SAWYER received a B.S. from the University of Maine, an M.B.A. from Northeastern University, and a Ph.D. in Marketing from Stanford University. He is currently an Associate Professor of Marketing at Ohio State University. Research interests include the measurement of the effectiveness of different advertising message and scheduling strategies and the improvement of research methodology.

JAMES SHANTEAU is Professor of Psychology at Kansas State University. He has a B.A. in Psychology/Mathematics from San Jose State University and a Ph.D. in Experimental Psychology from the University of California, San Diego. Based on his major interests in judgment and decision-making behavior, he has conducted research on consumer health-care choices, husband-wife decision making, and mathematical models of consumer judgment. He is on the Editorial Boards of *Memory & Cognition,* and *Journal of Experimental Psychology: Human Perception and Performance.*

TERENCE A. SHIMP is an Associate Professor of Marketing at the University of South Carolina. He received a D.B.A. from the University of Maryland. His research has concentrated primarily on the public policy implications of advertising practices. Recent research has included studies of the impact of deceptive advertising on repeat purchase behavior, tests of alternative theories of dramatic shifts in consumer behavior, and conceptualization of consumers' affect for brands as a function of their attitudes toward the brands' advertisements.

Author Index

A

Aaker, D. A., 177, *192*, 195, 199, 200, *213*, 227, *239*, 296, *305*
Aaron, I. E., 242, *261*
Abelson, R. P., 20, *41*, 96, 109, *120*, 135, 162, *147*, *165*
Abrams, K., 101, *121*
Achenbaum, A. A., 164, *165*
Adams, S. C., 129, *148*
Ajzen, I., 29, *38*, 102, 112, 117, *121*, 131, 135, 137, 139, *147*, *148*, 162, *165*, 200, *214*
Alesandrini, K. L., 66, 70, 73, *81*
Allard, F. A., 92, *124*
Alper, S. N., 94, *123*
Anderson, J. F., 91, 92, *121*
Anderson, J. R., 14, 19, 20, 21, 24, 25, *37*, *40*, 101, 118, *121*, 159, *165*
Anderson, N. H., 59, *63*, 155, *165*
Anderson, P. A., 91, 92, *121*
Anderson, R. C., 79, *81*
Appel, V., 137, *147*, *150*
Apsler, R., 45, *61*
Armstrong, G. M., 8, *9*, 195, 199, *213*, *214*, 295, *305*
Artley, A. S., 242, *261*

B

Baddeley, H. D., 25, *38*
Bandura, A., 116, *121*
Barbour, F., 114, 118, 139, *151*
Barclay, J. R., 202, *214*, 241, *260*
Baron, P. H., 30, *38*
Baron, R. S., 30, *38*
Bartlett, F. C., 241, *260*, 265, *287*
Bartz, W. H., 49, 56, *62*
Battig, W. F., 98, 99, 108, *125*
Bauer, R. A., 127, *147*
Beard, A. D., 111, *121*
Becker, J., 66, *81*
Begg, I., 108, *121*
Belk, R. W., 45, *61*
Bennett, P. D., 51, *61*
Berdine, W. R., 198, *214*
Berger, S. M., 103, *121*

Atkinson, J. W., 52, 59, *61*
Atkinson, R. C., 15, *38*, 265, *287*
Aulls, M. W., 55, *61*
Austin, J. A., 45, 47, *62*
Austin, J. L., 176, *192*
Ausubel, D. P., 77, *81*

Subject Index

A

Activation, 21–22
Advance Organizers, 77
Ads Compared to Other Types of Prose, 257–258
Affective Responses to Ads, 89–91, 134–138
Agricultural Ads, 256–257
Analogies, 77–78
Attention, 16–17, 22–23, 30–34, 87, 161
Attitude Formation and Change,
  conveyed by prosody, 226–227
  expectancy-value models, 138–141
  Fishbein-Ajzen model, 28–29, 139
  mediators of, 28–30
  political attitudes, 270–276
  preferential communication effect, 111–113
  prior preference, 268–270, 279–286
Attribute-specific Belief Research, 206–208
Automatic Decoding, 89–92
Automaticity, 16–17, 34
Awareness, 103–109

B

Behaviorism, 6
Beliefs, 109–111
  Prior beliefs, 266–286
  (*See also* Attitude Formation and Change)

Bounded Rationality, 163
Brain,
  Hemispheric lateralization, 91–92, 137–138, 157
  EEG, 91
Brand Loyalty, 267
Brand Name,
  Recall of, 98, 191
  Prosody of, 224–226

C

Cereals, Breakfast (Study of Ads for), 180–184, 188–190
Choice Rules, 114–115, 162–163
Chunking, 75–77
Classical Affective Conditioning, 116–117
Cognitive Responses to Ads, 28
Cognitive Structures, 28
Comparatives, Incomplete, 205–206, 227–229, 243
Computer Metaphor, 4
Computer Science, 6–7
Conceptually-driven versus data-driven processes, 18
Concreteness, 98–99, 104–109
Concretization Memory Techniques, 71–75
Connotative and Denotative Responses, 89–91, 224